WITH SAILS WHITENING EVERY SEA

A volume in the series

The United States in the World

edited by Mark Philip Bradley, David C. Engerman, Amy S. Greenberg, and Paul A. Kramer

A list of titles in this series is available at www.cornellpress.cornell.edu.

WITH SAILS WHITENING EVERY SEA

Mariners and the Making of an American Maritime Empire

Brian Rouleau

Cornell University Press
Ithaca and London

First published 2014 by Cornell University Press

Printed in the United States of America

Library of Congress Cataloging-in-Publication Data

Rouleau, Brian, author.
    With sails whitening every sea : mariners and the making of an
American maritime empire / Brian Rouleau.
        pages cm — (United States in the world)
    Includes bibliographical references and index.
    ISBN 978-0-8014-5233-8 (cloth : alk. paper)
    1. Sailors—United States—Social conditions—19th century. 2. United
States—Foreign relations—19th century. 3. Sea-power—United
States—History—19th century. I. Title. II. Series: United States in the
world.
    G540.R68   2014
    331.7'61387097309034—dc23   2014024630

Cornell University Press strives to use environmentally responsible
suppliers and materials to the fullest extent possible in the publishing
of its books. Such materials include vegetable-based, low-VOC inks
and acid-free papers that are recycled, totally chlorine-free, or partly
composed of nonwood fibers. For further information, visit our
website at www.cornellpress.cornell.edu.

Cloth printing   10 9 8 7 6 5 4 3 2 1

To the memory of my mother and father

Hail Land of light and joy! thy power shall grow
Far as the seas, which round thy regions flow;
Through earth's wide realms thy glory shall extend,
And savage nations at thy scepter bend.
Around the frozen shores thy sons shall sail,
Or stretch their canvas to the Asian gale.

—Timothy Dwight, *America*, 1790

Contents

Acknowledgments

    This book, like most others, owes many debts to many people. First, let me thank the terrific group of scholars who mentored me along the way. Danny Vickers was the original inspiration for what appears here. I walked into his classroom at the University of California, San Diego, a student of East Asia and stepped out an American historian. His boundless enthusiasm for the subject, effortless brilliance, and willingness to nurture students have amazed me. The University of Pennsylvania, meanwhile, introduced me to Mike Zuckerman and Dan Richter. Mike has improved me in many ways, both as a historian and, perhaps more important, as a thinking human being. More than anything, he has never failed to challenge me to become better, to consider more carefully, and to delve deeper, even as he has humored me more than once when I lost my way. It is his special ability to some-how approach any issue from all sides at once. That talent has immeasurably sharpened and enriched what appears here. Last, but by no means least, is Dan Richter, to whom I am perhaps most indebted. He does not need me to rehearse the merits of his dazzling and penetrating intellect here, although I have benefited immensely from it. More important, Dan deserves to be commended for taking a chance on a book to which he might never have seen himself contributing. His dedication has been unyielding, and I will always remain most grateful for that. Dan has no doubt been exposed to more of this book's (and my own) growing pains than anyone else, and yet he somehow always knew just what to say at exactly the right moment to nudge me back on track. It is one of his many gifts as both a mentor and a friend, and I will always feel indebted to him for that reason. Kathy Peiss, Kathy Brown, Steve Hahn, Ron Granieri, Rick Beeman, and many other faculty in Philadelphia also contributed significantly to the fantastic educational environment at Penn, out of which this work grew. Jason Colby and Jason Opal provided many insightful comments as the project progressed. Finally, thanks to the series editors, Mark Bradley, David Engerman, Amy Greenberg, and Paul Kramer; Michael McGandy; Max Richman; Susan Specter; and everyone else at Cornell University Press who helped make this a better book.

Since joining the history department at Texas A&M in 2010, many friends, colleagues, and staff have done much to provide a welcoming and stimulating academic environment. I would like thank everyone in what is a very large department. The members of the Atlantic world and U.S. in the World clusters have provided particular insight and inspiration. Quince Adams, Carlos Blanton, Al Broussard, Walter Buenger, Rebecca Hartkopf Schloss, April Hatfield, Andy Kirkendall, John Lenihan, Brian Linn, and David Vaught have donated generous amounts of time to mentoring a young colleague. Olga Dror, likewise, helped a rookie Texan learn how to two-step. Last but not least, here's to my fellow assistant professors, Side Emre, Felipe Hinojosa, Lisa Ramos, Dan Schwartz, Katherine Unterman, and Erin Wood. From writing groups to Friday dinners, I feel as though I never could have thrived in Aggieland without your good cheer.

Friends from all walks of life have also made the book possible. Though I am sure to forget a few, many come to mind. Josh and Maggie Keegan Gross and their entire family have been a joy in my life. In San Diego, I met and have been glad to know Vitria Adisetiyo, Mike Friedman, Leo Goldbard, Erin Hoppe, and so many others. And in Philadelphia, Greg Ablavsky, Kate Baldanza, Stephanie Corrigan, Ushma Domadia, Lauren Fox, Cassie Good, Katherine Hill, Matt Karp, Sean Kiley, Will Kuby, Andrew Lipman, Vanessa Mongey, Dael Norwood, Matt and Shelley Schauer, Patrick and Laura Spero, and Karen Tani made my time at Penn not only enriching but downright entertaining.

Beyond social debts, however, there are institutional and financial debts to be acknowledged. Many institutions have provided funding and other forms of support. The University of Pennsylvania offered invaluable financial assistance in the form of multiple research and writing fellowships. Texas A&M University also allocated significant amounts of money and leave time that contributed mightily to the finished product. The College of Liberal Arts, the Department of History, the Glasscock Center for the Humanities, and the Scowcroft Institute for International Affairs deserve particular mention for helpful travel and research disbursements. In addition, the Independence Seaport Museum in Philadelphia (with a special thank-you to Matt Herbison), the New Bedford Whaling Museum (with special thanks to Mark Procknik), and the Peabody Essex Museum in Salem, Massachusetts, each offered generous short-term research fellowships. Moreover, the staff at those institutions provided enormously helpful assistance as I navigated the archives. I would also like to thank dedicated librarians and curators at the Clements Library, the Chrysler Museum (with special thanks to Melanie Neil), the Historical Society of Pennsylvania, the Library of Congress, the Marblehead Museum, the Mariners' Museum, the National Archives, the Naval Historical Center, the Mystic Seaport Museum, the New-York Historical Society, the New York Public Library, the New Bedford Free Public Library, the Providence Public Library, the Scott Polar Research Institute (with special thanks to Lucy Martin), and the University of Pennsylvania Rare Book Room. At Texas A&M's Evans Library, Joel Kitchens and Carolina De Leon have patiently tracked down many a resource. Randall Bond has shared a wealth of bibliographic knowledge. In addition, I would like to thank the extraordinary group of fellows and scholars who comprise the McNeil Center for Early American Studies. It has long been my academic home away from home: a source of great conversation, even better friends, and quite simply an extraordinary place to be.

Portions of chapter 3 were published in "Maritime Destiny as Manifest Destiny: American Commercial Expansionism and the Idea of the Indian," *Journal of the Early Republic* 30, no. 3 (Fall 2010): 377–411; copyright © 2010 Society for Historians of the Early American Republic, all rights reserved. Portions of chapter 4 were published in "How Honolulu Almost Burned and Why Sailors Matter to Early American Foreign Relations," *Diplomatic History*, first published online June 18, 2013, doi: 10.1093/dh/dht105; by permission of Oxford University Press on behalf of the Society for Historians of American Foreign Relations.

Finally, let me end where I began, with my family. To Grandma and the memory of my grandfather, to Grammie C, and to Carol and Jerry, thank you for your constant encouragement. To my sisters, Lauren and Allison, the first and longest-lived friends I have had in this life: as my most steadfast supporters, you two are owed a debt that words do little to pay. My mother and father both passed away as research and writing were in progress. I never got the chance to say good-bye to either of them; this book, a project they were eager to see finished, is perhaps the best and most lasting tribute I can offer. It is dedicated to their memory, their love, and their devotion to their children. Last but not least, let me say thank-you to Katherine. As a source of happiness and laughter, of insight and inspiration in my life, she has no peer. I may study the past, but her love has me most excited about the present and the future.

London

Boston
New York — Salem
Baltimore — New Bedford
Nantucket

San Francisco
San Pedro
San Diego
New Orleans

Charleston

Flores

Faial
Azores

Lisbon
Cádiz
Tangiers

Philadelphia

Funchal, Madeira

Midway Island

Las Palmas, Canary Islands

Magdalena Bay
Mazatlán
Havana

Honolulu
Lahaina
Hilo

Mérida
Veracruz

Port-au-Prince
Les Cayes — Antigua

Acapulco

Praia, Cape Verde

San Juan del Sur
Aspinwall (Colón)
Panama
City

Monrovia

Guayaquil
Tumbes

Nuku Hiva, Marquesas

Pernambuco (Recife)

Callao
Paita

Apia, Samoa

St. Helena

Tahiti
Society Islands

Rio de Janeiro

Valparaíso
Talcahuano

Rio Grande
Montevideo

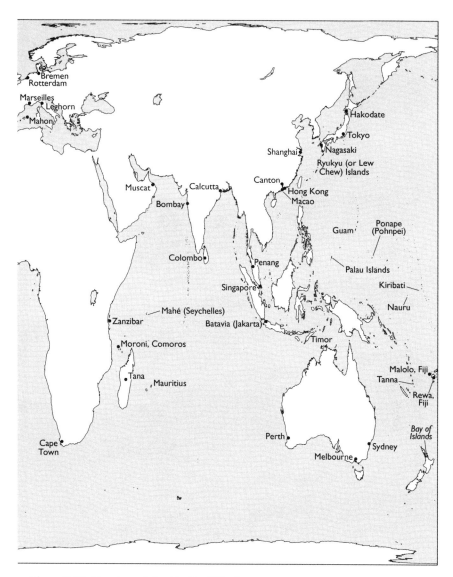

Figure 1. World ports regularly visited by U.S. sailors

WITH SAILS WHITENING EVERY SEA

Introduction

"Born to Rule the Seas"

Alexis de Tocqueville gazed east toward the ocean when he prophesied American power. Witness to the bustle of the nation's waterfronts—their clamorous shipyards, thriving exchange houses, and legions of sailors—this most famous tourist declared that the United States "will one day become the first maritime power of the globe [because] they are born to rule the seas as the Romans were to conquer the world." A veritable chorus of the young republic's citizens arose to accompany him. Toasts printed and reprinted throughout the Union celebrated the aqueous ambitions of Americans, "who may soon command the ocean, both oceans, all oceans." The *Southern Literary Messenger* boasted that "every ocean will swarm with their ships," while "their language, their science, their literature and their religion will pervade all the kindreds and tribes of heathendom." Most grandiloquent of all may have been *De Bow's Review*, which asserted that "every sea and navigable water under the face of heaven, sees the white wings of our shipping, and hears the bold voice of our mariners." And while "great has been our progress," they exclaimed, "there is a prophetic voice which tells us that we have but begun to enter upon that bright and glorious 'empire of the seas' which is yet to be ours."[1]

The political front manifested no less enthusiasm for the sea, ships, and sailors. Representatives from across the nation rushed to swear fealty to the goal of global maritime expansion. At a nineteenth-century moment witness to increasing tension over the disposition, slave or free, of the nation's territorial empire, combative regional interests appeared unified beneath billowy banners of American canvas. Observers rejoiced most in ubiquity, "commerce, carried in our own ships, found in every sea," the arms of the nation "so greatly expanded." "Almost limitless," exulted a senator, "extended to every sea." Orators jousted with Great Britain, "our only rival upon the seas," and pronounced with evident pride the expectation that national shipping grew at a pace that was soon to crown the United States "first commercial nation upon the globe." And it was the nation's sailors who made such lofty aspiration possible. The courage and daring of "our hardy and enterprising countrymen" extended the republic's reach around the world and "added to the common stock of the *whole* nation." Mariners, many maintained, were national objects amid a federally fractured people.[2]

This language of maritime boosterism pervaded the popular and political discourse of nineteenth-century America. The nation boasted of the commercial fleet's "incessant belt of circumnavigation," a feat of globe girdling that one newspaper imagined as U.S. crews who "sail around Cape Horn and others round the Cape of Good Hope, by which courses they frequently meet in the midst of the Pacific and exchange salutations." Speakers stood to applaud the technical perfection of American sail and steamships, the bravery and prowess of the American sailor, and thus, by extension, of the American man. Iconography made mariners emblems of patriotic pride and presented the ocean as the site of past and future national triumph. Long before Alfred Thayer Mahan's influential treatises on navalism, Americans were hearing how "the premonitions of the future point ominously to the sea."[3]

Histories of the nineteenth-century United States, however, remain wedded to decidedly land-based ideas of expansionism and empire. Even to this day, much of U.S. history has been hijacked by what has been called the "territorializing vision" of academic and popular discourse. The reigning paradigm postulates that nations are inherently discrete, bounded terrestrial units. But that supposition is an anachronism that mistakes what the nation became with what it once was and aspired to: only recently have "continental presumptions" come to control the country's cultural geography. As a result, the limits of the North American land mass tend to function as the end of our inquiry into the republic's nineteenth-century history. Working under those assumptions, the maritime world has been conceived of as a boundary, as something separate, as the natural limit to any nation-state. This book, however, seeks to reimpose the original meaning of the word "maritime," which was defined not as something confined to the water but rather that which bordered or touched the sea. The watery world, in that earlier conceptualization, was not a disconnected space deserving of distinct lines of inquiry. Rather, the emphasis was on continuity between land and ocean. As late as the nineteenth century, writers often referred to the globe as *terraqueous*, a term that connoted the interrelationship between the terrestrial and the aquatic. That connectedness should inform our conceptions of early U.S. expansion. Nineteenth-century Americans envisioned national empire extending onward into the Atlantic and Pacific, not halting at their shores.[4]

The concept of empire, as observers at the time never tired of exclaiming, included interlocked and interconnected landward and waterborne components. It was not simply that America would extend from sea to shining sea. Rather, saltwater itself was spoken of as a field for national domination. Familiar synecdoche had it that the "commerce of the United States whitened every sea," while others noted "the unparalleled extension of our commerce, now whitening with its sails, the remotest waters of the world" and "our ships from San Francisco to China and our Whalers in the Pacific . . . [which] whiten the Ocean." Sailors, said one congressman, were "the men whose enterprise explores every land, and whose commerce whitens every sea," while another account foretold that the world's "wilderness" places, once "whitened by the numerous sails . . . of adventurous commerce," would "be made to blossom like the rose" and "resound with [the] busy hum . . . of Civilization with its humanizing blessings." The swelling canvas of American vessels came to stand for an entire expansionist enterprise. As Timothy Dwight expressed it in the poem that prefaces this volume, the arrival of the republic's ships promised uplift: the "stretched canvas" of America's seagoing community would eventually "bend" the Earth's "savage nations" toward civilization's light. Or, as one sailor put it, the masts and spars of the nation's vessels meant that "daily do our whalers . . . and merchantmen display the flag of their Republic to civilized nations and savage tribes, creating new wants for, and siring a new language to, the natives of the Pacific isles."[5]

A repetitive appeal to the image of sails whitening every sea thus saturated the country's speech at the time. It was a mantra meant to express the nation's ambitious pursuit of commercial supremacy overseas, of U.S. dominance in the global carrying trade, and of transoceanic commerce as

Figure 2. "Yankey Tar." The discourse of maritime empire was not necessarily confined to elite circles. In their diaries, memoirs, correspondence, and sketchbooks, American sailors often represented their work overseas as integral to national commercial expansion. In this drawing, a Jack Tar in typical seaman's garb plants the country's flag atop an ocean wave. Courtesy of the New Bedford Whaling Museum, catalog #A-135.

a conduit for American-led enlightenment. Referred to interchangeably as the nation's "maritime empire," its "empire of the seas," and an "empire of the ocean," this expansionist ethos positioned American omnipresence throughout the globe's shipping lanes and harbors as an imperial aspiration. The "prize was the commerce of the world," as one orator claimed, and when sailors "spread the white sails of our ships on every sea," the "flag of the United States" would be "a flower that adorned every port and blossomed on every soil the world over." The country's chief competitor in this quest was Britain, an empire that had long relied on similar rhetoric to describe its own goals. Americans inherited those aspirations; to declare that the republic's sails whitened every sea was only tantamount to contemporaneous claims that British dominions constituted an empire upon which the sun never set. Henry Clay, after all, proclaimed that "Britain sickens at your prosperity, and beholds in your growth—your sails spread on every

ocean, and your numerous seamen—the foundations of a Power which at
no very distant day, is to make her tremble." But the advocates of an American maritime empire almost always saw their aims as conjoined with those
committed to territorial expansion. As the republic extended its dominion
across what would become the continental United States, ships and sailors were spoken of as the means to provide pathways by which bountiful
harvests and manufactured goods might be integrated into a burgeoning
world market.[6]

This book attempts to incorporate oceanic encounters into our understanding of the experience of manifest destiny in the nineteenth century.
Indeed, invoking the image of canvas covering the world was how Americans most often expressed their sense of the young nation's maritime manifest destiny. Maritime empire—the quest to see American sails spread across
every sea—was central to the experience of expansion in the early republic
and antebellum eras. The pivotal drama of the nation's early history—a
meeting of and exchange between many cultures—cannot be neatly and
narrowly contained on North America's land mass. Confining the story to
the continent obscures the early United States' global engagement, leaving us with the mistaken impression that only the achievement of overseas
empire at the turn of the twentieth century heralded the country's entrance
upon a world stage. We focus on manifest destiny as a matter of territorial expansion—largely in teleological anticipation of the Civil War—only
to forget the highly active role nautical U.S. nationals played in enlarging
America's planetary presence. When Senator James Bayard of Delaware rose
in 1852 to remind his countrymen of their nation's true extent, he had
them envision an eagle with "expanded wings," the raptor's unblinking eye
"watching over their meteor flag wherever it is unfurled." With a whale
fishery that prosecuted its "bold and successful industry" in "every sea" and
a merchant marine located "in every climate, and throughout the wide
extent of the habitable globe," the republic seemed boundless. Pioneering,
in other words, had its watery practitioners as well, and frontiers could be
composed of both remote coasts and distant deep water.[7]

Nineteenth-century America's massive maritime sector thus provides us
with the opportunity to investigate the multiple means by which the United
States, from very early on, became entangled in events overseas. Before
1898, that deceptively pivotal year of imperial jubilee, earlier generations of
seafarers, ambassadors in the forecastle, established intercultural relationships
that later travelers, tourists, missionaries, and diplomats would engage with,

build upon, or work to disown. During the antebellum era's peak years of sail, U.S. merchant and whaling fleets sent hundreds of thousands of young American men on voyages to all parts of the globe. At a time when most in the United States rarely traveled outside their respective counties, seafarers and the journals they kept provide a window into how a cohort of largely ordinary Americans were learning to think about the world and their nation's place within it. The experiences of sailors abroad provide an ample starting point in the effort to open the borders of what can rightfully be called American history and complicate the perception that world history is not relevant to the nation until its twentieth-century ascendance to superpower status. Illustrating the seagoing sector's vibrancy during the long nineteenth-century challenges the narrowing of interests that characterizes a good deal of scholarship on the era.[8]

Given their global ubiquity, seafarers should be allowed to join the growing cast of characters deemed responsible for shaping early American foreign relations. As the definition of diplomacy continues to evolve beyond formal state-to-state interactions, nonstate actors have emerged as valuable historical agents in enlarging our understanding of international affairs. Not all—not even the majority—of global interaction can be accounted for if we exclude informal or "unsanctioned" national representatives. Certainly not in the nineteenth-century United States, with its relatively low diplomatic profile and anemic State Department. Seafarers, far and away the largest community of Americans abroad in the first half of the nineteenth century, seem ideal and yet entirely neglected candidates in the effort to expand the evidentiary base in foreign relations historiography. Most studies assume that working people, deprived of the means to travel, engaged the wider world through dime novels, fairs, and other cheap amusement. But diplomats, travelers, and evangelists did not dominate U.S. overseas networks during the first half of the nineteenth century; those connections were largely populated by sailors. Despite the disproportionate attention granted to elites in the study of early American foreign relations, waterborne workers were the country's international face at the time.[9]

The state, it seemed to many, was absent in early diplomacy. Or if not absent, then overshadowed by those in the maritime community who "pry into the remotest regions" where local communities "behold the flag of our Union for the first time in their lives displayed—not from the gaff of one of our ships of war, but from the masthead of a whaler." Filibusters, Forty-Niners, temperance crusaders, African American colonization societies, Confederate expatriates, and numerous others were part of an array of individuals who embedded the United States in global affairs long before the seizure of its overseas empire, but each of these populations traveled networks pioneered and maintained by the nation's maritime community. They arrived at destinations where American seamen had long interacted with indigenous people and places where missionaries in particular never ceased to complain of the pitiable precedents produced by maritime "depravity." Nautical men crafted the channels along which other actors flowed outward into the world and often set the terms by which those groups could relate to their hosts. Observers at the time certainly noted that sailors "carry missionaries, embassadors, opera-singers, armies, merchants, tourists, scholars to their destination: they are a bridge of boats across the Atlantic; they are the *primum mobile* of all commerce." Yet for contemporary scholars of U.S. relations with the wider world, this single most sizeable cohort of Americans abroad has remained hidden in plain sight.[10]

Sailors were nineteenth-century America's largest class of representatives overseas, and thus the principal engine of its internationalization at the time. Maritime history *is* the history of early U.S. foreign relations. Including the ocean in America's master narrative fundamentally alters basic assumptions and trajectories governing that account. An isolationist dark, we have been told, prevailed until elite observers during the "global dawn" of America's Gilded Age began to articulate a more cosmopolitan outlook. Others insist that fin-de-siècle missionaries constructed the nation's first self-consciously global networks, while the post-1870 transatlantic immigration boom, for many more scholars, was the moment when the United States earned a truly transnational outlook. Some historians contend that nineteenth-century commodity chains and the consumption of goods from afar produced the circuits that first connected America to the world.[11]

These arguments by no means fall in the face of maritime material, but they must be reconciled with the very real ways in which the authors' protagonists circulated a world populated by an already influential cohort of working-class diplomats. They fail to appreciate how seamen carved the conduits along which King Cotton, King Wheat, and the other connective tissues of global commerce embedded the United States in broader capital flows. And even as seafaring labor allowed men and women of all classes to tastefully adorn their homes with imports and set their tables with exotic foods, mariners also made possible the surge of both forced and free migrants across the ocean. American missionaries and consular officials—regularly confounded by what they construed as the misbehavior of sailors—could only *wish* that isolationism characterized their country's conduct. It is more accurate, then, to see the late nineteenth century not as the international awakening of a slumbering continental giant but rather as a moment when control over the country's overseas foreign relations decisively shifted away from the maritime community's nonstate actors and into the hands of the state and state-allied interests. It is a narrative arc that must account for the decline of the mariner's influence in the face of consolidating elite authority and the use of that clout to clear the world of what was, across the nineteenth century, increasingly seen as a "rabble" whose chronic misbehavior jeopardized both the good name of the United States and the nation's significant overseas investments.[12]

But if sailors had an impact abroad, they also had one at home. Maritime encounters in the nineteenth century formed a large portion of the foundation for both public opinion in the United States about various other countries and peoples and developing ideas about the American people among the globe's other populations. The maritime realm reveals the permeability of national boundaries and how American history in the eighteenth and nineteenth centuries developed in dialogue with other parts of the world. The lives of sailors were linkages—conduits of information about race, nation, gender, and class—between the outside world and an emerging U.S. republic. An abundance of ships and sailors drew locations around the world into an American orbit, even as contact with the nation's maritime community allowed "foreign" peoples and places to exercise a reciprocal influence upon the United States. The watery regions between territorial nation-states facilitated intercultural encounters that proved powerful in the articulation of both similarities and differences between people. And as media outlets in the United States reported on those encounters, the images, descriptions, and qualitative distinctions between people manufactured by maritime actors helped shape popular conceptualizations of America in the world. The republic's sailors became sensory agents of the nation's commercial empire, or, in the words of one early nautical treatise, "the eyes and ears of the nation." "Then almost the only wide and constant travelers," seamen were touching, tasting, smelling, and seeing much of the world at a time when the lives of other Americans remained mostly local. Their experiences abroad, once recorded, were soon disseminated as influential insight.[13]

But while nineteenth-century Americans found themselves awash in maritime information, maritime history remains poorly integrated into the master narratives of nineteenth-century America and U.S. foreign relations.

Most maritime historians focus almost exclusively upon life aboard the ship at sea and continue to treat sailors as an isolated, eccentric enclave of men. Meanwhile, if and when diplomatic historians consider the ocean-going world, they fixate on the navy and an elite cadre of officers as agents of state power overseas. In isolation from one another, these fields have produced valuable and insightful historical knowledge, but it may be more fruitful to fuse subfields that are ordinarily segregated. The lives of sailors, after all, included far more than what happened at sea. Mariners were working men who spent considerable portions of their time ashore, interacting with a wide array of the planet's people. These interactions, in turn, constituted the bulk of early America's engagement with the world. If envoys and naval officers did conduct diplomacy, as we will see, it was often aimed at containing what they considered the "rambunctious" foreign relations of their working-class countrymen. So if the roughly 100,000 men who departed the republic each year during the antebellum era were in fact the largest and most influential population of Americans overseas, then the story presented here is less a maritime history than it is a history of the United States in the world.[14]

Although the word "sailor" itself often conjures something alien—the stereotype of Jack Tar, tattooed, tanned, swearing, womanizing, and hard drinking—seafarers are best considered agents in the internationalization of U.S. history. The idea that mariners represented "a peculiar class of men" or inhabited "a world unto themselves" does more to demonstrate bourgeois dominance of the sailor's public presentation than it does to illuminate the actual lives of men who labored afloat before the Civil War. The failure of mariners to comport with certain middle-class ideals did not necessarily render them so distinct as to justify their segregation from the larger history of the nineteenth-century United States. Indeed, to suggest otherwise is in many ways to reproduce the very rhetoric employed by the era's merchants, politicians, and other powerbrokers. Such individuals justified harsh disciplinary measures designed to extract labor from seafarers by claiming that maritime workers were in all ways "different" or "distinct" from other thinking and feeling people. The U.S. state, meanwhile, predicated its special dispensation to regulate the working lives of sailors on the notion that seamen were "strangers" to the customs and mores governing life ashore: "we do not look for the manners of a drawing-room on board of a ship," as one federal judge put it. Conceptualizations of the sailor as a singular, exotic "species" were popularized by people attempting to rationalize the power they exercised over the lives of seamen, and one unfortunate by-product of that process has been maritime history's gradual separation from bigger narratives about foreign relations and the United States in the world.[15]

Yes, sailors practiced certain distinctive rituals, dressed in specific garb, and spoke a special argot. But this was true of many different skilled tradesmen and vocational cohorts during the antebellum era. And yes, American sailors were notorious for distinctive markings and badges of status such as tattoos. But an inventory of that India ink reveals decidedly shoreside concerns: the two most common designs consisted of religious iconography and patriotic insignias. Mariners, therefore, are best thought of as "working men who got wet," individuals invested in their national origin and articulate about their own instrumentality in world affairs. They displayed sensibilities, attitudes, and opinions—about such key concepts as race, patriotism, masculinity, and honor—that suggested their close connection to ideologies operative ashore. This project proposes to investigate how American working men abroad chose to deploy those ideas, how foreign settings altered their meaning, and how peoples overseas influenced and were influenced by aquatic interlopers. Hence the usefulness of a term such as nonstate actor, an encompassing nomenclature that enables us to shed some of the stigma, strangeness, or "difference" usually associated with the word "seafarer." Nonstate actor is a term that better describes the republic's seamen ashore, many of whom identified as native-born U.S. citizens engaged in a consequential national project of commercial expansion. Nautical subject matter thus has more to teach us when it is de-exoticized, and thoroughly incorporated into broader narratives that detail the construction of U.S. empire in the nineteenth century. Sailors have much to teach us when captured off the ship's deck, intermingling with foreign populations, and acting as informal agents in the construction of the nation's foreign relations.[16]

The following pages, therefore, explore the records American men kept while laboring overseas, as well as documents maintained by those U.S. officials—consuls and naval officers—who were charged with monitoring, caring for, and disciplining the nation's maritime community. Each thematically organized chapter discusses one of several modes of encounter. These recurrent ideas or trends represent the larger concepts, methods, and principles through which American sailors interacted with the wider world. The separation of numerous themes into independent chapters, however, is not meant to suggest their mutual exclusivity. When and wherever applicable, the substantial overlap between categories of analysis that have been divided to attain some modicum of narrative coherence will be addressed. With that in mind, chapter 1 begins by noticing that nineteenth-century

Americans were awash in information from nautical sources. The antebellum era's seaports were also its largest producers of print, and sailors were, for a variety of reasons, the most literate cohort of working men in the United States. Those factors combined to make seamen active contributors to public discourse in America about the wider world and its diverse inhabitants. Seafarers supplied information about foreign peoples and places and became crucial intermediaries in the diffusion of observations gleaned overseas.

The second chapter investigates the many instances in which sailors staged blackface minstrel shows while traveling abroad. In their willingness to apply the burnt-cork mask and "jump Jim Crow" for indigenous groups around the globe, seafarers played a crucial role in disseminating American racial categories to an array of audiences. Maritime manuscripts also allow insight into how racial formation in the early United States was a global work in progress rather than a continental construct. Race was not produced exclusively by people in the United States, but was both forged in and thought applicable to an international context. The global diffusion of minstrelsy provides a focal point in the effort to describe ideas about racial difference in the United States as something that developed in dialogue with many places.

The third chapter considers how domestic rhetoric about Native Americans shaped how the republic's citizens abroad understood peoples they encountered. Frontier language and the discourses of civilization and savagery became one means by which American men comprehended the otherwise baffling diversity they encountered while abroad. In addition, expansionist rhetoric helped to legitimate violence against so-called Indians overseas and to authorize U.S. intervention and commercial intrusion into "underdeveloped" environments and economies. For a maritime community anxious to ennoble its own labor in terms that were reminiscent of the conflict and the Indian clearance characteristic of the continental frontier, manifest destiny seemed applicable around the world.

A fourth chapter discusses the form and substance of violent altercations between Americans and those they encountered abroad. It reads barroom brawling and harborside tumult as "diplomatic fisticuffs," that is, as sites for the enactment of a distinct, working-class, and masculine foreign relations agenda. The quarrelsomeness and disruption of the so-called sailor spree overseas was not anarchic but purposive, often targeted at racial inferiors whom white American seamen hoped to remind of their subject status. Yet the rampant rambunctiousness of sailors also created diplomatic headaches for the United States. In response to a perceived crisis in the stability of international mercantile capitalism brought about by mariners' misdeeds, a phalanx of missionaries, diplomats, and naval officers organized under the banner of "waterfront reform." They worked to implement disciplinary measures designed to prevent unruly sailors from jeopardizing profits derived from "peaceable" commerce's continued practice.

Of course, one stereotypical focal point of any mariner's "rowdiness" ashore was women. The myth of the sailor with a "girl in every port" has done much to obscure the complexity of relationships between seafarers and women overseas. Chapter 5 explores the intimate realm of the U.S. maritime empire and argues that sex and ideas about sexuality were crucial to mediating relations between seamen and the societies overseas through which they moved. Sailors became conversant in the sexual mores of a wide array of peoples, but the state and other authorities, in the form of consuls and Christian evangelists, scrutinized those sexual relations and attempted to exercise power by limiting "acceptable" forms of intimacy in their dominions. Moreover, the planetary forum in which sailors read the bodies and behavior of women suggests that rationalizations about inequality between the sexes had a transnational foundation in the nineteenth century. Within the seafaring community, in the nation's largest seaport cities, and traveling through print culture that often originated in those very cities, detail and debate emerged about American womanhood in a global context.

The sixth chapter acknowledges that sailors were the largest single community of itinerant peddlers in the world. American men came aboard ships expecting to trade with the globe's inhabitants, and these exchange relations dictated a significant portion of intercultural encounters abroad. Barter, however, looked very different than the sorts of transactions that sustained global mercantile traffic. Rather, the underground dealings of impoverished mariners in port represented a sort of shadow economy that was itself crucial to sustaining more profitable commercial connections between the United States and the wider world. American sailors helped integrate the nation into a global network of port city subsistence-level economies, even as their employers traded in the staples and consumer goods that enabled more affluent citizens at home to "buy into" empire.

Finally, an epilogue traces the significance of the decline of the deepwater maritime industry. By 1870, the largest community of Americans overseas were no longer common sailors but wealthy tourists. This was a meaningful transition with implications both for how U.S. citizens abroad came to be known and how the country introduced itself to the wider world. The work of overseas empire would now consist, in part, of erasing the allegedly discreditable legacy left by American sailors. Labor pools aboard global shipping, meanwhile, were more and more dominated by nonwhite peoples whom shipping firms and ship's officers believed were both more "tractable" and more cost effective.

Throughout the book, however, certain evidentiary issues have shaped the argument that is (and can be) presented. It is best, therefore, to address these several concerns up front. First off, the material utilized here skews the story in large part toward a specific subset of literate mariners with a presumably more reflective mindset than other sailors. This is offset, to some extent, by the use of depositions and consular files wherein non-literate seamen would provide statements signed with an "X." But many of the primary sources consulted—diaries, logbooks, correspondence, and memoirs—represent the narrative efforts of only the smallest fraction of a much larger workforce. They were written almost entirely by white, native-born Americans.

This amounts, in the end, to a notable silence surrounding nonwhite or foreign-born sailors in this account. While seafarers on the whole were a literate cohort of laboring men, nonwhite mariners generally exhibited far lower literacy rates. One finds much less material from which to draw meaningful conclusions about their encounters with people overseas. Of the very few diaries kept by black sailors that survive today, the most closely studied has been that of Charles Benson, a steward aboard the Salem ship *Glide*. Yet given his position on the vessel (stewards were usually viewed with suspicion by ordinary sailors, who were prone to describe them as the officers' "pets") and his race, Benson's journals exhibit, in one scholar's words, a pervasive "sense of isolation." It may be that black mariners wished, on some level, to distance themselves from the prejudices of white shipmates; Benson himself called "most all sailors" a "pack of fault finding ignorant men." But his is a rare voice. The perspectives of African American, Native American, Pacific islander, and immigrant seafarers, therefore, are largely absent from these pages. However, despite the diversity of the maritime workplace, native-born white American men still comprised an aggregate majority within national shipping prior to the Civil War. A study of their experiences abroad retains significance, even if it does not represent the most complete picture possible.[17]

Still, the absence of truly diverse perspectives is, in itself, a serious prob-lem, for, as mariner Richard Boyenton remarked in an 1834 journal entry, sailors were "a hetregenious mass of incongruity." Part of the issue here is occupational: a group of laborers called "sailors" worked aboard a vari-ety of vessels—whaleships, merchant traders, naval warships—each with its own rules and routines. The finer distinctions between these craft and service branches have been discarded to accommodate a more unified analytical framework, but the larger problem of flattening out the heterogeneous maritime world is connected to race and nationality. To put the issue bluntly: the "white" and "American" character of antebellum labor aboard ships flying Old Glory can be greatly overstressed. A project focused on the cross-cultural exchanges of American men abroad must acknowledge that sailors did not need to step off their ships to experience the international; vessels themselves *were* international meeting grounds. Although this book focuses on intercultural encounters abroad, several excellent articles and monographs chronicle the foreign relations of black sailors, which focused on circulating insurrectionary ideology between slave revolutionaries in Haiti and the broader Atlantic world and between northern free states and southern slave states. In other words, there are many good studies of life afloat that detail the racial and ethnic landscape aboard ships, depicting the sea as a sort of saltwater Babel. But while native-born, white U.S. citizens worked on craft that contained multitudes, most never seemed to stop identifying with their particular racial and national affiliations. More often than not, these men seemed to construe their appearance abroad and their interactions with other peoples through those special lenses.[18]

Indeed, the argument here, in part, traces growing disaffection with seafaring labor among white American men during the nineteenth century. That sense of estrangement proceeded from the intolerable poverty and confused racial politics life afloat generated, things that were unacceptable exactly because native-born white U.S. citizens were not supposed to experience the degradation they did at sea. The ocean is sometimes described as a heterotopic space divorced from the divisive prejudices of landward society and productive of supranational and multiracial collaboration among its assorted inhabitants. The cooperative possibilities presented by the sheer diversity of seafaring labor, however, seem to have become realities less and less often across the nineteenth century. This makes sense, given scholarly portrayals of the early republic as a place where American "national manhood" and "white manhood" increasingly became coequal and mutually constitutive propositions. As race science and romantic nationalism hardened prejudices at home, men who self-identified as white American sailors appeared to approach peoples overseas with varying degrees of suspicion, if not hostility.[19]

Finally, it should be recognized that the group studied here, deepwater sailors, were in fact unusual in an American maritime trade more oriented toward coastal and riverine traffic. As one recent survey persuasively argues, America was and is a "brown-water nation with a blue-water conscious- ness" whose "domestic waterborne commerce exceeded oceanic commerce by multiples of three and four." Another historian has noted that across the human past, the vast majority of the waterborne world has consisted of "alongshore peoples" who avoided the open ocean in favor of coastal envi- ronments. These are important points that demand consideration. But even if literate, white, native-born, saltwater sailors were the smallest percentage of the nation's maritime laborers, they were still the largest community of nineteenth-century Americans overseas. For the study of U.S. foreign rela- tions, that fact remains paramount.[20]

This was a large and broadly influential group of individuals who saw part of their labor abroad as ambassadorial in nature. Seafarers were im- mersed in an expansive and often public debate that was meant to define the new nation's role in the world and settle the question of how, exactly, Americans should introduce themselves to other peoples. Sailors exposed trends, tensions, and disagreements within the republic's nascent maritime empire that, when considered as a whole, represent a crucial if overlooked component of early U.S. foreign relations. Thus, rethinking mariners and what their labor represented can yield dividends. No less an authority than Herman Melville concluded of sailors that any "romantic view of them"—whether as exotic other, cosmopolitan revolutionary, or hedonistic nihilist—"is principally had through romances." The story told here of en- counters between working American men and individuals abroad remains attentive to the admonition of the famed whaleman and novelist to eschew any quixotic idealizations. It is a complex story of seafaring laborers who in the course of their multifarious voyages assaulted others even as authoritar- ian officers abused them, could be cheated and kept poor by swindling ship owners while they simultaneously stole from destitute shopkeepers, and who might find fellowship with diverse men even as that camaraderie was constructed in the context of the brutal mistreatment of women overseas. There are, in other words, no simple answers or easy explanations in detail- ing the lives of this miscellaneous mass of men. But the story, no matter how convoluted, still remains worth telling because national connection to the planet during the first half of the nineteenth century was principally nautical in nature. It is to that conflicted and conflict-ridden history of the early United States in the world that we now turn.[21]

Chapter 1

Schoolhouses Afloat

Mark Twain, remembering a Missouri boyhood distant from the ocean, in fact "incalculably far from any place," nevertheless spoke of American nautical daring as "in everybody's mouth." Recalling reports about the exploring expedition to the Pacific Ocean of U.S. naval officer Charles Wilkes, the famed author commented on "the noise it made, and how wonderful the glory!" People throughout his town were abuzz with new discoveries of lands and peoples that had previously "existed rather as shadows and rumors than as realities." Talk of the Wilkes mission thus joined a host of newspaper reports, editorial pieces, museum displays, panoramic spectacles, geographic textbooks, and other public forms by which the maritime community played a role as arbiter of the international. Twain's anecdote offhandedly ascribes to oceanic laborers partial responsibility for the image of the world, the "innumerable perceptions and beliefs based on everything from maps to hearsay," held by American residents. A small town on the then-western edge of the United States was animated by talk of global engagement: mariners allow us to accommodate the provincial and the planetary.[1]

Several factors combined to make Samuel Clemens's claims about sailors and nautically sourced information possible: high literacy rates among seamen, plentiful publications in port city hubs where mariners congregated, and the insistence with which many waterborne workers stressed their important role in American society. Moreover, a democratizing republic's reading public expressed more and more of an egalitarian interest in the lives of ordinary men, even if, as in the case of mariners, they were seen as living extraordinary lives by the standards of the time. Thinking about waterborne work as odd or "of interest" was itself a new development. Maritime labor—a pursuit that had in the seventeenth and eighteenth centuries served as a fairly ordinary stage in the maturation of men in America's coastal communities—looked increasingly like a distinct vocation whose practitioners had something special to say. Earlier generations of mariners in North America had published less often exactly because their work afloat was considered a normal, if temporary, vocation pursued by those who were expecting to eventually put down roots ashore. As the nineteenth century rolled around, however, and seafaring became a more exotic calling, its practitioners spent time justifying their time afloat and describing their working lives. The result of all that explication was a veritable explosion in the number of published seafaring narratives.[2]

The efflorescence of nautically themed media, in turn, reveals the danger associated with consistently conceiving of seafarers as men who occupied their own distinct and largely detached "watery" sphere. In doing so we overlook the connective function seafaring laborers often played; wide audiences in the United States read accounts of maritime exploits during the first half of the nineteenth century. Those publications were perused exactly because nautical life—hierarchical during a democratizing age, dependent on corporal discipline amid the rise of inner-directed individuals—increasingly looked like a foil to nineteenth-century modernity. Yet the more sea-voyage narratives were published, the better saltwater experience was integrated into the national consciousness. This chapter uses that fact in order to consider two interrelated issues: the manner and the terms by which members of the American maritime community used print to craft for themselves a highly public role in national life, and how sailors, as narrators, became important linkages between the United States and the wider world. Their frequent and widely circulated commentary on adventures, events, and occurrences abroad helped embed audiences at home in the United States in global currents of information. Seafarers, simply stated, served as crucial intermediaries between the United States and the wider world. American ships would become schoolhouses, educating audiences at home about cultures abroad.[3]

Mariners, therefore, did more than simply introduce America into the wider world. They also helped globalize the United States, and enhance what one scholar has called the "geographic consciousness" of the republic's readers. During the antebellum era, seafaring memoirs, autobiographies, and newspaper articles supplied by members of the maritime community all provided a point of contact between the domestic and the international. Sailors had any number of motivations for becoming authors. Some books read like captivity narratives, others were meant to enflame patriotic sentiment by detailing the cruelties of impressment and other British abuses at sea, and others told stories of reform and religious conversion. Yet at the core of them all was travel and the tales of new, different, or "foreign" sites such travel granted access to. Publications billed as "maritime memoirs" were as much travelogues as anything else. As mariner Charles Erskine noted, "We cannot all be sailors and travelers, and visit foreign lands; and so I intend that some of these strange places—the sunny islands of the Pacific and the frozen regions of the Antarctic—shall visit you." Mariners were, in his estimation, the "fearless pioneers of civilization who go forth in contempt of danger and death, to add to the sum of man's knowledge of the world" and "widen the boundaries of civilized existence." Or, as Ralph Waldo Emerson more succinctly summarized, "Chiefly the sea-shore has been the point of departure to knowledge, as to commerce." Mercantile pursuits might have motivated most voyages, but sailors also contributed to an economy of knowledge that made their observations of peoples and places overseas a marketable commodity.[4]

How sailors engaged with the wider world, how they narrated those events, and how those accounts were rebroadcast and interpreted among audiences at home point to the deeply consequential qualities of the American maritime community. Sailor stories shaped popular renderings of otherwise remote climes and their distant denizens. Such narratives suggest the potentially rich interplay between maritime escapades and the public record by which American readers might make reasonable judgments about peoples and events overseas. Shipboard laborers supplied much of the current that coursed through global circuits of knowledge. That in itself seems significant, given that most studies position working people as individuals who merely consumed the intelligence that other, higher-status sources generated. Mariners offer us the opportunity to examine a large population of ordinary individuals who in fact went into the world, engaged with foreign peoples and environments, and helped produce information.[5]

The first task these printed accounts assumed for themselves was to regularly remind readers that American sailors were everywhere, extending the nation's influence, contributing to its grandeur, and helping to promote the dissemination of valuable data. "Our commerce extends to every nation, and to every clime," began one such piece. "England alone pretends to compete with it," the article continued, "and even she is compelled to admit the invincible enterprize of American seamen." "Neither the inhospitable snows of the North, nor the burning regions of the South," the same author asserted, "can defeat our hardy sailors; the elements themselves have been made subservient to our use, and the riches of earth are pouring into our store-houses." Because creation was populated by "a divided and broken up human family that dwells upon the disrupted face of the earth," only the seaman, a "common carrier of all the physical, scientific, moral and religious productions of the world," could make those parts whole. Another report, this time from the *Sailor's Magazine*, reminded readers "how much we are indebted to the sailor": "He visits every clime, and brings to us the products of the most distant lands. He encounters storm, and peril, and dangers of every name, facing contagion and death, that he may minister to our luxury, as well as necessity, and while we are sitting quietly at our firesides, and reposing at ease on our beds, the sailor is braving the tempest, and causing a tide of wealth to roll over the land."[6]

But sailors also enjoyed emphasizing the important role they played in internationalizing America. They were well aware of their own instrumentality in building bridges between the nation and the wider world. George Little, reflecting in 1846 on his career afloat, dubbed seamen "great links [in] the chain which unites nation to nation, ocean to ocean, continent to continent, and island to island." Moreover, he continued, "an American sailor, when abroad, should recollect that he is a representative of his countrymen" with the "power to convey to those among whom he mingles a favorable impression . . . or to excite their prejudice against the name of an American." It was primarily through sailors, he concluded, that Americans would "gain a good name among foreigners." Jeremiah Reynolds, attached to the navy's Pacific squadron, reflected in his voyage narrative that the unique charge of the nation's nautical portion was to bear "our flag . . . to every portion of the globe, to give to civilized and savage man a just impression of the power we possess." That sailors moved freely across national boundaries made their role one of "impressing on others our spirit and efficiency," while at the same time learning of the "ability and resources" of other peoples so as to disseminate such useful knowledge at home in the United States. Sailors, Reynolds reminded his readers, while "rough and hardy," still wished to be thought of as their country's loyal representatives, willing and able to "account for wrongs suffered by their unoffending and unprotected countrymen."[7]

Sailors, in other words, used nationalist and expansionist narratives to include themselves in early nineteenth-century chronicles of burgeoning commercial empire. One of the recurrent themes of the seafaring stories the republic's mariners produced was the effort to position waterborne workers as valuable citizens. The affluence of America attested to their influence, even though seafaring careers themselves were not often financially rewarding. We "build the stately warehouses which overflow with the fabrics of every clime, erect the magnificent and splendid mansions which beautify and adorn our seaports, and construct the most beautiful specimens of naval architecture that float on the ocean." All such fruits of waterborne commerce were the sailor's gift. These appeals echoed contemporary testimony of antebellum workingmen's parties—of which sailors were often active members—to the role of producers in society, of the dignity and importance of manual labor in making wealth tangible. "Our labor has done it all," trumpeted one tract. Sailors "built and manned the ships which navigate every ocean." Seafarers stuffed cargo holds with the exotic commodities that "furnished the houses of the rich with all their comforts and luxuries." Waterborne workers allowed "those who fill the high places of society" to "feast their dainty palates on luxuries culled from every clime."[8]

In other words, many seamen depicted labor overseas aboard ships flying the stars and stripes as a badge of respectability. Global commercial expansion was particularly important to what one scholar has described as the process of "unbecoming British." To fly the American flag aboard ships in distant ports, anchored right beside His Majesty's vessels, was to offer proof that the United States had crawled out from under colonial dependency upon Great Britain and now traded freely as a peer of the globe's other great empires. Likewise, sailors' participation in the Revolutionary War and the War of 1812 (the latter conflict fought in part over "free trade and sailors' rights"), not to mention the experience of impressment, bolstered the republic's mariners' special claims to significance. Seamen in turn asked—at times in angry undertones—for acknowledgment as important actors in American aggrandizement. As later chapters will show, authorities overseas were skeptical of such claims, contending that mariners' misbehavior disrupted commerce as often as their labor facilitated it. And yet the persistence with which sailors asserted imperial utility and patriotic solidarity with citizens at home ought to reveal the significance of those ideas as the foundations of an American community among seagoing peoples who were often represented as outside national reach. Many in the maritime realm considered themselves to be some of the nation's chief delegates in the wider world. Early trade voyages were invested with meaning exactly because the country's small and underfunded government could not afford (and was ideologically indisposed) to maintain many foreign legations. This made the captains and crews aboard ships particularly important because they, and not any formal ambassador, would, as one newspaper in the early republic thought, generally "be the first who shall display the American Flag in those distant Regions." It was the responsibility of individuals aboard ships to render the nation "respectable by integrity and benevolence in all your conduct and dealings."[9]

Other observers and opinion makers shared these beliefs. One editorialist at the *Sailor's Magazine* remarked in 1832 that the nation's seamen "are visiting every port in the world, they are mingling among the nations, they have intercourse with every kindred and people and tongue, and are situated to exert a mighty influence, holy or sinful, according to their characters." The New Bedford Port Society asserted that mariners were "by no means unimportant as it regards our national character." Unquestionably "the most numerous and frequently the most important ambassadors of nations," shipboard laborers "supply the principal elements from which the conclusions are formed in distant regions, of the people who send them forth." Reporters claimed that "American Seamen possess immense power, either for good or evil. Their influence is like the element they inhabit—it surrounds the globe, and is felt through every part of the world." Another tract thought that mariners and the maritime sector more broadly were "the bearer[s] of our honor and our fame to every foreign shore," they are "the representatives of his country in every port . . . [and] by him, is [the] country in a greater or less degree estimated."[10]

That many of these testimonials about America's vibrant maritime sector were published suggests that some sailors were not simply avid consumers of words; they were producers as well. During the antebellum era, the United States shipped into the world tens of thousands of active observers, armed with pen and paper and anxious to report on the wider world for readers at home. Moreover, a burgeoning American print culture combined with democratic demands for the "common man's" voice ensured a healthy market for mass-produced seafaring narrative and maritime memoir. It was no accident that early America's most active media centers were also its largest seaports. Mariners often printed accounts of their exploits abroad, and they discovered a demand for their knowledge of overseas locations.[11]

Mercantile associations such as Salem's East India Marine Society or New York's American Geographical Society charged sailors with the tasks of keeping detailed journals and collecting "curiosities" abroad that would both enhance understanding about foreign peoples and places and provide intelligence about potential markets for American produce. Seafarers and, most crucially, maritime literacy were to be enlisted in the work of transcribing data that could advance the often interrelated objectives of science and commercial empire. Herman Melville famously scorned "the cosmopolite philosopher" employed by institutions of higher learning and dismissed fixations on the Enlightenment-driven exploration of individuals such as James Cook. Their individual efforts to educate others about the wider world, after all, represented nothing more than the collective "lifetime commonplaces" of ordinary sailors. Let those so-called sages, Melville instead suggested, "fire salutes to the honor and glory of the whale-ship, which originally showed them the way, and first interpreted between them and the savages." Class, the author implied, shaped the diffusion of knowledge, inasmuch as the social status of one's informant seemed to confer more or less legitimacy. "Respectably" sourced information was more likely to be archived, circulated and remembered, even though it represented only the smallest fraction of overseas travel performed. His diatribe was meant to remind readers—and historians—that a search for the true motive force behind the dissemination of information should look beyond the leatherbound, multivolume voyage narratives of wealthier travelers.[12]

In claiming that the sea "was my Yale College and my Harvard," Melville spoke to larger truths. His ruminations were echoed by the editorial boards of local papers that published fawning pieces trumpeting the "powerful claim which Seamen, as a class, had on all ranks of the community." Waterborne workers "had been from the earliest ages to the present time, the most important agents in the great work of maritime discovery," and "neither Vasco da Gama, nor Columbus—neither Anson, Cook, or Vancouver, would have been enabled to prosecute their perilous but successful voyages without the aid of the Seamen." Sailors produced and disseminated knowledge; they educated and informed. Hence J. Ross Browne's claim that "we are indebted to [American whalemen] for the extension of our commerce in foreign countries, for valuable additions to our stock of knowledge, [and] for all the benefits resulting from their discoveries and researches in remote parts of the world." Or another seafarer's praise for "the profuse store of knowledge brought by every ship's crew," which was "distributed together with India shawls, blue china, and unheard-of curiosities from every savage shore." William Phelps claimed that he had published his maritime narrative because "a man who has passed thirty or forty years roaming over the globe must be laden with rich experiences, unless he has passed along with his eyes shut, which, if imparted to the many who have not been much abroad, cannot fail to interest and enlighten them." One periodical's published list of reasons "why seamen ought to rejoice in their going out" recorded that first and foremost, "it is by means of foreign intercourse that knowledge is spread throughout the world"; without sailors, "the progress of knowledge must necessarily be very slow."[13]

But customarily, the role of seafaring in literature is reduced to the output of a very few individuals: Melville's *Typee* and, more famously, *Moby Dick*; yachtsman Jack London's *The Sea Wolf*; the hyperrealism of merchant sailor Joseph Conrad's *Lord Jim*. But even if maritime experience shaped their literary concerns, these individuals are treated emphatically as writers. Sailing seems to be a scribe's avocation while he pursues his truer calling. The presumption becomes that time spent among the ocean's illiterate and motley rabble of renegades enabled these authors' compositions to express cross-class and racial sympathies that were unusual for their respective times and places. One concludes that the literati did not emerge from below decks; instead they passed through them and, in doing so, gave voice to the voiceless. The reality, however, was far more complex. Attentiveness to the historical record reveals that famed sea authors did not write alone. Rather, they worked in a profession that was prone to produce piles of print.[14]

Reading, writing, and education helped diminish the dreariness of maritime labor. For what truly struck mariners, what they could not complain enough of, was the sheer *boredom* of life at sea. "It is well known to all who have crossed the ocean," mariner Richard Cleveland wrote, "that a passage at sea presents little of interest." Repetitive language helped textualize the tedium: his journey showed him little else than "the same unbounded and unvaried horizon, the same abyss of waters, [and] the same monotonous routine of duties to be performed on board." At least one American editorialist for a port city periodical sympathized. Before condemning the notoriously unrestrained behavior of seafarers ashore, he cautioned, observers ought remember that these were men "returned from a long period of confinement," only recently freed from "the monotony of the tossing waves and a routine of service within the walls of a single ship." A useful comparison helped make this point. The seaman who returned to land, this author thought, resembled "the student released from his studies; each in his turn, gives the reins to other propensities of his nature."[15]

In choosing an academic analogy to illustrate the confinement of common sailors, the writer proved more accurate than he likely intended; it was precisely the dullness of the deck that inspired mariners to convert their ships into schoolhouses. Their lives were regulated by a system of watches that ensured regular intervals of rest every twenty-four hours, and seafarers looked for ways to fill that vacant time. Options varied. Story-telling, dancing, singing, sewing, wrestling, and any other number of diversions worked to combat the weariness of routine. Periods of idleness, however, also provided the opportunity for reading and writing. Accounts of life at sea document sailors engaged with one another in joint acts of literary production and literacy instruction. Henry Wise thought that with pleasures aboard ship "limited," the "chief resource" for seamen seeking entertainment "was reading"; sailors "sought the library and poured over handfuls of ponderous tomes of physics, history, or travels." "Books," he concluded, "find their true value on shipboard—cut off from all amusement of the land, we derive the full benefit by reading." Another sailor, who tellingly titled his memoirs the reflections of "A Roving Printer," stated quite matter-of-factly that leisure time aboard ship "is generally spent by the crew in reading and writing." George Little, on a trading voyage to South America, thought that the "monotony of a sea life" was broken only by one's ability to find active mental engagement. Aboard his ship one Sunday afternoon in 1811, he noted how "on one side of the forecastle might be seen some engaged in painting vessels, landscapes, &c.; on the other were a group writing their journals; while a third set were learning navigation, taught by a young shipmate . . . [while still others] sat reading the Bible." The scene of a ship's deck crowded with scholars did not seem to surprise Little in any way. Rather, he rattled off the roll call of various people's occupations with a nonchalance that suggested the ordinariness of the day.[16]

By the end of the three-month voyage, Little had adopted an instructional role for himself; in his spare time, he saw to it that his "messmate, Jack Sawyer, made rapid progress in learning to read." Other men made sure that "the elementary branches of education were taught": "It was a common circumstance to see, in a clear day, from twenty to thirty of the crew" on deck "engaged in study." "Indeed," Little declared, "the forecastle," the section of ship reserved for common sailors, "was more like a school than anything else." Several historians have documented how an Atlantic maritime subculture stressed fraternal bonds between shipmates beyond the polarizing proclivities of race and nation. While those claims can be overstressed, it does seem significant that camaraderie at sea could develop as a function of reading, writing, and the learning of those skills. Scholarly accounts tend to locate the coalescence of connections between diverse crew members in the regular rituals of masculine performance. Treating one another in barrooms, patronizing brothels, and mutual resistance to the sometimes brutal abuses of officers are the behaviors more regularly cited as producing unity among sailors. Yet of seemingly further-reaching significance were the scenes Little described of men joined in the shared pursuit of basic to more advanced literacy. As Little put it, while his shipmates "differ[ed] essentially" from "associations met with previously to embarking on a sea-life," he still felt "contented and happy" because their mutual efforts to impart knowledge caused them to "feel an indescribable interest" in one another. Charles Erskine told a similar tale of his life afloat, where, during one of his earliest voyages, a shipmate taught him to read: "I went down to the berth deck . . . and told him that I wanted to learn to write." The man immediately "made some straight marks and some that were not straight on a piece of paper, and told me to copy them in ship-shape fashion." With enough practice, Erskine soon mastered the alphabet and with that came a rudimentary literacy that later blossomed. William Abbe, another foremast hand, noted in his journal simply that he "commenced to teach Johnny to read, sitting with him in the steerage." Later in the voyage he reported, "I have now 3 or 4 scholars and teach in the forecastle reading, writing, arithmetic, [and] geography."[17]

Literacy, however, entailed more than what sailors learned. It was also a weapon they attempted to use in an effort to push against stereotypes of themselves as ignorant rubes. Whaleman William Whitecar found that his fellow sailors were not the boors popular culture depicted, but rather, "thoroughly conversant with the leading topics of the day, and each, like every true American, had his individual opinion of the merits of newspaper notorieties, politics, and other matters that engross the American mind." Another sailor thought the books stacked in the confines of his ship ought to suggest that seafaring people were more than "mere machine[s]—a mass of bone and muscle." Henry Mercier, a sailor in the U.S. navy, consciously referred to his shipmates as "Literary Tars." Anticipating the suspicion that designation might arouse, he asked "should it be considered a strange or unaccountable coincidence if we had our book-worms on the forecastle of a tight Yankee frigate, as well as in the drawing room?" Adopting the truly international perspective his mobile profession allowed for, Mercier testified that "the 'march of mind' is abroad, and making rapid strides in both the hemispheres." "Why then," he persisted, "should it not on its journey take a sly peep amongst the man-of-war?" After all, the mariner reasoned, "when sailing on the boundless Ocean for weeks and weeks together, each day bringing forth the same dull, unvaried round of employment . . . what can be a greater resource to help dispel [boredom] than the interesting or amusing volume?" Some sailors, then, used literacy to advocate for their own enlightenment, to equate, in Mercier's words, the forecastle with the "drawing room." Reading might help close the cleavages of class and status that, as Melville had complained, increasingly distanced common sailors from the "respectable" quarters of antebellum American society.[18]

Estimates vary depending on the period under consideration, but most scholars agree that by the mid-nineteenth century, somewhere between 80 to 90 percent of the nation's citizen-mariners had at least rudimentary reading and writing skills. The New England origin of many of these men (arguably the most literate society in the Atlantic world) and the collective educational dimension of shipboard life combined to make the country's Jack Tars (as the men who so often dealt with that sticky pitch were colloquially known) one of the era's most literate cohorts of working people. At sea, individuals read widely and, for lack of alternatives, thoroughly. Sailor literacy itself was a highly contested subject among some nineteenth-century reformers who thought men before the mast were ill influenced by, in the words of one evangelical periodical, "their adherence to the light trash in the form of cheap literature which floods our land, and is generally found in our forecastle." In response, missionaries inundated departing ships with Bibles, temperance tracts, and proselytizing pamphlets, while several religious organizations established sailors' reading rooms in foreign ports and offered literacy instruction. Whether or not seafarers used their lessons to pious ends was another matter entirely. Most seemed indifferent to missionary meddling, and a few were hostile. A navy foretop man named Nathaniel Ames, for example, argued that "sailors universally are extremely fond of reading and are far better judges of books than they are allowed credit for." Thus, when reformers "stuffed ships full of [a] gloomy species of tracts," they "defeated their own object." Port city trade organizations such as the New York Mercantile Library Association or the Seamen's Library Company of New York had better luck establishing subscription libraries that departing mariners patronized. The U.S. navy likewise provided its vessels with libraries that seamen and officers could borrow from freely. One surviving 1839 catalog from the USS *Narragansett* noted that volumes could be checked out for fourteen days, with a fine of two cents per day thereafter. The list of subscribers ran the gamut from a commodore to several coal heavers. Another observer noted that the USS *Vincennes* had "a good collection of books on board," which "under the direction of a librarian" provided "for the recreation and improvement of the crew."[19]

Moreover, books and other printed material became a sort of currency between sailors and among ships at sea. Richard Henry Dana Jr., undoubtedly the era's best-known American sailor author, reported that during his voyage around Cape Horn, the ship often met with other vessels eager to trade in the written word. Referring to a whaleship they met with at sea, Dana recorded that "we exchanged books with them—a practice very common among ships in foreign ports, by which you get rid of the books you have read and re-read, and a supply of new ones in their stead." Rummaging through the chests of new acquaintances in search of something fresh for the eye gave sailors a pleasure they deemed inexpressible to people ashore. Dana claimed to have loaned everything he owned while at the same time admitting himself guilty of "borrowing and reading all the books there were to be found." "Anything," he exclaimed, "even a little child's story-book, or the half of a shipping calendar, seemed a treasure." That Dana, a Harvard student on nautical sabbatical, should have cherished books seems unremarkable. But he spoke of swapping printed information as an almost universal habit in the maritime circles he traveled. If anything approaching a global "information superhighway" existed in the early nineteenth century, here was its operation: sailors exchanging books, magazines, and newspapers from one ship to another over the course of a voyage.

That information leapt from ship to ship and found its way into circulation among networks of American print. Maritime penetration of the public imagination was regular and routine. When Dana later published his experiences afloat as *Two Years before the Mast*, he merely contributed to a much larger international exchange of reading material that seafaring life had allowed him to tap into. And just as Dana's vivid descriptions of California would prove instrumental in improving national knowledge of and interest in that increasingly desirable territory, so other seafaring narratives educated audiences about America's presence in the world. Seafarers helped feed and shape the flow of public information in the early United States.[20]

Sailors, in fact, often spoke of being immersed in a feedback loop wherein previously published voyage narratives inspired their own desire to travel overseas. Those individuals then published their own accounts, encouraging additional travel by subsequent readers of those accounts. Take, for example, the case of Alonzo Sampson, who went to sea, he said, because "a desire for travel and adventure was a leading trait of my character from a child." That desire had been stimulated by "books descriptive of foreign countries, and accounts of voyages by sea," which "possessed a wonderful interest for me, and were sought and read with the greatest avidity." When Frederic Hill "firmly decided" that he "would be a sailor and nothing else," he attributed the choice to his "favorite seafaring books." John Sleeper, meanwhile, claimed that his "wish to go abroad [and] visit foreign countries and climes" had been stimulated by his "strong attachment to reading matters relating to ships and sailors." Some mariners, thus, were drawn into a world of their own creation.[21]

Early American books, newspapers, and travelogues were not simply objects which word-hungry sailors squabbled over aboard ship. Rather, periodicals were littered with accounts that testified to the important role members of the maritime community played as intermediaries of information. The burgeoning mass media of the nineteenth century intersected with a contemporaneous expansion of the reach of American shipping to make the country's public sphere reliant on mariners for facts from abroad. Before media companies paid large numbers of foreign correspondents, sailors served that function. Indeed, so valuable was oceanic intelligence that the Harbor News Association was founded in 1849 to pool the resources of several large New York papers in order to station press agents in Halifax, Canada. That Nova Scotian city, the North American port closest to ships returning from Europe, became an informational hub that telegraphed to the United States transatlantic news supplied by vessels, their seamen, and the newspapers those individuals carried. Officers and ordinary mariners were interviewed for countless stories as their ships returned to port. Before the transatlantic communication cables that accelerated the dissemination of data, newspapermen prowled hectic harbors in Boston, New York, and Philadelphia for the latest reports from distant locales.[22]

Port city newspaper accounts were subsequently circulated around the country as other dailies and weeklies reprinted stories. To be an informed citizen aware of the outside world and its affairs was to be dependent, to some extent, on mariners. Both the republic of letters and the imagined community of nationhood, which championed the sophistication and knowledge conferred by literacy, traced a portion of their origins to waterborne workers who were often assumed to be illiterate and ignorant. The *Boston Courier* made that relationship explicit when it observed that "the great mass of dwellers upon terra firma, who contrive, by burning the midnight oil, to enlighten themselves, if not dazzle and illuminate the world," were indebted to "the mariner's bravery." Sailors supplied both the information readers enlightened themselves with and the spermaceti by which lamps and candles required to read were lit.[23]

A good deal of the newspaper coverage of nautical subjects attempted to embed the knowledge acquired by aquatic actors overseas in nationalistic narratives. Sailors became exemplars of American achievement, epitomes of audacity. Covering the discovery of an island in the Pacific by one of the country's whaleships, the *New York Sun* thought the episode uneventful not because the land lacked potential value but because the moment was just one of many demonstrations of American nautical nerve. It was only another "bold Yankee navigator" doing "what they have often done before, explore regions and lands . . . in perilous seas which other nations have not had the daring, enterprise, and perseverance to achieve." The *New-Bedford Daily Mercury* struck a similarly wearied tone when it printed excerpts from a whaleman's diary for their readers' edification. "As far as mere discovery goes there is little left to be done in the Pacific. Our whalers have cruised over, or crossed, nearly all the ground that had hitherto been untraversed." Americans were urged to consider their country's contributions to the science of geography and to remember that sailors extended the nation's reach into faraway places. As another periodical reminded readers, America's "'old salts' are better acquainted with these seas than any other seamen in the world" and often helped otherwise learned men revise maps "incorrectly marked by geographers." What little Americans knew of many places— particularly the Pacific, given its distance from the Atlantic world—was often derived from nautical sources.[24]

In addition to the maritime community's contributions to mapping and "discoveries," many news stories chose to highlight sailors as a crucial foundation for news and views from abroad. "We are indebted to Captain Upham of the ship *Corinthian*, recently arrived from the Pacific Ocean, for the following details," one typical 1835 account began. A "robbery and outrage, committed by one of the savage sovereigns of the South Sea Islands" was the subject of this particular story. The ship's company, its captain, and the *Boston Mercantile Evening Journal* recounted the events "as a warning to all who may be disposed to place reliance on the good faith of those untutored barbarians." With its lurid description of hostage-taking, showers of spears, and fierce Pacific islanders "singing the war-song continually," this newspaper narrative sensationalized events to titillate readers. It no doubt served the practical purpose of warning future voyagers of potential danger, yet it also meant to present images and convey characterizations of native peoples in the Pacific basin as violent, savage, and untrustworthy. Other papers picked up the report: within a month it reappeared in other Boston publications and news outlets scattered throughout New England's hinterlands. As it circulated in interconnected media markets, this self-proclaimed "warning" about the South Pacific's barbarous residents shifted in scale. What had been a minor altercation between a few individuals far away from the nation's shores entered the consciousness of the public as a recorded event capable of shaping American public opinion about distant peoples.[25]

Published accounts frequently testified to the brokering function the maritime community played between the United States and the wider world. In August 1800, readers in Boston, Salem, New York, and Baltimore had access to "extracts of a letter from the surgeon" aboard a Providence ship recently back from China. In an 1832 story that circulated through much of New England, the *Nantucket Enquirer* claimed to be "indebted to Captain Worth, of the ship *Rambler*, arrived at this port from the Pacific, for some information relative to islands visited by him during his voyage." Another episode at Lynn, Massachusetts, involved "letters received in town from . . . the brig *Charles Doggett*" describing people and events at the "Feejee Islands" in 1834. In 1836, relying on information from mariners who returned from those same islands, New England and New York newspapers alerted readers to certain "melancholy intelligence": with the "arrival at Edgartown of the ship *Cyrus*, Capt. Hussey, from the Pacific Ocean" came word of the murder of several American sailors and a call for the navy to "revenge the loss of so many valuable lives." Subsequent information provided by seamen gave one editor license to portray "Feejee Islanders" as "the most treacherous of any in the Pacific Ocean" who "seldom show the whites any quarter so fond are they of eating them." Mentioned only in passing was the fact that "all the accounts we have from the Feejees tell[ing] of their inhuman treachery" came from a singular source: "our whalemen."[26]

An 1865 edition of the *Boston Daily Journal* began another story by noting that "Thomas Ross, a colored man, one of the crew of the gunboat *Tioga*, called upon us yesterday and gave an interesting account and showed us some of the effects of a four years' compulsory residence among the cannibals of the Pacific Islands." When Ross and several shipmates survived a shipwreck, they "were immediately seized by the natives, stripped of their clothing, and at once inducted into the modes and ways of life peculiar to that people." The account stressed that "no harm was done them," though they were "compelled to adopt all the fashions of the natives," including perforated earlobes, which gave Ross a "grotesque appearance." Newspapers offered storytelling sailors a public platform from which to claim authority for themselves as veritable encyclopedias. Individuals such as the "colored man" Thomas Ross must have appreciated the influence their experience abroad commanded, given the more widespread marginalization nonwhite peoples contended with in nineteenth-century American society.[27]

Newspapers also regularly published letters sent home to families of seafaring men, thus widening the potential audience for maritime correspondence. The *Nantucket Inquirer*, for example, circulated an "Extract of a letter from Captain Richard Macy, Master of the Whaling Ship *Maro* to Josiah Hussey, Esq., of Nantucket" describing life in the Fiji Islands. That same story later appeared in at least five different newspapers.[28] The *Boston Daily Advertiser* presented "an extract from a letter from the third mate of the ship *Awashonks* of Falmouth, to his parents in that place" with the hope that its contents would prove interesting to readers. At times affairs tended toward the bizarre. In 1870, the *Salem Gazette* reprinted "several letters, from Mr. J.S. Russell, of our city," who "accompanies the U.S. [Naval] Expedition to Midway Island." Russell's principal fixation was the island's tropical climate, which "colors a white person, to a most complete shade of brown." The destabilization of his interconnected senses of regional and racial identity intrigued him. "Our party," Russell continued, "looks more like natives of the tropics, than genuine New Englanders." Could an authentic Yankee have a dark complexion? The possibility that "we may become quite black before summer is ended" even crossed his mind, throwing into sharp relief a larger discourse about the suspect whiteness of the nineteenth-century's seafaring citizens. The expectation that at least some mail would be published surely shaped how writers narrated events abroad. Mail might assume a scripted or even censored quality as mariners performed a particular role: that of the initiated guide responsible for making the exotic intelligible. Publication was more likely if the sailor reporter sensationalized events or rendered a scene in particularly striking terms. Decorum and decency, on the other hand, required the omission of particularly colorful episodes. What united most of these printed letters was an implied invitation for readers at home to invest themselves in the exoticism, extent, and wonder of the nation's maritime empire.[29]

But though letters home proved a popular medium through which to inform readers of events overseas, sailors need not have been literate to contribute. Those incapable of a signature might still grant oral interviews to curious newspaper correspondents. New York and Boston papers ran the stories of Horace Holden and Benjamin Nute, American mariners who returned home after spending five years "in slavery among the savages of Palau." Reporters "sought an interview" with the recently redeemed captives "and in a long conversation obtained from them [several] particulars" about their imprisonment. Likely unable to point out Palau on a map, American readers relied on maritime informants to learn what they needed to know about those Pacific people. "Cowardly and servile, yet most barbarous and cruel," the island's inhabitants, according to these seamen, seemed to "combine in their habits, tempers, and dispositions, the most disgusting and loathsome features which disgrace humanity." As an indication of that atoll's atrociousness, "our informants assure us that they were frequently indebted to the tender mercies of the men for escapes from death at the hands of women," who "outstrip the masculine in cruelty and savage depravity." Both the interviewers and the interviewees "regard[ed] as remarkable" a society where the "gentler sex" was the more vicious of the two. This reversal of gender roles justified condemnation of Palau and the conclusion that the island's indigenous population "are a very listless, idle people with very little intellectual powers."[30]

The regularity with which these missives, commentaries, and snippets were published is worth noting because it suggests how ordinary it was for individuals perusing papers to find information from abroad supplied by maritime actors. Typically, scholars have focused on particular flashpoints as moments when the public relied on seafarers for knowledge of or perspectives about a particular place or people overseas. Many officers and seamen who had experienced captivity in the Barbary states of North Africa, for example, turned to print as a way to valorize their own actions, complain about government policy, make ends meet, or draft very thinly veiled abolitionist attacks on slavery in the United States. Collectively, those narratives provided descriptions of distant regions and the customs of their inhabitants. Similarly, the United States Exploring Expedition, which circumnavigated the globe from 1838 to 1842, produced piles of print that helped familiarize American readers (like a young Mark Twain) with far-off places. These extraordinary events, however, never stood alone. Rather, they tapped into the broader popularity of published seafaring stories and the more regular appearance of nautical knowledge in a variety of printed media.[31]

But print was not the only medium through which nautical knowledge made its appearance. Even the theatre, on rare occasions, provided an opportunity for seafarers to serve as informational links between the United States and the wider world. Sailors were, of course, stock characters in eighteenth- and nineteenth-century British and American theatre, but some productions offered seafarers themselves the opportunity to dramatize their experiences overseas. In 1817, for example, the Philadelphia Theatre ran a play entitled *The Armourer's Escape, or, Three Years at Nootka Sound*, detailing the captivity of John Jewitt, one of two survivors of a massacre aboard the brig *Boston*. As it anchored off present-day Vancouver Island in 1803, Jewitt's vessel was attacked by a band of Nuh-chah-nulth Indians in retaliation for outrages committed by previous captains and crews. Jewitt was spared because of his skill as an amateur metallurgist and lived with the indigenous community for three years before his rescue. The circumstances of this extensive sojourn were recorded and published as *A Narrative of the Adventures and Sufferings of John R. Jewitt*, which was later adapted for the stage by American playwright James Nelson Barker. The production tapped into a number of extant genres and anxieties such as Robinson Crusoe-esque survival, captivity narratives (both Indian and Barbary), and dramatizations of U.S. expansion, but what was unusual in this case is the fact that Jewitt played himself. He and other sailors—particularly in plays about the Tripolitan Wars and American stagings of British nautical playwrights such as Charles Dibdin—helped dramatize their role as intercultural intermediaries. Americans who saw these melodramas were regularly reminded of their country's maritime connections to the world and the nation's dependence on seamen for depictions of peoples overseas. Relations between sailors, actors, and the audience were mutually influential. Playgoers' expectations about the "savagery" of supposedly uncivilized peoples overseas forced Barker to sharpen the edges of Jewitt's memoir, which as originally published had portrayed the Puget Sound's indigenous peoples with at least a modicum of sympathy. Hardening attitudes toward Indians as irredeemably barbaric (as chapter 3 will discuss in detail) would come to have consequences for how future generations of American sailors depicted native communities overseas.[32]

Sailors influenced the world's public presentation in the United States with more than words, speeches, or dramatic readings. As Thomas Ross noted above, mariners were often prepared to proudly display "some of the effects" they regularly acquired in distant lands. They returned home with objects—each telling their own story—that were displayed in various public and private forums. Even people from far away were exposed to the American gaze through maritime mediation. The no doubt bewildered "Birilip, a young native of the Feegee Islands, brought to this country by Capt. Eagleston in the ship *Emerald* [and] being exhibited at the Baltimore Museum" could testify about the capacity of seafaring to familiarize Americans with the unfamiliar. So too might the "three natives of Nuku Hiva, in the South Sea . . . [whom] the ship *Lion* . . . has brought to this country." The editors of the *Providence Patriot* could only "trust they will be treated with kindness and hospitality," having been "adopted into the great American family" by several seamen. The United States Exploring Expedition, meanwhile, returned home with a Fijian leader named Veidovi (spelled "Vendovi" in accounts at the time) who was suspected of having played some role in the murder of several American seamen. Veidovi died of tuberculosis very soon after arriving in New York, where city papers joked that this "cannibal of the 'first class'" had expired "in consequence of having nothing but roast beef and salt pork to eat." And yet those same sources expressed their hope that the corpse "may be placed in some Museum where [people] may be able to see it," revealing how ordinary it was for the public to depend on seamen as their source for the "exotic." The pickled head of "his Feegee Highness" was ultimately preserved for display and stood alongside a wide array of artifacts other seamen supplied from abroad.[33] How else to explain the intelligibility of Stephen Douglas's refrain—articulated over and over during his famed debates with Abraham Lincoln—that when the authors of the Declaration of Independence announced that all men were equal, "they did not mean the negro, nor the savage Indians, nor the Fiji Islanders. They were speaking of white men." The country's expansive maritime sector made such a claim conceivable because it familiarized people with "distant savagery."[34]

The transfer of individuals, however, was far less regular than the more ordinary way that seafarers provided the basis for imaginative connections between the United States and the wider world: the circulation of exotic "souvenirs" from distant shores. For many American men working away from home, collecting objects overseas and distributing them in their communities of origin achieved important ends. The items themselves were prestige goods that proved where one had ventured and publicly demonstrated the difficulties one had overcome in acquiring such curiosities. Yet for men who worried about a potential fraying of family relations, friendships, and romances as a result of distance, collectibles helped cement a sense of continued connectedness to shoreside communities. The goods often became keepsakes. Sailors who wrote about purchasing them often mentioned their hope that the objects would evoke distant lands, foreign craftsmanship, and, more generally, the strange, the distant, and the unique. Every voyage had its cohort of collectors, men who bought fanciful mementos, gathered odd animals, and plucked particularly striking plant life (some of which remains pressed between the pages of journals to this day). The aggregate impact of all this gathering provided a key way for ordinary Americans to connect to the larger world of global commerce.

Longer traditions of intercultural contact between mercantile capitalism and societies ashore made it possible for local economies overseas to develop sophisticated understandings about the tastes and desires of Euro-American maritime travelers. Enduring economic interconnection generated the growth of specialized sectors that were attuned to the needs or curiosity of working men in the seafaring community. Niche commercial districts developed as craftsmen began to produce items meant to satisfy the specific demands of visiting sailors. Many places acquired the rudiments of what might be termed a tourist economy, one that depended on a regular influx of mariners to sustain a mode of existence. Local artisans trafficked in exotic objects and souvenirs that American seamen then circulated at home. Bayard Taylor, traveling in the company of a U.S. naval squadron, remembered time spent ashore east of Taiwan at the Lew Chew (now Senkaku) Islands in the 1850s. "We were all anxious to procure some souvenir of the Island," he said. Consequently, "the sales were brisk and rapid, and most of the articles went off at a premium." Beads would buy nothing, though, for the island was emphatically a cash economy. Taylor "reckoned that there were at least a hundred dollars spent on the occasion." But although the native vendors conversed in currency, the traveler still felt as though their hosts "had lost 'the run' of us." The enthusiasm men showed for "Japanese silks, brass hair pins, straw sandals, fans, tobacco pouches, vases" and other finery "seemed to puzzle and bewilder the Loo Chooans," and such "recklessness of expenditure [was] quite beyond their comprehension."[35]

Taylor's mention of souvenirs aligned closely with other accounts kept by seafarers traveling throughout the world. Sailors were avid collectors who gathered over the course of a voyage mementos that exhibited craftsmanship distinct to distant places. As one diarist noted near the equatorially situated Jarvis Island, "a canue came alongside and a few of the natives called upon [us]," bringing "some rude specimens of their carving which will be quite a treat for our friends at home." Robert Weir, aboard a ship anchored at Madagascar, expressed his ambition to "get several spears, shells, and different kinds of cloth," while in the Comoros, he wanted to "trade for a few shells to remember the place by, perhaps Emma would like some." Frederic Hill, aboard a ship anchored along the Chinese coast in 1850, mentioned that "we made many purchases of curios, at prices that would now seem marvelously low, and returned to Hongkong, at the expiration of our visit, loaded down with presents for our friends at home." One sister wrote to her brother in the navy after he sent several souvenirs home, "We have had a good deal of fun opening boxes and getting out the curiosities. Fanny says the house is quite a museum." Seafarers helped American residences become international spectacles.[36]

Other men in the maritime community reported on portions of the world similarly familiar with the propensity of sailors to stock up on particular kinds of goods. Charles Wilkes, the commander of the United States Exploring Expedition, commented on the sailors' crazed engagement with "the trade in native curiosities" at New Zealand. Mats, carved whale's teeth, and a local cloth made from tree bark were popular, but no item seemed to titillate as much as the "tattooed heads" natives collected and cured. Wilkes himself admitted to purchasing "two preserved heads of New Zealand chiefs." Charles Judd's experience proved far less macabre, but he too had multiple opportunities to explore ashore and collect souvenirs. Residents in Madeira, despite the imposition of a quarantine, managed to come aboard in large numbers, bringing with them "the usual quantities of feathers, flowers, Dago caps, etc. etc." in which "some invested largely." Further south at the Cape Verde Islands, the men again reveled in "buying curios as souvenirs," though "the stores were oddly arranged and caused us much wonderment." That this was all usual for the navy man suggests how usual it was for those who were selling as well. Another sailor anchored at Canton marveled that "at meal hour our deck resembled a fancy Bazaar" populated by "villianious looking men reeking with filth . . . comming aboard to dispose of the most splended specimens of workmanship in gold silver ivery satans glass feathers at a price merely nominal."[37]

Purchasing brought the men into close contact with varieties of humanity some found personally revolting, even as it simultaneously forced a recognition of their attention to craftsmanship and ingenuity. People might be dismissed, but the fruits of their labor were subject to a different set of standards. Furthermore, the equation of the ship's deck to a floating mart reveals how mariners infused some maritime contact zones with ready money, sparked demand, and so proved instrumental to early economic development in ways that mercantile balance sheets fail to show. Industry abroad, from the makers of "Dago hats" to the tanning of human heads, was shaped, in part, by the influence such a large contingent of itinerant citizens exercised. Artisans and vendors around the world began, increasingly, to specialize production for a lucrative trade in curiosities directed at the tastes of maritime laborers. So widespread and popular was this trade that by the 1850s, museums and collectors were warned to keep a close eye out for "spurious" souvenirs from the Pacific, given that entrepreneurial seamen hoping to profit from a trade in forgeries "had learned the manner of preparing them from native medicine men." They then peddled "inauthentic" items as the genuine article.[38]

But sailors were also thought appropriate candidates for gathering more "substantive," scientifically valuable items as well. Charged with collecting specimens and goods by various port city marine, geographical, and anthropological societies, sailors became mediators who helped Americans attain a sense of connection to the outside world via material goods. Sometimes literally so; many seaport museums hired retired sailors as guides to their collections, asking them to narrate their overseas experiences and contextualize items. One patron at the East India Marine Society's collection in Salem remarked that the "effect of the ancient mariner" guide was "as if one had been transported in a moment to far off tropic lands, where palms were waving in air serpents and strange beasts lurking in the jungles." Clothing, shields, spears, artistic productions, and all varieties of goods were brought back to the United States in the chests of sailors ready to sell their finds to families and institutions keen on displaying such objects as badges of distinction or to satisfy a paying public's curiosity. Indeed, one seafarer described an odd scenario at Hong Kong in 1854, where, "trying to observe something new or remarkable," he thought that "more was to be learned by a visit to the Chinese Museum in Boston." "You can get as good ideas of China by visiting the Museums in the U.S. as you can get by going to Canton," he insisted. Artifacts deeded to museums by mariners returning from East Asia a generation earlier had spoiled travel for later sojourners.[39]

Phrenologists might make blanket requests for the remains of different racial groups to the crews of various vessels. If sailors were already collecting human heads as souvenirs, why not put that impulse to some "useful" scientific end? Gathering "indigenous" body parts was instrumental to imperial projects around the world, and in doing so, seamen tapped into what one scholar calls a broader "circulation of human skulls" that enlisted soldiers and settlers in the West to gather Indian remains for study and classification.

Amateur ethnologist William Goddard, for example, requested that individuals aboard a Marblehead brig "bring home for me, the Sculls of a male and female Hindoo, those of people of the age of twenty years or upwards would be preferred." But be careful, he warned, to collect specimens "entirely perfect in every respect, with complete sets of teeth." Similarly, Edward Shippen, on liberty at one of the Canary Islands, described a shipmate of his busily "excavating some of the singular arched Guanche graves." By the time he was finished, he "had quite a bagful of skulls and bones and stone weapons slung over the back of a donkey." Whaleman John Martin, in Australia, raided an aboriginal cemetery "to procure a skull of one of the natives for a friend of mine in Wilmington," though he knew the natives "would spear any one found molesting their graves." Sailor William Phelps, meanwhile, straddled lines between pseudoscience and entrepreneurship as he used his time abroad to help commission, create, and transport a supposed "mermaid" for academic study in the United States. It had "the skeleton of the upper part of a female baboon, connected with the tail of a fish, neatly put together and furred all over." Later, a board of surgeons inspected it and "pronounced a genuine mermaid." Phelps thought it was a prototype for what P. T. Barnum's museum later exhibited as the "Feejee Mermaid." Seafarers were scouring the earth, collecting specimens, and contributing to what passed for academic discourse.[40]

Indeed, the "science" of racism, which was marshaled to justify enslavement and territorial expansion in the continental context, proved no less useful to sailors making inroads for commercial empires overseas. Many seamen showed themselves to be at least casual students of racial science, given the detail-oriented nature of their accounts about the physiognomy of peoples around the globe. Their familiarity with rhetoric about skull shapes, bodily form, and blood purity should not be surprising, given the omnipresence of that speech in antebellum printed material and popular culture. Sailors were exposed to that language at home and used it to describe a variety of human groups overseas. They may have felt comfortable weighing in on these debates because of the democratic rhetoric that infused scientific practice in the early United States. The study and observation of people and culture was still thought to be within the purview of lay people, despite the mounting objections of a professionalizing cadre of experts. That fact and the heterogeneity of both the United States and the maritime world made, in the words of one historian, "every citizen, if not an ethnologist, at least a spectator on matters of race." Given the complexity and diversity of the wider world seamen stumbled into, a retreat into a usefully universal organizational schema proved helpful. Yet the relationship between the maritime realm and racial theorizing was reciprocal. In printing many of their observations in widely accessible memoirs and narratives, seafarers encouraged broader public engagement with a more globalized racial question than we are accustomed to think of at the time. The issue of physically manifested, immutable human difference was more than a debate about the condition of enslaved Africans or removed Indians.[41]

Sailors thus lent the weight of their experience overseas to contemporary discussion. N. Byron Smith contrasted Portuguese-speaking inhabitants from the Azores with those born in the more southerly Cape Verde Islands: the former had a "somewhat dark or olive complexion, [but] had no African blood in their veins," while the latter "showed more or less of it," seemingly "so black that coal would almost have made a white mark upon them." In New Zealand, Smith showed himself ready to read bodily form for the insight racial theorizing assured him it contained. Native Maori populations "in color very much resemble the North American Indians," he argued, but "instead of the thin, spare forms, harsh and strongly marked features, and high cheek bones of the Indian, they are rotund in form with smooth though not handsome features." Yet the comparison to Indians failed to account for "there lips, [which] are rather thick, though not as much so as those of the negro." Smith's notions of the indigenous population as "a wild and savage race" derived from the complex array of features he read like a map for the behavioral characteristics one should expect from such a cross-pollination of "Indian" and "Negro" characteristics. The precision with which he was able "know" peoples overseas as substandard by mere appearance later expressed itself in a categorical dismissal of the Pacific basin's nonwhite individuals. Smith doubted it was even feasible "to bring them to that high standard of intellectual superiority possessed at the present time by the Anglo-Saxon race."[42]

An equal attention to racial detail pervaded other maritime manuscripts. Charles Lane described the natives on Guam as people of mixed ancestry, exhibiting characteristics both Spanish and Chamorro. "The people are of a very dark brown, swarthy complexion," he began, while "their features are very small, with the exception of the cheek bones, which are prominent." His eye moved further down the body: "they are well formed, small limbs, and very small feet." Horace Putnam wrote of Mocha's inhabitants that "there black piercing eyes and there yellow skins bespeak the true Arab blood," while in Canton Albert Freeman assumed a phrenological affect in his claim that Chinese "skulls are thicker than a negroes," so that "what would kill us is fun to them." Such a skeletal defect allowed them to "lay around in the hottest places they can," because "it doesn't affect them." All things considered, Freeman concluded, "they are a queer race."[43]

Similar words legitimized the severity of labor African Americans were required to perform at home in the United States. Cranial density and hardihood of constitution intertwined to form the basis for exposing slaves to harsher living conditions, and peoples overseas showed themselves susceptible to similar charges. Given the burgeoning coolie labor trade between East Asia and the Americas and the involvement of U.S. shipping interests in that traffic, the ramifications of such observations should not be understated. Freeman himself off-handedly remarked that the Chinese "are as a general thing quite as black as our Southern negroes." In so doing, he only echoed claims circulating in popular media that sailors were attentive to. A contemporaneous article in the *Democratic Review* ranked China's inhabitants among the "dark species of man" supposedly inferior to Anglo-Saxons. These analogies must have made the process of densely packing such men in a ship's hold for their own "Middle Passage" across the Pacific seem somehow less criminal.[44]

Most of the quasi-classificatory language seamen used appeared in the 1840s and 1850s at a moment when "learned" treatises on race such as Josiah Nott and George R. Gliddon's *Types of Mankind* or Samuel George Morton's *Crania Americana* began to appear in the types of monthly magazines and periodicals sailors are known to have carried with them aboard ship to counteract the long hours of tedium. But while Nott and others admitted that their studies of "ethnography, etc." were apologias for slavery that focused on what he called "niggerology" and the "negro question within the United States," sailors discovered application for such science in more remote corners of the earth. Scholars have noted that the implications of scientific racism far outlasted the "slavery question" in the United States, sanctioning the animosity of northerners toward nonwhite persons even as human bondage became viewed as increasingly illegitimate. But to find maritime journal entries mirroring the vividly catalogued racial characteristics of African Americans and Indians at home reveals the global breadth of emerging discourses on the hierarchically arranged human family.[45]

The maritime world's connective links thus contained contradictory multitudes. Many scholars have pointed to the currents of resistance and revolutionary rhetoric—particularly among black seafarers and the question of Haiti—that circulated through ships and in shoreside communities. So terrified by the implications of that potentially destructive influence were antebellum slaveholders that they passed a series of Negro Seamen's Acts that required the imprisonment of any newly arrived African American sailors for the duration of their vessel's time in a southern port. Many white seafarers, though, circulated information that did not challenge the racial status quo but rather affirmed the ruling orthodoxy. The cosmopolitan maritime world could, paradoxically, contribute to the entrenchment of ethnocentric sentiment at home. Transnational currents were not inherently subversive of the nation-state's imperatives; they might instead, at times, reify power relations rooted in racial authority.[46]

If the ship at sea attained the characteristics of a floating schoolhouse, it is important to note that as the nineteenth century wore on, primary lessons included the science of biologically rooted difference. That discipline increasingly found expression in the way sailors wrote of their encounters with peoples overseas: they fixated on bodily distinctions. Previous generations may have been generally interested in color or complexion, but those characteristics appeared to weigh equally with civilizational achievement, technological aptitude, climate, and religious practice. N. Byron Smith would have sounded strange in 1800, speaking of sloping skulls, angular cheeks, bone density, and blood composition. When he wrote in the 1850s, though, he echoed any number of his maritime cohort, as well as literature that was widely read at the time. American ships, the antebellum public record enjoyed proclaiming, were involved in a vast campaign to whiten every sea. But that recurrent theme of whiteness could refer to more than mere sails. American racial ideology had powerful international as well as domestic foundations and applications. As U.S. canvas whitened every sea, so many in the maritime community would construe their obligation to bring a different, ideological, and in many ways more powerful breed of whiteness to bear upon that "wide extent of the habitable globe" that was subject to American incursion.[47]

Yet the relationship of white American sailors to racist ideology was extraordinarily complex, not least of all because labor conditions afloat were often equated with slavery ashore. Indeed, it was often the case that printed paeans to the sailor's significance appeared in newspapers owned by the very same merchants and shipping concerns who acted in ways antithetical to the interests of sailors. People who celebrated sailors were often accused of treating their employees afloat too much like bondsmen. Seamen were of course aware of that contradiction. They complained of their slavish lot, and the difficult conditions of life aboard ship inflected their public presentation of seafaring labor with undertones of frustration. Given the complicated politics of the position of white seafarers in national society—which venerated their achievements as a vanguard of civilization even while subjecting them to economic marginalization as the nineteenth century progressed—sailors needed an outlet to exhibit the contradictions that governed their lives. Blackface minstrelsy became one space seamen used to navigate the inconsistencies that shaped their experiences abroad. Sailors were not simply embedded in the era's popular culture; they were themselves active students of and participants in it. And yet, so were the many individuals abroad for whom sailors performed these shows. Local audiences attached their own meaning to blackface spectacles and worked to integrate an American theatrical tradition into their own cultures. The early foreign relations of the United States, therefore, were often conducted on decks and other improvised stages. Nothing better illustrates that fact than maritime minstrel recitals.

Chapter 2

Jim Crow Girdles the Globe

The ship *Lagoda*, while anchored at Honolulu, hired several Hawaiian crewmen who were renamed to reference popular African American caricatures such as "Jim Cuff," "Jim Crow," and "Uncle Tom." David Kanaka later became "Sambo" to his shipmates. Frederick Schley, ashore at Guayaquil, Ecuador, spoke of the "naked, dirty negroes" who wandered the streets there as men who all "showed the Sambo." William Abbe's whaleship halted at the Cape Verde Islands for provisions in 1858, where he found a beach "lined with darkees . . . flinging out their arms and gesturing in the most excited manner in the true negro fashion." Simeon Stearns remarked at Fiji that the natives were "black as jet, their hair or wool [with] as many 'bights' in it as any Cuff in the whole state of Virginia." In Africa, William Weaver watched a dozen natives load provisions aboard his ship; although he had never been there before, he found the men more familiar than foreign: "They are as black as hell and remind one of Old Virginia, where we see so many of them, the same Old Coons."[1]

Again and again, and in all corners of the globe, white American seamen remarked upon the similarity between peoples overseas and stock characters that populated the era's popular theatre. The blackface minstrel caricatures of "Jim Crow," "Jim Cuff," "Sambos," and "Coons" became the measure of their supposed analogs abroad. Counterfeit "Africans" on American stages—with their manic antics and comic chatter—became prominent players in sketches sailors made of environments overseas. "Real" black peoples abroad could be identified only by their resemblance to the racial forgeries of white performers at home. The appearances and behavior of strange peoples overseas became intelligible to mariners thanks in part to information they acquired while attending minstrel spectacles in the United States. Thus William Abbe's insistence above that Cape Verdeans cavorted in the "true negro fashion" or Charles Mervine's minstrel-influenced rendering of a Haitian man in Aux Cayes as "black as the Ace of spades, and so open countenanced that when he opens his mouth his head is half off, his lips is like two peeled beets in a black jar, and his hair curls so tight that he has to open his mouth to shut his eyes." Mervine merely echoed observers of American blackface entertainment who described actors' "lips thickened and lengthened with bright red paint to such a degree that their mouths resembled slices cut in a ripe watermelon."[2]

Theatre, minstrel shows, circuses, and curbside artists performed race in antebellum cities, pandering to the stereotypes and caricatures that increasingly influenced how mariners overseas envisioned other peoples. But blackface also influenced opinions among people abroad about seamen themselves. As an 1835 edition of the *Sailor's Magazine* reasoned, "we judge of other nations by the individuals we see," just as Americans "estimate the character of our Brethren of other States in the Union by the specimens we have seen of their citizens." But given the logical relationship between appearance and assessment, it seems significant that the individuals through which Americans would be judged often materialized in the shape of blackface minstrels. Whatever conclusions the outside world's inhabitants reached about the United States would be derived in part from maritime minstrel recitals. Many mariners, in fact, appeared *anxious* to perform American racial caricatures for people they encountered overseas.[3]

To some extent their eagerness is unsurprising; blackface minstrel shows were among the most wildly popular modes of entertainment available to antebellum citizens. By the 1830s, minstrelsy, a theatrical form with roots in the earliest decades of the nineteenth century, had been transformed into mass entertainment by the likes of men such as Thomas Dartmouth "Daddy" Rice. A white traveling actor who worked developing towns along the nation's western rivers, Rice reportedly observed and then replicated on stage the song and dance of a crippled enslaved stable hand from Louisville. Using burnt cork to blacken his face, appearing in the garb of a "plantation darkey," and speaking dialect associated with peoples of African origin, Rice initially inserted his act as a short accompaniment to longer dramatic productions. That routine quickly became the minstrel megahit "Jump Jim Crow," named after the song's chorus in which Rice, in affected speech, claimed to "Wheel about, an' turn about, an' do jis so / Eb'ry time I wheel about, I jump Jim Crow." Rice's number, which debuted in 1828, grew in scope as the actor responded to enthusiastic audiences by continuously adding new verses and steps. By 1830, the flutter of his feet—and a growing army of imitators—had ignited a popular cultural wildfire. Rice regularly packed houses in New York, and he had become a transatlantic sensation by 1836 after completing tours of England and France. It was with minimal exaggeration that an 1855 retrospective in the *New York Tribune* could claim that "never was there such an excitement in the musical or dramatic world; nothing was talked of, nothing written of, and nothing dreamed of, but 'Jim Crow.'" Indeed, it appeared as though "the entire population had been bitten by the tarantula; in the parlor, in the kitchen, in the shop and in the street, Jim Crow monopolized public attention."[4]

Yet stories of blackface minstrelsy's plantation origins like the one Rice told are likely apocryphal. He and many of the era's best-known racial caricaturists, after all, grew up in Manhattan's racially integrated dockside districts. There they would have witnessed many different pseudo-theatrical spectacles, from masked mummers to free blacks dancing for eels, oysters, and loose change. Historians now agree that this vibrant urban culture of song, dance, and holiday exhibition among the city's poorest white and black residents is the more likely source for minstrel material. Blackface, in other words, traced its origins to cross-racial contacts along the New York waterfront. And this harborside location provides a window into one of the phenomenon's more curious and understudied dimensions: international nautical performances staged by seafarers. Baltimore, Philadelphia, New York, Boston and their immediate environs—that is, the country's largest seaports, its gateways to the wider world—hosted thousands of minstrel shows annually in theatres whose seats were packed with sailors. The famed establishments of showmen like E. P. Christy, Daniel Emmett, and Henry Wood opened their doors to largely white, male audiences, many of whom, upon witnessing the display, thereafter hopped aboard vessels bound outward across the globe. There are few better examples of the sailor's role as a connector in multinational webs of cultural exchange than his effort to spread blackface minstrelsy's songs and dances throughout the nineteenth-century world.[5]

For sailors already prone to singing and dancing as popular marine pastimes, ships' decks served as readymade venues for the execution of minstrel shows abroad. Seamen seized the opportunity to perform before mixed crowds of fellow mariners, local officials, and indigenous peoples. The enthusiasm some sailors showed for reproducing American racial spectacle overseas suggests not only their own warm embrace of the era's popular theatre but also their aspiration to familiarize foreign societies with the nation's cultural landscape. In the foreground of that landscape lay the questions of class, race, and slavery that blackface performance worked to articulate.[6]

Other individuals living abroad sang and danced their own routines in response. Mutually exchanged performance became a means for beginning dialogue between people who were otherwise unable to "speak." Dramatic routines that in the United States threatened to close off collaboration across the color line were crucial to sustaining early contacts between white American seamen and racial "inferiors" when rendered abroad. Minstrelsy became, in effect, a ritual designed to construct intercultural solidarities, while the performance (and readaptation) of blackface form by other peoples abroad demonstrates that sailors were key agents of cultural interpenetration in the early history of the United States in the world.

But if international minstrelsy began as a tool that allowed peoples at potential odds with one another to temporarily unite in shared, mirthful experience, by the end of the nineteenth century, indigenous hosts found that these initially innocent antics portended dramatic changes. By entangling individuals overseas in the Anglo-American racial order, minstrel performance contributed to broader processes that bent the lives and labor of nonwhite peoples toward the world's imperial powers. The international "color line" was constructed in the wake of introductions that "Jim Crow's" antics helped facilitate. In short, nineteenth-century blackface entertainment had a global dimension. Minstrelsy took on new and evolving meaning(s) in an international context. At the very least, a transnational history of minstrelsy challenges the notion of its "quintessential" connections to race, slavery, and Civil War in the United States. Blackface, instead, becomes only one variation in a more globally diffuse catalog of masked performances, all of which had different resonances and were used in multiple contexts to achieve a range of ends.

The best documented of these episodes occurred during Commodore Matthew C. Perry's famed 1852 mission to "open" Japan. President Millard

Fillmore, with the staunch support of Secretary of State Daniel authorized the use of four vessels to establish formal diplomatic . mercial relations between the United States and Japan. America's p. in the Pacific had grown steadily over the nineteenth century, and the U.S.-Mexico War secured permanent frontage for the nation along ι. globe's largest ocean, hungry eyes gazed on the lucrative prize that was East Asian trade. Japan presented the prospect of new customers for American goods and, more significantly, a strategic location for coal depots trans-oceanic steamships required. The expedition itself would be an instrument for forging another link in what Webster and the mercantile interests he represented began to call the "Great Chain" of saltwater commerce that connected the United States to the wider world.[7]

Using supposed Japanese mistreatment of shipwrecked American sail-ors as a pretext for armed intervention, officials charged a reluctant Perry (who had expected to spend the remainder of his career in the comfort of a Mediterranean sinecure) with the difficult task of convincing that relatively hermetic realm to associate with what its leaders considered to be a barba-rous outside world. Perry's fleet, an assemblage of the United States Navy's most modern steam warships, bristled with cannon meant to impress upon the Japanese the violent alternative that continued isolation would entail. Other scholars have made much of the "gifts" to the ruling *daimyo* included as part of the expedition. In the printing presses, Colt weaponry, telegraphic demonstrations, and miniature steam locomotive, they find a "technologi-cal imperative" behind America's civilizing mission. Without denying the centrality of industrial expertise to American imperial agendas, though, we need to ask why a minstrel show organized by the squadron's white sailors became central to narrative and pictorial accounts of the expedition.[8]

We do know *what* the Japanese saw, if not *how* they saw it. Certain por-tions of the show found their way into the pages of expedition journals. Those reports reveal a flurry of affected speech, "dancing that surpassed all," and slapstick comedy routines that one observer thought would cause the Japanese commissioners to "[die] with their laughter." Perry's official interpreter S. Wells Williams asserted that "the exhibition was a source of great merriment to them and every one present, for the acting was excel-lent." Others also believed the performance a great hit among the Japanese, though one man took enough time to consider the question of reception: "The guests seemed quite pleased—they laughed a lot—but why? Perhaps even they did not know." John Sproston, a midshipman aboard the *Mace-donian*, likewise commented on the confusion such novel entertainment might have created. "When the sable gentlemen made their appearance," he began, "a murmur of astonishment arose among our simple guests"; "wooly heads, shirt collars of ample dimensions, and black faces contrasting with black and yellow striped coats, ruffled shirts and the usual parts of a darky band were truly new sights to them."[9]

The commodore himself recorded the event, albeit tersely. The treaty commissioners "were entertained on deck with the performances of the very excellent corps of Ethiopians belonging to the [ship] *Powhatan*," wrote Perry, who praised the "hilarity which this most amusing exhibition excited." He invoked the famed American minstrel proprietor E. P. Christy and depicted the Japanese laughing "as merrily as ever the spectators at Christy's have done," so much so, in fact, that one man draped his arm over Perry's shoulder for support as he doubled over, and, as the commander complained, "crushed my new epaulettes." Francis Hawks, the expedition's official chronicler, concurred with the commodore: "[the] exhibition of Negro minstrelsy . . . would have gained them unbounded applause from a New York audience even at Christy's." And importantly, as Hawks made entirely clear, the minstrel show was the *sailors'* initiative, or, in Perry's words, "got up by the sailors."[10]

Portraying sailors as particularly invested in the minstrel portion of the expedition's program encourages us to compare that event to the more "official" components of Perry's mission. The commodore paid close attention to the appearance of ships, weaponry, uniforms, and other ceremonial equipment among the American delegation. His diplomacy consisted of gifts, niceties, and calibrated decorum, all designed to display the nation's power and prestige. This was all part of what scholars have long pointed to as the "theatre" of empire: the waving flags and booming cannons meant to stage the supposed superiority of "civilized" peoples. Yet George Preble, one of the expedition's lieutenants, remembered Perry confiding to the men that their own (and more literally) "theatrical" contribution to the mission were crucial: "The Commodore . . . said the success of his treaty depended upon the success of the entertainment." Hence, declared Preble, "we did our best." It was understood, in other words, that the crew's minstrelsy was their own form of diplomatic ritual. In denigrating African Americans, they communicated the United States to Japanese onlookers in some essential way. And if broadcasting race was a primary motive of the minstrels overseas, there is some evidence to suggest that this gambit was successful. For while many Japanese found *all* outsiders to be fundamentally barbaric, later accounts of prejudice in the Meiji empire note that

Figure 3. Japanese minstrels. This 1853 Japanese print depicts the antics of a U.S. naval minstrel troupe, the Corps of Ethiopians belonging to the USS *Powhatan*. A playbill distributed to the audience promised songs and dances of "the plantation 'niggas' of the South." Unknown Japanese artist, *Telegraph, Dance on Ship, Music and Singing on Ship* (detail), 1853. Watercolor on scroll, 12 × 50½ in., object number 52.55.1. Museum purchase and gift of Mr. and Mrs. Victor Spark as a memorial to their son, Donald W. Spark, USMCR, 1923–1944. Courtesy of the Chrysler Museum of Art, Norfolk, Va.

diarists consistently referred to black peoples in particular as "pitifully stupid, grotesque, dirty, unmannered, physically repulsive subhumans . . . with faces resembling those of monkeys." In that sense, supposedly "American" minstrelsy could be seen as a tool for sustaining not only white national identity in the United States but also national or cultural identities in Japan and elsewhere that were predicated on black inferiority.[11]

Those developments took place, however, over the long term. In the short term, American accounts persisted in emphasizing the positive response of audiences abroad, as when Francis Hawks noted that minstrel shows "produced a marked effect even on their sedate Japanese listeners, and thus confirmed the universal popularity of 'the Ethiopians' by a decided hit in Japan." Literal diplomatic breakthrough became a function of the comic skewering of blackness overseas. Hawks felt that the two countries became closer to one another in shared mirth over the counterfeit faces of African peoples. The chronicler even emphasized that it was this moment, after the performance, when a Japanese commissioner named Matsusaki chose to embrace Perry, exclaiming "Nippon and America, all the same heart." It is crucial to stress the "universal popularity" that Hawks (and others) ascribed to the "Ethiopians" and "Jim Crow." The sources for mutual understanding—as simple as a collective chuckle—were founded in the ridiculous (mis)representation of black people. The goodwill generated by minstrelsy was, observers thought, a potentially unifying force. The Japanese, at least, would have understood the diplomatic significance of minstrel gymnastics, given that musicians, actors, and other performers had long accompanied ambassadorial legations visiting from Korea and Okinawa. As early as 1635, the shogun requested that the Korean court, in addition to the usual retinue of nobles and courtiers, "send a troupe of equestrian acrobats." Americans were clearly not the only people invested in viewing the popularity of national cultural forms as evidence of a favorable diplomatic reception. But they were very aggressive in insisting upon the concord created overseas by the burnt-cork mask.[12]

Aboard the USS *Powhatan* at Hong Kong in December 1853, for example, Thomas Dudley noted that "we are amusing ourselves and friends on shore. . . . Minstrelsey and balls have been given on board two of the [flotilla's] steamers, and we have done our share . . . winning merited applause for [our] excellent endeavors." Several months later and further north along the Chinese coast, "all Shanghae was invited [aboard ship] and came, first we gave them 2 hours entertainment from the negro minstrels [for whom] there was unbounded applause, all went off first rate, then we had refreshments, and then a grand ball." Later still, the ship's "minstrels gave performances which delighted the residents of Canton." And in a letter home to his sister dated December 20, 1853, Dudley went on in great detail about the regularity with which the navy's sailors turned blackface actors:

> We have a minstrel band of 9 performers, that do beat Christy's all hollow. One of them does up Lucy Long tip top, and they are always well received. Every Monday we have a performance—alternatively the theatre and "nigger band"—on these occasions the ship assumes a gala appearance and great things are done. The Captain has a great supper for admirals, governors, and other big fish. The Wardroom for Lieut and less fry while we of the steerage entertain the still smaller fry, such as midshipmen, passed mids, etc. etc. The suppers are great, as is everything else. The Susquehannah has a theatre every Wednesday, the Winchester on each Fridays and the Mississippi on Tuesdays, so you see we do not lack for that kind of amusement. Society in China there is not and so we are obliged to turn our ships into playhouses, to interest the men, and amuse ourselves.

In claiming that ships were consistently converted "into playhouses" for the exhibition of a well-practiced "nigger band," Dudley dramatically illustrated the far-reaching influence of American minstrelsy at the time. His insistence on blackface's palliative impact abroad, meanwhile, echoed the use of racial theatrics to help "reform" the inmates of insane asylums and prison populations. In the international context, minstrelsy's practitioners often spoke of the shows as embraced by local populations who were desperate for the edification a "superior" American cultural form could provide.[13]

Diagnosing China as devoid of "society," Dudley prescribed racial caricature as an elevating panacea. His assurances that all who bore witness were enamored of the display (the troupe "merited applause" in Hong Kong; they "delighted" in Canton) echoed other observers who were likewise invested in recording Jim Crow's sensational reception around the world. Here lay a gesture toward the imperialistic potential of cultural productions: a perception that America's mass entertainment was embraced by "admirers" overseas living in a social vacuum and desperate for the fulfillment promised by an outside power's theatrical ingenuity. The phenomenon is reminiscent of the "sonic conquest" of the American West, where mastery of the continent was measured, in part, by the replacement of savage "whoops" and wild noise with the acoustics of civilization. Many, in fact, saw minstrelsy as an antidote for the absence of musical acumen overseas. After all, Japanese singing, as one disgruntled hearer complained, was little more than "a kind of a cross between the half wail, half-vocal screech of the Chinese, a boy dragging a stick over the palings after him, and a severe asthma," while Chinese street theatre was dismissed as mere "caterwauling." Boasting of the endless international appeal of blackface celebrated the beginnings of U.S. penetration and domination overseas, but it also negated the need to question or challenge the minstrel show's potentially problematic representations of slavery and black culture. Affirmation abroad, then, ensured the medium's perpetuation at home, which, in turn, further guaranteed regular exportation of minstrelsy overseas and the deeper entrenchment, eventually, of racial stereotypes about African Americans.[14]

We cannot know how universal the delight truly was. One wonders, for example, if Joseph Jenkins Roberts and his entourage, representing Liberia's black leadership, were amused during their sojourn aboard the USS *Saratoga*. The ship's purser described Roberts and company being rowed aboard in August of 1844 for a formal dinner. "In the evening," he pronounced with evident pride, "we brought out all our forces for the amusement of our distinguished guests, [and] the negro band sang 'Old Dan Tucker,' 'Jim along Josey,' and other ditties of the same class, accompanied by violin and tambo-rine." It was thought, by this white diarist at least, that such celebrated company should command only the finest entertainment. If the colonizationist Roberts shared abolitionist Frederick Douglass's views, then he found black-face entertainers to be nothing more than "the filthy scum of white society, who have stolen from us a complexion denied to them by nature, in which to make money, and pander to the corrupt taste of their fellow white citizens." Indeed, from Governor Roberts' point of view, it may have been evidence of the very bigotry that necessitated the "repatriation" of freed slaves.[15]

Yet what makes the exhibition odd, at least by the standards of the time, was exactly that black guests comprised its audience. Performances in the United States were strictly segregated; African Americans were almost always denied entry to the show. Minstrelsy afloat, on the other hand, frequently involved the integration of audiences as performers sang and danced before mixed-race crowds of indigenous inhabitants and nonwhite crew members. The multiracial maritime world did, of course contain multitudes, and it would be fascinating to learn what black or Indian mariners thought about the minstrelsy of their white shipmates. Unfortunately, we lack the evidence by which to make definitive judgments.

We do know that white sailors showed enthusiasm for the ritual wherever they traveled. In Hakodate, a relatively remote whaling port in northern Japan, a group of men aboard the bark *Covington* in 1858 came ashore to witness the traditional theatrical practice known as Kabuki. Quickly bored with the entertainment (the actors "were not what would be called 'stars' at home," one sailor quipped), the mariners provided their own, as described by seaman Albert Peck:

> There were about fifty sailors collected here and after witnessing the performance for a while the stage was taken possession of by them and there being fiddlers banjo players &c. amongst them a negro concert was improvised and the stage resounded to the steps of the Juba dance with varieties which gave immense satisfaction to all in the theatre.

All, that is, save the Japanese actors, who, Peck noted, "appeared highly indignant at being interrupted in their performance and driven from the stage." During the three weeks the vessel remained in port, the theatre was repurposed for minstrelsy and homage was paid to William Henry Lane, also known as Master Juba, the famed African American dancer in New York's Five Points slum.[16]

Horatio Bridge, an American officer patrolling for illegal slave traffickers off the coast of West Africa, observed that the size of a ship hardly mattered when measuring its musical capacity. For while frigates and ships of the line were automatically assigned a band, even smaller vessels would scrape together something of the sort, because "there are always good musicians to be found among the reckless and jolly fellows composing a man-of-war's crew." Bridge remembered regular evening entertainment at sea that ordinarily involved minstrel favorites such as "'Jim along Josey,' 'Lucy Long,' 'Old Dan Tucker,' and a hundred others of the same character." They were "listened to delightfully by the crowd of men and boys collected around the forehatch, and always ready to join the choruses." Original compositions such as "Ethiopeana," "The Virginia Mammy," and "Nigger in a Daguerreotype Saloon" appeared as nightly entertainment aboard other naval vessels. Charles Mervine thought that the USS *Powhatan*'s carpenters spent much of their voyage building stages so that the men might "give a shine tonight called the 'Powhatan's Minstrells.'" Another observer remarked that "every morning . . . the cooks and sailors get together forward with a banjo and tambourine, singing all the nigger melodies with a voice and taste that would make the Christy Minstrels applaud." Henry Wise, meanwhile, enjoyed coming off his watch to hear shipmates "chanting Virginia melodies" while performing "a complicated series of jigs, called the double shuffle." Minstrelsy, then, was embedded in the daily routine of many a ship.[17]

Naval squadrons more generally seem to have been potent vehicles for the diffusion of minstrel performance. Even before venturing to Japan, the federal government had played an active role in securing America's position in the Pacific. Building on the piecemeal efforts of individual commercial ventures, in 1836 Congress authorized the largest exploratory expedition ever sent into the region by any nation. A variety of objectives motivated the venture, some scientific, others economic and political. Departing in 1838 with a fleet of six ships and nearly 1,000 sailors, Lieutenant Charles Wilkes eventually led the United States Exploring Expedition on a four-year circumnavigation of the globe that was chiefly celebrated for the discovery of the Antarctic continent.[18]

Yet exploration is often a mutual act, as the squadron's sailors tacitly acknowledged by offering minstrel performances to inquisitive Polynesian and Melanesian onlookers. Charles Erskine, a member of that expedition, wrote in his memoir that while traversing the Pacific Ocean the crew aboard the *Peacock* "treated the natives to a regular, old-fashioned negro entertainment." The "natives" were Fijians from Rewa held hostage while awaiting the progress of a manhunt ashore for a key player in the massacre of American sailors some years before. Attempting to entertain their "guests," the sailors smeared grease on their faces and began to shuffle across the decks. Referring to the black dandy "Zip Coon," a common minstrel character who parodied the "ludicrous airs" exhibited by some northern free blacks, Erskine claimed that "Juba and Zib Coon danced and highly delighted them, [and] the Virginia reel set them wild." Next, two of the crew tied themselves together, were draped in a blanket, and mimicked the braying of a donkey, while their "comical looking rider, Jim Crow Rice . . . made his appearance." Expedition commander Charles Wilkes thought "the dance of Juba came off well [and] the Jim Crow of Oliver, [the ship's carpenter,] will long be remembered by their savage as well as civilized spectators." Indeed, it was the audience, "half civilized, half savage," which "gave the whole scene a remarkable effect." The wild popularity of minstrelsy afloat was further hinted at by Wilkes, who claimed that the "theatricals were resorted to" in large part because "the crew of the *Peacock* were proficients, having been in the habit of amusing themselves in this way."[19]

It seemed that wherever the fleet moved, the crew insisted on replicating American minstrelsy overseas. In Tahiti, an attempt by officers to stage for the natives a rendition of Friedrich Schiller's *The Robbers* fell flat when the "savage" audience began to grumble that there was too much "*parau*," or talk. A group of sailors saved the show by smearing their faces and demonstrating "comic songs" that were popular in America. Wilkes noted in an aside that the Tahitians believed that "the rendition of this slow-talking and quick-footed caricature of blacks" was the real thing "and could not be convinced it was a fictitious character." Given that much of what could be considered a successful minstrel show in the United States depended on a knowing interplay between performer and audience, a spectator's inability or unwillingness to acknowledge the spectacle's fiction created a radically different dynamic. The failure of native viewers to separate costumed from concrete blackness marks an essential difference between minstrelsy abroad and in the United States, where audiences and performers generally recognized the genre's conventions and caricatures. When witnesses were unfamiliar with the spectacle, as in Tahiti, the show's meaning was up for grabs.[20]

What, exactly, could non-English-speaking observers who attended performances have gleaned from the shows? Japanese spectators might have projected on the minstrel performance their own understandings derived from Kabuki: both theatrical forms used masked actors, slapstick, and song. Perhaps the Fijians Charles Erskine claimed were "set wild" by Jim Crow saw in the routine nothing more than a variant of the *meke* dancing indigenous to the islands. At the very least, we have some evidence that Fijians may not have construed minstrelsy's meaning as primarily racial. Rather, as one observer at Rewa noted, African Americans throughout the islands were called "'kuke' (cook)." "All black people they call cooks," the mariner explained, because aboard American ships visiting Fiji, "the cooks [are] generally negroes." The designation "kuke" entitled black mariners to little regard, exactly because food preparation was a low-status task; "cooks are the meanest people in the Feejees," it was explained. One Fijian informant remarked that with all of the soot and smoke of a constantly burning kitchen fire, it was "no wonder that the 'kaisi paplangi' (foreign slave) should get black entirely by having to cook and prepare the food for a number of chiefs (white people) continually." As this passage suggests, islanders who saw minstrel shows may have seen the "stigma" or "humor" of blackness as occupational or status-oriented rather than racial. As the shows crossed borders, their meaning changed hands. Because of the scant historical evidence about how indigenous viewers perceived sailor minstrels, the reflexive condemnation of blackface's message as racist is likely an oversimplification.[21]

It might be most fruitful to consider maritime minstrelsy in a much larger universe of performances exchanged between sailors and other peoples around the world. Often unable to speak one another's languages, groups thrown into sudden contact relied on song and dance routines as communicative devices. Therefore, the same Fijians for whom Charles Erskine and his shipmates "jumped Jim Crow" in turn treated the sailors to a show. Once the guests were seated by their indigenous hosts, "a big muscular native . . . commenced beating . . . on the Fiji drum with a small war club [while an] orchestra consisting of a group of maidens began to play some on two joints of bamboo." And as this was occurring, multiple men identified as chiefs, with "wreaths of natural flowers and vines twined around their turbans . . . [and] their faces painted in various styles, some wholly vermillion, some half vermillion the other half black," began to sway in formation. Erskine found the accompanying music "anything but musical"—it "would fail to be appreciated by a Boston audience" his witticism went—but nevertheless thought the show on the whole enormously entertaining. And so, with "a loud clapping of the hands . . . [thus] ended the matinee." Sailors may have blackened their faces to "speak" with spectators abroad, but this

Figure 4. Fijian dance. American maritime minstrelsy might best be seen as part of a broader series of practices wherein peoples who were unable to communicate verbally instead exchanged song, dance, and performance as a means to mutual intelligibility. Here, Fijians dance for a party of Americans who had earlier jumped Jim Crow for the islanders' amusement. "Club Dance," illustration by J. Drayton, in Charles Wilkes, *Narrative of the United States Exploring Expedition*, 5 vols. (New York, 1856), 3:190.

behavior must be set alongside those same spectators coloring themselves "vermillion" (or any other number of shades) in an effort to reciprocate.[22]

No doubt the precise meaning of the Fijian "matinee" was blunted by Erskine's cultural tone deafness. This was no different than the equally confused responses registered among indigenous onlookers witness to minstrel shows. What mattered was the capacity of a song-and-dance routine to create constructive relations between peoples who otherwise might have been suspicious of each other. In an earlier period, for example, Erskine referred to natives at Tierra del Fuego as contemptible beings "little above the brute creation" and "lowest in the scale of humanity." Unable to share a tune or even a few steps with such "savages," Erskine spoke summarily of the absence of common humanity. Yet later in his voyage, New Zealand Maoris came across far more favorably exactly because entertainment engendered sociable relations. While ashore with a cohort of shipmates, Erskine was amused by a series of what he called "love dances," "war dances," and "peace dances." In turn, and, "to give them a rest," a gang of sailors "danced several 'fore-and-afters' and 'all fours,'" though "the 'Sailors' Hornpipe' 'took the cake,'" as "the natives [appeared] overjoyed with it." The "New Zealand ball," as Erskine called it, did not end until very late; "we did enjoy skipping the 'light fantastic toe' with those fairy-like natives." Both parties could construe the gestures of a dance as gestures of goodwill. Many more mariners began to notice the significant role that performance played in intercultural encounters.[23]

Somewhere in Micronesia, a sailor discussed a dinner ashore followed by "a grand dance" with "women singing and keeping time by clapping their hands." At "the close of each dance, the white portion of the audience would cheer the performers," and in exchange, someone "struck up [a] violin" and "all hands joined" in what was referred to as a regular blackface "breakdown." Another observer, meanwhile, spoke of sailors skylarking before Tahitian onlookers, who, in exchange, "gave us one of their old dances." The performers "seated themselves round in a ring" and "commenced making a kind of grunt," until "two of the party sprung up into the middle of the ring and began dancing, and making all sorts of grimaces and most violent licentious motions of the body." With "gestures more violent," they "wrought themselves to the highest pitch of excitement" to a point where "every blood vessel was much swollen, and the perspiration ran in streams down their faces" before the group eventually "kicked up their heels and fell on the deck, which was the signal they had finished." Described in clinical terms, these dances were stripped of their indigenous ritual significance, just as blackface, in an international context, disengaged from its original significations surrounding race and slavery in the United States. Instead, they attained new, ad hoc meaning for parties struggling to communicate. Charles Rockwell, a naval chaplain stationed off the coast of West Africa, spoke of his time alongside the coastal Krumen people as punctuated by regular intervals of entertainment. "Sometimes," he began, "when the sailors were at leisure in the evening, they would collect the Kroomen on board together upon the forecastle, and get them to show off some of their native dances." Their steps, Rockwell commented, "had not a little of the kick and shuffle peculiar to the negro dances with us" and was, in other words, somehow authentically African because it resembled the sham steps of white entertainers in the United States. The music, however, left something to be desired because of its "loud, harsh, monotonous" qualities.[24]

The squadron's seamen used these occasions (and the Krumen) to stage impromptu blackface routines. "Zip Coon," the caricature of the ostentation of free blacks, made his appearance after the ship's surgeon gave one native dancer "an old uniform frockcoat, with bright yellow buttons and a standing collar." With "his coat buttoned up to his chin, in true dandy style, and his bare black legs appearing below, like those of a peacock under his plumes," the unwitting actor, as Rockwell sarcastically surmised, "made no contemptible figure." The ship's crew certainly thought so, for "many were the jokes which the sailors cracked upon him." Yet their derision merely masked the indispensable role Krumen played aboard ships off the coast of Africa. Coastal Krumen (the name is almost certainly pidgin for the English word "crewman") served as a regional labor pool aboard Euroamerican vessels, performing the rough and dangerous tasks of piloting vessels through unfamiliar waters while also facilitating communication and supply with peoples ashore. White sailors justly fearful of tropical maladies indigenous to Africa were all too happy to have Krumen handling the heavy lifting, and yet their specialized knowledge and temporary position as pilots offered them status and privilege aboard ship that were uncommon for black men in the United States.[25]

Even as this Krumen "Zip Coon" mocked black claims to pride, white American sailors inhabited a maritime world populated by "savage" peoples who were necessarily empowered aboard ship. For men who had come from a segregated republic, this duality proved difficult to sustain. Mariners thus turned to ridicule in the confines of a harmless stage show in part to vent their resentment. Satirizing black pretensions to power and prestige was a common practice among white American sailors. "Negro masters," held at bay domestically, nevertheless made themselves known abroad. It annoyed many working men along the maritime frontier. They wrote in jaded terms of "black authority" overseas. Nathaniel Morgan, for example, spoke of a soiree on Timor where a local dignitary was entertained aboard. "The particulars would make an amusing volume," he began. For "is not this a great occasion? Just think of it, a real genuine Royal levee between one Capt. Slumman L. Grey of this infernal old blubber hunter and a half dozen half civilized he and she ignirant Portugee Negros." Morgan appeared unable to restrain himself. "Kings! Nobles! Lords! It is amusing to observe the profound courtesy and respect with which our Capt. is treated by these half bred Negro royalists." He mocked his captain for remaining receptive to the flattery of illegitimate—that is, black—aristocrats and felt contempt for the "grandeur" of nonwhite royalty. Similarly, as William Stetson and his shipmates stood on the *Arab*'s deck watching a member of Hawaii's royal family proceed ashore from, a barge, Stetson noted that "our boys had but little respect for black royalty." Maritime minstrelsy became yet another venue to work through the frustrations of white men beholden to black authority while overseas. Real threats were rendered manageable by white men whose masked playacting reduced black peoples to mere punch lines.[26]

More aggressive overtures, however, were summarily punished by a command structure that was most interested in protecting profit and property. Souring relations with Krumen would be bad not only for the ship's discipline but also for business more generally, given their indispensability in African waters. This was the lesson taught to Abraham Lyell, who was convicted of assault on the person of a "Kroo-man" and sentenced to imprisonment and loss of pay. When asked why he had done it, Lyell confessed to feelings of frustration that "Kroomen . . . had pretty much their own way" aboard the USS *St. Louis* and said that the outburst was meant to prove that "a nigger was not his equal." White sailors aboard other ships were often brought up on similar charges. Blackface antics that derided black laborers aboard ships brought laughter and acclaim, while more physical displays initiated punitive proceedings. Given a choice, seamen became more and more likely to opt for the "peaceful" policing of boundaries that minstrelsy offered.[27]

And indeed, sustaining peaceful—if not always comfortable—relations seems to have been the most common consequence of mutual performance. The visual and aural spectacle of song and dance served to entertain each side of a cultural encounter and thus sustain at least limited dialogue over the course of ships' visits. Small moments hint at a larger trend whereby peoples on both sides of a societal divide parlayed performance into at least momentarily mellow relations. One 1840 account, for example, published as "A Whaler's Journal" in Boston's *Daily Advertiser*, mentioned that after the crew attempted to amuse individuals native to an unnamed Pacific island with minstrel antics, audience members later approached the vessel, "and on the occasion of their visit had bedaubed their faces with a species of dark compound." The indigenous inhabitants, in other words, had blackened their own faces as they approached a ship where sailors had recently done the same. This was performative reciprocity meant to buy both goodwill and goods themselves. Not coincidentally, the author remarked, "a general traffic soon commenced." Food was provided to the seamen, while the natives stocked up on valuable iron implements. "We gave some hooks to our islanders," the account continued, "and the poor fellows manifested their joy by the most joyous capering about the deck." The dancing looked very similar to steps the seamen had previously exhibited ashore; "their 'wheels about' were not quite so systematic as those of 'Jim Crowe,' but they were on the whole quite as extravagant." The anonymous whaleman called this bizarre decktop bazaar "trading in pantomime," for after all, "neither party understood a word of the other's language." But peoples who appeared before one another in painted faces found enough in common to begin bartering.[28]

John Erskine's voyage narrative noted that Kanaks, the Melanesian people native to New Caledonia, came aboard there "to get up a dance on the main deck, which we lighted with a few lanterns for the purpose." The observers were skeptical about its artistic merits, for "like most savage performances of the kind, the movements consisted in twisting about the body . . . loud whistlings . . . abrupt yells" along with "a general clapping of hands, one performer playing a bass on his hip." Yet it seems unsurprising that in the next sentence, Erskine remarked that the entertainers "all begged to be allowed to sleep on board," and "a space between the guns [was] allotted to them." Having ingratiated themselves with a performance, individuals might leverage that trust and goodwill into advantageous economic or political relations. And indeed, the next morning, an active trade began between sailors and Kanaks that gave the latter a means to acquire goods that were important to status in the local community.[29]

Other individuals appeared willing to adopt the minstrel form as a means of securing favors. In one example, Whare, a Maori, "made himself a general favorite on board" a warship by "executing some of his native dances," which "earned him the sobriquet of 'Jim Crow.'" The crew on another ship dressed an interpreter they had hired at Vanuatu "in a delightful Christy minstrel dress." These natives were individuals who found in Jim Crow and minstrel aesthetics an access point to American maritime culture and the privileges it could help provide. What was condescendingly comedic for sailors could be good business for native practitioners. For a contact zone like the ship's deck to function—and thus allow for the exchange of goods, technology, and ideas—some conventions had to be established. Before the later development of Pacific-wide lingua francas meant to facilitate communication, minstrelsy and reciprocal performance by indigenous peoples became what one scholar calls the "creole language" and "extravagant gestures" needed to sustain relations in the spaces between various cultures. In that sense, minstrelsy abroad functioned much like its early manifestations at home in the United States, where white and black waterfront workers, canal builders, and ditch diggers constructed a "mudsill mutuality" by trading steps and songs after work.[30]

Yet other observers saw something less than harmless, humorous, or positive in the free exchange of song and dance, for it appeared as though indigenous actors might be indulging in mockery of their racial or civilizational "betters." If white sailor minstrels meant, in part, to poke fun at the pretensions of pretended black aristocrats, that fact must be set beside the willingness of Pacific peoples to use similar forms to caricature the idiocy of white interlopers. Richard Henry Dana, while loading cowhides in California, took note of one of his Polynesian coworkers' capers and remarked that "by the occasional shouts and laughter" of nearby Hawaiians, "it was evident that he was singing about the different men that he was at work with." Unable to understand their language, Dana nevertheless deduced that "they have great powers of ridicule, and are excellent mimics, many of them discovering and imitating the peculiarities of our own people before we had observed them ourselves." Mariner Richard Cruise, at the other end of the Pacific about the time Dana wrote, pronounced the *haka* dancing of New Zealand Maoris—with its "gestures of the body . . . and contortions of the countenance"—to be "very violent, and often frightful." Closer inspection, however, led him to believe that the songs that accompanied the dance "observed, with a degree of ridicule, that no two white men ever moved their arms and legs in the same manner." Comic reproaches were soon followed by strains that seemed to express "their hopes that other ships would come among them, and their wish that the white men would trade with them for muskets and powder."[31]

Thus the Hawaiians whom Dana admits were regularly abused by his shipmates and cheated by officers and the Maoris whom Cruise condescended to could employ humorous or pointed airs of their own to poke fun or pursue political position. Polynesians, Dana thought, "sing about persons and things which are around them, and adopt this method when they do not wish to be understood by any but themselves," and so subverted to a small extent the authoritarian pretensions of outsiders seeking to profit from their labor. Indigenous inhabitants, then, were never the passive recipients of minstrel or theatrical performance; they were not the "local" receptacles for a "global" force." Instead, they demonstrated an avidity for artistic display aimed at the same complex ends that blackface performers aspired to.[32]

Other observers also commented on how widespread all of these minstrel forms were becoming and how common it was for other peoples to repurpose blackface in pursuit of their own ambitions. Bayard Taylor, an American who wrote of his global travel in 1859, illustrated an interesting scene while in India. As he was dining with an English gentleman, their meal was interrupted by a Hindu troubadour who began to strum a mandolin for whatever coins the men might spare. But "to my complete astonishment," Taylor gasped, the musician "began singing 'Get out of the way, Ole Dan Tucker!'" Enjoying the Yankee's surprise, he proceeded to strike up a litany of the era's most popular minstrel songs, including "'Oh Susanna!,' 'Buffalo Gals,' and other choice Ethiopian melodies, all of which he sang with admirable spirit and correctness." Further along in his travels, Taylor again spoke of minstrelsy's global influence: he heard "Spanish boatmen on the isthmus of Panama singing 'Carry me back to ole Virginny' and Arab boys in the streets of Alexandria humming 'Lucy Long.'" And yet, for whatever reason, it was the sound of "the same airs from the lips of a Hindoo" that he had been "hardly prepared" for.[33]

George Colvocoresses anchored at Tahiti aboard the USS *Vincennes* only to observe that "the females here have certainly a very great passion for singing." The women, however, did "not confine themselves to their national songs" but would "strike up some one of our own which they have learned from the whalers, and which seemed to be as familiar to them as to any of us." And in 1841, in Mérida, Mexico, diplomat John Lloyd Stephens was welcomed ashore by a local brass band playing the minstrel song "Jim Crow" under the erroneous impression that it was the U.S. national anthem: "The band, perhaps in compliment to us, and to remind us of home, struck up the beautiful *national* melody of 'Jim Crow.'" An honest mistake, Stephens thought, given the frequency with which American naval bands were used for minstrelsy overseas. Audiences abroad habitually reappropriated what had been played and performed for them, and that reappropriation further demonstrates the unstable meaning of these minstrel performances. Peoples overseas discerned what they wanted to in the show's song and dance. Maritime minstrelsy thus helps undermine simplistic narratives of coercive cultural imperialism. It demonstrates how localities resisted the imposition of U.S. cultural norms by reshaping minstrel material to suit their own needs.[34]

Perhaps the clearest (and most entertaining) attempt to reuse specifically minstrel-like forms for the ridicule of maritime norms took place in Rewa, Fiji. There, a whiteface performance staged for both natives and sailors mocked the archipelago's American arrivistes as clumsy, tactless, and ignorant. In short, Fijian artists bent on denigrating white mariners appropriated all of the traits exhibited by black caricatures in the minstrel show. It was the islanders' contribution to a broader performative dialogue between recently acquainted peoples. The scene, which took place in the early 1840s, was described by a seaman named John Jackson who understood the local language, and, his comments merit extended quotation. Fijians, he began, "sometimes amuse themselves with masquerades," and Jackson remembered that at one such gathering, "an individual . . . took the character of a white man, and performed it so well, that he caused great mirth." The man

> was clothed like a sailor, armed with a cutlass, and as a substitute for bad teeth (which is a proverbial characteristic of white men amongst these people), he had short pieces of black pipe-stems placed irregularly, which answered very well. The nose on his mask was of a disproportionate length (which they say is another prominent feature, adding nothing to the beauty of white men). His hat was cocked on three hairs in the sailor fashion, and made from banana leaves. In his mouth was a short black pipe, which he was puffing away as he strolled about, cutting the tops of any tender herb that happened to grow on either side.

Jackson was then careful to note that these performances were staged by the lower classes of Fiji for the amusement of royalty and that in all other ways and instances, commoners were expected to observe a strict etiquette before their betters. The counterfeit white mariner proved amusing precisely because he violated with impunity what were otherwise inviolable norms. "This mimicking sailor acted his part cleverly," Jackson elaborated, "and paid no attention whatever to decorum." Rather, he strutted about puffing away at his pipe as unconcerned as though he was walking the forecastle . . . [until] some of the masqueraders reminded him that he was in the presence of Tui Drekete. He immediately asked who Tui Drekete was, and could not be made to understand, till some of them looked in the direction the king was sitting, when he pointed (which is greatly against the rules), and asked if that was the "old bloke," walking up to him bolt upright and offering his hand, which the king smilingly shook. The sailor then told him he had better take a whiff or two with him, as it was the best tobacco he had smoked for many a day. The king, willing to make the best of the amusement, took the pipe, the spectators making the air ring again with their shouts and laughter, 'Vavala gi dina, dina sara' (a real white man, a real white man!).

The humor here focuses on the comical appearance of white sailors—almost certainly American whalemen "because," as Jackson remarked, "most of the ships that visit Feejee are Americans"—and the inability (or unwillingness) of those individuals to behave appropriately. An "invading" cultural form could be used by indigenous individuals to construct oppositional depictions of those who had initiated the encounter.[35]

These were clearly multilayered events. It was not simply that satirizing sailors allowed Fijians (and, presumably, other peoples staging similar shows) to depict what they saw as the boorish and ridiculous qualities of alien peoples. Rather, these theatrics granted Fijians a certain amount of creative license to transgress the rigidly observed boundaries of their own social structure. White seamen were in part the advanced guard of encroaching and disruptive maritime empires. And yet their unruly qualities could be repurposed by, as John Jackson thought them, underlings who assumed a seafarer's identity to enjoy otherwise unthinkable liberties in the presence of local notables. Leveling actions and gestures connoting informality—pointing at the king, refusing to prostrate, direct communication between "high" and "low"—became possible in the nonthreatening and humorous confines of these whiteface performances. Native audiences clearly would not buckle beneath the burden of a blackface art form designed in part to satirize nonwhite peoples. Rather, as mock seafarers themselves became the theatrical vessels of local political critiques, indigenous actors at Fiji and elsewhere showed the creative potential born out of cross-cultural connection. This was the embodiment of the new and "odd" emerging out of the crucible of contact, or, as sailor Frank T. Bullen later reflected, one of those "queer transmutations" resulting from the "closest, most intimate, and,

I dare to say, most beneficial contact" between the "dusky denizens of one of the most retrograde, hide bound of nations with the sturdy upstanding Puritans of England's prime."[36]

Fijians adopted the persona of the sailor as their embodiment of free-spirited subversiveness in the same moment that nineteenth-century Americans came to construe nautical life as retrograde for its hierarchical and thus servile nature. Perhaps in an ordinary and thus "safe" theatrical forum, Fijians were simply prepared to grant the "lowliest" of creatures permission to speak the unspeakable. If so, this would not make the islanders' performances very different than blackface shows, which often featured "lowly" slaves heaping scorn on more elite figures. Given that potential similarity in aims between Fijian masquerades and American minstrelsy, it seems appropriate that the two probably intersected at Rewa. It was there, after all, that the United States Exploring Expedition had "jumped Jim Crow" and set the local population "wild."

And so, even as they blanketed the world, minstrel tunes that were nominally derisive of nonwhite agency were repackaged for local use, as work songs, satirical entertainment, or a source of income that preyed on homesick Americans who were anxious to hear what blackface show runner E. P. Christy saluted as "*our* native airs." Clearly there were peoples around the globe who would dispute the possessive tone of Christy's comment. Hence the hesitancy with which we must assign any definitive interpretation of minstrelsy's meaning to overseas audiences. Minstrelsy was immensely complex; contemporary scholars who have examined song lyrics and playbills reveal that it simply cannot be boiled down to the exhibition of exploitative racial imitation. The routines contained many targets and abundant burlesques, all of which changed over time. Just as the content of blackface performance shifted over the course of the antebellum era (class-based protests against capitalism and critiques of elite pretension were gradually replaced by more overtly racist representation of black peoples), so also did its aesthetics and target audience. Yet we must also appreciate shifts in meaning as minstrelsy crossed borders, something Jim Crow was prone to do from the late 1830s onward.[37]

The words, music, and form of blackface was in the hands of more and more people overseas, and we should remain skeptical of studies that situate blackface shows solely in a national political debate over race and slavery. Bondage and the biological distinctions between peoples were certainly crucial ingredients to minstrelsy in its American or even in its transatlantic iterations. But in a more global context, blackface begins to look like a single variant in a variety of masked performances indigenous to myriad cultures. From creole comedians in Cuban theatres who parodied that island's largely African heritage via the painted body of the *negrito* to the more widespread Atlantic world practice of "playing Indian" on stages, international impersonation ran rampant. As the pace of global interconnection quickened over the course of the nineteenth century, that multiplicity of masquerades became more significant in both the making of intercultural introductions and, later, in the reification of racial boundaries. Nowhere does this become more apparent than around the Pacific basin. There, Jim Crow did not enter a cultural vacuum but rather appeared in a continuum of costumed and colored dances circulating the region. When minstrels made their appearance abroad, nearly identical idioms overlapped and collaborated. Blackface's "wheels about and turns about" were simply added to a vibrant trans-Pacific ritualistic culture already characterized by dramaturgical exchanges and interlocking influences. Minstrelsy integrated nicely into long-standing theatrical practices used to conduct diplomacy in a region of the world that had been woven together long before the arrival of Euroamerican ships.[38]

The most famous of these polyglot performances still takes place to this day in Nagasaki, Japan. There, the Kunchi festival features rites and rituals meant to evoke that city's special status as a previously "closed" country's singular gateway to the wider world. Nagasaki's manmade Deshima Island, after all, served as a Dutch East India Company trading outpost, not to mention the Japanese source for information from abroad. It is appropriate, then, that performance art there celebrates the city's status as a cultural crossroads. Many years before a corps of minstrels aboard the USS *Powhatan* staged seriocomic antics, Nagasaki hosted lavishly costumed troupes of actors and dancers decked out in ornate face paint and enlarged collars meant to pantomime European sailors and traders. The grotesqueries of the *ketoujin* or "hairy barbarians" proved loose analogs for later minstrel representations of comically inferior black peoples. Amid chants, music, fireworks, and slithering dragons, individuals witnessed replicas of billowing sails announcing the appearance of people from afar.[39]

Kunchi itself stood alongside more widespread sixteenth-century Japanese soirees where revelers (some reputedly with painted faces) engaged in *nanban* drag shows meant to mimic the garb and mannerisms of then-recent arrivals from the Iberian Peninsula. It is all more broadly characteristic of the Pacific's international maritime districts and captures the cross-current of cultural influences that characterized life in those crossroads. Jim Crow simply stepped into that long-vibrant exchange. Minstrelsy and its seeming counterparts overseas were largely devoted to similar ends: to meet and greet, to stage the new and strange and render it acceptable. Sailors and Fijians traded tunes inside what one witness called a *bure* or *buri*, a "townhouse for public meetings, and to entertain strangers," while the *haka* dance performed for Joseph Clark was one "which the Maoris called 'entertaining strangers.'" Was not the ship's deck simply another *buri*, a space allotted for cultural merging and designed to facilitate dialogue between strangers? Was not Jim Crow simply another dance meant to do the same, that is, to entertain strangers? In a regional environment that for centuries prior had facilitated cross-cultural exchanges through theatrical practice, blackface performers were quickly made to feel at home. If, for sailors, minstrelsy was a diplomatic tool, other peoples abroad performed their own masked songs and dances with a similarly diplomatic objective.[40]

Of course, this discussion of actors' intentions and audience reception must remain speculative. There is little to no direct evidence on either front, only inference drawn from context, exactly because the motives of shipboard performers were so murky and multifarious. For just as whiteface performance in Fiji might work to puncture the sanctity of hereditary privilege, seafarers, members of a motley multiracial workforce, could use minstrelsy to complain about class distinctions afloat. The translated playbill Matthew Perry distributed among Japanese spectators may have promised selected songs and dances of the "plantation 'niggas' of the South," but this takes on added meaning when one considers the frequency with which white sailors compared their hard lot afloat to that of the slave ashore. Given the minstrel's characteristic application of dark hues to white skin, there was, for example, a delicious double-meaning in mariner Justin Martin's claim that it "would be better . . . to be painted black and sold to a southern planter rather than be doomed to the forecastle of a whale ship."[41]

Top-deck stages, in other words, were spaces where power could be reclaimed. Maritime minstrelsy may have used slave imagery and melodies as part of a systematic critique of nautical life as "like slavery." The comic display became a clever means to mask reproaches that officers would otherwise have termed "mutinous." William Good, serving on the USS *Merrimac*, learned that lesson the hard way when, in 1857, he was manacled and placed in the ship's brig for exclaiming that his lieutenant was "more fit to be a nigger-driver than a gentleman." The irony of this otherwise unremarkable court martial lay in Good's rating aboard the vessel as a "Musician, Second Class." Perhaps he might have had better luck drawing the enslavement analogy while engaged in minstrel antics with his fellow band members, for this more direct outburst cost him a reduction in rank and forfeited pay, not to mention the indignity of imprisonment. Some officers regretted minstrelsy's appearance aboard ship precisely for its sometimes subversive quality, its capacity to loosen tongues in a dangerously free expression of dissatisfaction among men accustomed to complain of their lot as slavish. J. Willett Spalding, aboard a ship stuck in Hong Kong while coaling in 1854, thought the mariners' "burnt-cork dramatic performances . . . a thing not at all calculated to improve discipline," for they made "'Rome howl' much oftener than good sailors should." Another officer wondered about the unruly impact of "animal spirits" unleashed by blackface spectacles.[42]

The performances of sailor minstrels seem to be further complicated by the fact that the characteristics ascribed to the caricature of black individuals appearing in those shows aligned very closely with the stock sailor's own stereotypical traits. "Jolly Jack Tar," as common seamen were often denoted, was alternately celebrated and excoriated for his jovial, carefree, boisterous, child-like temperament. Stories, plays, and other literary productions often (though not always) introduced sailors as comic relief. They were depicted as ignorant and improvident buffoons, oddly costumed in distinctive dress, and speaking the peculiar occupational argot specific to seagoing peoples. In a word, mariners were often seen as "other," and, in terms of their popular representation, not always distinct from racial groups skewered along very similar lines. Seafaring characters and maritime-themed songs even became popular portions of the minstrel's repertoire, as when Mark Twain noted that blackface performances "were a delight to me as long as the Negro show continued in existence [including] sentimental songs such as 'A Life on the Ocean Wave' [and] 'The Larboard Watch.'" For observers outside the maritime world, it did not seem a dramatic leap from the ship to the minstrel stage. After all, sailors were called "Tars" exactly because their bodies were often covered in a thick coat of black glue that was useful for caulking a vessel's seams.[43]

Stereotypes about sailors perpetuated by popular culture were omnipresent enough to become the basis of legislation and jurisprudence. Congress justified the federal government's unique oversight of maritime workers by citing their notoriously diminished mental capacities, while the Supreme Court, in cases such as the (in)famous 1897 case *Robertson v. Baldwin*, repeatedly pointed to sailors "as deficient in that full and intelligent responsibility for their acts which is accredited to ordinary adults." That same language, when applied to peoples of African descent, had for generations justified slavery and segregation. And while the two were not perfectly comparable—black peoples were "biologically predisposed" to inferiority while sea service simply transformed otherwise capable men—the parallel nevertheless extended so far that seamen's advocates referred to the *Baldwin* case as the "second Dred Scott decision," while the *San Francisco Examiner* opined that "the difference between a deep-water sailor and a slave is $15 per month."[44]

There was less distance between "Jovial 'Jack Tar'" and the minstrel show's "Happy Darkey" than many sailors might have liked. Even as some white mariners interfered with the ability of African Americans to control their own self-presentation abroad, seamen at home endured similar struggles in a transatlantic popular culture that perpetuated ridicule of sailors. Minstrelsy afloat thus proved no less complicated than its counterpart ashore. In maritime culture, blackface performances became places to work through multifaceted issues. The metaphorical "blackness" of the white sailor overseas; the appearance of nonwhite authority figures abroad; the need to protest through parody the authoritarianism of shipboard command structures: nautical blackface operated simultaneously at multiple discursive levels. If what an audience actually absorbed from that entertainment was ambiguous, the motivations and intended message of mariner performers was no less so.

The jury may remain out regarding the *precise* meaning of seafarers' performative proclivities. But at the very least this was, as Bayard Taylor noted, a process with imperial implications. Remarking on Jim Crow's growing global ubiquity, the traveler declared that "Ethiopian melodies well deserve to be called, as they are in fact, the national airs of America" because they "follow the American race in all its emigrations, colonizations, and conquests, as certainly as the Fourth of July and Thanksgiving Day." Journalist J. K. Kennard likewise remarked that for all the time it took Britain to "encircle the world . . . 'Jim Crow' has put a girdle round about the earth in forty minutes."[45] The *New York Herald* thought minstrelsy was "heard in every circle," with "Jim Crow here—Jim Crow there—Jim Crow everywhere," and the *Boston Post* agreed, proclaiming that "the two most popular characters in the world at the present time are Victoria and Jim Crow." The global significance of an empire-building queen could be compared only to the imaginative empire already erected by American showmen. Although minstrelsy at home was a crucial platform for expansionist rhetoric, the performance of blackface overseas was also a nod to colonialism. It helped

promote the beginnings of prejudice. Ideas about the inferiority and incapacity of nonwhite peoples were implicit in the representational politics
of minstrelsy. Its meaning overseas may not initially have been racial, but
the show's influence ultimately trended in that direction. Populations the
world over became entangled in a hierarchical matrix of legally sanctioned
inferiority that was Anglo-American in origin but global in implication.[46]

Only too late did some Pacific peoples learn of the dangers lurking
behind what were at first glance innocent antics. Fijians, Kanaks, Tahitians, Tongans, and many others who had once hosted blackface performers soon discovered what the asymmetrical power relations undergirding
minstrelsy's portrayals of race could mean for those who were seen as essentially "black." The mutual misunderstanding of masked performance on
the middle ground of the ship's deck had at first made possible the opening up of creative and constructive relationships, but Jim Crow eventually
distinguished itself as the harbinger of an aggressive racialization campaign
unprecedented in its systematic sorting of supposed difference. Historian
Eric Lott argues that minstrelsy became a field for expropriation wherein
"black people were divested of control over elements of their culture and
generally over their own cultural representation." Expropriation, it seems,
was a fate shared internationally by other nonwhite peoples. By the end of
the nineteenth century, thousands of Pacific islanders had been kidnapped
and forced to board ships destined for Australian and South American plan-
tations in a practice called blackbirding. American vessels and U.S. citizens
played prominent roles in this coercive process. Many indigenous peoples
died, and most never saw their native lands again. These transplants, who
mixed with unfree "coolie" labor from China and South Asia, were then
further corralled and controlled by their new host societies during what
one historian calls a coordinated, worldwide, late-nineteenth-century "segregation mania."[47]

"Jim Crow" stuck his foot in the door, and what followed was Jim Crow
law: a collection of legislative initiatives designed to preserve racial hierarchy and promote the economic interests of elite sugar, cotton, and mining
concerns across the Pacific. The White Australia Policy—just one of several
state-sponsored segregationist edifices known as the global Gilded Age's
"Great White Walls"—proved remarkably reminiscent of the race-based re-
strictivism practiced by Redeemers in the U.S. South. The similarity is not
surprising, however, given the prominent role Confederate expatriates, run-
away whalemen, and white beachcombers played in Australasian politics.
The Pacific chapters of the Ku Klux Klan these men formed constituted,

in one British observer's 1870 words, an "American party, that objects altogether to dealing with the nigger on terms of equality" and was in favor of "carrying matters with a very high hand." One-time witnesses to and participants in the crippled slave Jim Crow's tricks, many Pacific peoples had by then come to more literally embody his deracination, enslavement, and segregation. After conducting interviews with American sailors who profited from the blackbird trade in Tahiti, one British newspaper even opined that conditions there were "worse and more inhuman than the old African Slave Trade."[48]

Sailors were not, of course, directly responsible for the imposition of those discriminatory political regimes. Policy emanated from administrative desks and settler-colonial institutions above the seaman's pay grade. And yet, mariners made important introductions—no matter how benign, initially—that would eventually metastasize into a cancerous international color line. William Reynolds, attached to the same exploring expedition that danced minstrel steps at Rewa and across the Pacific, was one of the few to reflect on the potential implications for Polynesian peoples of U.S. racial restrictions that were already entrenched by the time he wrote in 1840. Impressed by native hospitality at Samoa, he "could not help thinking, what would be the reception of these people in *our Land*?" The question was not answerable in any but the most unpleasant of terms. After reflecting on it, Reynolds claimed, "my pride as a white man melted away." Yet it was, in some sense, too late for a guilty conscience. Sailors had opened a dialogue that had progressively more discriminatory implications for peoples overseas, and they did so in the guise of Jim Crow. Indeed, it seems instructive that although Reynolds felt sadness at Samoa, only months later he would revel in the slaughter of Fijians as "a great saving and a general blessing to mankind at large." The "sooner they are exterminated as a race, the better," he bluntly surmised. For all of blackface's communicative potential, one side of that conversation did not care much, in the end, about the ultimate fate of categorically "inferior" people, wherever they may be.[49]

Along the increasingly expansive pathways pioneered in part by nineteenth-century American sailors, Jim Crow—first as antics, then as racial regulation—made his way deeper and deeper into what western cartographers recorded as some of the world's most remote real estate. Even Antarctica, the most isolated of those outposts, bore silent and icy witness to minstrel activities. Charles Wilkes's United States Exploring Expedition might have discovered that southerly continent—and along the way working hard to circulate blackface's manic ballet throughout the Pacific—but the conquest was, in a sense, incomplete until Jim Crow himself had stomped his seal into the frozen earth. In this case, he did so at the behest of British mariners, who, by the 1850s at least, appear to have further disseminated blackface performance by adopting American minstrelsy as a shipboard ritual of their own. And so when famed polar explorer Robert Falcon Scott's HMS *Discovery* arrived in 1902 at the planet's southern extreme, one of the first initiatives implemented to stave off boredom during the long and cold winter was a regular theatrical schedule. Eventually, one witness wrote, the men "undertook to organize a nigger minstrel troupe," with "all the Sambos [soon] busy blackening their faces and hands and dressing." Temperatures of forty degrees below zero did not seem to dampen the sailors' enthusiasm. Men rechristened themselves the "Dish-cover Minstrel Troupe," donned elaborate costumes of oversized bowties and undersized hats, and told jokes in "the nigger language."[50]

As more serious investigative work began, the stage was disassembled to make room for additional equipment. And yet it seems significant that just as Japan was "opened" by the strange diplomacy of minstrels, so too would

Figure 5. Antarctic minstrels. When blackface minstrelsy became a truly global phenomenon, racial theatrics were performed even in Antarctica. Pictured here are the mariner minstrels of HMS *Discover* at their South Pole research station, ca. 1902. "Minstrel Troupe," P83/6/1/1/80. Scott Polar Research Institute, University of Cambridge.

Antarctica begin to unveil itself before those blacked up for the occasion. In both instances, and in the many in between, seemingly inhospitable places were rendered cheerful, friendly, and familiar with a few daubs of dark grease and a little dialect. Across the nineteenth century and well into the twentieth, at a time when actual African Americans were largely restricted in their travel, seafaring men claimed their lineage as a useful tool in the breaching of borders and bridging of cultures. In the parodied immobility and ignorance of one race, mariners built cultural bridges that allowed those individuals following in the wake of Jim Crow's seafaring sojourn to construct the more fluid and interconnected international order we are familiar with today.

Most observers, however, seemed to overlook the means by which Jim Crow made his appearance overseas. Traveling troupes no doubt played their part. But atop the ocean wave stood ready-made performers prepared to replicate the nation's most popular form of entertainment for a diverse array of spectators. By blacking up around the globe, young American men brought the baggage of American history to peoples far removed from the nation's shores. Minstrel shows were laden with the burden of the country's past—racism, degradation, misappropriation, all hiding in plain sight between the notes of cheery melodies and plantation "airs." Yet blackface minstrel characters were not the only caricatures to materialize overseas. Many white sailors from the United States were, in fact, also prone to perceive Indians abroad in the peoples they encountered. We are accustomed to seeing manifest destiny as what cleared the North American land mass of whoever and whatever impeded national territorial expansion. The aquatic variant of an ideology that is often thought of solely in terms of continental aggrandizement, however, helped open the world's oceans to the spreading sails of American commerce.[51]

Chapter 3

Maritime Destiny as Manifest Destiny

But here's to the lad whose fearless heart,
On land and ocean free,
Directs his feet to range alike
The forest and the sea

The boy who is at home the same
On rock, and tree and spar,
In whom we find at once combined
The hunter and the tar.
Who loves the gale that splits the sail,
Or bows the towering tree,
Who knows the for'c's'le and the camp,
The forest and the sea.

Who an anchor or a rifle ball
With right good will can cast,
Content before the hunter's lodge,
Content before the mast.
To whom the deaf'ning thunder's crash
Is source of lightsome glee,

When threat'ning storms in anger lash
The forest and the sea.

Who lights his fire in sylvan glens,
Where cliffs o'erhang the deep,
And 'tween the howl of wolf and surf
Goes calmly to his sleep.
Who never seeks from danger's face
The path by which to flee,
But meets unmoved the terrors of
The forest and the sea.

So begins a much longer poem extolling the virtues of young American manhood during the 1850s. Here, a courageous spirit of enterprise helps light the world's darkest and most remote spaces; here, sailors help pioneer an expansive global frontier. Yet what makes this ode so intriguing is its claim that *both* "the forest and the sea" comprised the country's wilderness. This early nineteenth-century insistence on the basic equivalence of woods and water as coextensive fields for American ambition, a claim common to the era, has not trickled down into twenty-first-century historical accounts. Instead, westward territorial growth receives a disproportionate share of academic interest, thus misrepresenting a moment when the country's attention in fact extended outward across both mountains and ocean. The world's saltwater spaces, therefore, should also be seen as frontiers populated by American men, even if the frontier imagery that survives today is dominated by buckskin clad mountain men rather than canvas-clad Jack Tars. In fact, national expansion—the heady and exuberant spirit of manifest destiny—was waterborne as much as it was landbound. It seems fitting that this particular copy of the poem was found carefully clipped from a newspaper and pasted to the pages of an ordinary sailor's 1851 journal. As he roved the Atlantic and Pacific over the course of three years, these verses clearly helped one young man explain the meaning of his sojourn to the aquatic edges of the early republic.[1]

In fact, sailors regularly used the rhetoric of manifest destiny to describe both the peoples they encountered overseas and their own participation in the process of commercial expansion more generally. As they strode out of burgeoning eastern cities and onto the ship's deck, mariners struggled to make sense of the world they encountered. Demographic studies of seamen have long pointed to their youth, poverty, and lack of formal education. Not well read in classic works of geography, sailors no doubt relied on the experiences of their better-traveled shipmates in order to anticipate the sorts of societies they might encounter in the course of a voyage. Many were American seamen departing from American ports, and we can reasonably expect that these individuals carried a host of assumptions about such issues as savagery, civilization, and the boundary between the two. These were understandings about the world that were shaped by popular culture, by the very act of coming of age as working men in the United States, exposed to penny dreadfuls and a flash press full of regular allusions to America's "heroic" conquest of savage space.[2]

The most pervasive evidence of this are the obsessive references citizen sailors made to American Indians as they traveled across the globe prior to the Civil War. Ideas about North America's native peoples played a major part in helping the nation's seamen comprehend an otherwise baffling array of cultures. Whether as savagery embodied or anti-modernism personified, Indians figured prominently in the imaginations of many mariners as they moved from port to port. Men coming out of cities and towns that were increasingly bereft of a significant Indian presence still claimed privileged knowledge about primitivism. And in "knowing" natives in North America, they claimed to know all their incarnations. Diaries, logbooks, and other accounts suggest that the creation and continued expansion of the United States had bestowed on American men a belief in their own capacity to understand and interact with the "savages" that circled the globe.

The first substantial population of Americans to travel abroad regularly left the nation's shores unprepared to appreciate the very real cultural complexity and demographic variety they would encounter. Sailors advanced across ocean space only to retreat into powerful long-standing ideas about Indians as undifferentiated savages who at best provided novel spectacles and at worst proved to be implacable foes. Of course, not all sailors used comparisons to Indians. Many hailed from maritime towns where Native American seafarers were a common sight. Others would know of Pacific islanders and other exotic persons from tales of travels circulating among the seafaring men they interacted with on a daily basis. And, as the second chapter suggested, "blackness" competed as a construct for identifying foreign bodies overseas, minstrels tended to provide the initial introduction for American sailors to peoples who were later spoken of as having some essentially "Indian" quality or qualities. This "Indian" designation was largely (though not entirely) confined to peoples white American sailors encountered in the Pacific. It was closely related to the overseas expression of the tropes of manifest destiny and described not just people but an entire matrix of civilizational achievement and material life.

Sailors, therefore, had an "Indian" mode of existence in mind that could be—but was not necessarily—connected to complexion. It was with a paradoxical mix of wonder, nostalgia, and hatred that nineteenth-century white American men approached so-called Indians overseas. In the run up to the Civil War, popular notions of Indians as a declining, even "doomed" people influenced perceptions overseas, generating curiosity if not melancholy among observers. When "blackness" and its accompanying slurs appeared abroad, it never contained quite so contradictory a set of understandings. Peoples of African descent, after all, were not in sad decline at the nation's edges. Rather, they were more often spoken of as a pervasive problem in the republic. There was no pathos surrounding a "vanishing African" because black individuals were more firmly (and dangerously) entrenched in antebellum society. "Blackness" generated levels of anxiety at communal, sectional, and national levels in ways that were more clear-cut than "Indianness" did. The former almost universally implied disparagement or contempt; the latter did not.[3]

Sailors had at their disposal a stock frontier "savage" from the American case that could be applied to other "savages" on other frontiers. Persons of supposedly "Indian" extraction who crossed paths with American seamen overseas, in turn, suffered the heavy burden of a nation whose past they were not a part of but yet were profoundly and unfortunately implicated in. In holding so-called Indians abroad accountable to stereotypes that had been established at home, the country's seamen revealed how American history might ensnare even those who lived outside national borders. The phenomenon also tells of tables turned entirely. Historians of European exploration, contact, and colonization in the Americas note that initial witnesses to "discovered" Indians depended on earlier characterizations of Irish, Saxon, and Greco-Roman bodies to describe the exotic. By the nineteenth century, Native Americans had become the stereotyped frame of reference that was applied to peoples encountered outside the continental context.[4]

As Thomas Bender has suggested, "other histories are implicated in American history, and the United States is implicated in other histories." That sailors brought their ideas about Indians in the United States to bear on the world at large supports this observation. Categories of analysis such as race and areas of study such as nineteenth-century Native American history are often artificially bounded by the imposition of impermeable national boundaries when a more porous conceptual framework is called for. Without failing to appreciate the very real ways that nationalism in the United States depended on racial thought and Indian enemies, we must push beyond lines drawn on maps. For many people living in antebellum America, racial theorizing was an analytical tool in both a national and world-historical sense. It explained the apparent triumphs of the white community in the United States *and* around the globe. Jacksonian narratives that described savagery receding before a civilized empire of liberty were thought to be applicable to both the American wilderness and larger portions of the planet.[5]

Accounts that continue to privilege westward migration as the crucible of American racial ideology do not tell the complete story of an era when the nation's maritime destiny seemed as manifest as its landward one. Historians have much to learn from the decades when multitudes of white American seamen plied the oceans in search of trade, ambassadors representing a country and a race they deemed superior. In a period when many scholars point to territorial expansion as the preeminent fixation of the national political economy, a parallel strain of maritime expansionism existed that should not be seen as necessarily opposed to or in conflict with its landward counterpart but rather as developed in concert with it and dependent on nearly identical forms of oratorical flourish.[6]

At the time, "frontier" constructs had a range and meaning beyond that later recorded by more territorially minded scholars from Turner onward. Robert Walker, President James Polk's treasury secretary, spoke in 1848 of "our *maritime* frontier upon the Pacific [being] now nearly equal to our Atlantic coast, admirably situated to command the trade of Asia and of the whole western coast of America." Other speechmakers spoke of U.S. ships instigating "a new commercial era" wherein the republic might realize "her destiny . . . as the centre and emporium of the commerce of the world." The Cincinnati *Daily Enquirer* concurred, proclaiming that it was the Pacific basin's "manifest destiny to become a portion of the American domain." These words swelled a chorus of voices fixated on an oceanic dimension to the idiom of national expansion. Sailors proved receptive to such rhetoric, as it suffused their labor abroad with a noble purpose. While politicos littered newspaper articles and popular oratory with visions of an American frontier that ever extended into the setting sun, seamen who shipped into that space imaginatively peopled it with Indians and others who had long been the objects of national interest, if not national conquest. Whether clearing paths toward Texas's cotton fields or the fabled China market, Americans used images of Indians and the frontier to authorize and legitimate their deeds.[7]

Complexion was the most common point of reference by which American seamen used ideas about Indians to domesticate what was foreign to them. When Samuel Shaw's ship the *Empress of China* lay anchored off the coast of Java in 1794, two canoes approached the vessel proposing some exchange. Peering down into the smaller craft, Shaw noted that "these people are middle-sized and well-made—complexion similar to that of the North American savage, with regular features and a pleasing countenance, though their teeth are excessively black." He recorded only that some of the sailors bought monkeys from them for a few bits of old cloth and that both parties went their separate ways well satisfied. The innocuousness of the arrangement was made possible, in part, by a reversion to familiar faces and skins, namely those of the "North American savages" Shaw so mundanely invoked in his brief journal entry.[8]

Charles Lane, a young man on shore leave from the New Bedford whaler *Henry Taber,* wrote home from Guam to a cousin in New York State in very similar terms. The island, he claimed, was "inhabited by a wild race of men" who "in complexion resemble our North American Indian." The men "were nude," he stated, while the women "wor a piece of calico around their waistes." None of that information seemed to concern him; it was simply a way to make a place unknown to his correspondent somewhat intelligible. The young mariner expressed greater enthusiasm over the killing he made at a local haberdasher's: "I got me about forty hats, enough to last me the rest of this voyage; and good hats they are too!" Fifty years earlier, William Haswell also very casually noted that in Guam, "50 Indians" had approached to meet his ship with fruit and hogs, while another sailor, at Tonga, thought the "'Hula Hula' dances" of the local population, in "gestures, songs, and dances very much resemble those of the North American Indians."[9]

William Allen, who kept a journal aboard the whaleship *Samuel Robertson,* lamented to himself that native women in the Marquesas islands, while "glowing with passion," carried with them a "disorder which caught from one of these women is much worse than the same in America, makes old men of young ones," and "seems to be a real poison to a white man!" But how could one resist, he seemed to ponder, for these were no "dusky savages" but rather had "clear skin as much lighter than our american indians as ours is lighter than a mulattoes." For Allen, frank sexual encounter became forgivable only when he estimated that Indian women overseas were fairer skinned than those in the United States.[10]

Whatever the relative modesty or immodesty of a particular encounter, American men abroad used their ideas of Indian physiognomy to make clear through contrasts the contours of the wider world. This process was not confined to the South Pacific. Horace Putnam, serving before the mast aboard a brig named, conveniently enough, the *Cherokee*, wrote of the Arab inhabitants of Zanzibar that "there complexion is of a coffee colour nearly the same as our Indians [with] eyes invariably black, deep set in the head." The Indian comparison allowed him to conclude that "no one can imagine more fierce or terrible beings, the very personification of the Devil." David Edwards, anchored at Tangiers, took the time to note in his journal that the city "was full of filth crawling in every direction" and the "people here are a set of loathsome looking objects darker than our Indians speaking generally." A preconceived understanding of the importance of appearance also aided Edmund Gardner when his ship halted off the coast of present-day Namibia to seek water in 1803. A search ashore quickly led to contact with the locals. "Their coloring was not African," he stated, "but a shade or two darker than the Indian." The Indian body provided an important point of reference in the process of categorizing people who were new to the sailors.[11]

American men also understood certain women through the lens of standing cultural categories about female natives in North America. When a whaleman named George Attwater sailed into Hawaii aboard the *Henry* in March 1822, he spied a collection of outriggers heading toward the ship. His shipmates suggested that he follow their lead by shaping crude knives out of spare iron hoops. Attwater quickly did as told and soon enough collected in trade a small pile of fruit for his trouble. It seemed as though everywhere he looked, "there ware a canoe of Indians and squars" ready to barter; indeed, "canoes as thick around the ship as toads after a rain." In rendering the encounter, Attwater found it more suitable to describe the females as squaws rather than women. A host of assumptions about Native American women was attached to that word that had now become applicable to their "relations" elsewhere.[12] Fifteen years later Joseph Osborn and several shipmates, coasting along Fijian shores onboard the bark *Emerald*, came to the town of Bowe for a variety of sea cucumber used in the China trade. Seeing their native trading partners engaged in festivities, the men ambled over to observe but were quickly called upon to participate by "a saucy set" of dancers. When pulled in by one of the women, Osborn wrote that "the Old Squaw gave me a terrible hugging in which I was well smeared with oil [but] the Old Lady seemed greatly pleased with me." The succinctness of other accounts points to the reflexive relationship observers ascribed to "native" and "Native American" femininity. A log kept aboard

the ship *Fortune* at the Pacific island of Nauru noted sailors "lyin
tradeing with Natives for Fowls, Cocanuts and Squaws," while W
son saw in Hawaii "pretty squaws well behaved and somewhat c
The preexisting stereotype of the Indian squaw demarcated the boun
of civilized femininity, revealing a complex gendered component to t
encounters overseas.[13]

Wherever one traded or traveled, he could choose to find an Indian
likeness. Even as Native Americans receded from the lived experience of
more and more Americans at home, they continued to appear before the
thousands of men who spent their lives most distant from the nation. The
significance of the fact that these references kept appearing in correspondence and journals should not be overlooked. Letter-writing and the keeping of diaries, both aboard ship and in the maritime milieu, were profoundly
public acts. Mariners regularly shared, read aloud, and traded missives and
other records among themselves, thereby propagating bodies of knowledge
about omnipresent Indians. So while removal and warfare decimated Indian
populations in the United States, citizens laboring overseas readily located
replicas among foreign peoples and consistently shared those findings. They
measured themselves against Indians, used Indian analogies, and made Native Americans out of others in order to return to that familiar metric. The
repetitive exchange of written material meant that other seafarers and correspondents at home—who might share letters and report the information
their sailor relations provided—all became implicated in the creation of
knowledge circuits that persistently located "our American Indians," to use
William Allen's phrase, in distant territory. The transmission of American
racial attitudes overseas and their reinscription among mariners revealed
the depths of dependence on Indian referents possessed by persons raised in
national popular, political, and literary cultures imbued with Native lore.[14]

Seeing others as Indians or using comparisons to Indians was not simply a rhetorical strategy; it suggested a particular manner of approaching
the world. The possessive "our" that preceded "Indian" in some accounts
communicated the familiarity of otherwise unknowable people. The claim
to ownership modified behavior—for example, by affecting Shaw's tactics
during and expectations of trade with native "Indians" in Sumatra—and
shaped how seafarers handled intercultural contact. Degrees of difference
emerge in the sources: certain individuals wrote as if they saw other peoples
as actual Indians, while others merely likened those they observed to Native
Americans for ease of understanding. The use of an analogy is not a refusal
to acknowledge differences between and among indigenous peoples, but

analogy does imply in the mind of the invocator at least a rough equivalency between the objects in question. Even if some persons did not discover Indian facsimiles overseas, many appear to have found enough in common between indigenous peoples at home and abroad to call on a language of correlation. The comparative schemas and linguistic overlaps are significant because they suggest an ongoing dependence on long-standing domestic categories of race in efforts to conceptualize global encounters.

Reliance on Indian equivalencies often went beyond the issue of appearance. Behavioral markers that white Americans considered specifically "Indian" became yet another means by which they familiarized the strange. John Browne, who shipped out as a whaleman in the 1840s, returned from shore leave at Zanzibar to scrawl his few impressions of East Africa. One among them was what he called the "haughty air" of those "worthless scoundrels." Initially complaining that "like all savage nations . . . [there was] nothing like sprightliness or vivacity about them," Browne concluded with a common comparison: "They pride themselves, like the North American Indians, on their power of concealing of every emotion." For Browne, savagery exhibited itself in the deportment of self-possessed men who were wrongly convinced of their own importance. The Arabs who wandered the port cities of the African horn proved convenient analogs to American Indians and thus compounded the disdain Browne expressed for two peoples he found comparable in their insolence and idleness.[15]

Robert Coffin observed the practice of trade in Polynesia and was himself instantly reminded of life in the United States. Having caught a sperm whale in Pacific waters around 1855, he and his shipmates began to knock out the teeth, partly because the men enjoyed the craft of scrimshaw. The main purpose, though, was the utility of the teeth as currency; as Coffin noted, "the Polynesian savages it is as important a treaty article as wampum among our Indians." Coffin assumed a universal fascination among "savages" with trinkets and toys rather than items of any real value. To Coffin, teeth functioned in the South Seas in the same way as beads had in America. His comments reveal the disconnections between reality and image that had appeared in the minds of white Americans by the 1850s. Wampum had a sacred function in what remained of Northeastern Indian confederations, who were, by and large, integrated into the broader cash economy. Still, fictional depictions and New England mythologies that were prevalent at the time Coffin wrote retained the anachronism, which in turn shaped the manner by which the mariner wrote of encounter abroad. Immediately prior to the Civil War, when Indians were less a part of the lived experience of most white Americans, observers depended on hearsay and (mistaken) literary evidence for their notions of "Indian" behavior. Not everyone's experience was the same. Ezra Green mentioned neither whale's teeth nor wampum at the same Society Island chain Coffin visited but still found "Indians" there in 1839. When several shipmates deserted on the island of Moorea, the natives turned out en masse to pursue and capture them in order to collect the $150 reward. "Indians that have learnt the value of money will do anything at the risk of life or liberty to obtain it," a disgusted Green sighed.[16]

But just as at home, it was often what Indians did not do, how they did not behave, that came to count for more in describing their likeness abroad. William Whitecar, a whaleman aboard the ship *Union*, discovered this to be the case while anchored off the coast of western Australia in 1856. Sent ashore with a party of men in order to water the ship, he came across a group of aboriginals whose appearance and behavior inspired a small discourse. "These people are in the extremest degree indolent, [with] words and blows being equally useless" as an inducement to work. Even after the briefest of encounters, Whitecar concluded that "these Australians contrast very unfavorably with our North American Indians, being possessed of all their bad qualities, without a single one of their redeeming traits." The young seaman did not elaborate on what exactly redeemed one people and damned the other. Whitecar seemed more certain about the definitive quality of inaction in delineating the Indian lifestyle both at home and, as he discovered, in the antipodes. Another mariner concurred, writing of Tahitians that "these Indians act just as much as is necessary for man's happiness" and no more. Lurking behind such talk was a sense that perhaps the far-off places of the earth were not so unfamiliar after all, given the unifying force of a mythology of Indian characteristics.[17]

Perceptions of a transoceanic "Indianness," though, had some potentially insidious consequences. In "knowing" Indians the world over, American men knew also how to deal with refractory natures. The episodic racial violence sailors visited upon native peoples could take on greater significance than the regular sort of fraternal fisticuffs (discussed in chapter 4) that otherwise occurred ashore. In some instances, the "Indian" label or analogy authorized use of extralegal violence as a way to redress grievances. The language of mariners was rife with assertions of the incapacity of Indians, both at home and abroad, to comprehend anything other than brute force.

Simeon Stearns, a young mariner working a voyage that circled the South Pacific, jotted a quick note to himself after some unmentioned incident at

Tonga. He declared flatly that "I believe there is no way to satisfy an Indian when he is bent for war but to kill him [for] these people know no law but that of might." Echoing those sentiments, Joseph G. Clark, whose vessel had been robbed of some articles by a group of South Sea islanders in 1840, noted that upon receiving orders from the captain to prepare a small punitive expedition, the vessel rocked "with enthusiastic applause, as we wished to show our superiority to the savages." He later testified with pride that a small village had been burned to the ground and its food stores and canoes destroyed. William Clark, who saw the same incident, remarked that when the captain gave orders to burn the town, "this was good news for the men as they wanted some sport for they considered it nothing more."[18]

William Reynolds was equally willing to shed "Indian" blood as recompense for some offense. In a journal he kept in 1841 while part of the United States Exploring Expedition, Reynolds elaborated on the outrage he and others among the crew felt as they learned of the deaths of two men at the hands of several Fijians. "The seamen were excited to fury . . . and wanted to go after the Natives and fight them at once," he wrote. "Kill, kill, was [the] cry and they had no idea of sparing any one." By the end of the day, Reynolds thought that more than 100 men from nearby villages had been slaughtered. No apology was forthcoming: "It was bloody work," he admitted, "but all the lives in Feegee would not pay for the two we lost." Extending mercy to such people, he wrote, was mere romantic foolishness. His morbid reflection was only that "I regard the bloody fiends as I do the sharks, and feel the same kind of inward joy in killing them in battle, as I exult when one of those monsters of the sea is torn from his hold on life." Identifying variously demarcated "Indians" overseas authorized speech that focused on the necessity of chastisement and even the potential benefits to "civilization" of annihilation. Charles Erskine, another sailor accompanying the expedition, penned a ballad chronicling the same Fijian violence in terms of the "Indian": "We are the men our chieftain led / O'er dark Malolo's plain," the song began, "Before us hosts of Indians fled / And left two hundred slain."[19]

Verbal misunderstandings, thefts, even murders were not unheard of among sailors in all parts of the world. Yet in the supposed Indian country of foreign shores, offenses that in some places were the province of consuls and magistrates took on a special meaning for American men as grievous assaults against civilization punishable only through violent retribution. Their nation's history had taught these seamen about the unresponsiveness of savage minds to anything other than naked aggression. Men who

Figure 6. "Town of Rewa." While overseas, seafarers often observed communities they described as having fundamentally "Indian" characteristics. Such a designation often legitimated brutal assaults against "savage" enemies. "Town of Rewa," illustration by A. T. Agate, in Charles Wilkes, *Narrative of the United States Exploring Expedition*, 5 vols. (New York, 1856), 3:109.

traveled beyond the boundaries and borderlands of the continental United States carried with them a belief in the efficacy of the racialized vigilantism that was thought to be winning more of the West for white Americans at home.[20]

The polemic white seafarers unleashed on "Indian" peoples abroad may have functioned as an outlet for potentially explosive enmities that could not be expressed in the confines of a ship. White men forced to labor alongside people they styled "Indians" could not assault such individuals with impunity. The native peoples seafarers worked with directly were generally, if grudgingly, tolerated. Abusing them might provoke the ire of officers and jeopardize the safety of all aboard a vessel; the success of a voyage depended on cooperation. Still, such compatriots aroused complaint. Journal entries often functioned to air animosities that could not otherwise find expression.[21]

Indeed, what appeared to gall many white American men about maritime labor was its potential to reverse the generally dependable racial hierarchy of the United States. Many complained bitterly about being forced to live and work alongside the "savages" ship captains hired as short-term hands at overseas ports. These men fixated on the insult to the dignity of their racial and national station that work beside "Indians" represented. When a captain on a nearby ship hired Pacific islanders (generally referred to as "Kanakas," from *te enata*, which in various Polynesian dialects means "the men"), William Stetson, who was at Maui aboard the whaleship *Arab*, used the occasion to write forcefully and lengthily on that subject. Luckily, he began,

> we still have a crew of white men in this respect we have all the voyage been more fortunate than the generality of whalers, as when men desert, the skippers either from necessity or choice usually ship a lot of wild kanakas or some like specimens of other nations, and therefore a white man in the forecastle is frequently a stranger in his own house, and very lonely. It is for this reason that many desert from whale ships, who, if they were associated with their own countrymen and civilized people, instead of living amongst a set of barbarian cannibals would never think of leaving. There are but very few whalers so long out from home as we are with a crew of white men in the forecastle. The *Christopher Mitchell* was one of those few and hence it was that we used to enjoy ourselves so well with her crew we were all "kindred spirits."

Stetson's obvious frustration derived from what he felt was the threat to white racial kinship that interracial labor environments represented. Affective ties to countrymen and country—arguably more important to people thrust so far from all they knew—began to look unsustainable while in the presence of "inferior" human specimens. This, according to Stetson, led to desertion among the white portion of the crew. Not caring to see the fundamental power relationship between "civilized" and "savage" peoples their country had accustomed them to overturned, white American men fled the scene. Stetson did not blame them. When he experienced racial integration aboard ships, he spoke not of encompassing fraternalism but a deeply felt sense of loneliness, bitterness, and isolation. White mariners noticed, in one man's words, that cruel captains "could no longer get *men* to ship with [them]," and so they were "obliged to take *things*," Kanakas, "a species of brute upon two legs," "bare-assed niggers," better fit "to go to the devil" than to serve next to "civilized" shipmates.[22] Naval reformers and other activists in the industry complained similarly about the national disgrace of white American men having to serve alongside such mongrel "filth."

Stetson and many others wrote in an antebellum context when whiteness and citizenship were more closely intertwined categories. To them, their "countrymen" were those they unequivocally referred to as "white men." In more and more vituperative tones across the era, they strenuously objected to maritime labor as the site of an unacceptable agglomeration of Anglo-Saxon and inferior races.[23]

Other sailors advocated direct action against offensive peoples rather than desertion. Elihu Wright, writing from Honolulu in 1823, told his brother about the collective violence he and his American shipmates engaged in against "Indians" they considered interlopers. Because it had become "fashionable to leave ships here," he began, the captain sought replacements among native Hawaiians. The crew thought that solution unacceptable and vowed to see that "the damned indians would jump overboard and swim on shore faster than he could bring them off in a boat." The fact was, Wright wrote, "most of them live in a very filthy situation"; the men "did not like to have them," and so "threw them overboard." But, Wright concluded, "I will say no more about this filthy race, as I hope to leave them soon." The connection between their being "Indians" and undesirable, a lesson learned at home in the United States and thus one that needed no explanation for the benefit of his correspondent, motivated Wright and his shipmates to physically protest the master's effort to integrate their home afloat. For some American seamen, "Indians" had the potential to become more menacing than an abstract idea or adversary: they threatened to become co-workers. Men such as Stetson and Wright reacted with hostility to the competition for work and the depressing effect on wages that Pacific islanders and other non-white laborers had within maritime industry. When they expressed their frustration, though, they returned to racial nomenclatures prevalent in the United States and fixated on savagery. Those categorizations legitimated verbal abuse, at times violent reprisal, and revealed how seemingly American ideologies had a global reach and ramification. Anxieties about conditions in the seagoing labor environment, anxieties that escalated as the nineteenth century progressed, were made expressible through readily available racial portrayals.[24]

Yet merciless violence or a reinforced sense of American superiority were not the only responses that so-called Indians abroad elicited. Hostile reactions, of course, were not the only ones possible, and some men were either accustomed or prepared to accept the idea of "Indian" colleagues. Encounters outside the homeland sometimes inspired introspection and empathy rather than indignation. Matthew Perry, en route, ironically, to force open Japan at gunpoint, mused philosophically about scenes of English colonial cruelty he witnessed while anchored at Cape Town, South Africa. Initially condemnatory of British depredations, he reflected that "we Americans have no right to rail at other nations for the wrongs they have inflicted upon aborigines of countries seized upon by them . . . [as] we are not far behind in the frauds and cruelties committed upon our own native tribes."[25]

Captain Amasa Delano, aboard the ship *Perseverance* en route to China, took time ashore at Chile to ponder hypocritical policies toward native peoples as well. As he saw it, the problem was hemispheric in nature and endemic not only to the United States but to all countries that claimed to stand beneath the banner of civilization. "The native Indians . . . are treated in the south in the same manner as they have been in the north." They were warred upon, harassed, and distressed by Chilean settlers. Delano surveyed areas surrounding the few ports he stopped at and noted that Spaniards "had robbed and despoiled the unfortunate Indian of all that was dear to him." The American captain seemed to sigh as he remorsefully concluded that "thus, thinks I to myself, goes the world:—one man robs another of his country, his wealth, and his liberty; and then says he is a brute, and not a Christian."[26]

Delano's comments seemed to affirm the common belief that the Spanish colonial regime had practiced distinct forms of cruelty, but he also expressed an awareness of injustices against Indians wherever they took place. He was in all other ways derisive about Spanish customs and society, but on the specific subject of native peoples and their treatment, honesty obligated him to admit the flaws of his own countrymen. Some looked on the world and found a community united in opposition to the "savagery" of a universal "Indian" type. For others the appearance of indigenes abroad inspired a recognition of more common human traits such as cruelty and avarice. Perry and Delano saw conquest stripped of the quasi-millennial, nationalistic overtones it had attained in their own homeland and admitted to themselves the hollowness of it all.

Richard Henry Dana Jr., author of the widely read *Two Years before the Mast*, showed no less sympathy toward Hawaiians, or "Kanakas," as he shuttled between the hide-trading depots of 1830s California. In several instances, he praised his native co-workers, referring to one particular man nicknamed Hope as his *aikane*, or "lifelong companion." "I really felt a strong affection for him," Dana admitted, "and preferred him to any of my own countrymen there." The feeling appeared to be mutual, for Dana thought "there was nothing which he would not have done for me." Clearly, then, not all feeling toward Pacific peoples was negative, and not all white sailors relied on comparisons with Indians. Yet Dana's concern for non-white shipmates was matched by the callousness of others, a posture that became more common as the nineteenth century progressed. At one point, requesting medicine for his Hawaiian friend, Dana was rebuffed with an incredulous "'What? [For] a damned Kanaka? Oh! he be damned!'"[27]

The Harvard student turned foremast hand channeled much of Perry and Delano's sanctimony about the abuse of native people. "The greatest curse to each of the South Sea islands," thought Dana, "was the first man who discovered it." As he embarrassedly confessed, it had been "white men" like himself who, "with their vices, brought in diseases . . . now sweeping off the native population." In Dana's grave estimation, Hawaiians "seem to be a doomed people," suffering "the curse of a people calling themselves Christian." Here is what has been termed "imperialist nostalgia," a mourning for what one himself has contributed to the destruction of. A popular habit of thought in the United States, penitent profession was common among members of the maritime community overseas. It should be remembered, though, that Dana's temporary position aboard the ship—he did not consider life afloat an occupation and in fact used his formidable family connections in Boston to avoid that fate—meant that he was not forced to view "Kanakas" as competitors who lowered wages and disrupted Anglo-American fraternity. Unintended consequences shade Dana's sympathy, though, for in registering protest against the inevitable "doom" of Pacific natives, he simultaneously advanced the cause of a "civilization" that was engaged in attempting to reinvigorate societies deemed beyond repair and thus ripe for seizure.[28]

The men who routinely expressed regret about the consequences of empire were usually officers or gentlemen, revealing a class divide aboard ships that influenced the perception of "Indians" abroad. Perry and Delano's perspectives align them much more closely to views espoused by the Whig Party and political platforms that were less condemnatory of "savagery." Individuals of higher status, themselves more likely drawn to the Whigs and their emphasis on order, may have been socialized to a somewhat more sympathetic attitude toward Indians. Native Americans, Whigs suspected, were suffering at the hands of Democrats, a supposedly vulgar and ferocious rabble who eagerly populated continental frontiers. The frauds and injustices committed against so-called Indians abroad no doubt provided an opportunity for these men to rehearse personal political grievances rooted in their domestic struggle against an empowered, mobocratic lower-class polity. For these officers, the sailors serving in their forecastles must often have formed a closer approximation to brute savagery than generally peaceful native peoples who were being thoughtlessly despoiled. For instance, William Murrell, a sailor aboard the frigate *Columbia*, recounted the repeated harangues of his commanding officer, who thought the mariners "a set of skulking sons of bitches, and . . . only wished . . . they might die and be damned." Commanders, in other words, often expounded on the expendability of sailors beneath them in the same way that some of those same mariners spoke with disdain about "Indians" abroad.[29]

An inherent muddiness results when applying racial attitudes and observations to the political arena, where no clear polarization between sympathetic Whigs and vituperative Democrats existed. There were multiple styles of masculinity in the antebellum era, none of them hegemonic. Yet the difference between ordinary mariners who were embracing an opportunity to "show our superiority to the savages" and officers who were exhibiting dispassionate remorse does help to illustrate the period's diverging models of manhood. One more aggressive, the other restrained, the former more attractive to working-class men, the latter to middle- and upper-class individuals. The American maritime community was in no way an undifferentiated mass. Divergent representations of "Indians" abroad exposed the cleavages of class and status characteristic of such a large labor force.[30]

Most ordinary men serving aboard American ships overseas were not so prone to a sympathetic consideration of the "Indian point of view" as their officers. Or if they were, their conclusions took an entirely different tone. Twenty-two-year-old Francis Allyn Olmsted, a traveler whose whaleship roamed the South Pacific in February 1839, made a note to himself that was remarkably Jacksonian in its affirmations of white civilization's historic triumph over so-called savagery. He urged his fellow citizens not to sneer at the American seaman, for "many of the fertile islands of the Pacific would now be untenanted, except by the indolent savage, and the enterprising colonies upon them must long since have become extinct, were it not for [our] frequent visits." Further still, he wrote, white persons and property have often "been protected from the ruthless and capricious dispositions of the natives by the timely arrival of a whaler with his brave crew inured to danger in its most formidable aspects." George Little, in another memoir, recapitulated Olmsted's argument. He argued that commerce would always lead sailors "among the less informed, uncivilized portions of mankind." Nothing more than good sense suggested that a white man "possess[ed] a mind of a higher order than the savage, and is by him looked up to as a superior being." American seamen, therefore, should at all times "set before the savage a copy for his imitation." American mariners more generally positioned themselves as their country's foot soldiers on the frontier's frontlines. Their bodies became national symbols, emblematic of America's mushrooming influence abroad. They stressed their role as commercial ambassadors and bearers of white civil society overseas in order to check comparisons middle-class observers made between seamen and "savages."[31]

The editorials of port city newspapers, trade journals, and the Democratic Party press also spoke of the existence of "Indians" around the globe. Those at home in the United States with any degree of familiarity with the literature sailors generated became complicit in affirming the truly global sweep of American incursions into and improvement upon "savage" territory. Other observers incorporated seafarers' contacts abroad into the discourse of expansionism with an enlarged sense of America's presence on the oceanic frontier. Edgar Allan Poe reminded American readers that "our pride as a vigorous commercial nation should stimulate us to become pioneers in [the] vast island-studded ocean." Herman Melville noted that "the whale-ship has been the pioneer in ferreting out the remotest and least known parts of the earth," adding that "if American and European men-of-war now peacefully ride in once savage harbors, let them fire salutes to the honor and glory of the whale-ship, which originally showed them the way, and first interpreted between them and the savages." The treatment of Native Americans at home, then, was underpinned by confirmation received from abroad that "Indians" and "savages" were in full retreat around the world. Reinforced by narratives that glorified the progress of civilization in distant lands, the expansive program of the continental republic received fuller sanction.[32]

Popular media reinforced the proposition that both territorial and aquatic expansion mutually sustained one another. One observer remarked that "New England furnished gratuitously a pioneer service, opening up the byways of old ocean to all, in the shape of her whaleships." Another wrote, "These master seamen of the young republic [are] as truly pioneers as their kinsmen, who, with axe and rifle on their backs, are pouring through the passes of the Alleghenies to subdue the West." Seafarers laboring along the nation's maritime frontier found encouragement to connect their activity to the removal of Indians that characterized the subjugation of the continent, while settlers in the West often used nautical imagery. Popular literary culture reflected that interdependence. As the earlier sea fiction of James Fenimore Cooper (who was a widely read author among seafarers) transitioned into the more familiar, territorially oriented Leather-stocking tales, it gestured toward the fused marine and landed frontiers. So did the output of the nineteenth century's most prolific dime novelist, Ned Buntline, who intermittently wrote about frontier figures such as Buffalo Bill Cody and Kit Carson, but also produced an equal number of maritime melodramas, such as *The King of the Sea* and *Cruisings, Afloat and Ashore.* As one literary scholar argues, a "metaphorical interchange" entwined nautical and terrestrial contact zones in early American literature. Both the public and seafarers were reading accounts that often used language to describe an overlap between commercial and continental expansion, between sailors and pioneers. Those individuals seem not to have discouraged the comparison. One mariner on a South Atlantic sealing expedition remarked that just as a "frontiersman cares for no luxury beyond fresh meat, coffee, and salt, so it was with us," while Washington Irving described overland travelers "bravely steering . . . across the continent, undismayed by danger, difficulty, or distance, in the same way that a New England coaster and his neighbors will coolly launch forth on a voyage to the Black Sea, or a whaling cruise to the Pacific." When George Ruxton claimed that without the "daring enterprise" of "hardy" mountain men, the American West "would be even now a *terra incognita* to geographers," he sounded a lot like national newspapers proclaiming "but for seamen, a great portion of the world would now, and ever, be a vast terra incognita." In one element, mariners became "the bearer of commerce and harbinger of civilization and improvement," and in another, "rude hunters" were "the hardy pioneers who have paved the way for the settlement of the western country." The appearance of "Indians" overseas seems less surprising, given this symbiotic relationship between the fused frontiers of land and sea.[33]

Decades of extirpative warfare and removal policies, however, subtly shifted how Americans came to measure so-called Indians abroad. Men in both the 1790s and the 1850s claimed to find "our Indians," that is, American Indians, in terrain far removed from the United States. The possessive pronoun signified white American ownership of a more universal racial type visible the world over. The meaning of the phrase "our Indians," however, changed over time. A people who represented a realistic presence and even a threat to white American sailors in the earliest years of the republic became the subjects of abstract pronouncements in the years immediately preceding the Civil War. When John Hayes briefly scrawled from Cape Town in 1787 that the Hottentots in South Africa "prove as troublesome to back Settlers here as the americane Indians do to the backsettlers in our country," Indians came across as a force to be reckoned with, a legitimate threat and impediment to territorial expansion around the globe. Hayes departed in 1787 from a nation whose army still suffered regular defeat at the hands of native peoples.[34]

Francis Olmsted, on the other hand, observed "Indians" abroad from a more comfortable perch in the 1840s. He spoke in tropes, alluding to a "vanishing race" of Indians at home and, as he learned, overseas. Evidence gathered on a whaling voyage around the world revealed an amorphous, widespread force known as "progress" that proved too much for the Indian constitution. A stopover in Hawaii, for example, convinced him that "the total extinction of the nation is inevitable, and these humble islanders must shrink away before the irresistible march of foreign enterprize." "Like the aborigines of our own country," they too would "become exterminated." Whaleman William Myers, who was anchored at an unnamed island, wrote of "being confronted by a race in decay, for here in the Pacific, the natives are slowly, but surely, diminishing in numbers." From their perspectives in a time where removal was an operable policy and Indian defeat east of the Mississippi had been achieved, Olmsted, Myers, and others spoke of native peoples everywhere as lamentably, if inevitably, doomed. They could afford to philosophize about the fate of indigenous peoples with a certainty that was not available to earlier observers.[35]

Whereas observers such as Hayes described "Indians" abroad from concrete experiences of their abilities and power, subsequent accounts depended for their standard of comparison on stereotypes of Native Americans that were prevalent in popular culture. William Reynolds articulated that shift in perception in an 1838 letter to his sister, whom he told of welcoming aboard, in his words, a "chief" from the coast of New Zealand. "We often have him to dance and sing after the manner of his nation—'tis as good as a play," he wrote. The man's body looked "just the same as the pictures in the Penny Magazine represent." Theatre and cheap periodicals had become Reynolds's point of reference for ideas about how so-called Indians behaved both at home and abroad. Seafarers in the 1830s and 1840s ventured from coastal cities where a person was more likely to encounter men "playing Indian" than actual Indians themselves. Stagecraft, "redface" performance, and the bedecked bodies of Tammany Society or Red Men lodge members marching through the streets increasingly became the more probable point of reference for city and town dwellers who were shipped overseas and sought native peoples. Men in the early republic left a nation in which Indians located east of the Mississippi were potentially a part of their lived experience. Reynolds, writing after removal, explicitly referred to popular consciousness—"the Penny Magazine"—as the source of his knowledge. A half century of maritime observation that began with a real wariness of Indian capacity slowly but definitively moved toward more elegiac forms of expression rooted in fictive depictions of native peoples as a noble but unavoidably ruined race the world over. Some mid-nineteenth-century seamen felt distant enough from the experience of seeing North American Indians that they could even claim so exotic a mantle for themselves. Charles Erskine, who was at an island in the Tuamotu Archipelago, wrote that the natives "gathered round and stared at us, just the same as we would at a tribe of Indians walking on our public streets." One sight was as rare and as worthy of wonder as the other.[36]

While nominally detached from the processes of continental expansion and Indian-hating that were coming to define national citizenship and white racial identity, seamen expressed a sense of belonging and connection to their country by implicating themselves in the American struggle against barbarism. They did so more readily as the nineteenth century progressed. Earlier observers could not seriously link receding Indians to an aggressive racial or national pride; eastern confederations were still politically and militarily powerful then. Under those conditions they identified "Indians" abroad through physiognomic comparisons precisely because Indians were present in so much of the early republic's life. Subsequent generations of mariners found the occasion (and ability) to express triumph, intertwined as it was with race pride, over a removed enemy at home and their ostensibly disappearing counterparts overseas.

The crowing over the ascendancy of American whites that was characteristic of later diarists simply does not appear in the initial records. Later "Indians" abroad were enlisted to reflect new realities: of "Young America's" reckless rise to power, of Anglo-Saxon superiority, of a shift from uncertain balances of power on the frontier to assertive proclamations of imperial inevitabilities. It is instructive that maritime imagery infused portions of the Democratic Party's most aggressive faction. "Young America sighed that there were no more Mexicos to conquer on this continent [and so] . . . in Panama he fell in with the outpost of the advanced guard of the army of occupation—the sailor of manifest destiny views, who was waiting for his country to overtake him." The free-floating ambition of Americans overseas became tied to the country's sailors. This development undermines distinctions that are traditionally drawn between continental expansion and the overseas imperialism of the later nineteenth century. Just as westward settlement was justified as the appropriation of lands vacated by a dying people, intrusive commercial expansion was also legitimated by perceptions of the cultural deterioration of the original occupants. Simeon Stearns, for one, certainly thought this way. Returning from a few days' liberty at the Bay of Islands, New Zealand, he remarked in his journal that "with regard to the inhabitants . . . it is sufficient to say they are Indians and Indians are the same all over the world. . . . They are a poor miserable set of Devils not fit to control themselves or worthy of the land they occupy."[37]

In arguing that New Zealand's "Indians" were unfit to inhabit the land they occupied, Stearns advocated a removal policy that was more global in sweep than even Jackson and his Democratic colleagues in Congress conceived of. So did mariner William Clark, who in 1840 wrote that Hawaiians were "wretched," "a near approach to the beast" and that their "Islands [were] much too fine a country for such a people . . . not worthy of such salubrious air." The sailors' proposals illustrate the change in tone that is visible in maritime talk of "Indian" encounters across the first half of the nineteenth century. Observers in the latter part of the eighteenth century and the early nineteenth century tended to use comparisons to Indians almost exclusively as an explanatory or classificatory device. Superficial similarities became a means to describe and make knowable alien peoples and environments. While such comparisons were condescending in tenor, they were largely benign in intent.[38]

By the 1830s and 1840s a noticeably more strident and militant tone had emerged in many sea journals. Over time, racial ideas about Indians had hardened. Disparaging commentary, fantasies of violent encounter, and the invocation of removal-oriented or extirpative behavior—what has been called in other contexts the "anti-Indian sublime"—appeared in the writings of many white American voyagers. The virtues of civilized forbearance were replaced by a discourse of justifiable vengeance. The United States Exploring Expedition's sack of Malolo, Fiji, pointed to that broader change, and it was a shift mirrored by changes in antebellum political and literary culture. As Jeffersonian talk of assimilating and incorporating Native Americans gave way to Jacksonian discourse about Indian intransigence and the necessity of a harsher approach, the speech of sailors overseas followed suit. The literary front manifested a similar change too, as the thoughtful and complex frontier stories of Cooper began to compete with more sensationalistic penny-press productions that explicitly glorified expansionism and frontier violence. While the transition was not seamless, it reflects seafarers' engagement with Democratic Party politics and the popular press. Sailors read partisan pamphlets and newspapers that circulated in the working-class districts of America's seaport cities, and they found ample applicability overseas for the expansionistic rhetoric characteristic of both the era's politics and a broader cult of national aggrandizement.[39]

N. Byron Smith demonstrated as much by accessing a language of manifest destiny unavailable to earlier generations of seamen. Held over in Hawaii while his whaleship prepared for another season in the Arctic, Smith strolled the deck circa 1853 and reflected on the island's natives as their canoes darted in between the harbor's larger vessels. He sensed "a doom that seems to rest upon the race, felt even by themselves." "Certain it is," Smith continued, "that they are fast fading away, like many other barbarous nations." Growing up in 1840s Sag Harbor had taught this young man enough about American history to enable him to isolate a cause for "race decay" in the Pacific: "the onward march and spread of the Caucasian race, which 'Manifest Destiny' seems to say shall have absolute dominion over the whole earth." The young mariner returned over and again to his certitude. Referring to a biblical passage colloquially translated as "it should be perfectly clear to anyone," the seaman repeated that "the destiny of these islands is so evident that he who runs may read." Reflection did not engender melancholy, though: "It is well that it is so," he indifferently intoned. Henry Wise, attached to a naval squadron circumnavigating the Pacific in 1848, shared a similar opinion. "Hopelessly and inevitably," the mariner wrote, Polynesians "must look forward to the rapid future when their lands will be in strange hands and when the few remnants of their race be slaves or puppets to their white masters." But this was not cause for commiseration. No matter how "sad the picture, the results bear no comparison to the benefits accruing the world at large in acquiring a foothold in these islands, which from their position and resources are destined to become of vast importance to commercial enterprise in the Pacific." Whaleman Edward Perkins, surveying "the broad track of American enterprise" as it circled the globe, believed that "at no period of our national existence have American interests been so manifest in the great Western Ocean." "Laws, literature, and commerce" were gifts the wandering workers aboard U.S.-flagged vessels bestowed, even as "the kingdoms and tribes" with which they interacted faded into obscurity. Elias Trotter similarly saw the history of his country's expansion played out in other places across the globe; in New Zealand, "like unto the young days of our now prosperous republic, more land was needed by the settler as he swelled his little own" while "the natives receded."[40]

In making these arguments, Smith, Wise, and others predated by several years the views of *De Bow's Review*, which wrote of Hawaiians that "the race must soon become extinct, [as] the experience of . . . American Indians has proved that aboriginal races can no more change their habits of life than the leopard can change his spots." Or they may have read some recent edition of the San Francisco newspaper *Daily Alta California*, which wrote of Hawaii in April 1851 that "the native population are fast fading away," the result being that it was the "inevitable destiny of the islands" to "pass into the possession of another power," namely, "our own." Seafarers of the mid-nineteenth century were no less steeped in the rhetoric of manifest destiny than landsmen and no less willing to resist its usage in far-flung ports and places: "Manifest Destiny" applied to, in Smith's words, "the whole earth." Commercial and territorial expansion proved to be overlapping interests in Hawaii that were expressible in analogous terms. All was connected as part of a broader pattern that characterized the territorial and watery West, where racial ideas about Indian "inferiority" legitimated imperial ambition. Deep water was as much the locus of early American geopolitical design as fertile soil. The persistent talk of "Indians" abroad suggests that the United States bought what William Seward called "the ultimate empire of the ocean" on terms very similar to that of its continental empire.[41]

Mariner William Phelps, for example, presented his argument for the overlap between terrestrial and saltwater expansion when discussing the case of California. During the 1830s, as a participant in the Boston-based cowhide trade between the American Atlantic and a Mexican-controlled Pacific coast, Phelps witnessed firsthand what he felt was the influence of waterborne workers in extending the interests of the nation. As he reckoned, it was "the knowledge obtained through this traffic [which] in a great measure led to the acquisition of California" and "produc[ed] an extension of civilization unprecedented in the history of the world." And "in after years," the sailor swore, "when our children are reaping the blessings of peace and prosperity in this fair region, beneath the broad folds of the 'Star Spangled Banner,' should some curious person ask, Who first displayed the glorious emblem on this majestic river?," the answer should be: seafarers. "Vessels of Boston," sent "for the purpose of trade and discovery [were] the first to exhibit the flag of our country to the wondering savages of these solitudes." Like literature glorifying the efforts of pioneers on the land, Phelps's account (erroneously) stressed both the emptiness of "discovered" territory and the awe the appearance of American agents inspired. But before mountain men, prospectors, settlers, or soldiers had arrived on the scene, the Pacific frontier, as this mariner enthused, had been "whitened by the numerous sails of adventurous commerce." The nation's canvas spreading across the world's seas became one way to express or portray the multiple mediums along which manifest destiny might travel. Mariners may have insisted that sails preceded rails in the West, but it did not matter which came first, for one aided the other and all united to promote the same goal of enlarging American influence.[42]

In the antebellum era, it would seem, one did not need to venture along overland trails to find Indians. Americans harbored ideas about them that were so ubiquitous and powerful that they could be found wherever one traveled, and their characteristics could be ascribed to people who were demonstrably unrelated. Indians symbolized a tradition of thought that helped create a sense of national place and direction in a wide variety of settings. In continuing to confine "Indian country" solely to the North American continent, we fail to take into account the more expansive boundaries of native ground held by citizens who shipped out in the nineteenth century. "Indian country" was less a clearly defined area and more an idea or imagined border used to demarcate a racialized geography of not just a continent but the world. It separated people that were increasingly understood to have distinct destinies, one ascendant, the other despoiled and in decline. Americans laboring abroad described the battle between civilization and savagery not as continental but rather as global in nature. Rhetoric about "Indians" and a frontier discourse gave men who were far away from the United States the means to attach themselves to the sense of mission and purpose their countrymen ashore ascribed to the rising star of their own race and republic.[43]

Sailors were not immersed in a free-standing maritime culture that was disconnected from landed society, though they are often given no identity other than that conferred on them by their vocation. Citizenship, though, did not end at the water's edge, and native-born sailors were not divorced from national life. They insisted on their inclusion in it by enlarging the republic's field of inquiry into questions of Indian fates and white racial supremacy. "Marginal" peoples who are otherwise sidelined sometimes seek to access power and identity by clinging more fiercely to specific national, ethnic, and imperial ideologies, and that is precisely what seafarers did. The issues on many of their minds while they were far from the country's shores integrated them into the mainstream, even though other observers stigmatized sailors as irregular people, incomplete men, and suspect citizens. Mariners were sensitive to such attacks and vociferously denounced savagery abroad to compensate for insecurities generated by physical detachment from the nation. They would act American by implicating themselves in the national struggle with Indians. The rhetoric of "Indian-speak" constituted an imaginative link that closed distances between sailors and their homeland. The empirically incorrect—yet intellectually satisfying—act of locating "Indians" overseas suggests the indispensable emotional and psychological role native peoples played in early American national thought.[44]

Alfred Thayer Mahan gave the fullest expression of this frontier justification for commercial expansionism overseas as he surveyed, from the 1890s, the passage of nearly a century in which American shipping surrounded the globe. Speaking of the republic's economic incursions into China, the famed naval theorist noted that American spheres of influence there did not emerge from overt aggression but were in effect invited by the decadence of Asian culture and its inability to resist more "virile" nations. The history of the United States taught him that "incompetent races" repeatedly fell "back and disappeared before the persistent impact of the superior." In China, as had been the case in North America, the right to control territory and wield power went to those willing to put that land to some productive good. Musing about whether his country ought to pursue a mercantile agenda in Asia, Mahan inserted an atavistic Indian-speak in the logic he presented in affirmation of commercial expansion. "Will anyone seriously contend that the North American continent should have been left forever in the hands of tribes whose sole use of their territory was to contravene the purposes of human life?" Mahan's query contained its own response. Westward territorial expansion, for him, produced historical data that was applicable to new economic and imperial agendas in the Far East. In the words of one historian, "the Indian past manifested the Asian future."[45]

Certain continuities surely united "Indian warfare" and later imperial conflicts in the Philippines and China. Yet when Mahan spoke at the turn of the twentieth century about a "frontier past" and its influence on contemporary commercial enterprise, he tapped into a more widespread language that members of the antebellum American maritime community had adopted. Seafarers, political economists, politicians, and the public sphere had long spoken of finding "Indians" abroad as a means to both comprehend and conquer exoticism. The foundation for Mahan's argument was the cumulative experience of the many young American men who had been sent to labor aboard ships in the early republic. They returned home to report of the same "Indians" whose legacy in the United States Mahan appealed to in justifying intrusive economic expansion overseas.[46]

The dependence of maritime authors on Indian tropes reveals how economic and cultural relationships between the nation and world were to some extent constrained from the outset by a refusal on the part of itinerant Americans to acknowledge the diversity of peoples and pasts around the globe. For these authors, distant persons and places that exhibited essentially "Indian" characteristics could, under certain circumstances, be subjected to invasive economic incursions, corrective violence, or "civilizing" programs. In effect, they suffered under the weight of the renderings of American history that sailors and others constructed. Moreover, some evidence exists to suggest that indigenous populations were sensitive to that burden.

For example, Samuel Kamakau, a Hawaiian political leader who witnessed the influx of American maritime and missionary interests on those islands, wrote in 1841 of his fear that "if we do not gather our strength now, after many generations our children would be like the American Indians—a race without history." The archipelago's later monarch, Queen Lili'uokalani, also loathed the sight of her people "relegated to the condition of the aborigines of the American continent." Pacific peoples more generally used the Indian example to fill colonial offices with petitions opposing "land reform" measures meant to enable whites to become owners of island property. Do not "open the doors for the coming in of foreigners" one such document reads, for "we are afraid that the wise will step on the ignorant, the same as America and other lands." These concerns of natives for their own vanishing history and the corollary fear that it would be overwritten by the tragedy that was the story of the North American continent moves a long way toward making the point that transnational encounter ensnared wide swaths of the world in historical processes that are often read as merely continental in scale. But just as in North America, where indigenous and Mexican peoples are recorded as resisting or readjusting colonial categories imposed from without, Pacific islanders also contested the potential perniciousness of their classification as Indians. Polynesians, Melanesians, and other Oceanians constructed cross-island and interethnic alliances devoted to sustaining at least some autonomy in the face of Euroamerican intrusion. Ironically, this was partly enabled by the accelerated pace of U.S. commercial expansion in the region: joint service aboard ships as a localized labor pool connected previously disparate islanders. Many nineteenth-century Americans may have lumped these individuals together as "Indians," but beneath the surface of that process countermeasures were burgeoning that would dispute such a designation and construct alternative grounds for cooperation among the Pacific's native peoples. They articulated a different destiny for themselves than the vanquishing and vanishing that seemed so manifest to the early republic's aquatic interlopers.[47]

Yet in insisting on the transnational, transoceanic nature of the "Indian" question, mariners sought an attachment to a nation that increasingly labeled them as a morally deficient outsider class as the nineteenth century progressed. This was a bitter pill indeed for many seamen to swallow. Waterfront reformers helped propagate long-standing stereotypes of sailors as irresponsible and infantile, something akin to the noble savage. And so it was that the same scorn and contempt crews heaped on "savages" overseas would soon be brought to bear on themselves at the hands of middle-class activists seeking to civilize America's benighted harbor dwellers. Of course, one of the most grievous habits reformers attempted to correct was the notoriously quarrelsome nature of sailors. Violence against "Indians" abroad was often committed under orders from officers, but a much wider array of altercations were perpetrated in direct violation of the command structure. Interpersonal conflict overseas, however, was never so anarchic or inconsequential as we might imagine. White American sailors often threw punches and drew knives in defense of national or racial prerogatives, even as that proclivity itself became the subject of diplomatic consternation.[48]

Chapter 4

A Maritime Empire of Moral Depravity

In November of 1852, they descended upon Honolulu in droves. "Vengeance!" was their cry. American sailors, enraged after one of their number had been killed by an overzealous prison guard's club, swarmed the city to punish those deemed responsible. The targets of the nearly 4,000 rioters, as one of many witnesses described it, were symbols of religious authority and a repressive government: "Last night the crews of the ships went ashore and raised a great disturbance . . . knock[ing] down the fort to get the man that killed the sailor," not to mention "pull[ing] down the station house to set it on fire." Another bystander spoke of anarchy as the sailors' "hitherto smothered rage now burst forth in curses loud and deep." The port's hospital, said to be staffed with corrupt orderlies who mistreated sick seamen, was surrounded and pelted with brickbats. Frustrated by puritanical legislation passed by missionaries who were well placed in the archipelago's government, crowds also fell upon the homes of Rev. Richard Armstrong and other superintendents of souls. Particular care was taken to retaliate against native Hawaiian peace officers as well. Rampaging mariners worked to ensure that "the Kikos [police] dare not show themselves for fear of the mob" by "knocking down every Kiko they could find."[1]

American officials Elisha Allen and Luther Severance pled with the men for order, but to no avail. Most of the city's residents fled to the countryside. Some local notables barricaded their homes and prepared to meet force with force. William Parke, Hawaii's marshal, requested that King Kamehameha III call up the native militia to quell the disturbance. The proprietors of bars and taverns hoped to weather the storm by dispensing food and liquor so the sailors' wrath would not turn against them. All conceded that when united, armed, and angered, the workers of the U.S. whaling fleet "had possession of the town" and could act with impunity. Authorities thus moved to conciliate the men before spreading fires consumed nearby ships and their immensely valuable cargoes of oil. A speedy trial was promised for the man who had killed the imprisoned sailor, while leniency would spare those who were principally responsible for the riot. After almost three days of unrest, Honolulu finally found peace, but the charred ruins of several important local institutions was to demonstrate for all the significance of America's maritime laborers in shaping the nation's early foreign relations—and the perils of underestimating their influence.[2]

For the Hawaiian government, the Honolulu riot of 1852 soured relations with a republic that seemed unable to control its citizens' depredations. The incident helped scuttle the early efforts of American missionaries to ensure the annexation of Hawaii; the royal family instead chose to pursue closer ties with Britain and eventually with Japan as potential counterweights to the danger of destabilization U.S. influence posed. But the inability of the native constabulary to deal with the sailors' uprising also fed a contradictory impulse toward the centralization of police power in the hands of foreigners thought to be more capable of managing their fellow *haole*, or outsiders. Troops of white guards gained authority that would eventually manifest itself in the militias that were later responsible for toppling Hawaii's native government. Indeed, as the Hawaiian marshal's memoirs had it, paramilitary companies formed in the aftermath of the riot "were carried on for some years, and perhaps . . . might be considered the ancestor of the present organization, the Honolulu Rifles," the gun-toting group of "concerned citizens" most directly implicated in both promulgating the Bayonet Constitution and deposing Queen Lili'uokalani. At a mid-nineteenth-century moment before the American state possessed the power and the will to protect the claims of its people in Hawaii and elsewhere overseas—no matter how dubious the claims—private seafaring citizens took it upon themselves to settle disputes and avenge insults. Those actions had consequences for the societies in which sailors acted.[3]

A combination of complex factors contributed to Hawaii's ultimate fate. Sailors never acted in a vacuum. The local political context always played a role in the unfolding of events in the American maritime community overseas. The sense of crisis surrounding the 1852 riot in Honolulu, for example, was almost certainly increased by recent developments in the archipelago. Only a few years earlier, the "respectable" violence of land reform, the so-called Great Mahele—which largely dispossessed native peoples by dividing the islands' commons into privately owned tracts—had wrought havoc in Hawaiian society. In addition, whispers about invading filibusters from California were omnipresent. And yet very little serious attention has been paid to the role of American sailors in the unfolding of the nation's foreign affairs there and in other places around the globe. Rather than the significant nonstate actors they were at the time, the early republic's mariners are treated as nonentities by scholars. Their behavior abroad is read as immaterial, as little more than the drunken escapades of a dissolute class. For a variety of reasons, we know more of gossip about filibustering invasions than the reality that American and Hawaiian officials struggled mightily with what they saw as a daily onslaught of supposedly "degenerate" sailors. Indeed, King Kamehameha III chose not to order an investigation into the rumored invasion from California exactly because, in the words of one U.S. commissioner, "so great is the number of American seamen here [and] so prone are they to have difficulties with their officers and with the police" that it proved a large enough task simply "to manage all these disputes." And yet, despite those declarations of what might be considered the sailors' "daily filibustering," historians of the Hawaiian Islands speak in dismissive terms when describing "seamen on shore leave" as "a boisterous . . . rabble, whose ideas of pleasure were not over-refined; too frequently their tastes rose no higher than the grogshop and the brothel, and a brawl with a native constable was entered into with real zest."[4]

However, events in Honolulu reflect much more than the drinking habits of an unchecked "rabble." Repeated incidents that were similar in nature—if not in magnitude—to the 1852 riot occurred in other places where sailors resisted the imposition of authority and discipline. During those episodes, American mariners used violence to insist on the importance of their labor overseas and demand inclusion within the diverse cast of characters responsible for introducing the United States to the wider world. N. Byron Smith, a seafarer who was present at the Honolulu Riot, remembered the "men talking excitedly in the barrooms about 'what shall we do to vindicate our rights?'" He saw the violence not as chaos but instead as a mode of political agitation, a demand for "rights" that spilled out into the streets. Our willingness to listen to such demands will in turn provide a more complete and accurate understanding of the shape and trajectory of early American foreign relations.[5]

Despite the disproportionate attention granted to middle- and upper-class individuals in the study of early American international affairs, sailors were the nation's face around the world in the early nineteenth century. Our account of America's foreign relations is incomplete if we exclude seafaring peoples. It is more accurate, then, to see the late nineteenth century—the global dawn of the Gilded Age—not as the international awakening of a slumbering continental giant but rather as a moment when control over the country's overseas diplomatic activity decisively shifted away from the maritime community's nonstate actors and into the hands of the state and state-allied interests. A new narrative arc must include the decline of the mariner's influence in the context of the consolidation of elite authority and the use of that clout to clear the world of the riotous "riffraff" that nearly burned Honolulu to the ground in 1852.[6]

That uprising, in fact, pointed to the precise problem with American seafarers' activities abroad. In the eyes of national consular and diplomatic authorities, sailors approached the wider world far too pugnaciously. Close readings of nautical journals and records of U.S. consuls, however, reveal a population of young, white working men who were acutely sensitive to personal, national, and racial honor. These individuals, variously termed by historians, in other contexts, "martial men," "roughs," and "jolly fellows," were aggressive, aggressively patriotic, and actuated by a closely held concern for reputation. They were a group who found in harborside tumults with foreign peoples a means to measure both their own masculinity and that of the people they encountered overseas. The quarrelsomeness and disruption of the so-called sailor spree overseas was purposive, not anarchic. It often targeted racial or national "inferiors" whom white American seamen hoped to remind of their subject status. Therefore, barroom brawls and other altercations on the world's wharves, quays, and coasts are best thought of as "diplomatic fisticuffs," that is, as the enactment of a distinct, working-class, and masculine foreign relations agenda.[7]

Seamen were not alone in their fondness for the rough and tumble, of course. In the early republic, male milieus more generally—from raucous frontier towns to urban sporting clubs and fire companies—seem to have bred boisterousness. Seafarers were one part of a larger (and largely working class) culture of interpersonal violence. But observers at the time believed sailor behavior to be *particularly* consequential because it affected the nation's global reputation. From the point of view of politicians, the State Department, diplomats, and missionaries, the misdeeds of mariners shaped the attitudes of other peoples and cultures toward America and Americans, and that had very real ramifications in the fashioning of American foreign relations. Every barroom brawl, stabbing, or other violent incident jeopardized connections the United States (and its commercial class) had built with foreign governments (and their own merchants). Efforts to control rambunctious sailors became a diplomatic imperative. The antebellum quest to "reform" reprobate seamen must be seen as less a domestic than an international undertaking, as an endeavor meant to address a perceived crisis in mid-nineteenth-century global capitalism. As one advocate of maritime uplift argued, had churches, libraries, and government-funded boarding houses been more prominent overseas, "the disgraceful occurrences of the fall of 1852 would probably not have been witnessed in Honolulu, nor would Americans have had occasion to blush at the conduct of their countrymen."[8]

Yet men who often took offense over slights to both their masculine honor and their national honor were not easily dissuaded by pleas for pacifism. The language and actions of seamen reveal their enhanced interest in demonstrating the strength and dignity of their homeland. To claim victory in these seemingly small skirmishes was to confirm much larger truths about the bellicosity—and hence, superiority—of the young republic. A spirited display of patriotism was often performative, symbolic, or rhetorical within the boundaries of the United States. But for the many thousands of Americans who went out into the world aboard ships to meet other nationalities, rhetoric easily gave way to action endowed with more literal meaning. Mariners sought to demonstrate their country's preeminence and protect its reputation before audiences ill-disposed to accept the argument for American exceptionalism. Sailor William Stetson believed as much; he wrote of the violence he and his shipmates visited on the bodies of Chileans at Talcahuano as a "necessary and indispensable amount of broken heads, black eyes, and bloody noses." Indispensable because such exploits were the means by which the American "crew of the [ship] *Arab* got their name up in Talcahuano." Given the fighting ability and fierceness of his compatriots, Stetson blustered that "no doubt . . . if we visit the port again we will immediately be recognized." His braggadocio staked the reputation of American men in foreign ports on their ability to throw punches and break heads.[9]

Fists often flew along the fissures created by national allegiances. On November 16, 1859, the Nagasaki consular court heard the testimony of Thomas Case, an American whaleman who had been beaten by five men from HMS *Cruizer*. Affidavits from some of the British seamen revealed that Case entered the Commercial Hotel, interrupted a celebration, and struck a Sergeant Smith square in the jaw. He then turned and fled while the group sat stunned by the sudden assault. "Can we stand this, men?" was the call to arms that snapped five aggrieved Englishmen awake. They followed Case, caught him, and retaliated in kind. When brought before his consul, the American remained unrepentant. "Earlier in the day," he explained, "the Sergeant began to throw out hints and slurs against Americans, he saying five Americans were not as good as one Englishmen." Rather than suffer this abuse of his countrymen, Case decided to silence the man by splitting the very lips that had uttered such vile slander. In another incident, this time at Nagasaki's Oriental Hotel, two American sailors were punished for fighting with British seamen they had goaded as "damned lime juicers" and "lime juicer sons of bitches." In Singapore, a British sailor brought charges against his American attacker, claiming that "the accused called me a lime-juicing son of a bitch, struck me in the face . . . [then] seized a hatchet and said he would cut me down with it." Those slurs were based on the Royal Navy's practice of staving off scurvy through the distribution of citrus fruit throughout the fleet: Britons became "limeys."[10]

In a country electrified by the patriotic stakes of events such as the 1860 prize fight between the American John Heenan and British subject Thomas Sayers, such sparring between republicans and royalists seems unsurprising. Yet the hostile climate produced by those regular bouts abroad seemed to defy cheerful proclamations of imminent American and British commercial cooperation rooted in a shared racial heritage. The *American Whig Review* may have predicted the "Englishman and American of the nineteenth century meet[ing] amid the palmy groves of Ceylon, or the coral isles of the Pacific [to] hail each other as brother [and] shout the watchword *Onward, onward*," but much of the surviving documentary evidence suggests no love lost between the mother country and her former colonial possessions.[11]

Rather, American seamen were able to put into practice the sort of anti-British animosity cultivated by belligerent Democratic newspapers and fiery Fourth of July oratory. A disjuncture existed between the peaceful visions of empire concocted in mercantile armchairs and its rough practice by the sailors those merchants employed to bring such pacific prophecies to fruition. Much like Honolulu, the British colony of Cape Town, South

Africa, learned that lesson the hard way in 1850, when American seamen from several whaleships and "the sailors on shore from the U.S. Sloop-of-war Portsmouth . . . concluded to try their hand at taking the town." Eye-witnesses could "not recollect what the original provocation was, but the riot became serious." The mariners "went in on their muscle" and bested the local police in pitched battles before "the military were called out" to reestablish order by bayonet. The situation looked no different in Guam, where a local theatre catering to seafarers was reduced to pandemonium when Americans in the audience "refused to hear" the house band play "God Save the Queen." A "general row" ensued, with "'the Britishers' flung neck and heels out of the windows." And with the same obvious pride that suffused the accounts of other working American men overseas brought to blows with a still-hated enemy, the witness made clear that "every day thereafter, while we remained in town, the Yankee sailors paraded up and down the streets, as a challenge to their historical foes."[12]

These men attempted to clarify for U.S. consuls that on the waterfront large matters lurked behind small stories. And while at the Oriental Hotel and other barrooms around the world violence spilled out into the street for the spectatorship of indigenous populations, those same native spectators often became targets for roving gangs of American seamen. Many white American sailors eagerly sought to test their strength in relation to a variety of persons they considered racial inferiors. Brawling became a sort of ethnography in the American maritime community. It allowed for the combatants to make very particular observations, and those observations then assumed the status of cultural characteristics. The ferocious foreign relations of American sailors and their antagonists abroad represented an intercultural clash of norms about manly honor and violence as a form of vindication.

For example, William Allen, aboard the *Vandalia* at Macao, wrote of "the most hidieous scenes occur[ing] daily," many of the ship's sailors "comming aboard with faces battered and bruised and swolen in consequence of fighting . . . with the Portoguese soldiers." Yet the violence hardly seemed indiscriminate. Men, "for pure love of the thing," left the vessel with what he called "a very musical patriotic pugalistic frame of mind," seeking people to abuse. At Penang, Richard Walsh went ashore with a group of men who immediately "began fighting, daring any number of Malays and Chinamen to 'take it up.'" Carousing about the town, the sailors "were the terror of the natives while their leave lasted." One particularly boisterous individual drove "50 of these natives out of a field." "Stripped to his trousers" in true bare-knuckle fashion, he swore he "would make some of them fight."

Instead, the locals fled, closing their shops "lest the sailors should turn them upside down." Their cowardice led Walsh to conclude that "we could have whipped the whole of them, for these people are all afraid of European fists." Whaleman William Whitecar similarly remarked that South Asian aborigines "are possessed of no courage"; he came to that conclusion after watching a shipmate scatter "a score of them before [him] with a good sized cudgel." What many men chose to remember about their travels in foreign places was tied to the outcome of violent encounters. Seemingly inconsequential fighting led to consequential cultural pronouncements concerning the relative fitness of particular peoples. Hence Albert Freeman's observation, as he and his shipmates barreled through Canton, that "the Chinese always give way to a foreigner, and are as timid and cowardly as man can be."[13]

Violence, moreover, was not simply contained in an *act* of aggression. Violence was also the *fantasy* of one's capacity to conquer another. It was a language that encompassed bravery and cowardice as ethnic qualities, a lens that colored the nature of interactions between American men and other persons abroad. One officer in the Perry Expedition to Japan, for example, remembered "hearing one of our 'old salts' growl out today, 'for his part he could any day lick a hundred of such fellows in petticoats, who hid themselves behind canvass forts and used paper pocket handkerchiefs.'" Mariners spoke of their combativeness as a quasi-diplomatic tool that ensured respect for the flag and American Anglo-Saxon manhood. Playing up the servility of a race cowed by the mere threat of comeuppance at the hands of seafarers allowed men ordinarily disempowered by a ship's hierarchical command structure to have a taste of agency. As this individual suggested, there was the diplomacy of the elite, with its elaborate dress, niceties, and kowtowing, and, there was the diplomacy of the roughs, where fists finalized matters. Boasting of any group's fear of those relatively tiny instruments became tantamount to talk of the ability of a state's army or navy to compel respect or obedience.[14]

And what many sailors from the United States proved unable to endure was their travel to locales where nonwhite peoples enjoyed measurable authority. Seafarers came from a nation that self-consciously celebrated whiteness as instrumental to rights, privilege, and the exercise of power, but they soon found themselves in places where race played little part in the constituted social order. Empowerment of black peoples overseas—as soldiers, police officers, customs officials, and the like—struck many American observers as particularly problematic, but other elevated "racial inferiors" elsewhere were no less reviled. While anchored at the Caribbean island of

Antigua, Thomas Dudley wrote home to his sister with the shocking news that "the police officers are niggers and arrest white people." Unsurprisingly, he thought "it wouldn't set well on me to have a nigger arrest me." That whole corner of the globe took on a corrupted feel to Dudley, given the liberties all black people there seemed to exercise in their dealings with whites. "Here," he fumed, "a black man is as good as a white one," "the niggers will not hesitate to curse or fight a white man," and "one can't walk along the streets without getting sauce from some black man or woman." Dudley wished himself at home, where segregation ruled and deference to whites was the expected stance for peoples of African origin.[15]

The fraternalism of the sea did not always take precedence over more pressing loyalties such as race and nation. Elias Trotter, aboard the whaleship *Illinois*, expressed a particular animosity toward the empowerment of nonwhites when he stated that a friend of his in the forecastle "gained the good will of the whole crew" after fighting a particularly "pompous" black man, "an over eaten nigger filthy in appearance and bad in disposition." "Twill not answer," Trotter summarized, "for one man and especially a coloured man to dictate to American feeling men." In so overtly connecting race feeling, national feeling, and violence, Trotter made clear what other accounts imply. To combat dictatorial racial others, colored men attempting to impose on "American feeling men," as Trotter put it, was to fulfill the promise of white privilege that many citizens at the time supposed made the United States so wonderful a place. His remarks capture the core of complaints white seamen made about labor overseas. Close, even intimate contact with subordinates was part of the job, an unavoidable occupational hazard. Yet it hurt feelings. Deeply internalized racial antipathies that were central to habits of thought in the nineteenth-century United States and constitutive of basic human relationships there were destabilized abroad.[16]

Violence, then, became one means to oppose indecent inversions of proper hierarchy. Anything that smacked of assertive nonwhite masculinity aroused the special ire of many white working-class men overseas. In Nagasaki, for instance, a mariner named William Baird struck a boatman who had the nerve to claim that "he was as good a man as him." Peter Hawkins, similarly aggrieved, stabbed a local vendor for calling him a "white son of a bitch." Offended in Callao, Peru, Thomas Murray threw punches after crying out "I am no son of a bitch, but a white man!" At the Bay of Islands, New Zealand, a boat steerer named Mac Martin, hearing that a "large negro" had been "bragg[ed] up as a 'Bully Man,'" took such "big talk as a kind of challenge," "remarked that he could 'whip any nigger that ever was born,'" and

gouged the man into submission. Pernambuco, Brazil, was nearly turned
upside down in 1856 when festering tensions between white seamen and
black dockside workers finally exploded; men aboard the American brig
Fairy began to mistreat local fruit sellers, saying "they would kill every
Portugee son of a bitch on board." They soon linked up with other of their
countrymen to terrorize the harbor and, in the words of the ship's second
mate, "commenced to abuse, beat, and threaten to murder the niggers."[17]

At Santiago, Cape Verde Islands, the U.S. consul complained to State
Department superiors that U.S. sailors conducted themselves toward black
vendors in "ways as ugly as ingenuity could invent, [with] numbers of natives" reporting to him of "being beaten, having their clothes torn; Monkeys, Tamarinds, Oranges, &c. thrown into the sea." Alonzo Sampson
detailed the systematic mistreatment of the local population at Hong Kong,
complete with descriptions of sailors who "amused themselves with upset-
ting peddler's stands, tearing down the Chinamen's shops," and, "the most
delectable fun" of all, "catching two or more Chinamen, and tying them
together by their tails or queues." A court reporter at the U.S. consulate in
Shanghai confirmed the existence of such cruelty when he recorded in
affected dialogue the testimony of numerous Chinese boatmen requesting
an indemnity from the American legation for ill treatment suffered at the
hands of U.S. sailors. On multiple occasions, they claimed, seamen "abused
them, called them 'damn fool,' 'damned Chinamen,' and 'damned Chinese
sons of bitches.'" Frequently, they "makee fight me, and I must run away in
sam pan." They "makee swear at sam pan men, say 'damned Chinamen,'" all
the while attempting to provoke confrontations with those who dared to
stand their ground.[18]

But stand their ground many of these men appeared to do. The individuals overseas with whom sailors fought were not anonymous punching
bags but people who also viewed these brawls as the public vindication of
personal honor. They resided in local communities from Rio de Janeiro to
Shanghai; were protective of reputations in their own immediate circles of
friends, family, and acquaintances; and seemed to find in the outcome of
contests with seamen a similar sense of self-worth. Depositions recorded in
consular offices and at naval courts-martial provide an opportunity to capture the perspective of men and women assaulted by marauding mariners.
According to his indictment, Edwin Haley strutted ashore at an unnamed
foreign port declaring "he would like to have a clip at [a] damned black
son of a bitch" and that "he would allow no nigger to strike a white man."
But he met his match in the form of a dare from a black pilot named John

Jalls, who stood before the court with great pride to declare that "if he was on shore he could whip two men like the accused" and that "if [Haley] wanted to fight me on shore any time, I would see him." Master's mate George Howard confirmed this sequence of events in his deposition, stating that Haley then came before him to complain that a "damned nigger has been talking about me and when I asked him about it he challenged me to fight." White sailors were more often the instigators, but challenges could be issued on either side of the color line.[19]

The large numbers of black men who appeared in judicial records detailing affrays overseas is itself telling. Very few African American sailors left written records of their experience abroad, but courtroom testimony suggests that time spent beyond U.S. borders decoupled many men of color from the deferential attitude expected of them at home. Anthony Dyer, master of the *Echo*, responded to the charge of assault laid against him by denouncing the ship's cook as an "insolent negro" guilty of gross insubordination. The man spoke loudly, spoke often, and when reprimanded proclaimed he "would talk to General Andrew Jackson that way if he pleased." Silas Fitch, aboard the whaleship *Charles Phelps*, claimed to "have seen many negroes" in his day, but, he complained, he had to leave home to find "the proudest and the sassyest darkey that I ever saw." In other words, these were all black men who, when abroad, chose to speak more freely than they ordinarily might. Sailors repeatedly commented about "sass" received from peoples of African descent, or, as one man in Antigua noted, "I never saw so saucy a nigger before"; "if he'd talked in Virginia as he did on our vessel, he would certainly have had 9 and 30 lashes the next morning." Seafarers could threaten them, as did George Thayer, who, when faced with an "impudent" black man, exploded: "You damned nigger, if I had you back in Georgia, I would sell you." But that was the point. This was neither Georgia nor Virginia. Nonwhites abroad, as a livid J. Ross Browne spat, "presumed upon [their] equality to a degree that was insufferable." This state of affairs produced tension.[20]

In response, verbal violence between marauding sailors and locals was particularly prevalent. Men may not have spoken one another's languages, at least not fluently, but posturing and insults seem to have been broadly intelligible. This was all the cacophony of maritime empire, where individuals on all sides shouted at one another, daring and goading prospective adversaries in highly public displays of bluster. Frederick Schley and his shipmates, anchored at Batavia, proceeded to provoke nearby Malaysians, whose blackened teeth (stained from chewing betel nuts) and "complexion

black as the negro's" made them "as ugly as I suppose the Devil to be."
However, the Malaysians did not remain silent, instead jeering back "that
dogs have white teeth!" The seamen then made a move to fight but were
deterred when their assailants drew their swords. Belligerent resistance to
bullying mariners happened elsewhere, too. An anonymous diarist spoke of
shore leave in Canton as plagued by "the sneers and hooting of patriotic
Chinese," who were "impertinent in their carriage." "Constantly today we
heard the epithet 'Tanqin' (Red Devil) with motions expressing a desire to
cut our throats." Aggravated by effrontery exhibited by a people he thought
should be "as servile as possible," the man muttered that "I would like to
have caught [them] off their own dunghill." But, outnumbered and intimi-
dated by hostile Chinese aggressors, he could only retreat to the safety of his
ship and issue paper threats. Washington Chase, another mariner, described
a series of altercations between American men and native Chileans that
he thought derived from local prejudices. He wrote that Valparaiso, after
all, was populated by an ignorant lot who "at night will often insult and
otherwise ill-use strangers, [whom] they consider Burros, or asses, and they
take pleasure, and frequent occasion, to address this epithet to foreigners."[21]

Courtrooms, meanwhile, became sites where supposedly inferior peoples could articulate grievances and, as accusers, exercise a measure of power
over people who claimed they had none. At San Juan del Sur, Nicaragua,
for example, a translator was provided so that a native vendor could bring
charges against a gang of American sailors who had robbed him. "They took
a tin pan containing money," the man explained, "called me a damned nigger, and threatened to give me hell if I said anything about it." But complain
he did, and he probably found satisfaction with the result. The defendants
denied the theft but were nevertheless found guilty and sentenced to reduced pay and a year's lost liberty. Cokananto, a native Fijian, was also given
a translator so that he could relate his grievances against America's maritime
empire. The deposition, signed with an "X," complained of mariners who
"interfere[d] in the affairs of the Chiefs of these Islands," who "shot a number of men," "rob[bed] canoes," and generally "conducted [themselves] very
badly." "I should be very glad to see these persons removed from the Feejee
Islands," he concluded. The U.S. commercial agent at Fiji very much wanted
the same thing and worked closely with naval commanders and ship masters to ensure that discipline aboard American ships was adequate. Tahitians
likewise bombarded the American consulate with complaints about U.S.
citizens with whom "it was difficult to keep harmonie and peace . . . since
fighting and every other disorder were frequent if not constant." One

missive addressed "His Excellence the President of the United States of America" and implored him to do something about men who "in defiance of our laws" committed "every wild and violent act" and whose behavior "put a stain on the nation's character." Prominent in this correspondence were lectures about law and its seeming absence among Americans abroad. What sort of chief or ruler was His Excellence the President, these letters implied, if he could not restrain his own subjects?[22]

In another episode, a representative from the Chinese village of Kim Ting, outside Canton, likewise used the machinery of maritime empire to carve out some measure of protection for his own people. Before the U.S. consul, he complained of sailors "who by extortion enter mens houses, threatening their families so that the people of the village are enraged and resist the determination of the intruders." He asked that the consul "absolutely restrain the American merchant sailors from entering the villages and causing confusion among innocent people." The response that came one week later expressed regret and promised inquiries among shipmasters, punishment for the guilty parties, and future vigilance to prevent similar outrages. That this exchange took place in 1843, one year after China's humiliating defeat in the First Opium War, seems significant. Local inhabitants could seize upon the wanton violence of maritime actors as a means to embarrass foreign intruders, extract apologies, or even demand concessions from them. The respectful tones that characterized such correspondence also served to enhance the legitimacy and prestige of indigenous political actors, for it contrasted sharply with the rough language mariners used to instigate imbroglios abroad.[23]

Many native deponents, in fact, had the pleasure of watching maritime aggressors chastised in consular courtrooms. A man at Shanghai whose name went recorded as Ah Foo, along with several other boatmen, helped bring suit for manslaughter after one of their number was killed by John McKenna, an American sailor. "He fightee me," Ah's testimony explained, and "said he would chuck all the Chinamen overboard." And McKenna was, apparently, a man of his word. He shoved someone off the side of the ship, and the victim was knocked unconscious and drowned. Asked to answer for his crime, the sailor pointed to what he believed was the insolent behavior of a Chinese vendor who refused to cower. The man "laughed in my face," McKenna swore; "he stood there on the gangway and gave me all the cheek he could give me."[24]

Conditioned to command racial inferiors, McKenna could not abide one who refused to be commanded. The sailor's appeal for clemency depended on the status of the deceased as a "damned Chinaman." The

American legation, however, saw the matter from the point of view of the remaining Chinese boatmen who initiated the suit. His interrogators scolded McKenna, expressing disgust over the seaman's apparent nonchalance after having killed someone: "You seem to have treated it as a matter of no moment," their reproof went, "so slight an affair as not to go down into the boat to see if the man was dead or alive." The mariner was slapped with a sentence of several years' imprisonment, and the Chinese complainants received the court's apologies. Decisions about the consequences for fighting did not automatically favor mariners. Many men who left the United States determined to dominate instead met their match overseas among individuals who were not inclined to roll over.[25]

The racism of U.S. sailors, therefore, had very real consequences in the development of American foreign relations. In lashing out against peoples abroad they deemed inferior, sailors worked aggressively to entangle the world in a racial order that was Anglo-American in origin but global in implication. A shove in the street, a kick to the groin, a slur, or a derogatory gesture provided for indigenous communities the evidence of the pernicious influence of imperialism (and imperious maritime interlopers) over their daily lives, and it fomented hostility among those who were involved in or witness to that behavior. The memory of those episodes worked further to perpetuate enmity toward Americans as the harbingers of destruction and suffering. Thus, maritime violence seemed like a contagion demanding quarantine.[26]

Elisha E. Rice, U.S. consul at Hakodate, Japan, said as much in describing the descent of the crews of the ships *Adeline* and *Rapid* on the town. "A more vicious and abandoned set of men I never saw," he complained to his superior. The men "commenced a regular system of plunder, rowdyism and drunkenness." They "entered dwelling houses and stores at pleasure and helped themselves" to the contents, "beat the owners" who complained, and "otherwise illtreat[ed]" the natives. Rice even attempted to have the ringleaders jailed, but "they went so far as to *deny my authority to interfere* and defied me to arrest anyone." The power in making relationships with local populations, in other words, did not lie with the republic's appointee. It was claimed by men whose power was rooted in physicality, men who were repeatedly referred to in official correspondence as "ruffians," men who seemed to glory, if anything, in ruining the good name of the United States abroad. The outraged diplomat could only throw up his hands in disgust, deriding any whose sympathies were directed at those he sarcastically referred to as "the 'much abused sailors.'"[27]

Although the tumult at Hakodate is in one sense a relatively minor incident, it reveals why we should take sailors seriously as agents of American foreign relations. Elisha Rice's protest to the State Department suggests the influence mariners exerted overseas, infuriating as that influence could be for their "betters." A conscientious sailor named Albert Peck, who witnessed these violent episodes, shared the consul's consternation. "Most of those [seamen] on shore began taking anything they had a fancy for," including gallons of rice wine, which further fueled the destructive rampage as American mariners moved "up and down the streets tak[ing] whatever they came across" and abusing merchants who resisted. Peck, for his part, "was sorry to see this go on as it . . . would detract from the good opinion they had begun to form of us." Later travelers, in other words, would be forced to confront this legacy of violence and the suspicion and mistrust it had generated.[28]

Other officials appeared to concede that sailors were responsible for making (and breaking) American foreign relations. State-appointed diplomatic representatives existed more to clean up the damage created by the maritime community's hordes than to exert positive control over international affairs. For example, when he was approached by representatives of the Tahitian monarchy incensed about the depredations of American whalemen, the U.S. consul could only advise them to give such men a wide berth. "Do you consider the white man a dog?," he asked. Native residents needed to understand that Americans were unaccustomed to being ordered around by what they thought of as "uncivilized" peoples. Resistance would simply "cause trouble and perhaps the loss of life, for the seamen will assuredly come on shore armed." The diplomat himself could do very little. Placating sailors directly would do more for Tahiti, he implied, than working through "official" channels. A consul's report to Congress in 1853 on conditions around Shanghai similarly bemoaned that an unruly underclass of sailors "roam about the suburbs of the Chinese city, getting into constant broils with the natives, in which both sides use weapons, and dangerous wounds and even death are the consequence." The diplomat demanded help dealing with so "turbulent [a] class"; his own effort, he complained, "only exposes me to ridicule, as ultimate failure is the result." These officials were not alone in their admitted impotence; many other diplomats professed similar exasperation. Reading such correspondence raises questions about who, exactly, was in charge overseas.[29]

Thus when consuls and other observers witnessed the omnipresence of disorderly American seamen, they did not celebrate such pugilistic displays, as did sailors, but rather, they despaired of the consequences. Stephen Rowan, a naval officer anchored with the Pacific squadron at Tahiti in 1828, watched American whalemen fighting with indigenous men and stealing from canoes that came alongside vessels. "Rascally behavior," he thought. And "what then," Rowan worried, "can be the opinion of other people respecting us?" The answer was dismaying: "They can look on us in no other light than as pirates of the worst cast." Francis Ripley, a wealthy traveler rounding Cape Horn for California, came to similar conclusions after witnessing a fistfight between a few American sailors and some Portuguese in Rio de Janeiro. "The majority of our vessels," he seemed to sigh across the page, "will give the United States a very bad name in all the stopping places of the world." The reason was simple. Seafarers, "while a hardy set of men," seemed to accomplish little more than violent confrontation when they went ashore. "They fight with the natives" immediately upon touching dry land, "disgracing themselves and the place from which they came." Like Rowan, Ripley was concerned: the sheer number of "rowdies among them will so far counteract the impression made by the better class that Americans will get a bad name round the whole coast."[30]

But beyond the question of mere bloodshed, nautical villains were also bad for business. The "disorder" elite observers complained of usually referred to anything that threatened the secure conduct of trade. The U.S. consul at New Zealand's Bay of Islands wrote to inform the State Department that the "vicious propensities" of "our own countrymen" were "sowing seeds of dissent amongst the natives, thereby impeding our Commerce in their progress of trade amongst them." Because of the depredations of U.S. sailors at Fiji, the U.S. commercial agent there reported, vengeful natives cut off subsequently arriving ships and murdered their crews, and, as the American official concluded, "commerce has had to pay the penalty at the same islands." A "fear that other ships in the Pacific will suffer as the news spreads to other islands" heightened the sense of urgency. A consular officer in Canton concurred. "Small trifles" from which "disturbances have been created," he recorded, endanger "the lives of all the foreigners here . . . but also . . . a large amount of treasure and valuable property." These events were almost always the result of the "constant riots between seamen and the Chinese rabble." Thomas Miller, the assistant secretary of state, wrote to the U.S. legation at Hilo, Hawaii, about the American government's diplomatic embarrassment when Russian officials in Washington, D.C., repeatedly complained about "gross outrages" and "lawless proceedings" emanating from American whaleships anchored along the Siberian coast. Miller wrote that such episodes were "very injurious to our . . . interests in the North Pacific" and suggested "the great need [for] vigilance in preventing such unlawful acts." Punishments meted out were meant to rein in sailors' destructive tendencies and allow "respectable" people to go about their business in every corner of the globe visited by American ships.[31]

Yet these concerns were not confined to formal diplomatic channels. Their regular appearance in national print media suggests broader public familiarity with the national "problem" of maritime violence. The *Sailors Magazine and Naval Journal*, for example, editorialized on the subject: "In no place in the world is the character and conduct of seamen more deserving of consideration than in China, for nowhere else does so much depend on their deportment." Trade, fretted the writer, was often "hindered or stopped in consequence of the ill conduct of sailors." The regularity with which mariners became embroiled in "riotous scenes of the greatest enormity" tended to "keep alive in the minds of the Chinese, the most unfavorable opinion of our character." The "bad conduct" of seamen "put in jeopardy the property and persons of many." Such behavior endangered the enterprise of more "upright" Americans by engendering indiscriminate hostility toward all foreigners in China. During diplomat Nicholas Trist's first posting as a consul in Havana, Cuba, he wrote similar-sounding pamphlets that complained of "the number of vagabond American sailors who infest this port, and give so much trouble to the authorities." The "peculiarly reckless character of [the] crews" of American ships caused commerce to suffer, as incessant imbroglios cost ship captains the time and money required to deal with them. Naval chaplain Charles Stewart also published a lengthy screed to denounce the many "thousand instances of oppression, insult, and cruelty" perpetrated by "nominally civilized men" aboard "ships ploughing the seas." Their "aggression and barbarity" worked to "shroud the stripes of America in reproach."[32]

Port city newspapers were littered with sensationalistic stories of violence between American sailors and indigenous communities abroad. In late 1843, the *North American and Daily Advertiser* published a story with the headline "The Troubles in China" that reported riots in Canton connected to "a quarrel between some sailors and Chinese shopmen." The same year, the Boston *Daily Atlas* wrote of sparring between white seamen and black innkeepers in an article entitled "Outrage and Streetfight." Enough stories of this nature were published to create what could almost be called a genre. Most journalists concluded, as did the *Daily Evening Traveller*'s editor in 1865, that sailors often "sinned against" their foreign hosts, making in most instances "the 'white man' . . . more in fault than the 'untaught savage.'" Newspaper accounts emphasized the repercussions of maritime violence for future American interests in the Pacific and beyond. For example, the Honolulu *Friend* complained of the "many sad examples of injustice and dishonesty" perpetrated by mariners "so *burnt into* the [natives'] souls" that they cause "relentless war . . . wherein the innocent are made to suffer for the guilty."[33]

Figure 7. Fight aboard the *Orray Taft*. Men took pains to record the results of overseas brawls in their journals, suggesting the significance seafarers attached to those fisticuffs. Anonymous journal kept aboard the ship *Orray Taft*, 1864. Courtesy of the New Bedford Whaling Museum.

Each man's commentary suggests the linkages early nineteenth-century Americans constructed between their country's reputation and its expansive commercial fleet. They recognized that the behavior of American seamen would be one of the primary means by which the world would judge the republic. The unruliness of those men proved deeply troubling. As mariners fought for their country, other Americans agonized over that fighting. The more violently seamen insisted on defending the dignity of the United States (and the racial ideals they believed represented those of their country), the more indignant observers became about the potential embarrassments sailors offered the nation. Spectators at the time bore witness to the omnipresence of American seamen around the globe and struggled to define its precise impact on the opinions foreign peoples would form about the United States. Most of those men fixated on the carnage that cultural encounter seemed to generate and bemoaned the inability of the "better sort" to alter the perception that Americans were an obstreperous set of people.

All of this aggression was particularly vexing to officers and consuls, merchants and missionaries, because it conflicted with their ideas about the "civilizing influence" of commerce. Such individuals celebrated trade as a panacea for all varieties of chauvinism. Rev. John Warren's oration on the subject, for example, lauded "the connections that may be formed by commercial intercourse" as "not only a source of wealth" but also "a reciprocity of kind offices [that] will expand and humanize the heart, soften the spirit of bigotry and superstition, and eradicate those rooted prejudices, that are the jaundice of the mind." In 1851, U.S. Representative Gilbert Dean crowed that "civilization follows in the peaceful track of the merchant ship and her brave crew," while at almost the same time a senator announced that "it is the mission of commerce to civilize the world. It is commerce, aided by steam, that is to carry those principles of liberty and enterprise which have given this country its prominence and its glory throughout the world to the other races and nations of mankind." John Erskine, wandering the Pacific, thought quite explicitly that "trade [would be] the way to civilize all these races and open up fresh channels of commerce." Ships were supposed to be conduits of knowledge, uplift, and mutual regard. The problem was, according to Erskine, that "the undisciplined crews of vessels" turned prospective partnerships "into little better than plundering expeditions."[34]

These men and others peddled a so-called gospel of commerce that heralded economic interconnection as a peaceful alternative to martial relations between peoples. It was a discourse rooted in Enlightenment-era philosophy that promised to end war by tearing down mercantilism's protectionist barriers and promoting mutually beneficial exchange relations. This set of ideas gained traction in America following its conflict with Great Britain in 1812, which was fought over the principles of "free trade and sailors' rights." The United States set itself apart from European rapacity, some argued, because its foreign relations agenda was dedicated to the inherently peaceful aims of trade. Deep structural paradox resulted when, in service of those avowedly amicable ends, merchants hired sailors who were given to fighting with many of the world's inhabitants. Though some people thought commerce a tranquil alternative to empire's more brutal aspects, it often brought peoples into contact who found such association offensive and who used the occasion not to preach peace but to instruct in intolerance.[35]

Something, then, had to be done to stem the tide of nautical belligerence. Some public forums still celebrated sailors in the aggregate as "useful citizens" who "discovered islands and continents" and "opened intercourse between almost all tribes, peoples, languages, and tongues on the globe," but such paeans were platitudes. American diplomats and missionaries painted a far different picture of, in the words of one evangelist, those "white-faced heathen" known as mariners. Prone to sickening displays of viciousness, men of the sea needed to be restrained for the good of the entire economic, religious, and civilizing project that was included under the heading of "United States commercial expansion." Descriptions of seafarers as "rogues," "rascals," and "miscreants" appeared more frequently in communications within the nation's diplomatic channels, expressing a growing sense that the rambunctiousness of sailors needed to be contained before more catastrophic damage was done. Transformation of the sailor's habits, pursued through a variety of methods, became a common answer.[36]

During the antebellum era, waterfront reformers—mostly evangelical Christians inspired by a series of transatlantic religious revivals known as the Second Great Awakening—founded organizations dedicated to the advancement of the sailor's material and spiritual condition. Associations such as the American Seamen's Friend Society pressured ship owners and mercantile firms to donate money that would be used to distribute Bibles, build churches, erect boarding houses, provide reading rooms, and establish banks for the benefit of sailors. Much of the effort to "improve" the mariner's lot focused on the nation's largest seaports, but it had an international dimension as well. Various crusaders built institutions for the benefit of American seamen in such heavily trafficked towns as London, Callao, Honolulu, and Canton. Commercial hubs where sailors swarmed became attractive targets for those seeking a solution to what middle-class activists increasingly referred to as the recklessness of the nation's nautical ambassadors. While such efforts are typically understood as one part of a larger domestic reform movement (and a relatively insignificant cause when compared to abolition or temperance), we might better view them as part of a consequential and coordinated international assault on the threat to the stability of the mercantile economic order mariner misdeeds posed. Powerful interests aligned behind this crusade, linking their proposed solution to a perceived crisis in global capitalism to the language of religious uplift. The steady, sober, spiritually sound habits of businessmen needed to become those of sailors as well. The gospel of commerce was to be buttressed by an evangelical gospel devoted to containing a seemingly ungovernable group of men.[37]

"Proper" authorities, the argument went, would not regain control until they had taught mariners the virtues of sobriety and self-respect. American foreign relations overseas now hinged on toughening the temperament of sailors, the nation's largest and most influential class of representatives. With the many "villainies [that] have been practised" by mariners on his mind, the U.S. consul at Canton argued it was "absolutely necessary to retrieve the character of Americans here," and presumably elsewhere. "Character"—a concept central to reform movements of the long nineteenth century— became a word repeated in diplomatic correspondence, and spoken about as crucial to the commercial contacts that sustained the nation's place in the world. Missionaries saw in their efforts to convert sailors a dual benefit: the preservation of the valuable economic relations mariners jeopardized and the creation of additional evangelists who would spread the Word as they traveled the world. Reformers saw great potential in the global presence of American sailors. Mariners, "confined to no place," men of "extensive influence," if brought to Christ, could prove instrumental to "the spread of truth in the world." Sailors were to become itinerant evangelists in a double sense: of the nation, and, given proper exertions, of the word of God. As one rapturous waterfront prophet enthused, "Let the seamen of our land be converted . . . and an influence is brought to bear upon the missionary enterprise which will give it a mighty impulse; the Gospel will have free course and be glorified throughout the world!"[38]

Missionaries at home and abroad, of course, were businesspeople as well. And until later-nineteenth-century reforms instituted a salary system, unpaid U.S. consuls also depended on commercial activity to earn a living.

Thus, each had a material interest in assuring that rowdy seamen did not menace the main chance. In a published tract, harborside activist Orville Dewey encapsulated the struggle to protect commerce by promoting creed. He expressed the widespread hope that by reforming sailors, the work of converting the world could proceed with far fewer obstacles. Conversion, however, meant a turn toward the principles of both godliness and liberal capitalism.

> The cause of Christianity in heathen lands suffers grievously for the vices of sea-faring men. On all pagan shores our missionaries complain of this influence. How natural the inference of unchristianized people against our religion! They reason from what they see. A missionary is sent among them to teach them a better religion than their own. *He* is a good man: grant it. Yes, they say, but this is the priest; what sort of people, what sort of parishioners has he? And, lo! a throng of wild, lawless, dissolute, drunken sailors! The conclusion is fatal.

He issued a warning: leave mariners unchecked, and "our commerce must suffer for it," for the "cause of Christianity" was tantamount to that of commerce. Another evangelical publication reasoned that given the thoughtless thuggery of seamen abroad, "it can never be a matter of indifference with commercial men, whether they commit a valuable cargo to the hands of honest men or to the hands of rogues and swindlers." The plan was to civilize the savage sailor. This would promote peace in the world's "heathen" communities and goodwill toward the United States, those being the true engines of profitable economic interrelationship.[39]

Consuls and other official observers reacted similarly to the seemingly wanton destructiveness of American sailors. Although they did not use religious rhetoric, their aim was also to control laborers who were seen as destructive to the "peaceful" goal of the spread of civilization. To some American diplomats, that meant using the law as a managerial tool. Reams of State Department records provide evidence of sailors being hauled before consular tribunals and subjected to fines, imprisonment, or hard labor for all varieties of "disorderly" conduct. A reputable nation could not tolerate such disreputable behavior among its principal laborers overseas, least of all a republic rooted in the rule of law. In response to the "frequent collisions and bloodshed" mariners instigated, therefore, one diplomat pleaded with the State Department to help "prevent the extension of present evils, and save our reputation for a law loving and law abiding people." For much of the early modern era, European jurists had conceded that the western Atlantic world was "beyond the line": an anarchic space where power became the principal determinant of political legitimacy. In the later eighteenth century, a concerted effort developed among British and American authorities to turn those "zones of violence" into "zones of law" capable of anchoring civilized society. Sailors, however, had by and large slipped through the cracks of that endeavor. As late as 1850, the U.S. consul at St. Helena complained about the "lawless crews" of "our mercantile marine" who adhered to a retrograde doctrine of "'might makes right.'" "More prompt and energetic measures" were requested from the State Department so that "refractory seamen may be punished" and a respect for regulation restored.[40]

Some observers advocated for the application of force to combat the crisis. Henry Wise, a U.S. naval officer, celebrated in his journal a Pacific Ocean where "the enterprise of our hardy fishermen has driven the ships of all other nations out of the field of competition." Yet the sudden arrival of over "twenty thousand seamen" quickly bred "a long catalogue of atrocities" in which sailors and natives reciprocally visited violence on one another. He thought it "high time the government should take measures," perhaps a squadron of well-armed ships "constantly cruising and touching among these groups [that] would tend in a great measure to shield the whalemen from hard usage and the natives themselves from the imposition which is so often practiced upon them." Throughout his disquisition, it is nearly impossible to determine who Wise felt was more savage: sailors who were "lost to all the habits and tastes of civilized society" or the "barbarian cannibals" and "goblins" he thought inhabited Polynesian islands. For the United States, maritime empire meant the subjugation of its own waterborne workers as much as, if not more than, it meant the administration of a subaltern colonized class.[41]

Lieutenant Thomas Dornin similarly believed that naval authority would be an antidote for sailor degeneracy. At Callao, he rated the "ungovernable dispositions of merchant seamen" as the parent of "many obstructions which interrupt commerce." Only able commanders unafraid of discipline could ensure "proper subordination" and thus see "our national character on the whole much advanced" and "a high value . . . set upon our friendship." In response to myriad calls for order abroad, Congress expanded both the scope of the national consular system and the size of the navy in the 1840s and 1850s. The court dockets of those newly enlarged institutions, meanwhile, recorded a noticeable uptick in the prosecution and punishment of mariner malcontents. And as antebellum America experimented with federal power at the saltwater edges of a thoroughly maritime state, locales overseas became the beneficiaries of a coerced workforce of convicted sailors. "Disorderly" mariners under armed guard did empire's dirty jobs. They built roads in Hawaii, swept streets in Callao, and dug gas lines in Shanghai, while entrepreneurs benefited from the fruits of this unpaid mudsill labor.[42]

Many sailors were quick to denounce attempts to "restore order" or "reform a degraded class of beings" as nothing more than pretention and imperiousness. They saw fines and imprisonment as a species of state-sanctioned extortion. One seaman raged that "two thirds of our foreign consuls are broken down gamblers and swindlers or some such thing who if they possess sufficient influence to get a consulship are all right as they can restore their fortune in a year or two by a systematic plundering of the sailor who is fair game for all." Another seafarer, who was denied a discharge by a consul even though he had suffered much physical abuse, "thought American consuls were sent to these places to protect and defend American citizens," but saw now that "you are good for nothing but to pamper to every captain's wishes." Efforts to apprehend, manacle, and punish disruptive seamen ashore brought comparisons to slavery. Ben Ely indignantly proclaimed that "no slave on shore ever suffered half so much injustice as in nine cases out of ten is practised on board our ships," but liberty at Mauritius gave him no greater pleasure, "for the inhabitants all look down upon mariners as a low and degraded set of beings . . . exposed to be treated like dogs and outcasts." James Bond seethed that undisciplined sailors along the South American coast were "hunted with blood hounds worse than fugitive slaves in the states."[43]

Charles Erskine thought ships' officers and admiralty judges guilty of the very viciousness they ascribed to waterborne workers. "Would His Honor consent to be struck with a handspike or lashed to the rigging and flogged?," Erskine asked. He understood that, "in this nineteenth century," it was not the people whom mariners maltreated but rather the sailor who "is most tyrannically abused." Just as the mercantile elite complained of violent seamen, sailors could (with good cause) protest against the abusiveness of their superior officers. An infuriated mariner whose captain regularly dashed him in the "face and eyes [with] a bucket full of urine that had rotted under the heat of a tropical sun" and who asked an American consul at Maui whether working men "were dogs undeserving of the treatment common to human beings" spoke for many others complaining of similar cruelty. So did his conclusion: "There is no law on this side of Land for the poor Sailor."[44]

The religious reform movement, meanwhile, considered seamen to be no better than savages and heathens. Missionaries in the Pacific showed such contempt for him and his shipmates, Cyrene Clark complained, that even "if they invite us to church, they shove us into the nigger's pew, by the threshold, saying 'That will do for you; wait there while I go up yonder and worship.'" John Jones also took time in his journal to complain about "Our Sandwich Island mishionarys [who] are always ready to take what small change a poor Devil has in his breeches pockets on Liberty Days and in return for it will tel you that you will certinly go to hell." As the riot of 1852 suggests, Hawaii more generally, given its position as a crossroads for American commerce, was the site of particularly violent contestation between sailors on one side and missionaries aligned with the archipelago's monarchy on the other. And whaleman William Stetson, for one, seemed both puzzled and mortified by the tendency of white American religious authorities to sympathize with "subhuman" Kanakas (i.e., Pacific island-ers). He went so far as to brand evangelists "more kanakas at heart than the kanakas themselves if such a thing is possible." A "sailor going ashore after having been a long time at sea," after all, "naturally desires to have a little fun," but "as soon as he is in the least degree noisy," the police are called to "pounce upon the poor sailor man." There was something terribly wrong with that picture: "One would think that in such a country as this, he might receive some little favor, or at least justice, from a white man, but instead of this, every opportunity to shove a sailor in 'chokey' and fine him is eagerly embraced." The sole function of missionary authority, from Stetson's point of view, seemed to be "to fleece the poor sailor men out of their money in the shape of fines, court fees, etc."[45]

A strange contradiction allowed the nation to release into the world a group of men that was primed to perceive themselves as superior to un-civilized peoples and at the same time produce a consular service that pun-ished assertions of that very same racial nationalism. White American sailors certainly opposed their own segregation as a special class of citizen who required reform or restraint. By maintaining their whiteness as the basis for inclusion within a community of civilized persons, mariners attempted to mitigate marginalization. Courtrooms in turn produced dialogue between sailors and their adjudicators abroad that exhibited rival visions of what constituted a functional foreign relations agenda. A "disorderly" seafarer awaiting judgment for fighting with African Krumen encapsulated that struggle. The court reporter's colorless prose noted that the accused, when asked why he had hit the man, recited a lesson learned at home in the United States, and "replied that 'a nigger was not his equal, and he be God damned if he would not knock a nigger in the head whenever one came his way.'" Another American mariner, John B. Smith, stood before a naval tribunal to answer the charge of fighting with Okinawan villagers in 1854. His defense hinged on an appeal to the sanctity of martial manhood. "Had it been expected that Americans should exercise an abject and cowardly submission towards the Natives, then I was to blame that when threatened with violence I was prompted by my manhood to retort.... Which of you would not have done the same?," he pointedly asked. The officers interrogating him had no patience for his appeals to racial and masculine camaraderie; Smith was docked pay, denied future liberty, and confined.[46]

These statements made aggressive attempts to underline sailors' Anglo-Saxon identity, even as their presences before disapproving tribunals suggests the contested nature of maritime demands for white racial solidarity. Seafarers sought the freedom to correct—violently, if need be—native populations the world over who refused to respect American manhood; bureaucrats protective of the state's agenda proved loathe to grant them that permission. The latter expected to manage maritime dominions through courts, fiat, and other technocratic mechanisms, but sailors saw tests of strength as the more efficient means. Indeed, hearings were important nodal points between competing notions of empire, honor, male obligation, and patriotism, between the de jure authority of "official" diplomats and the de facto authority some sailors claimed. Judicial proceedings became contentious themselves in large part because men saw the stakes their diplomatic fisticuffs entailed. Even with the odds stacked against them inside courtrooms more invested in protecting a command structure than investigating the particulars of any given case, litigants defended themselves in forceful if succinct terms.

"I shipped to fight, and if I did not fight, I would be called a coward," complained one individual sentenced to fifty lashes for brawling. Shipmates asked to testify in the man's defense also wondered why the court refused to understand this; "If he would run, they would call him a coward," the witnesses reiterated. No self-respecting man could simply walk away from an affray, not if he wished his dignity to remain intact. That was no doubt what mariner Thomas Allen meant as he defended his violent behavior by exclaiming, "if Christ struck me, I'd strike him back." In another case, ordinary seaman James Wright, arraigned for fighting while ashore in Peru, attempted to express similar sentiments more clearly. His statement, signed with an "X," suggests that men need not have been literate to remain articulate. "Gentlemen, assailed in this manner how was I to act? I put this question to your bosoms, as naval officers, as men, as Christians, is it not reasonable to suppose that man's very nature would urge him to endeavour to ward off blows?" Other men could be more effusive, if not as eloquent. Washington Pearsley, facing comparable charges at his own court martial and told he would be flogged, "threw his hat on the deck" to declare that "There's no use in licking me . . . you might as well lick the broad side of a shithouse as lick me!" He rejected repentance, as did many other mariners.[47]

Whatever imperatives the court claimed, in other words, would not supersede those of a mariner's masculinity and racial identity. And whether officers approved or not, the free expression of those concepts required doubled fists and swift kicks. Sailors claimed equality to their so-called superiors through narratives of participation in the noble project of commercial expansion, even as the disruptive forms this participation took threatened imperial objectives overseas. These were white men who seemed to be confused about why they would be punished for performing the good work of punishing lesser races. Yet given the regularity with which maritime laborers faced disciplinary action for their behavior, whiteness proved an unstable foundation upon which to construct a case for maritime rights and would become one among many challenges the American racial order faced overseas. Many seafarers became exasperated when it appeared as though they were being treated as an inferior caste, or, as one U.S. consul condescended, "a distinct and peculiar species of the *genus homo*." William Thacker expressed that aggravation best when he refused to even enter a plea at his 1858 court-martial, wondering aloud "What the hell is the use . . . when a man's word is considered no more than a God damned dog's here?" He sneered as the judge advocate convicted him of insubordination, remarking only that "he was condemned before he was brought in."[48]

The space between those two poles, between Anglo-American sailors as vulgar "dogs" that disrupted commercial agendas and as legitimate white working men, became the battleground on which many of the republic's seamen fought for a sense of themselves—and the respect of others—as members of the community of civilized peoples. Mariners exposed the tensions of commercial empire in that they straddled careful distinctions between colonizer and colonized. Their difficult relationships with the administrators of the U.S. maritime empire render hollow grandiose public pronouncements that American Anglo Saxons were "taking possession of all the ports and coasts of the world." The labor of seafarers, after all, con-tributed to an aggregate prosperity that observers heralded as evidence of national and racial exceptionalism. Yet the physical efforts of sailors them-selves to impose on foreign populations those very same notions of racial supremacy, their own attempts to take possession of the ports and coasts of the world, sparked condemnation among U.S. officials. This situation troubled the fiction of a simple dichotomy between subjugated native and white authority figure and suggested the ways in which class interfered with racial paradigms of power.[49]

With most elite observers prepared to see difficulties ashore as a product of the seafarer's inveterately dissolute character—the "habits to which sea-men are proverbially prone," in one diplomat's estimation—it was the rare voice that conceded that explaining maritime violence probably required an exploration of the structural deficiencies of mercantile capitalism. This was, after all, an oceanic economy terribly hard on its workers, and poor men poorly remunerated were perhaps disposed to cruelty, insubordination, and improper discipline. William Miles, an American consul stationed at Callao, admitted that while ashore in Peru, sailors lived "careless lives" characterized by much roughhousing. But that fact was directly connected, he wrote, to an exploitative "system in practice towards Seamen" characterized by "great injustice here and everywhere." Mariners in Macao, it seems, also proved an "expense and vexation to American residents" because "their conduct is so abandoned and insulting to the inhabitants of the place." Yet the chief blame, an official argued, lay with the nation's ship masters. To cut costs, they drove away their American crews and hired cheaper Asian replacements, thereby "land[ing] disorderly men without any money for their support." Abuses perpetrated by officers, a Shanghai official confirmed, "lead to constant desertion," thus "congregating ashore a band of dissolute and reckless indi-viduals . . . from whom I am daily apprehensive of hearing of some outrage committed upon the natives that could create a decided ill feeling against us among the Chinese." In the Pacific particularly, a sympathetic U.S. vice-consul noted, "crews [were] being engaged over a period from two to four years." Men so underpaid as to be "generally indebted to the ship" by the end of a voyage "become exceedingly restless and dissatisfied." Capitalism, all these onlookers implied, was implicated in the abuses for which it pun-ished disorderly seamen. Preaching the gospel of commerce, some witnesses warned, did not inherently soothe "savagery" of any kind, be it the sailor's or the Pacific islander's. Rather, civilization's multiplying "zones of law" bred "zones of violence." The two had been mutually constitutive all along.[50]

Turmoil ashore, then, was the inevitable result of unleashing impoverished and exploited individuals on the world. The hypothesis was that men became more aggressive abroad once they had become desensitized by the disciplinary violence and rank chicanery merchants and officers practiced. The reckless abandon of a brawl represented a form of resistance to the otherwise rigid regulations imposed by officers and employers busily maximizing profit margins. Abused men—"institutionally emasculated" men, in the words of one scholar—would reaffirm their manliness by seeking others to abuse. Or, as sailor Samuel Leech supposed, mariners "kicked and cuffed" who they could because, "being treated as inferiors themselves, [they] love to find opportunity to act the *superior* over somebody." Naval chaplain Charles Rockwell surely thought so. He censured seafarers as a class for the "guilt of shedding human blood . . . either in drunken quarrels with each other when on shore, or with the natives." But, he cautioned, "let us look at the facts of the case." Seamen, after all, "are under such despotic rule, and are, in so many ways, checked and restrained, that they become peculiarly selfish and sensitive as to what they regard as their rights and, where they dare to be so, are noisy and obstinate in defending them." Because authorities in "foreign ports . . . show him no civility," another man declared, the mariner is "often reckless in his conduct," but "were they treated as men . . . they would soon show themselves worthy of a reputable standing in the community." Only when sailors ceased to be in all ways beaten down would they stop beating others.[51]

These officials' complaints certainly spoke to larger trends in deepwater maritime labor. In the aggregate, as the nineteenth century progressed, voyages became more arduous, crew sizes were reduced, and real wages shrank. For common sailors, this meant harsher discipline, longer periods of time spent at sea, and more labor for each individual while afloat, all for diminishing compensation. Some of those charged with overseeing sailors believed that xenophobic outbursts were only symptomatic of those greater economic grievances. Their observations after 1830 or so connected an increase in "immoral conduct," as one missionary stationed along a heavily trafficked American shipping lane phrased it, with the fact that "voyages . . . are much longer than formerly [and] their success more precarious and uncertain." This assessment is surely true up to a point. But such claims also underestimate how deeply felt and fundamentally divisive more tribalistic concepts of personal, national, and racial honor could be.[52]

Novels such as *Moby Dick* have been enlisted to demonstrate the polyglot solidarities that emerged among cosmopolitan seafaring communities.

But these accounts often depend on idealizations that disregard the historical record. Melville's fictional account of Ahab's quest, to take only the most famous example, is based on the actual experience of the ship *Essex*, which was rammed and sunk by an enraged sperm whale in 1820. In the novel, white, Pacific islander, and black sailors were friends and comrades, but the real-life whaleship was a so-called checkerboard vessel where white seamen segregated themselves into separate quarters in order, in the words of one man, "to escape being so closely pent up with so large a number of blacks." *Moby Dick* ends with Queequeg symbolically saving the life of white shipmate Ishmael. In reality, the white crew of the *Essex*, cast adrift from their sinking ship, cannibalized their black shipmates to survive. Indeed, in a larger sense, it is instructive to note that when the first American sailors' unions began to mobilize against oppressive working conditions, they almost universally excluded nonwhite peoples from their ranks. Mariners collectively bargained for the removal of foreign aliens from the workplace and insisted on treatment commensurate with their elevated racial station. Mass insurgency among waterborne workers often proved ineffectual, with some exceptions, exactly because the old animosities of color and creed died too hard in the multiracial maritime world.[53]

The most enduring legacy of violence overseas materialized toward the end of the nineteenth century. By that time, life before the mast had become difficult enough to dissuade most white men from sea service entirely. And yet, ironically, the very class of officials who had sought to punish the physical expression of race hatred reconstituted those same crimes in service of the state. Policymakers may have worked toward the removal of riotous maritime actors, but they also showed themselves masters of appropriation. The gendered and racial discourses that helped provoke the Spanish-American War—the idea that the world was a proving ground, popular theories about civilization's enervating impact on men, and an attendant national need for aggressive, "strenuous" activity abroad against savage foes—had antecedents in the supposed virtues sailors derived from their own variety of "diplomatic fisticuffs."[54]

When a disciplinary committee convened aboard the USS *Wabash* in 1857 and convicted Charles Currell of assault and battery, he clarified his conduct by claiming that "I am an American, and I will defend myself, and I will not be trodden upon like a damned worm." It was his prerogative as a man and an American, in other words, to see himself redeemed in combat. His commanding officers did not agree; they saw the outburst as an impediment to proper order and yet another manifestation of the sailor's inveterate insidiousness. Yet by the turn of the century, expressions and actions similar to Currell's were being heralded in stump speeches as evidence of American pluck. Theodore Roosevelt became only the most prominent voice in a chorus of public speakers who sought to reinvigorate dwindling Victorian manhood through conflict with "barbaric" races abroad.[55]

"A peaceful and commercial civilization," the future Rough Rider intoned, "is always in danger of suffering the loss of the virile fighting qualities without which no nation, however cultured, however refined, however thrifty and prosperous, can ever amount to anything." The early nineteenth-century gospel of commerce had portrayed uncultured and unrefined sailors as disruptive brutes precisely because of their seeming addiction to violence. Curtailing seafarers' aggressive posturing, in turn, became both an economic and diplomatic goal. At this later 1890s crossroads, though, a problematic diagnosis was pronounced over the calm commercial world that the benevolence of business had helped create. For commerce, as some complained, only churned out effeminate citizens "content to rot by inches in ignoble ease" and "destined to go down before other nations which have not lost the manly and adventurous qualities." As one school reform commission protested, "the boy in America is not being brought up to punch another boy's head or to stand having his own punched in an healthy and proper manner." Policymakers, responsive to America's apparent "virility gap," began to promote aggression abroad as an antidote to the threat republican torpor posed. The state, in other words, learned to marshal, direct, and narrate belligerence that in the hands of an earlier generation of seamen had seemed anarchic and disruptive. Once adopted by the proper institutions, assertiveness achieved sanctified status as a buffer against the dangers of decadence. So it was that the path to 1898—a year replete with racialized violence enacted by Americans overseas—was constructed along tracks the nation's nautical class had long traveled.[56]

Too late, though, for Charles Currell. He and men like him, flexing their own power, refusing to be crushed like "damned worms," were not considered legitimate agents of a muscular foreign policy. Legislators came to parrot those pariahs only after safely containing most maritime malefactors in a steadily tightening net of military and diplomatic authority. Civilizing its own seamen had been the nation's duty before it could civilize the world. As one consul hyperventilated, legions of "American ships" heretofore arrived abroad only to paint a "perfect . . . picture of moral depravity, combined with everything disorderly, vicious, illegal, unjust, and impolitic."

If the fin-de-siècle United States did manufacture a "moral empire" overseas, it can only claim to have done so atop the wreckage of what earlier observers considered the mariner's "immoral empire." Violence had been one measure of sailors' supposed licentiousness; their relations with women would prove another.[57]

Chapter 5

An Intimate History of Early America's Maritime Empire

Any fixation on fisticuffs alone would, of course, lend the impression that the oceanic frontier was strictly a battleground. But like all frontiers, it was characterized by many varieties of interaction. The nation's water-borne workers most often simply mingled among peoples whom they occasionally mangled. The resulting intimacies, especially between sailors and women abroad, meant that early American foreign relations were often indistinguishable from sexual relations. Men who worked in the maritime community often pursued the latter and thus constructed the former. And nowhere is the relationship between those two subjects—the intimate and the diplomatic—more apparent than in the correspondence of Patrick Barry Hayes.

Hayes shipped out of Philadelphia in March 1831 aboard a southbound vessel and eventually found employment at an American firm in Brazil. The voyage through the Atlantic, though, proved hellish. The nicest phrase he could muster to describe his berth on board was "that filthy hole." The food received no higher marks, comprised as it was of "hash and god only knows what." The crew were distinguished for their rascality and consisted of "ten white men [and] eight black fellows, small niggers who looked more like monkeys than human beings." In any other time and place, such an offensive array as surrounded him on that ship "should have been stopped as Pirates . . . being a damned Piratical looking group." As it was, the racially mixed character of the vessel "was really beyond bearing for any white man." The ship's arrival in Brazil proved no respite.[1]

Having entered the city of Rio Grande by May 1831, Patrick Hayes soon ingratiated himself with a cohort of American men circulating the port. A motley set of clerks and itinerant seamen made up a group he referred to in his correspondence as the "Yankee boys." Days passed in attending to various work-related tasks, but nights found the men intoxicated and seeking the pleasures of female company. "Like all good fellow countrymen away from home," he explained to a friend in Philadelphia, "we ought to greet the arrival of strangers from our land [by getting] pretty damn drunk." On these occasions, Hayes boasted of displaying his "usual gallantry" and in the process becoming even "*more* fond if *possible* of ladies society than at home." Soon enough, admitted Hayes, the champagne began to take its toll: "You know my propensity of making a fool of myself when drunk," he wrote, "but never did I carry my self quite as far as this." The "Yankee boys," Hayes conceded, "are all a damned rowdy set and as drinking and whoring are almost our only amusements we know no end."[2]

From the carousing, therefore, came contact with Brazilian women, and from such intimate associations derived a host of judgments about the larger society of which the women were a part. Gender, sexuality, and racial ideology all intertwined in Hayes's account as the most convenient and powerful ways to understand the seemingly strange world of South America's largest country. Encounters with women led this waterborne worker into some frank discussions of coitus, and the subtext of these discussions revolved around divergent customs in his homeland and his temporary Brazilian home. He viewed the time he spent among the "fairer sex" of Portuguese society as an education in the mores of that portion of the world. Hayes and many other maritime laborers became savvy observers and interpreters of intimate activity abroad and attempted to extract information by "reading" women's bodies and the various sexual codes they encountered. Between the sheets, Hayes and his cohort found a more literal variant of the "pleasurable instruction" that elite travel writers strived for in their journeys. They formed judgments about gender, race, and politics predicated in part on the behavior of women they met overseas. These judgments in turn convinced them of certain truths about the United States. Descriptions of women, not to mention the pursuit of amorous ends, became a crucial tool for articulating differences between their homeland and the wider world.[3]

Sex and sexuality became yet another way to familiarize foreign societies with American national manhood. Patrick Hayes thus spoke in exhaustive detail of his "conquests" abroad as a demonstration of republican virility.

One of Hayes's friends, J. S. J. Grogan, received some of his more salacious wisdom. Maritime workers, as we have seen, were often very careful observers of the peoples they fraternized with, and that surveillance by no means excluded the intimate practices in place at any given location. A letter Hayes wrote in July 1831 began with the assertion that while he had been among Brazilians for some time, he had "but little relish for their manners and customs." In particular, he loathed "that *one* which you seem to think has been performed on my hole—which I can give you my *word* of honor still continues unscathed." Nothing "less than 100 gold dollars will even tempt me," he joked, before offering up a mock prayer asking the Lord to "deliver us from all evil—especially that worst of all evils, 'buggering.'" "I can assure you candidly," he continued, that it "is carried on to a great extent in this place." He described Brazilian acquaintances of his pursuing twelve- and fourteen-year-old boys, railing against the immorality of these arrangements, before halting abruptly with the claim that his "penis shudders at the idea."[4]

Another letter, this one written in 1832, pursued similar themes. Hayes remarked that "I have not become so much of a Portuguese as to use a boy." Anticipating his friend's astonishment, he continued with the assurance that "it is no joke, because I know for facts several men here who keep fine boys for their private amusement—what beasts!!" Accusations of pedophilia and homosexuality leveled against Portuguese-speaking men differentiated civilized eros from the reckless, aberrant perversity his hosts exhibited. Improper masculine pursuits and misdirected lust made Brazilians objects of humorous scorn. Hayes in turn constructed himself and his fellow Yankees as manly and virile, as exotic objects of desire in the eyes of native women accustomed to the company of effeminate "buggers." In his obsession with the unnatural appetites of "exotic" men, Hayes echoed American travel literature, adventure stories, and dime novels that were similarly invested in depicting foreign masculinity as fundamentally inferior. And in his expressed desire for female company, he displayed an enthusiasm for what one scholar describes as tales of "personal annexation" that pervaded the era's pro-expansionist press.[5]

Unsurprisingly, then, the bulk of Hayes's correspondence fixated on his escapades among "the ladies." He emphasized that the "Yankee boys," unlike their Portuguese counterparts, knew what comprised a "proper" good time.

In his estimation, nothing matched the "enjoyment of having a good *shag* in front from a pretty girl, of which there are no scarcity here." From what he saw, "every woman in the place could be got at." To another friend he excitedly explained that "there is no scarcity of common *strumpets*." Details emanated from that single declaration. "All shave their + which with the peculiar retrograde movement they have in the act, gives I can assure you a delightful and novel feeling to one who has the luck of getting a good-fuck!" Brazil, it was true, "possessed very little of ladies society," but Hayes claimed not to miss it "so long as a fellow can obtain a single leap when the state of his body requires it."[6]

He chose instead to locate "ladies society" back home in Philadelphia, construing Brazil as its antithesis, a playground for American men who were seeking only physical gratification. Exoticizing the bodies and sexual behavior of Portuguese women became the means by which he explained to his friend the vast cultural differences between life in the United States and life abroad, between "ladies" in America and the "strumpets" who strutted in streets abroad. Clearly aroused by the availability of Brazilian women, he used them as tools with which to draw larger conclusions about society there. The "looseness of the morals of the women," in Hayes's opinion, was ascribable only to "the want of education and the extreme jealousy of the men." And while Brazil was one of the world's largest slaveholding societies, Hayes's eyes opened to the absence of liberty only after spending time among Portuguese-speaking women there. He really did not blame the women for seeking out the company of American men, considering that "the poor devils . . . are all watched or rather *kept* like birds in cages more than human beings." He interpreted their sexual adventurousness as an attempt to seek "that Liberty which we are all so tenacious of and which we are so anxious to possess." Part of the purpose of this language was to authorize interracial sex; crossing that barrier, after all, was easier to justify when women were portrayed as desperately seeking carnal connection. The presence of American men in their midst, then, was itself a liberating force. The sexual prowess of the republic's citizens supposedly proved a "freeing" influence for caged women. Hence the political and diplomatic potency of their presence overseas.[7]

But even a certified hedonist like Hayes was careful to draw boundaries that served to distinguish himself as a white American man who was only *temporarily* transplanted and had certain ultimate allegiances to his own countrywomen. Race entered prominently into the distinctions drawn between home and abroad. In Brazil, he wrote, there are "many whores and girls who go in without scruple [and whom] you can pole for one gold dollar." Men in Brazil were an odd sort, though, for if they did not pursue boys, then "dark wenches are preferred by many [of them]." Not by Hayes, though: "Give me as white a girl as possible," he declared. But fair skin proved difficult to come by, for while he admitted that "there are many pretty girls here," "still few are what we would call '*real white*.'" In acknowledging a dearth of whiteness south of the equator, he appealed to a distinctive—even if fictive—community of white American men, the "we" who would not find anything in Brazil that measured up to their own standards of "real white[ness]" and thus of true beauty.[8]

Hayes looked on Brazilian society with American eyes and failed to appreciate the minute racial gradations that mattered a great deal to people raised in a world attentive to such detail. The United States had a far less nuanced hierarchy and did not often acknowledge diverse schematics of skin tone. Thus the careful distinctions Hayes failed or refused to see in Brazilian society caused him to disdain an appetite for "dark wenches." The "real white" women he lusted after attached him to those men of his own country who, while not unwilling to sleep with nonwhite peoples, nevertheless hid such attraction behind a rhetorical veil that lauded the virtues and purity of women who were untainted by black blood. Willing to admit that Brazil had its fair share of pretty girls, Hayes nevertheless maintained connections back home in his appeals to an American brotherhood that knew the supposed superiority of white femininity.[9]

Hayes always clarified the locus of his true loyalties. To his friend Robert Lynch, he wrote with the hope that "after a few years separation from friends and home, we shall see one another settled down at homes enjoying the pleasures and happiness of a steady comfortable married life." "None my dear Bob," he continued, "after all said and done is so pleasant as that state [where you] have one in whom you can place every confidence and every hearts secrets." To another friend, he asserted that "upon returning in a few short months to my native home," he would "have *one* who alone can make me *happy*." These statements could be interpreted in any number of ways: a guilt-induced call to reform or a formulaic homage to middle-class domesticity come to mind. More important are the ways that Hayes connected his country of origin with the potential for marital bliss and fulfilling female partnership. Whatever gallivanting he engaged in overseas, Hayes depended on a connection between his homeland and the promise of future stability with the company of an American woman. It was a promise of accessible whiteness, of dependable friendship and solace, and of comfort.

Only an American woman could deliver this desirable outcome, and the connection between "home," both nation and dwelling, and its female occupants appeared paramount in his imagination. Simultaneously espousing racist ideology while engaging in interracial intercourse and expressing a xenophobic nationalism while laboring alongside a diverse company of men, Hayes and others like him defy easy categorization.[10]

And Hayes by no means stood alone. His account of life and work abroad stands out for the intricacy of its detail, but not for its sexual subject matter. Hundreds of thousands of men in his position shipped out from the United States over the course of antebellum era and while abroad, observed, interacted with, and had sex with multitudes of women (and sometimes men). The women they encountered overseas, imagined at home, and remembered from past experience became common points of reference for young men striving to articulate either the qualities of a remote society or the superiority of its American counterpart. But this was more than the stereotypical "girl in every port" for which sailors were (in)famous. For these young American men, women were "objects" in more than a sexual sense, even as the desire for intimacy pervaded their rendering of female society abroad. Beyond those urges—or at least intertwined with them—lay a larger sense among seafarers that women had symbolic importance as the embodiment of any place's broader characteristics. The role of foreign women carried metaphoric weight beyond a night's carnal repose.[11]

But women overseas were not necessarily silenced by the scrutiny of sailors. They sought to use itinerant maritime populations for their own purposes, which suggests that seafarers mattered in the multiple places they roved as part of their working lives, not just in conversations about gender and sexuality in the United States. This chapter, then, is an effort to continue studies recently begun by historians about the relationship between intimacy and empire, or, what one scholar has called the "intimate frontiers" of imperial interrelationship. Within port city contact zones, sex, race, power, and regulatory impulses fused into highly charged combinations. The realm of the intimate was a contested arena where distinctions between people were constantly drawn and redrawn. Commercial expansion overseas created the opportunity for new (and sometimes transgressive) sexual and domestic arrangements, and those relationships were, in turn, implicated in both defining and defying racial categories that were fundamental to power relations between the republic and the wider world. Seafarers, in other words, created boundaries even as they crossed boundaries. And what was more, as sailors interacted with women, state and religious authorities bore witness to those conjugal and affective connections. Their frequent efforts to manage maritime intimacy signaled an international dimension to what was, in the nineteenth-century United States, a broader effort to police the limits of "permissible" relations among a supposedly oversexed rabble that was staining the moral fabric of American communities. Thus no account of early America's place in the world is complete without some investigation into the intimate dimensions of maritime life.[12]

Women overseas caught the eye of many male travelers in part because the homosocial world of the ship left individuals surrounded solely by men. Much like those who populated western mineral rushes, extractive-industry encampments, and fur-trading societies, seafarers spent large portions of their working lives in homogenously male company. The first words many mariners uttered when they came ashore expressed wonder at what seemed, by then, to be the sheer novelty of seeing a woman. As Justin Martin mentioned in a letter to his brother, "you wont get a sight at anything in the shape of a woman the whole voyage," so that "the first one you see when you come [ashore] will look so pretty that you will bite a piece out of her cheek before you know it." His liberty ashore at Hawaii, he admitted, was punctuated by "fine times with them," but, he warned, "they are right cunning, some of them (the girls I mean) . . . [and] bear plenty of watching." These mixed feelings were mirrored in many accounts of maritime life. Women were a sight for sore eyes, but frustrated mariners also found that many of the so-called fairer sex would not be passively manipulated. Rather, in dynamic intercultural encounters, women overseas pressed their potential advantages with men (perhaps literally in Martin's case) hungry for their company.[13]

Thus, seamen's marveling might quickly turn to aggravation as mariners projected their disappointment about people they came into contact with onto the persons of women. William Allen connected his sense of Callao as nothing more than a "collection of outhouses" and "jackass dung" to a decided disinclination toward that city's women. "Let me see," he sarcastically began, "in our country they call animals that wear bonnets and long togs, women, yes, I saw some women but such women!!" Problems abounded. For one, he griped, "they were as *black* as my hat or blacker." Moreover, they were "about as big round as they were long." So big, in fact, that he found their gait akin to a rolling barrel: "I see one fall down and instead of stopping as common folks do, after she was down she ended over and come on to her feet just like a cask." "I had heard much of the beauty of the

Spanish Girls," he groused, so "I was the more surprised when I saw such ungain creatures." The tone of the account altered little as he transitioned to a description of the surrounding environment that fixated on dirt, mud, and filth.[14]

Gender and geography were intimately linked by those mariners who sought beauty in both, found it in neither, and criticized accordingly. The entirety of midshipman Charles Blake's 1862 commentary at Cádiz consisted of this: "Judging from what little I have seen so far, I should never wish to go beyond the limits of the United States to see beautiful women." Whaleman George Blanchard wrote of St. Jago, Cape Verde, as though the features of the island and its females were one and the same. The "young ladies might rival the finest figures in our own Country," he conceded, were it not for their "faces, the best resemblance to which is their imitative companions of the woods, the monkeys." No, the mariner thought, "love could never nestle on the thick Black lips of a Portugee niggar." Lust, on the other hand, just might. He and his shipmates seemed willing enough to trawl brothels, and, "in purchasing one of these animals," he snorted, "you don't buy a Pig in a Poke, you see your bargain." Misogyny became topographic for this sailor; a distaste for the women he encountered became entangled with his rendering of the landscape. The "wretched, naked, [and] disgusting" environment was "like a woman's mind arrived at its utmost limits early in its existence—it never has improved—and like a woman—never will, untill it changes masters."[15]

But this talk of despair and disgust was partly the product of just how close the relationships between seafarers and women abroad could be. Younger, poorer, unattached mariners exhibited while overseas a good deal of dependence on the same women they often degraded for their racial "impurities." Older, advanced, and wealthier men—officers and other middle managers of maritime empire—usually had the means to live comfortably while traveling, were often married, and had families to consider. Common seafarers, devoid of resources, sought inexpensive room, board, comfort, and a measure of protection while ashore in unfamiliar places. Those services were often provided by women. In other words, the women overseas with whom most mariners interacted were rarely just prostitutes; they usually played multiple parts. Whaleman Dan Whitfield, for example, wrote of the washerwomen who approached the *Doctor Franklin* for laundry work that "they do not depend altogether on the washing they got for A Livelihood, But that they very often Picked up A sweetheart" in the process. Another sailor, aboard the *Samuel Appleton*, noted that laundresses piloting riverboats crowded alongside his vessel long before the anchor dropped outside Canton. They fiercely competed for "your wash-ee," but, he added, that was not all "they will do for a dollar, no matter how long the stay in port." Soon enough, the men he sailed with had selected their particular favorites.[16]

Meanwhile, what we might think of simply as brothels were multipurpose facilities that functioned as hotels, clothiers, pharmacies, and perhaps most important, moneylenders for sailors. Waterfront networks sprang up in scattered sailor towns constituted largely by female managers—for whom it made good business sense to cultivate a reputation for reliability—that offered transient men some sense of security. Accounts commented on the importance seafarers placed on maintaining amicable relations with these facilities and their proprietresses. Ezra Goodnough spoke excitedly of the need to get "his girl" at Mahé, a port in the Indian Ocean, a new dress, "for if i do not get her a new dress she will not remember me." These women in port were "our sweethearts," while a particular one would be "my wife," a woman who fulfilled more than sexual desires. Given the multiple functions wives served, perhaps we should reconsider the popular ballads that are typically dusted off to confirm the indiscriminate sexuality of sailor stereotypes. As one song had it, "I have a spanking wife at Portsmouth gates / A pigmy at Goree / An orange tawney up the Straights / A black at St. Lucie / At every mess we find a friend / At every port a wife." While undoubtedly a celebration of freewheeling sexuality, the song might also be read to imply the mediating role women played overseas in welcoming mariners ashore, securing their space and provision, and providing a safety net for men detached from established communal bonds. A man found a wife in every port if for no other reason than because he had to.[17]

Indeed, there is something meaningful about the regularity with which itinerant mariners described the women they met abroad as their "wives" and the transitory (but meaningful) relations shared with them as quasi-marital. Such language pervades maritime accounts of the sexual escapades of young men overseas to the point that its usage hardly seems accidental or incidental. The word "wife" connoted a degree of stability and (more to the point) dependence that other words did not. These women were not the mistresses or concubines who populated narratives written by wealthy travelers. Rather, sailors' accounts appeared to acknowledge that while women overseas served a sexual purpose, they performed other crucial tasks. Many white American seafarers made clear that the most permanent relationships they conceived of were located at home in the United States, usually with one of their own race. But forming pseudo-marriages abroad was a recognizable enough institution and custom to warrant regular comment

Figure 8. Dancing girl. Barrooms, dance houses, and brothels were crucial contact zones in America's maritime empire. Sex connected U.S. citizens to peoples overseas and became a means to many things: cultural observation, barter, and the exercise of power. "Dancing girl," from the journal of Frederick Smith, kept aboard ship *Petrel*, undated (ca. 1873). Courtesy of the New Bedford Whaling Museum, Logbook KWM 99.

as serial but not necessarily casual commitments. Whaleman James Hoberley, for example, noted while at Tanna, in the New Hebrides, that "we laid there about a fortnight, the Women came on board and every Man took a Wife to himself, we gave them Shirts and Tobacco which pleased them."

Aboard the ship *Ann Alexander*, "there wuz some of the Ladies came to be our Wives . . . one of them could satisfy all hands easy enough at least she did several and wanted more for a head of tobacco apiece."[18]

And as these accounts all make clear, gifts solidified those connections between American men and their caretakers ashore. Ezra Goodnough expressed genuine concern over the continued happiness of his special favorite. Paying women to care for him while abroad, he thought, was perfectly acceptable, for "that is more than the girls at home do," who "will not think of a poor Devil either for love or money." Above the Arctic Circle seaman Robert Strout spoke of one shipmate's relationship with an Inuit woman. He "made love to her" after "giving her all the presents" his limited income allowed, but when he approached his commander for more gifts, the captain asked him if "he had no more respect for himself than to fall in love with one of those lousy Squaws." Yet as soon as the ashamed seafarer "gave up his suit," the vessel's master himself "took up winter quarters" with the woman. "So much for Church members," Strout caustically surmised. At the center of this account is a woman who very methodically moved through the ship's company, extracting income for herself and her parents. Other men seemed less enamored of this economic relationship, even as their complaints gestured to the dependency of maritime classes on waterfront women. Joseph Clark complained about the many "arts . . . performed by woman . . . which are devised to defraud the mariner." These harpies, "degraded and unprincipled females," cheated sailors with "feigned smiles and hypocritical and specious graces . . . extorting from [them] valuable presents" without "even an apology." What fulfilled some men became for others a form of exploitation that confirmed the universally bad character of women; "*woman*," Clark spat, such creatures "dishonor[ed] the name." After emptying his pockets to pay for a night's pleasure in Peru, William Stetson noted with evident annoyance that "women rule the world everywhere." The resources he expended to please them proved his point, or so he thought. The men drew these conclusions, of course, without bothering to ask their companions whether or not they felt particularly empowered.[19]

Other arrangements prevailed elsewhere. In island cultures along the Pacific Rim, fathers, brothers, and other relatives often managed relationships between women and maritime laborers. Sex in these instances not only facilitated commerce but was in and of itself a commercialized practice; "modesty," as sailor Albert Peck pithily put it, was the only item "of no marketable value on board of a ship." Women at Kiribati, he reported, "were in the market for anybody with a piece of tobacco," which, on receipt, "they would hand to their husband or father or whoever it was that would receive it." Other men, Peck continued, simply marched their female charges "up to us, point at them, and say 'tobak.'" Such stark terms fail to capture the perspective of native women, who at times probably associated sexual encounters with prestige and potential access to material goods. One mariner, a rare relativist, thought so, judging that "by our standards, the women . . . would be called utterly immoral, but their freedom of conduct . . . is regarded by them as an injury to no one." John Martin remarked at Cape Verde that "the ladies of fancy . . . were in plenty and very free with their favours," but he also acknowledged that the women were only there "to make a certain amount," upon which they "return to their homes get married and lead a virtuous life." Maritime sexual clientele, then, were stepping-stones to respectability for many female inhabitants of port cities. Recently arrived men, for their part, were happy to contribute to that cause. Aboard the *Zephyr*, at Maui, a man remarked that "the girls swam along after dark of which most of the crew tack one," while the mate aboard the *Cavalier* showed a talent for both brevity and obscenity in remarking at Ascension Island that the sailors were "fucked to death." Ten years earlier, William Allen described a similar scene, "40 or 50 girls" surrounding the vessel, willing "to grant any favor for from a head of tobacco up to a thin shirt or 50 cents."[20]

Thus, anecdotal evidence abounds to support the larger point about sexual liaisons between mariners and women overseas, or as one man aboard the *Bowditch* phrased it, "what the whalers call refreshments that is to see the ladies." Commodore David Porter's assessment while at the Marquesas during the War of 1812 might apply more widely: "With the common sailors and their girls, all was helter skelter, and promiscuous intercourse, every girl the wife of every man in the mess, and frequently of every man in the ship . . . [so that] no one among them formed a connexion which was likely to produce tears at the moment of separation." But when maritime histories of the era conclude only that "the American man could not resist the proferred charms of these dusky beauties of the tropics," a larger world of foreign relations—of sex as a connective link that sustained longer-term relations on which the American maritime empire was built—is inherently lost.[21]

But use of the word "dusky" does point toward a crucial facet of these sexual-cum-international relations. Namely, that while masculine expectation and peer pressure created a climate that was ripe for erotic experimentation, by the 1840s and 1850s, the fact that they had crossed racial boundaries had become an integral component of how many men overseas

recounted those experiences. The titillation and transgression of sexual encounter now became about broaching the boundaries of monogamy *and*
race. Charles Lane's 1856 letter to a cousin recounted his infatuation with
an indigenous Guamanian named Marie. "A pretty girl," he claimed, but
one who had a "very dark brown, swarthy complexion." That revelation
made him halt to apologize: "I can hear your criticism, my dear cousin, but
you must remember I had been for ten months on the ship, and had seen
no young ladies in that time." George Harrison, whose ship lay anchored at
Rio de Janeiro, wrote home to his father of visiting the theatre with several
of the crew. He spoke of being there surrounded by "little negers . . . jab-
bering in their native tongue it is really amusing to a stranger." The men
patronized live arts "in order to see the girls" no matter what their color,
but only because the female form was "so great a novelty." "You must excuse me," Harrison clarified, quick to note that he "would rather go to one
of ours than go here." Options, however, were limited. And so, in another
sailor's words, "Spanish ladies" may have "lacked the fairness of complexion
so highly prized with us," but this did not bankrupt "the principal business
carried on in Talcahuano, Fucking."[22]

William Henry Weaver was one such individual who was invested in
how sexual mores and racial boundaries intertwined to separate America
from the rest of the world. Home was unsullied, while places outside its
borders revealed corruption and vice, thereby confirming notions about
the United States as a beacon in the midst of darkness and decay. Returning aboard from liberty in Madeira, he smugly recorded that "in no part of
world that I have yet visited, and I can say that I have more than two thirds,
seen girls that can compare with those of Yankee land." He admitted that
although he had met a pair of Portuguese women while ashore, "there was
something about them I can't fancy." They "will do well enough to make
love to," he conceded, "but no further," because "they are not white." With
these ruminations, he offered a clear sense of how foreign women registered in the minds of some American men. Sexual relations were not to be
confused with true affection. Anything beyond momentary gratification
and the meeting of needs that might arise while a sailor was in port was not
only racial but also political treason.[23]

As Weaver formulated it, national greatness aligned itself with both racial
and female purity. The unsurpassed beauty of white women properly embodied the nation. Seamen were not necessarily inclined to view all women
as short-term lovers. Sophisticated lines of separation divided sexually available women from romantically desirable ones. This left in the boundaries

of civilized American life the positive elements of male-female entangle-
ments such as devotion and chastity and expelled to the outer realm emo-
tions and desires that were increasingly understood in pejorative terms. In
legitimating sexual relations overseas, seamen expressed contempt for their
non-American partners as somehow degraded, ironically, for having been
cajoled into intercourse with them. These understandings of sexual life outside the republic appear as historical forebears to present-day ideas about
the "third world" as the appropriate or expected site for sexual tourism,
deviance, and turpitude. It was the internationalization of what one scholar
notes as the nineteenth-century trend of men practicing "self-restraint with
one class of women," only to "enjoy erotic pleasures and give vent to their
natural passions with another." Such attempts at compartmentalization were
put into play by Robert Weir, for example. His seafaring journal noted
that in order to "see some Arab women" at the Comoros Islands, he (and
several shipmates) "had to enter the house by force." They scattered several
families before there "soon collected a crowd from which we vamoosed
without much ceremony." Local headmen, irate after the intrusion, complained to the captain, but Weir only grinned to think of his return home
to the United States: "What a barbarian I'll be to show myself among ladies
society again." The difference between home and abroad hinged between
comparably worthless women waiting behind doors he might kick down in
search of sex and the American "ladies" into whose more polite company
he aspired to return.[24]

Yet for as much that seafarers spoke of the significance of race in delim-
iting desirable and undesirable women, the reality is that many sailors fraternized regularly with members of the opposite sex who would have been
considered members of an "inferior" caste at home in the United States.
Some, for that very reason, refused racially transgressive associations altogether, such as sailor John Winslow, who seemed to sigh with relief when
his vessel departed Madagascar: "the last of the princesses left us to night
and the ladies of pleasure I am verry glad to see them go for they are as dark
as mid night and for 2 yards of 5 cent cotton they afford all their charms
which are verry few as I wish for none of them neither princess nor subjects." Undoubtedly, a larger number of the maritime community abroad,
lacking Winslow's scruples, single-mindedly pursued women as objects of
sexual gratification and chose not to differentiate among them so long as
they served that purpose. The latter group are disproportionately reported
on, even celebrated in some ways, in large part because they comport with
the stereotype of Jack Tar. Written accounts, though, suggest far greater

efforts on the part of American seamen to sort through the mass of female humanity in order to confirm their own countrywomen's superiority. And yet, for all that this talk animated by race should have curtailed associations between white men and "inferior" ladies overseas, the fact remains that such women were indispensable intermediaries between ordinary seafarers and local populations.[25]

On both sides of the equation, sex was clearly an important integrative force between the United States and the wider world. It mattered a great deal to male maritime workers, but it was also an important source of wealth, status, and prestige to the many women who serviced America's itinerant global workforce. For as one naval officer estimated of the women he met in the world's port cities, "two thirds of those are common prostitutes dependent alone on transient men for subsistance." But despite (or perhaps because of) prostitution's omnipresence, intimacy and sexual access became another battleground on which the state and representatives of "respectable society" attempted to control the nation's foreign relations by claiming managerial jurisdiction over the erotic impulses of waterborne laborers. Historians of North America's borderlands have recently interrogated the ways that adjudicating intimacy became an important method of restraining and containing the "immoral" (and potentially destructive) impulses of low-status persons. Simply put, gangs of transient workers have often stood in awkward and suspect relationship to "settled" society. The appointed (and self-appointed) guardians of marital and sexual norms, therefore, clashed with a sexual culture among sailors—and other populations of largely young, single, working-class men—that seemed far too freewheeling and abandoned.[26]

As the nineteenth century unfolded, consuls, courts-martial, and missionaries aligned to impose greater limits on the perceived libertinism of sailors. Their erotic appetites were increasingly viewed as an embarrassment to respectability in the international community. Mariner sexuality—and that of "the rabble" more generally—was viewed as exhibitionist, nonreproductive, and detached from the responsibilities of fatherhood; three strikes against it in a transatlantic culture where the bourgeois ideals of sexual propriety and companionate heterosexual marriage were becoming dominant paradigms. Moreover, sailors' seemingly single-minded quest for physical satisfaction was thought to clash with the decorum that ought to dictate relations between nations. The quarrels, animosities, and other "petty" jealousies such relations engendered threatened the stability that was needed for profitable commercial intercourse. Seafarers, meanwhile, overworked and underpaid while performing the rough labor of maritime empire, often saw little reason to deprive themselves of pleasures they perceived as both a necessary respite and a fundamental expression of American masculine prowess. Sailors' complaints mounted against the unwanted interference of those who sought to inhibit sexual expression in the name of proper foreign relations. For many mariners (not to mention women overseas), sexual relations were absolutely necessary to the successful conduct of the "lower sort's" own diplomacy. Eros was an end in itself, but it also acted as a sort of currency that facilitated broader social and economic interchange.[27]

A common complaint among mariners was that their sexual appetites had been curtailed by the meddling of authorities. Thomas Morrison, aboard the whaleship *Avola* at an unnamed Pacific way station, grumbled that while "I and some others went on shore with great expectations, we got greatly disappointed [for] the Missionarys has got glory pumped into the natives good and at both ends." George Blanchard, without a woman in Hawaii, spoke in similarly bitter terms of "the missionary operation": "too infernal lazy to get a living at home," they "get appointed to some beautiful island of the Pacific" while "laying up the dollars" amassed by penalizing sailors via vice laws. The suppression of mariners' sexual urges by others, therefore, could be grounds for work stoppages and other disruptive acts. The Salem bark *Reaper*, for example, put into Fort Dauphin, Madagascar, in 1839 under threat of a general strike. Women were the issue. "Last night," the captain wrote, "slept on shore and let the girls come on board for the purpose of keeping the crew quiet this is hard but I am forced to do." In 1857, seamen aboard the *Parachute* threatened to riot at Hong Kong unless their erotic appetites were satisfied. As one journal keeper put it, the vessel soon became "as one of the dens of five points, New York," where "Chinese harlots . . . prominade the ships deck in all their scenic glory."[28] In a more serious incident on Maui in 1825, sailors aboard the ship *Daniel*, armed and flying a black flag, attacked the homes of several missionaries for their refusal to allow women aboard ship. Outside Honolulu in 1827, sailors on the *Dolphin*, angered by restrictions placed on women aboard vessels, "attempted to form a coalition to 'knock off the tabu.'" Shouting "'Where are the women?'" squads of men "commenced a riot," smashing the windows of various authorities' offices and threatening to pull down their houses. Only armed resistance by native Hawaiians beat the seamen back.[29]

Maritime empire's administrators were in a bind regarding sailor sexuality. Disapproving of its rough edges, they also recognized that men became far less compliant workers when they were regularly deprived of intimacy. Authorities considered aggressive sexuality a liability, and yet efforts to curtail erotic license often produced the very disruptions regulators sought to forestall. Complex negotiations came to determine the duration of shore leave. A managerial ethos dictated the attempts of officers, missionaries, and consuls to limit and control access to women's bodies at crucial port cities in the nation's maritime empire. If licentiousness could not be stamped out, then it could be rationed and, as much as possible, kept out of sight. Often, this meant limiting "lewd" activity to ships at anchor. Ambrose Bates, first mate aboard the *Euphrates*, believed that intermediaries ashore at any number of port cities saw negotiation over sexual favors as a top priority in a larger process meant to facilitate friendly relations. Fathers, brothers, mothers, pimps, and madams climbed aboard to "apply to me for a situation" for those women who comprised their "harems": "They come alongside every day in hope of obtaining leave to come on board," he wrote. Indeed, as he circled the world, Bates found himself "provoked to death with them." The matchmakers, however, generally "went off verry much displeased when I informed him that I allowed no women on board whilst I had charge." Their annoyance helps illustrate the instrumentality of women as connective links between ship and shore and, in a larger sense, between America's maritime community and its partners in enterprise overseas. Bates, in aggressively policing sexual activity, had jeopardized one of the keystones of hospitality in global commercial networks.[30]

Arrangements could not always be made, and even when they were possible, they did not please everyone. But many ships managed some form of compromise that kept sexual pollution confined to classes of people thought to be already degraded. Stephen Curtis, a rare scold among sailors, noted with stinging sarcasm that "every night, at sunset, a boat was sent ashore, for the laudable purpose of bringing girls on board of the ship." What was shocking to him, however, was that "this performance . . . was sanctioned by the captain." The ship's officers had negotiated the arrangement to prevent the "disruptions" associated with seafarers in search of sexual satisfaction. Another seafarer noted in matter-of-fact terms that "it is the fashion [for our ships] to run in to the land at night send 2 boats or 3 on shore and fetch off girls 1 to a man . . . and after a nights debauchery put them on shore and repeat the same night after night." At St. Helena in the South Atlantic, one vessel became, according to a crew member, "a perfect floating brothel," all arranged by the captain, who "appeared to be pretty well acquainted" with the women he sent aboard. Elite observers often begrudgingly tolerated such behavior for fear of retaliation, though they never failed to complain about sailors, whom they saw as "generally low, unpolished men" who left the "tinge of vulgarity" wherever they landed. And yet their presence was usually abided by locals, at least for a time. This complainant confirmed why that should be the case, even if he never connected the two: "the handsome girls . . . landing from the whalers" carried with them piles of "old greasy red or checked shirts." These textiles were the tangible benefits of a night's so-called vulgarity.[31]

For seamen (and the women they interacted with), intimacy smoothed all other economic transactions and cultural interactions. For authorities, international relations inherently attained a sexual flavor because they channeled the erotic energies of waterborne workers into productive and profitable relationships with host populations. Prostitution and sexual libertinism were thought of, to some extent, as allowable along the maritime empire's frontiers, as something "necessary" to sustain crucial commercial and diplomatic linkages. But as the nineteenth century progressed, authorities frowned on such sexual display as those broader links became self-sustaining and sexuality more clearly seemed a conduit of disease, decay, and degeneration. An evil necessity in distant outposts became more evil and less necessary as time progressed. Reform movements against prostitution and sexual "perversion," already a force in larger American cities, found their way to maritime outposts. Missionaries were often the ones to insist on amendments to policies on prostitution among ship owners and officers. For example, Daniel Wheeler's concern for the "daughters of Tahiti" caused him to "shudder for the awful and woeful consequences" the sexuality of sailors entailed. Yet missionaries knew that all their measures to "stop this overwhelming torrent of iniquity" were "abortive, and can never be successful, unless co-operated with on the part of the masters of the shipping." Religious officials (and some local communities) were growing ever more dissatisfied with half-measures designed only to "hide" rather than eliminate what they saw as the unseemly sexual appetites of sailors. Missionary to Hawaii Hiram Bingham and others sought to circumvent the authority of naval commanders who they saw as complicit in the "pollution" of Polynesian women by asking the American Board of Commissioners for Foreign Missions to pressure the federal government for independent inquiries into the conduct of "rogue" officers. "Happily for our American Republic and for the world," he wrote, "a just indignation extensively prevailed against the wrongs" sailors and their enablers inflicted. In the middle of the nineteenth century, such reformers put increasing pressure on the machinery of maritime empire to prosecute those who purveyed sexual "indecency."[32]

Intimacy thus received a good deal of institutional attention at the federal level. Some organizations were merely preventative, such as the network of nationally managed marine hospitals established at key ports and designed in part to curtail the spread of venereal diseases thought the sailor's trademark affliction. Syphilis, gonorrhea, and other infectious illnesses had long been recognized as a consequence of traffic between countries, to the extent that it becomes nearly impossible to disentangle commerce from maladies associated with sexual congress. When Cook islanders coined the phrase *kua pai au*, or "I am shippy," to describe the effects of sexually transmitted ailments, they laid the connection bare. Quarantines, hospitalization, and prohibitions were actively pursued as countermeasures against the death and depopulation for which sailors in particular were thought responsible. The British Empire might have been the first to license brothels, pass contagious disease ordinances, and establish formal medical inspections of sex workers, but America's maritime empire was characterized by ad hoc methods geared toward similar ends. Prophylactic measures to control maritime intimacies, however, were complemented by punitive ones.[33]

Fiercest condemnation was reserved for homosexual intimacy. Though same-sex encounters are rare in the maritime historical record, they provoked harsh responses when they surfaced. The American consul at Paita, Peru, for example, heard testimony from men aboard the ship *Emily Morgan* about the conduct of one John Fryer. His shipmates stated that Fryer had repeatedly tried "to have connection with David Stanton in his hindemost parts" and asked the official to remove him from the ship. "It was not save to have sutch a man on board of the ship," the sailors complained. Their request was "that he should be put on shore." Consular officials complied; Fryer was detained until his vessel left port, and during his detention he attempted suicide. The diplomatic legation at Fayal, meanwhile, heard testimony that the steward aboard the ship *Citizen* had been stealing into sailors' "berths when the lights were out" to take "there inexpressibles in to his mouth." That man too was cast ashore under consular authority. Naval courtrooms were sites for the severe punishment of what was often referred to as "criminal connexion" or "scandalous conduct" between servicemen, such as when sailor John Powers was dishonorably discharged and branded after "commit[ting] pollution on a man with his pants down." American authorities thoroughly investigated all such instances of so-called perversion in its maritime labor force and worked to expel those deemed responsible. Police power was employed to ensure, as much as possible, a heterosexual norm afloat. The United States could not be seen as a country that countenanced "abnormal" sexual urges among its representatives abroad. In most instances, the majority of men aboard the ships in question seemed willing to collaborate in the criminalization of queerness. Officials abroad may have tolerated prostitution and concubinage among sailors, at least to the point they did, in an effort to prevent the proliferation of male-to-male sexual relations.[34]

But while prostitution had its "advantages" in the eyes of consular officials, brothels were very closely monitored precisely because they appeared to genteel eyes to be clearinghouses for all sorts of wanton immorality. They seemed to breed the crime and disorder that diplomats considered a poor example to "uncivilized" peoples who themselves, in the eyes of white U.S. officials, were only tentatively climbing their way out of the savage state. The debauchery of profligate mariners seemed to be "teaching the natives mischief they never would think of" otherwise, and, as one consul complained, many "natives are quite bad enough without any farther lessons being taught them." Another evangelist, surveying a port in Madagascar where "fathers and brothers" brought "their daughters and sisters on board" to "sell all the virtue they possessed for a fathom or two of calico," thought maritime empire little more than a "floating scene of abominations" where people who ought to "look up to Americans as a superior race of beings" could instead "catch their vices." Missionaries fully recognized that their role would be not simply to impart Christian principles but also ensure that iniquities taught by sailors "must be *unlearned*." Public health crises in port city communities provided all the proof (and reproof) critics needed to condemn the supposedly limitless sexual appetites of sailors. "It is truly distressing to learn," as a typical account scolded, this one written from Patagonia, "that our own countrymen have plunged into the most loathsome debaucheries with this unhappy people, and rendered almost inveterate those polluting vices which carry death in their train, and spread a fearful blight over all that is lovely."[35]

But in this context, disease was not simply a biological agent. Rather, it was conceptual, and it connected venereal ravages with other troubling symptoms of moral decay. Seafarers were condemned, in particular, for exporting abroad what historians have described as an antebellum urban sporting culture that specialized in brothel riots and other forms of exhibitionistic violence against sex workers. In these bursts of destructive brutality, men engaged in elaborate displays of autonomy by asserting themselves amorously and using intimidation to coerce and control sexually active "public" women. In some sense a literal hunt for female company, these episodes assumed ritualistic characteristics among men who spoke of access to women's bodies as a sort of rebellion against the forced abstinence their working lives afloat entailed. Recall Justin Martin, who thought himself prepared to bite the first woman he saw after six months at sea. His metaphor and rhetorical flourish, however, spoke to certain realities; Walt Whitman thought New York City's "hardest houses" of prostitution were those that serviced sailors, and reports sent in to the State Department chronicled the appearance of similarly rough episodes abroad.[36]

At Nagasaki, Dutch officials contacted their American counterparts to ask for the punishment of U.S. citizens who had recently stormed a local brothel, beating several women and robbing their patrons. Victims testified that they "had just gone to sleep with the girls" when several American sailors broke in, "kicked us in the face and chest," threw down prostitutes, and broke furniture. A local shopkeeper, meanwhile, addressed the American consulate at Canton to complain of "a prostitute establishment lately got up immediately in the vicinity of our house, producing much disturbance, not only alarming my family but actually injuring my property." Sailors who belonged to a vessel with a U.S. flag had been busily "tearing off the tiles of the roof, breaking our windows, pelting our house with stones, casting away our flower pots, and alarming the fears of my family by hideous and savage yelling—all without any cause of offense on our part, contrary to the allowed usages of all well regulated and civilized nations." The man "beg[ged] leave therefore to request that this prostitute establishment be removed," so that "good order and quietness" might be "restored to the neighborhood," not to mention "safety and protection to myself, family, and property according to treaty." Here was an individual who studied the intimate affairs of American maritime empire only to conclude that as long as the republic countenanced reckless sexuality, it could not count itself in the ranks of civilization. Terminology typically wielded by conquerors was here instead employed to shame national officials into action: did not a "well regulated and civilized nation" such as the United States care about its international reputation? Many different people were paying attention to who seafarers slept with and using that information to draw conclusions, demand action, and exert power.[37]

What was the "nuisance" of violence against women at home in the United States threatened, when committed abroad, to devolve into national embarrassment. Consular records abound with episodic violence—beatings and attempted rape—visited on the bodies of women overseas. William Wilson, at Ponape, was very forthright in claiming that coerced sex, even with children, was common: "a man can get any girl he wishes small girls etc.," and "if they cry they are beat." Seaman Orson Shattuck was shocked at what he saw in New Zealand. "Miserable and unfortunate little girls" were compelled there "to give themselves up to our rugh and brutal sailors." A legation in Japan translated similar testimony from imperial subjects identified as Isohay and Denkitchi, who complained of a sexual assault committed against Isohay's wife, Isuya. On a Nagasaki bridge, Isohay claimed to have met "a foreigner who came up to them," pointed to Isuya, and said "'I want this girl.'" Isohay replied that "'this is my wife' but he insisted and then threw me down." "I said," the defendant concluded, "this is my wife and she is not your wife." The men struggled for some time before watchmen separated all parties and brought them to trial. Protecting the "honor" of local women appeared to be the principal motive behind a number of altercations between American seafarers and the societies that hosted them. Female bodies were often treated by mariners as something to which they were entitled, while communities ashore viewed the violation of wives, sisters, and daughters as particularly objectionable evidence of the erosion of their own sovereignty.[38]

Singular episodes, therefore, quickly devolved into mob violence during which larger portions of a municipality would turn out to resist the unwanted advances of sexually aggressive intruders. Matthew Perry mentioned that an entire Okinawan village appeared en masse to stone one of his squadron's sailors after the man took undue liberties with a local woman, while the Nagasaki consulate heard testimony from Nakiama and Enoya about "three sailors who came on shore," chased a woman, knocked her down, and were then themselves beaten when a crowd, "hearing the screams, came in great number." When irresponsible maritime workers committed sexual crimes—what the translator of a Japanese official's letter of protest pegged as "extravagances"—"many quarrels . . . [took] place." Because most of those crimes revolved around women and took place in or near brothels, consuls wrote often that "houses of this character are a great evil." "Many evils will be prevented and much trouble will be avoided," one consul felt, if such districts could be shuttered entirely. Indeed, evil was a word administrators returned to over and again to describe sex, assault, and mob violence inspired by unchecked intimacy: "it is an evil bearing alike on the peace and interests of all Foreign residents" overseas. International law raced to catch up with the mushrooming of such incidences as treaty makers inserted into diplomatic agreements language similar to that of an 1854 Compact of Friendship and Commerce between the Ryukyu Islands and the United States. Article IV of that accord explicitly stated that "persons from Ships of the United States" who "violently go into houses, or trifle with women, or do other such like illegal acts" would be arrested and imprisoned. Some sailors, of course, knew that their sexual appetites were being targeted in treaties. One man even feigned indignation, sarcastically commenting on how "little confidence has been put in our good taste." He thought that most women abroad were ugly and exclaimed that "there's not a man in the squadron who would touch one with a ten foot pole." Experience, however, had taught diplomats otherwise, and their negotiations reflected broad-based skepticism about any seaman's capacity for sexual self-restraint.[39]

This treaty language, however, only represents the application abroad of rampant suspicions surrounding mariners in the U.S. coastal cities they departed. Sailors there were deemed offensive for the ways that they defied emerging understandings of a functioning household. A large population of itinerant men who often left behind (and failed to support) struggling female and juvenile dependents did not comport with middle-class expectations. Missionaries and legal authorities often placed sustained pressure on the male maritime community to honor their manly responsibilities as heads of household and providers. This was the standing contradiction in the maritime community's intimate relations with the wider world: the more sailors used sex as an integrative device abroad, the more frequently they were attacked as social deviants who failed to comport with the norm of marital monogamy.[40]

Yet these obligations to wives and families at home proved difficult to meet because of the absences from home maritime work required. Commercial capitalism, as we have seen, increasingly demanded more and more of the deep-water sailor's laboring life. This, in turn, forced among mariners a dependence on prostitution overseas for any sort of intimacy. But that same mercantile system also bred bourgeois bellyachers whose disapproval of maritime vice rarely seemed to understand how their incomes and stable positions in society in fact depended on the working-class itinerancy they attacked as productive of so much evil. Indeed, the expectations attached to manhood ashore and manhood aboard ship were often directly at odds with one another, placing seamen in a difficult situation. The former, which treated men as rational, stabilizing influences in the home, clashed with the latter, which emphasized corporate fraternity among a loose brotherhood bonded by prowess in the arenas of drinking, fighting, and womanizing. The disjuncture between competing constructions of manliness left seamen open to reproach at home even as they gained a sense of superiority overseas by applying their own notions about the appropriate behavior and responsibilities of men and women.[41]

And while seamen assessed women as a viable measure of any particular culture, authorities in the United States came to scrutinize the lives of their own waterfront women as indicative of the abnormality of maritime life. Harbor towns populated disproportionately by wives and unsupervised children were thought to reflect poorly on men who left home for extended periods of time. To make ends meet, these women often labored at various odd jobs that took them out of their homes and away from female responsibilities such as housekeeping and childrearing. Worse still, from the perspective of city elite, was that these women and youths became a drain on public coffers; people who should have been supported by their husbands were instead dependent on the dole. The blame for this state of affairs was increasingly laid squarely on the shoulders of maritime workers. Wealthier, more established women, such as the wives of sea captains, had adequate resources to remain dependent and did not suffer such scrutiny. Theirs was, in many instances, a more private anguish over the failure to maintain with any regularity the companionate bourgeois household. But the struggling wives and families of common seamen encountered constant reminders of their deficiency in meeting obligations thought essential for "respectable" men and women at the time. This state of affairs could not have escaped the attention of mariners themselves, and it complicates the attention they paid to women overseas. For while they scrutinized the intimate realm of sex and affective relationships in foreign ports as evidence of the merit of any particular place, sailors departed from American coastal cities themselves subject to similarly judgmental forms of scrutiny.[42]

Policing the intimate in America's maritime empire, therefore, began in the nation's seaport cities. These were the so-called dens of vice where seafarers returned from abroad having been schooled in the arts of licentiousness and sexual libertinism. Waterfront reformers treated such districts as the chokepoints they were: spaces where the rottenness and immorality mariners had acquired overseas threatened to spread more widely throughout American society. With, as one purity campaigner put it, the "potential moral contamination of future husbands and fathers at stake," there was a tendency to treat the sexuality of seafarers as a kind of contagion. What began as a defensive operation—involving the implementation of various vice laws in the nation's Atlantic and Pacific gateways—had evolved into a global crusade against prostitution by the end of the nineteenth century. Organizations such as the Woman's Christian Temperance Union headed overseas as part of a transnational social purity campaign designed to eradicate the sin of the global sex trade. Historians eager to link the origins of American internationalism to the efforts of progressive reformers, however, should remember that the worldwide anti-vice movement was preceded by a mobile maritime labor force that had put a significant percentage of that prostitution on a paying basis. This was the symbiotic relationship between maritime empire and non-marital sex that the self-appointed guardians of decency fought to eradicate. But American sailors were often vocal in reminding officials that ready access to women's bodies was a key condition for their continued employment. What others labeled as degeneracy, they suggested, was to the waterborne workforce a crucial component of their difficult lives afloat. Long before American soldiers serving in foreign conflict zones stirred passionate debate over venereal inspection regimes and the ethics of prostitution, sailors had tested those tempestuous waters. To those who would fight to eradicate the global scourge of sexual impurity, the seaman's supposedly "sorry" model stood as a warning against inaction. Along the world's waterfronts—all of them, as one appalled observer thought, a "vortex of dissipation"—wrangling over the definition of deviancy became an excuse to exercise power.[43]

But these disagreements serve to mask what was broad consensus in America's maritime empire. After all, agreement existed among most men at sea—as it did for those on land charged with "controlling" rowdy mariners—that women were an inferior variety of humanity. A casual, even jocose misogyny pervades accounts of shipboard life. William Rogers recorded on a voyage from Salem to India in 1817 that upon catching a few fish the crew, unsure of the species, designated them "Old Wives, the reason was because *they were so snappish*." Richard Henry Dana Jr. filled several pages of his seafaring narrative with a dialogue about wives between the ship's carpenter and sail maker. The carpenter became dejected, "completely down in the mouth," after failing to receive letters from his spouse. The sail maker countered by telling him he had been "a bloody fool to give up his grub for any woman's daughter." His advice was never "to be made a fool of by anything in petticoats again!" "'You've hove your money away'" the counsel continued, "'but every man must learn once, just as I did.'" Still, the carpenter was dejected and, Dana thought, "bore with difficulty the jokes of the sailors, and with still more difficulty their attempts at advice and consolation, of which the sailmaker's was a good specimen."[44]

One candid letter, written at sea by mariner Richard Settle, hints at the regularity with which men fled "woman trouble" ashore by setting themselves afloat. "Some nights," he began, "we get together and spin yarns about home some of them will tell how some girl fooled them and some how they fooled the girls." The fourth mate, "Mr. Lunbat, he tell us some pretty good yarn about the girl that he has fooled and some of them he has ruined." "The reason he came out in this ship was on account of a girl that he ruined in Lindon Vermont . . . she was 7 month along before her father found it out [and] we have got 2 or 3 others that had to leave home for the same thing." The fact that this was a relatable predicament for several others aboard the ship suggests a more permissive attitude toward casual sex that would dictate relations toward ordinary men and the women they encountered overseas. But, more than anything, it pointed to the dismissiveness of these men about the specific needs the women they encountered might have had.[45]

Just as a young woman in Vermont was left to wrestle with the complications of child-rearing, so many women overseas would work to care for children left them by men unaware of their responsibilities or unwilling to fulfill them. Indeed, the hard labor of maritime empire was not performed by working men alone. Women who provided care and comfort to floating populations, bartered for sex, and birthed babies were in all ways essential to the functioning of a larger commercial machine. They must be counted among the laboring classes of the global mercantile matrix. Yet local societies struggled to integrate mixed-race children of uncertain lineage who emerged from maritime empire's many intimacies. Such juveniles had a questionable claim on the local community's resources, and U.S. consular officials also wondered aloud in letters to the State Department about the precise status of individuals who claimed wandering American men as their fathers. By the 1850s at least, the republic's legations abroad had begun to gather testimony from women about their liaisons with national citizens and inquire about the rights any issue from those unions had. "There are in this consulate," the commercial agent at Samoa noted, "a very great number of half caste children of American Citizens . . . by Samoan women." And, "as it is very probable at no distant day there may arise questions involving their rights as Samoans, or as Americans, I respectfully request that the Department will advise on this matter in order that all doubts may be settled." Similar requests for clarification came from other outposts.[46]

Take, for example, the case of a woman identified in Nagasaki consular records only as "Taka." Through the court translator, she complained of being "very sad daily" after bearing the child of an itinerant American laborer. She was ruined: "I cannot marry with any [Japanese] man" after sharing a foreigner's bed, and "thought often it would be better for me that I lost my life, but I do not so, having thought of the child, and I am now in great distress." The father of the child, who was hauled before the court, claimed that the woman was a common whore and that the child was one "made through lewd intercourse with some Japanese man." Taka could only reiterate that she had "been overwhelmed with a deep sorrow," so much so that she "went on the seaside one or two times for the purpose to commit my suicide by drowning," but "this was prevented for the grief of my young child to be left alone from me." Perhaps to play for the court's sympathy, she argued that "although I am of course a foolish woman . . . I am very angry against his conduct and believe that there is no difference of the humanity between Foreigners and Japanese." The magistrates were begged to order payment of reasonable child care expenses. But "expert" testimony from three European doctors dashed her hopes. Upon examining the child, they claimed that he was of wholly Japanese origin, and not a "half-breed." Taka was turned out empty handed, inspiring Miyagawa Fusayuki, the town magistrate who thus became responsible for the care of an abandoned woman and child, to formally protest what he called the "cruel and odious" conduct of American citizens abroad.[47]

The intimacy of maritime empire, then, did not end with sexual encounter but could continue over time as births increased in consequence of such trysts. A woman contemplating suicide while pleading for consular support might seem melodramatic, but the situation points to the narrow options and difficult choices of individuals who lived in the path of U.S. commercial expansion. The anger both Taka and her town elders expressed captures the quotidian struggles set into motion by seafarers' sexuality, the often desperate underclass of port city women servicing those men, and the adjudicatory American state. Most seafarers were not brought to account, at least not for their sexual exploits. The U.S. consular bureaucracy typically denied petitions for assistance on the part of female foreign nationals caught up in this intimate diplomacy, helping to codify an international (double) standard. Delegates depicted women's "normal" sexuality as restrained and placed the burden of responsibility for transgression squarely on their shoulders. More mobile seafarers, meanwhile, had moved on to tell jokes and sing songs that celebrated their special virility and glorified male heterosexual freedom.[48]

This sort of humor and sexism illustrates consensus about men's spiteful or at least suspicious attitude toward the opposite sex. Seafarers, simply stated, were not the picaresque heroes of their own ballads. Rather, what they observed abroad often served to reinforce fairly conservative attitudes and beliefs about women. Contempt for women (and at times misogynistic violence against them) increasingly became naturalized as it blanketed more of world. Indeed, the conclusions many sailors drew while overseas worked to undercut the claims of the antebellum era's burgeoning women's rights movement. Edward Upham, aboard the clipper *Great Republic*, wrote to his friend Charles, in Portland, Maine, detailing events in China. "Fifteen hundred miles from my Port," he began, and "yet I never before felt a stronger attachment for my *Country* than now." The "contrast is striking," marveled the mariner; "Yankeedom, with all its faults is without doubt the greatest–*dom* . . . that exists." And women inspired this patriotic discourse. The Chinese "are a funny set, as you ever saw," for "the men have as many wives as they can pay for, & the females will all *screw*, if they can get a chance." The "degraded females," of course, "yielded themselves" to those "who treat them like human beings," for unlike the United States, women in China "have no position [and] are mere slaves to the native lords and husbands." American patriarchal structures received reinforcement from abroad when the republic's male citizens became invested in fantasies of their own magnanimity and their nation's greatness, intertwined as each was with the supposed "better treatment" women enjoyed at home.[49]

Murphy McGuire, for instance, aboard the *Sunbeam* at Celebes, in the East Indies, observed femininity there for just one day before remarking that "American women were the most pampered and cared for in the world." Sailor Solomon Davis, at Montevideo, remarked on the unhappiness of the women he saw there and concluded that "the contrast between the sweet souls of Americans and other countries" must cause any reasonable person to "feel every day a greater regard and affection for" his country. A counterpart in the navy commented at Rio de Janeiro on the comparatively confined existence of Brazilian women: "by this manner of raising young ladies," he thought, "they have no confidence in there own virtues as the ladies of our country do." Philander Chase observed that "the ladies we saw on shore appeared so different from the fair ones of our own nation that I could hardly believe them the same sort of being." "How happy," he exclaimed, "that the beauties of our own America are yet so far [from them]." These men assured themselves that when American women were compared to their counterparts elsewhere, they were hardly in a position to complain. Time overseas invalidated the grievances women articulated at Seneca Falls and elsewhere by implicitly teaching some men that women in the United States had advantages their counterparts abroad did not. Maritime travel may have broadened horizons in some literal sense, but it could also curb men's receptivity to their countrywomen's critiques about constricted political or economic opportunities at home. How else to read Thomas Dudley's comments while ashore at a Japanese island, where, noticing that women were "doing all the drudgery," he penned a letter home asking readers to "think of this ye 'women's rights' women of America, and be very thankful with your present lot, and that you are not in Okinawa."[50]

The casual disinterest in the opposite sex a sailor named J. Ross Browne exhibited seems emblematic, though, of what underlay many of the observations made by the maritime community abroad, namely that most men did not find much different, and thus interesting, to say about the diversity of women they encountered. Registering his disgust with the standard of beauty among Swahili men in East Africa, Browne nonetheless admitted that while obesity was preferred on that strange continent, this was not so different, in a relative sense, from the equally arbitrary forms that attracted American men to their mates. Moreover, the fixation of African women on the trinkets handed out by sailors seemed to him similar to the admittedly finer but essentially similar "gewgaws" that fascinated ladies in the United States. Indeed, as mariner Charles Erskine smirked while in Singapore, the women were "very fond of shopping, a favorite amusement I find with the fairer sex the world over." Of course, when Erskine entered marketplaces, he did so to trade; women, on the other hand, were responsible for the more frivolous art of "shopping." Sailors' supposed cosmopolitanism could actually lead to some fairly retrograde conclusions about women's role in society.[51]

"Women are the same all over the world," Browne boldly, if contemptuously, concluded. "I have discovered that fact, at least, and that much information has been added to my stock of knowledge." So blunt a statement may have been obvious enough to other seamen that it did not warrant mention. Women simply amounted to little, perhaps because men began their voyages with a dismissive attitude toward the opposite sex and did not discover anything overseas to overturn such assumptions. The disdain

Browne expressed for what he discovered to be the *universal* failings of women differed very little from the *specific* shortcomings hinted at by other mariners in particular ports and places. Sailors on the whole assured themselves that as men, they at least had something in the way of superiority over half of the world's population. Interestingly, though, these epiphanies often derived from what was termed a trade in "trinkets" between sailors and women. It was a brisk business that preoccupied many others in the American maritime community and informed their impressions about the wider world.[52]

Chapter 6

Making Do at the Margins
of Maritime Empire

"Sam dont never get it in your head to come to sea as long as you can get your bread on shore." Walter Brooks offered this piece of advice to his brother Samson in 1850, halfway through a voyage into the Pacific. Writing to his family in Rochester, New York, from locations around the globe, Brooks titillated relations at home with stories of adventure abroad, all the while insisting that no one should repeat the mistake he made in shipping out. "I think if I was in america again I cood go to work and be contented," the mariner continued, "but it is no use growling now I will go bout with it if I can." It was not much later, though, that matters began to brighten slightly. "I have been sorry a great many times," Brooks refrained, "but I begin to like it better now." A sense of resignation pervaded all the reluctant wayfarer wrote, but the voyage, he suggested, was not without its few pleasures.[1]

The island of Fayal, in the Azores, became the first of several stops the *Gladiator* visited as it roamed the ocean. There, "only the captins boat went ashore," but that did not prevent Brooks from getting a look at the archipelago's Portuguese inhabitants, for "the natives come to the ship with boat loads of apples and grapes figs lemons chese the best chees I ever eat I tell you." The details of the local economy became his particular fascination. He was amused by the sight of men "trading close and knives for fruit some of the sailors traded half there close away fore fruit we cood get a bushel of fruit for an old jack knife." Weeks of near-putrid ship's stores had made the sailors wild to exchange what they owned for fresh provisions. Yet Brooks also marveled at the items a person might acquire abroad for what seemed to him a pittance. Rusted tools and shredded clothing befitting a trash heap at home somehow bought bushels of prime produce in more distant places. Understandings of economic value that American men grew up with were repeatedly overturned by their experiences in the marketplaces that sprang up around the world to cater to itinerant mariners.[2]

Brooks fixated on what could be bought and what it could be bought for. At the Society Islands in March 1851, he gushed that "we come to ankor and . . . got oranges and cocoanuts and all cinds of fruit there the natives are verry frindly." Moreover, the sailor "liked there manner of trading": "they come abord in there canoes as thick as hops with a basket full of fruit and ask you to bee there friend all the pay they wanted or got was an old shirt or something of the cind." The praise he offered the natives was tied to the willingness of indigenous peoples to exchange often and exchange fairly. In Brooks's mind, this meant acquiring exotic goods for what seemed to him mere trifles. His inability to comprehend the very tangible worth of sailor "discards" to local economies in Atlantic and Pacific islands reflects the one-dimensional ethnocentrism of Anglo-American valuations. Yet it was precisely those notions of value that shaped many intercultural interactions overseas.[3]

Praise for—or denunciation of—a particular place often hinged on the quality of exchange relations between commercially minded sailors and a no less commercially minded shoreside community. Walter Brooks was by no means the only mariner who scrupulously observed how goods changed hands around the world, and a survey of oceanic manuscripts provides valuable evidence of the microeconomic behavior of ordinary men buried beneath the macroeconomic thrust that was antebellum American commercial expansion overseas. Sailors' journals and letters provide a way to discover how the material goods of nineteenth-century Americans crossed international lines. In the impromptu markets that formed on the decks of ships at anchor and the cross-cultural bartering in port city bazaars, American men overseas found cause to interact, collaborate, and also dispute with the greater part of humanity. Indeed, it was individual trade that often brought working men abroad into closest contact with other peoples.[4]

Most scholarship on the development of overseas markets for American produce, however, focuses on the goods ships carried rather than the sailors who carried the goods. The gospel of commerce marshaled vessels and sailors to promote American prosperity, but what trade those ships conducted was measured in figures found in treasury rolls and balance sheets. To the extent that transnational economic interchange has been noticed, it has been either a story told from the perspective of the success or failure of merchants and brokerage firms or as a tale that measures middle-class consumption. Ideologies of domesticity and empire, meanwhile, have been shown to intersect in households that imported the exotic objects, foods, and fashions sailors shipped home. Transnational contact zones were fostered in the parlors and dining rooms where Americans literally "bought into" empire. But this emphasis on bourgeois ornamentation and the economic dealings of elites neglects the largest community of traders and consumers in any particular port: mariners and the relatively poor people they interacted with in coastal cities.[5]

As Tongan anthropologist Epeli Hau'ofa has observed, "Views of the Pacific from the level of macroeconomics and macropolitics often differ markedly from those at the level of ordinary people." The same lesson can be extended to the world's many maritime exchange districts. Neither Walter Brooks nor the Portuguese and Polynesians he bartered with cared very much about what the ship *Gladiator* carried in her cargo hold; they were there to buy and sell from one another. Businessmen, commercial agents, and their prosperous customers were not the only individuals who constructed consequential exchange networks in the eighteenth and nineteenth centuries. Seafarers also traded actively across the same oceans, and those smaller-scale economic relations were the primary means by which the majority of the globe's inhabitants came to engage commercially with Americans. Those many thousands of transactions were not measured in terms of tonnage or GDP.[6]

As clerks in government offices and merchants in exchange houses calculated one type of economic rationale to organize the world into sources of profit, sailors traded for the gratification of more immediate, subsistence-oriented needs. Maritime workers in the United States, after all, were consistently counted in the ranks of the working poor. As some of the most underprivileged wage laborers within port city communities, seamen were often only seasonally employed and at all times highly vulnerable to the frequent contractions of the business cycle. To help alleviate poverty's worst effects, therefore, they used a diverse set of subsistence strategies that historians refer to as the "economy of makeshifts," or, more evocatively, "scraping by." This usually involved some combination of bartering, pawning, pilfering, and other stopgap measures meant to prevent cash shortages and ensure survival. And, quite naturally, American mariners who went abroad expected to use those same subsistence strategies in order to provide themselves access to the comforts and pleasures waterborne work otherwise denied. To do so, they tapped into the informal economies of the Atlantic and Pacific. Thousands of American arrivals thus enlarged the size and scope of extant underground exchange networks. Even as the cargo these vessels carried integrated the republic into a global commercial matrix, sailors assured simultaneous American assimilation into alternative sub-economies that thrived just below the surface of mercantile capitalism.[7]

The systems of subsistence that American workers and individuals overseas practiced thus became inextricably intertwined. At times, these small-scale exchange relations functioned smoothly, ensuring ready access to food, drink, entertainment, and shelter. At other moments, sailors attempting to "scrape by" overseas came into conflict with peoples who had very different ideas about the behavior that undergirded "proper" economic interconnection. Tensions ran particularly high when truck devolved into outright robbery. Those episodes appeared with greater frequency across the nineteenth century. As voyages became longer and more exacting, as sailors' wages decreased, and as peoples around the globe showed increasing familiarity with and thus skill at swindling seamen, maritime laborers exhibited less patience for formal economic interactions and elaborate trade protocols. Instead, they more quickly and readily resorted to cheating or theft. The ever-more-dire economic straits of the American maritime community fused with hardening racial attitudes to legitimate larceny.

Those conflicts in turn jeopardized much larger international economic structures, destabilizing the predictability merchant capitalism thrived on. This became self-perpetuating: as traders protected proceeds by squeezing sailors, sailors acquired necessaries ashore by resorting to the unsavory means that consuls deplored and that menaced macroeconomic structures. What observers often failed to realize, however, was that the two economies—of sailor subsistence and business yields—were two sides of the same coin. One can neither be disentangled from nor understood without the other. The "respectable" realm of warehouses, counting rooms, and tastefully appointed middle-class homes was intimately connected to the "disreputable" dealings of mercantile capitalism's underground economic sphere. The latter was a murkier world of makeshifts—a shadow economy cast by the glow of gold that shipping firms amassed. Histories of nineteenth-century economic expansion thus remain incomplete so long as they fail to document the people who were making do at the margins of maritime empire, men and women whose labor underwrote the antebellum merchant marine's meteoric rise to global prominence. The history of burgeoning commodity chains that increasingly connected the United States with the wider world across the nineteenth century cannot be understood in isolation from the economic lives of waterborne workers who crafted them.[8]

While seafaring was a waged occupation, it necessitated living for long periods of time without ready money. Payment for the voyage did not usually occur until its termination, at which point ship owners carefully deducted the cost of clothing and provision sailors had purchased from the vessel's stores. Likewise, while captains doled out spending money to the crew for liberty in a foreign port, the amount was kept deliberately small in order to discourage desertion. Pocketfuls of coins, after all, made flight a more tangible possibility for disgruntled men. Impoverished members of an underclass who required creative coping strategies at home, seamen were practiced in the sort of extemporization needed to engage economically with the wider world.[9]

Sometimes a wardrobe became a source of income. William Stetson wondered at sailors going ashore, "receiving a dollar a day," yet still managing "to spend five times that amount." He found the answer to that mystery at Talcahuano, Chile, where "coats, pants, shirts, chests, and every other article for which there is any demand [were] disposed of, furnishing the cash for another 'time.'" Later, at Tumbes, Peru, Stetson said that sailors "falsified the saying that 'money is the root of all evil,'" given their ability to scrape by without cash. Another group of sailors at the Cape Verde Islands, finding "money rather scarce among us," quickly "exchanged our blue jackets for Spanish dollars." With their outerwear stripped, "all hands were ready for a bust." That included hiring donkeys for a trek through the countryside, purchasing "pockets full of figs and fruits," and a surprising degree of self-control: "the Captain said he was very much pleased indeed to find us all sober." Having sold their coats in Cape Verde, the men moved on to sell their "red flannel shirts, tobacco, knives, shoes &c parts of their outfit" on arriving in Rio de Janeiro. They understood the relative worth of these articles: "red flannel will sell here for $3 or $4 dollars shoes for the same." They went into a store and "immediately commenced bargaining for our articles which was soon finished to the satisfaction of both parties."[10]

Most seaports of any appreciable size spawned cottage industries to cater to the needs of seamen who were converting their attire and other personal possessions into cash. They took the shape of what one American mariner in New Zealand called "a house of entertainment for the sailors," where men had "money advanced to us at the rate of five dollars per day . . . together with twelve and one half percent interest." But the strategies sailors implemented to survive economically while abroad were familiar to them; they had honed such tactics at home. In Hong Kong, Alonzo Sampson was reminded of Boston's rougher economic districts. "The shops of the natives are small," he reckoned, and "over every door is the stereotyped and everlasting sign, 'Cheap John,' which sometimes reminded me of the sign 'Cheap Cash Store,' so often met with at home." "The shop keepers," Sampson continued, "like the Jews in some of our cities, hail every sailor that passes with a formula something like this: 'Come in John; every ting got, John.'" He meticulously catalogued what he paid for various articles and the value of the items sailors redeemed for ready money: "A fine pair of silk pants, $2; vest of the same material, $1.50; fine linen shirts, $1; shoes for 50 cents, and not bad shoes either."[11]

Journals make clear that sailors had a well-developed understanding of what sold where and for how much, not to mention interest rates associated with short-term lenders and pawnbrokers. Specific colors and cuts of cloths brought an understood price, and no doubt the business was transacted so swiftly and agreeably because the parties were familiar with the arrangement. Relationships of mutual dependence sprang up around the globe between working-class American men and local brokers who pawned and loaned to laboring men who did not have the letters of credit that sustained wealthier travelers. The travel narratives and maritime memoirs of officers and genteel passengers were littered with lavish details about elaborate entertainments local notables arranged for them. They danced, drank, and cavorted just as often as ordinary seamen did, but they could expect such hospitality as a mere matter of course, as a courtesy extended by their peers and business partners overseas. Mariners desired those same types of pleasure, of course, but they scrimped and scrambled to accumulate the necessary capital for them. Pilfered ship's stores or old clothing became collateral at port city pawnshops, barrooms, and boarding houses. On second glance, the men who were derided by skeptical observers as improvident—consumed by a "spirit of prodigality and wastefulness," in one scold's words—seem fairly shrewd in their capacity to calculate the exchange rates of items that crossed international lines. Employers who paid sailors paltry sums seemed surprised when waterborne workers "wasted" their wardrobes and personal effects on port city "trifles." For seamen, however, this was a coherent strategy they used to supplement the food, drink, and shelter that was provided for them on board.[12]

Sailors simply enlisted a set of skills that was unknown to those unfamiliar with what it meant to scrape by. Bourgeois observers alternately excoriated and romanticized mariners as men who lived carefree lives unburdened by the worries that weighed down society's more responsible members. Closer attention to sailor journals, however, shows a very different picture from the stereotype of the blithe seaman who disregarded tomorrow for the pleasures of today. In fact, careful calculation and self-discipline dictated most sailors' behavior, as with the working poor more generally. Plans for remaining solvent while abroad often began early in a voyage. When John Martin, for example, stepped aboard the ship *Lucy Ann* in 1842 he didn't even know the difference between stem and stern. But his new shipmates urged him to forget about the vessel's rigging; he would, they explained, himself need to "get rigged . . . with a supply of Tobacco; side combs, & handkerchiefs to trade for fruit & other articles." Skeptical at first about the initial outlay, the mariner noted that when his ship anchored at the Azores, tobacco functioned wonderfully as a means to earn friends overseas. "As soon as the boat touched the beach we were surrounded by the Portuguese white yellow & black, with you have tobacco, I have orange you trade me I trade you."[13]

Figure 9. Azorean marketplace. The shadow economy of the maritime empire consisted of the sort of small-scale trading, bartering, pawning, and pilfering that is taking place along the waterfront in Fayal, Azores, in this image drawn by an American sailor. "Azorean marketplace," from the journal of an anonymous sailor, kept aboard the ship *Sea Ranger*, n.d. Courtesy of the New Bedford Whaling Museum, Catalog #2001.100.4557.

N. Byron Smith also remarked on the particular importance of tobacco in securing goodwill abroad. While preparing to leave New York, Smith, "not being addicted to the use of that article," initially refused to stock up on the sot-weed. Conversation with some of the crew changed his mind. After the men told Smith that it "could be traded off to very good advantage in exchange for fruit, shells, and other curiosities [among] the natives of the Pacific islands," he purchased four or five pounds of Virginia leaf. Alonzo Sampson similarly discovered nicotine's role in sustaining the shadow economy. "We had no money," he (and other impoverished mariners) often complained, "but tobacco was a lawful tender, and for one pound we could buy a peck of figs, basket and all, or one hundred oranges." Other useful items were similarly described by seafarers as essential components of proper maritime equipage. Often, whatever could be safely stolen from a vessel's cargo hold would be dragged ashore and sold in the informal markets that operated alongside large-scale commercial trade. Admiralty court dockets were littered with prosecutions for theft aboard ship, suggesting the regularity of the practice and the sense that many sailors believed small-scale robbery to be a legitimate claim on employers who paid their workers poorly. Depositions show everything from bags of cocoa in Bordeaux, a ship's chickens in Liverpool, to (perhaps unwisely) the captain's coat in the South Pacific, all taken and sold in nearby underground economies. Local inhabitants appear to have seamlessly integrated such items into their daily economic lives. Or so thought one diarist who helped shipmates roll a small barrel of valuable whale oil ashore at Maui. Surreptitiously acquired, the stuff was "retailed out in small quantities and for it we obtained a large quantity of pumpkins, watermelons, musk melons, grapes, sugar cane, turkeys, ducks, hens, &c." Native Hawaiians seemed unsurprised by the sight of sailors operating an impromptu stand and were eager to deal: "Our immediate vicinity was thronged with Kanakas in a moment, all anxious to buy but still desirous of making a good bargain." The enthusiasm for such exchange is understandable, given the substantial price reductions of illegally supplied items, sans import duties and transshipment fees.[14]

The regularity of the shopping or stealing of mariners suggests the creation of niche markets very precisely oriented to the exchange of particular goods. Residents abroad knew what to demand of American seamen and what products interested the sailors. Seafarers seemed no less attuned. Smith's shipmates assured him a "very good advantage" should he follow their lead in procuring stores, while Albert Peck's fellow crew members alerted him to the fact that Cape Verdeans "could get no tobacco therefore we would find a ready sale for it." Maritime workers were often no less commercially minded than the men who owned the companies that employed them, but they were accustomed to very different definitions of commerce than those that drove macroeconomic dealings. This accounts for the differences of opinion about what U.S. travelers saw at places like the Azores: merchants saw poverty driven by indolence, while seamen like Sampson, tapping into the underground economy, believed that the "people of the place drive a thriving trade with sailors and whalemen at their stands in the streets, where they sell fruits and little articles of home manufacture."[15]

Before voyages began, seamen instructed one another about which goods were best suited to foreign markets and individual "advantage." Additionally, they informed each other about the very specific protocols that existed regarding how best to approach trade with residents in distant places. These discussions read like roadmaps, describing key developments that enabled sailors to gauge success in dealing with unknown persons. Sailors emerged from locations overseas educated in the economic customs of a place and desiring to remember particular lessons for future reference and the edification of shipmates. For example, William Speiden declared it "a general rule in dealing with the Chinese, to offer them about one half the amount they ask you and never buy more than one article from one store if you do." By "buying one thing from one shop, you are very apt to get a good bargain," he argued. William Clark thought the natives in Singapore were "characterized for their expertness in making a bargain." They would, "unless you are perfectly acquainted with their mode of dealing, charge you four fold for an article." He warned, "Keep your eyes open [or] you will be cheated in spite of your wits."[16]

Sailors' journals and letters reveal populations who used intercultural encounter to instruct one another in the etiquette of exchange. Whether a seaman was at a South Asian storefront, a Fijian hut, or the Baltimore wharves, he had to acknowledge the specific social rituals of trade there. The global shadow economy was always mediated by varieties of local custom. Successful bargaining required a willingness to eat sometimes unpalatable meals, engage in rigorous ceremony, and remain open to the tactile experience of exchange. While at Guam swapping fish hooks for fruit, one sailor complained of the native Chemoros that "once they saw that we possessed so much iron," the men became "entirely too affectionate": "too fond of embracing and rubbing noses"; that was "the very member we most desired to keep furtherest from their oiled offensive bodies." Yet the stench did not overpower his sense of humor. The natives' "talent for [finding] the most successful bidder" caused the mariner to remark that "iron has the same effect upon them as silver does upon a Yankee, it bought their friendship instantly." As he sat at a table with others in Fiji in 1851, William Myers had to decide whether or not to drink what he thought was an odoriferous native decoction that contained the saliva of several other men. When his turn came, he fretted when an interpreter told him that "the natives construed it into unfriendliness and that a refusal would only gain their ill will." Myers nonetheless reported that many "of our chaps refused to drink their fill." Myers ultimately drank and was rewarded with a meal and a more civilly disposed indigenous population. Purchasing security in their commercial relations, however, sometimes required sailors to quite literally hold their noses.[17]

Brokers often facilitated barter between those on ships and those on shore. Such go-betweens spoke the local language(s), were familiar with the markets, helped set exchange rates, and worked to prevent the degeneration of trade into conflict. Richard Cleveland's ship, anchored in Hawaii, "admitted a chief on board, who, while he kept the natives in order, and guarded us against having too many on board at a time, served us also as a broker, and very much facilitated our purchases." Edmund Gardner referred to a native he called a "shipkeeper" who assisted with trade and would clear the decks when the "Kannackas" became boisterous. When his ship anchored at a Pacific island, William Myers was approached by "a good looking fellow" who emerged from the crowd surrounding the vessel. All the natives "were anxious to secure to themselves individually a 'filende' (friend)," and soon enough, one introduced himself to Myers, repeating "my name Samuel, me you filende, you my filende." The system "was carried on all around till some of our chaps had each a dozen filendes" and in that manner "were more or less bountifully supplied with fruit according to the means of their native filendes." Another mariner at Tonga noted that "as soon as you land," the natives "throng about you, exclaiming in broken English, 'How de do my fliend? You be my fliend? Go my house, me got plenty fruit my house.'" The men exchanged tobacco for tropical produce, but "after supplying their 'immediate necessities' . . . [we] found they had stolen all our tobacco and pocket-knives." This Pacific-wide system of *taio* friendship bonds had long served to integrate outsiders and facilitate material exchange. With the arrival of Euro-Americans, it became a way for islanders to acquire manufactured goods and the status they conferred, even if some sailors saw it as nothing more than an opportunity for individuals to display their talent as "expert thieves and arrant rogues."[18]

From another point of view, though, this was how impoverished port city dwellers everywhere attempted to make ends meet. These rituals were not necessarily "exotic" or unique to Polynesia. In more developed Atlantic and Pacific ports, legions of bar owners, pawnshop proprietors, and boardinghouse keepers—a population generally referred to as crimps—helped ease a sailor's stay abroad and arrange for employment. They often spoke a pidgin English built around barter and reciprocity, a language, as one sailor had it, "picked up by intercourse with vessels." Thus Albert Peck, in the middle of the Atlantic and at an opposite end of the earth from William Myers' experience with Pacific "filendes," reported that he was approached at Fayal with an "'I Sam, s'pose you present me one old shirt no never been wore me present you one jackass cheese.'" Everyone needed a friend on the world's waterfronts, and the basic function of crimps and other brokers was in principle similar to that of the *taio*, beachcombers, and analogous intermediaries sailors interacted with at other places. Food, drink, and shelter was their provenance, and their power over sailors took the shape of debt incurred as men availed themselves of valuable services. Given the exploitative potential of any brokering relationship where seafarers felt somehow disempowered by individuals they depended on to facilitate trade, it should come as no surprise that complaints often arose. One man thought the "portagues Beech Combers" acting as go-betweens at the Gilbert Islands even "beneath the natives in principles or in fact anything else," while John Martin, at the Navigator Islands, observed that "when a ship arrives the white men flock on board they are called beach combers and a regular set of scoundrels they are." Too "lazy to work at home for a living," they preferred a life of ease, willing to "beg clothes, old trousers and [other] articles that the natives would not even touch with one of their spears."[19]

Port city crimps were no less controversial, and, indeed, they became a particular focus of nineteenth-century waterfront reform literature. One author characterized them as "land-sharks, land-rats, and other vermin" who infest "all sea-ports in the world" and "make the hapless mariner their prey." Their crime was to swindle indigent seamen and, "in the shape of landlords, bar-keepers, clothiers, and boarding-house loungers," "devour them limb from limb." But such screeds rarely did much to shrink the size or influence of the world's economic intermediaries, men and women who integrated recent arrivals into mercantile capitalism's shadow economy of survival. Rather—and as with similar objections to pawnshops, bucket shops, dolly shops (which specialized in low-value goods), and short-term lenders at home in the United States—the persistence and volume of those innumerable complaints only highlighted the necessity of underground actors to the perpetuation of larger commercial enterprises. The global network of boardinghouses for sailors proved a particularly important node for underground transactions and small-scale smuggling. Although one U.S. consul complained of the "native boarding houses for seamen at Callao, where they live when on shore, and lead careless lives as they do in all countries," carelessness was not quite how sailors saw the situation. Such places were needed sources of sustenance and scrip. So long as a "healthy" international market economy insisted on underpaying its waterborne workers, it would require the unhealthful vices associated with crimps and other intermediaries. The itinerant anonymity of seafaring life further heightened the need for such go-betweens. At home, individuals might call on friends, neighbors, or some trusted establishment for assistance. While traveling abroad in unfamiliar terrain, sailors in strange places required the guidance brokers gave.[20]

Thus, part of the working poor's work overseas was dedicated to arranging for life in foreign ports and along the intercoastal exchange networks that American vessels plied. Most common men before the mast, whether through intermediaries or by themselves, seemed able to find some method of meeting the demands of their marketplace counterparts. When seafarers stepped ashore to swap with native vendors, they connected broader systems of subsistence in place at otherwise disparate locations. The meetings at these meals, ceremonies, bazaars, and top-deck trades were negotiations between peoples who were not always similar culturally but who nevertheless were mutually accustomed to the demands of scraping by. As men and women rubbed noses, shared beverages, shook hands, and gesticulated wildly, they helped integrate the world's shadow economy of small-scale barter. By working at it, mariners could usually reach a settlement as to the value of one object versus another. From the ports of the transatlantic world to the small islands of the Pacific, mariners moved in circles where specie was rare and reasonable trades were more than acceptable. In this way, goods from disparate locales circulated around the world. Linen manufactured in the United States was redeemed in Rio for hats made there, which then found their way to the tops of heads of Fijian natives, having been exchanged for wood-carved curiosities that were stowed away, returned to America, and pawned there to make rent. Permutations of this flow of small-scale goods were endless.[21]

At Java, Jeremiah Reynolds saw that men "stripped their jackets of buttons to buy cocoanuts, chickens, and other palatable productions." Both

Figure 10. Barroom scene. Taverns and boardinghouses were among several key institutions in port cities that were instrumental in the functioning of the global shadow economy. Proprietors at these establishments provided room and board, loaned money, pawned clothing, and fenced stolen goods. This establishment in the Bay of Islands, New Zealand, hung American emblems to welcome its chief clientele, U.S. whalemen. Courtesy of the New Bedford Whaling Museum, Logbook KWM 276A.

sides seemed to feel they had made a bargain. Robert Browning, in Tahiti, noted that with islanders there, a "string of buttons is a great present, but of all baubles whale teeth are most valued by them." It "is emphatically their money," he continued, "for which they sell hogs, fowls, potatoes, and fruit."

Frederick Schley wrote home from Hawaii of "the ship surrounded by a swarm of Kanakas, each having some article for sale or barter, for which the most capricious prices or exchange were at times demanded." Perhaps "a fellow with a chicken or pig would want in exchange for it a piece of red or yellow bunting . . . and as he will not take money or anything else insted, he goes away disappointed." Others outlandishly "ask the same price for every thing they bring, without any mind of their relative value." But this was not Bedlam. Rather, this was how the maritime undereconomy functioned. Improvisation and making do contrasted with the standardization and consistency seaport merchants hoped to see in overseas markets. William Allen and his shipmates looked on as several Malay boats "came off to us bartering bannanas plantains yams sweet potatoes coca-nuts fish fowls eggs and sea shells." The sailors calculated that the natives would "give more for a rusty jack knife than they would for 10 silver dollars." Burr Kellogg discovered that New Guinea's "ignorant natives would take tobacco in trade sooner than money." An unknown diarist in Hawaii similarly remarked that "fruits, vegetables, and poultry could be purchased for a mere nothing, an old knife or an ounce of tobacco could get a fine pair of Chickens or as much fruit as would be conveniant to carry." As mariners arrived at faraway destinations, men and women felt one another out about what would work in acquiring what was wanted. Meaning usually became intelligible. In most cases, that is. David Porter misunderstood the words and gestures of fruit-bearing Nuku Hivans as a request "to have their heads and privates shaved"; it "was what they seemed most to desire," he innocently averred. Probably not, but the brisk trade he later reported meant that these individuals eventually understood one another. Behavior geared toward exchange helped disparate linguistic groups arrive at some kind of consensus.[22]

Indeed, there were moments when sailors satisfied by successful trading shed racist invective. Frank Bullen suggested as much while at the Bonin Islands, near Japan. He and his shipmates "got some food" there, "yams, and fish cooked in native fashion, for which the friendly Kanakas would take no payment." And "although they looked murderous enough to be cannibals," the natives were very obliging, suggesting to Bullen that "it does not do to go by looks always." Hospitality overcame his predisposition toward suspicion. So it was for Nelson Haley too. Byron Island in the Pacific seemed at first glance to be populated by "a surly looking lot of the blackest kind of cusses," but Haley tempered his opinion after finding chickens, vegetables, and fruit "piled up in unlimited quantities" for the sailors to enjoy. He wrote, "the natives were very peaceful, not showing any disposition to molest or steal anything." For Haley, blackness initially marked the indigenous population as suspect, but his caution was mediated by their attentiveness to the mariners' needs.[23]

When exchange relationships satisfied a seaman, a typically positive report flowed from his pen about the success of the voyage and the friendliness of a region's inhabitants. But trade relations only sharpened the prejudiced sensibilities of many other men. Often the threat of violence loomed over the economic relations of seafarers overseas because they regularly put persons their country had accustomed them to think of as racial inferiors in positions of power over white American men. An 1840 account published by a whaleman in one of his hometown newspapers, the *Boston Daily Advertiser*, spoke of Pacific islanders who contrived to steal fish hooks until the seamen used firearms to force an end to the practice. "The value of the hook was next to nothing," the man conceded, "but then we disliked the idea of being outwitted by a simple islander, and besides this, we did not like to establish a precedent to govern after cases." Such complaints inadvertently confirmed that individuals abroad were hardly "simple" but instead would work to maximize their own gains in seizing on sailors as a source of goods.[24]

The humiliation of being swindled by nonwhite vendors proved a common source of frustration for mariners abroad, threatening their self-image as members of an intellectually superior Anglo-Saxon race. John Browne remembered that after one of his shipmates was tricked into trading away a knife for an item of little value, the man became enraged. "This made him very angry," Browne understated. "I ain't going to be cheated by any dod-burned black-faced nigger no way you can fix it," the man raved. He told Browne that if only he could return to the scene of the crime with him, "he'd give that nigger a lickin' that would astonish me." Economic grievances also found racial expression in A.H. Beckett's journal as his ship traded rum and tobacco for ivory along the coast of western Africa. He spoke of his time there as exile from what constituted economic propriety. The place "would try Job's patience if he were here." It was inhabited, Beckett said, by "what I call saucy niggers," for "if you sell them a quart they want you to give them a gallon." Yet the native Africans had to be placated or they would simply stop trading with the sailors. The frustrated mariner acknowledged that fact but reiterated: "it requires the patience of Job to deal with these niggers." Journals and memoirs often became the only places where many mariners could create the sense of personal control they lacked in exchanges with uncooperative, thieving traders. The pen may not have been mightier than the sword in a literal sense, but it would have to do. Facing similar intractability in Bombay, William Rogers concluded that "I think the Hindoo a low, cheating, brutal race, but a short remove from brute creatures." Racially and commercially charged language intertwined to define entire peoples based on their economic selves. These complaints were reminiscent, however, of similarly frustrating encounters at home in the market stalls of Charleston, Baltimore, and New York operated by African American men and women and in trading posts in the west and southwest with Native Americans and Mexicans. Larger portions of the world's urban and frontier economies were sustained by supposedly "inferior" people who were repeatedly accused of disorderliness and thievishness by their white American customers. Seafarers tapped into that running discourse.[25]

The contents of a single narrative sometimes illustrated how the reputation of an environment depended to some extent on the hospitality it offered to a sailor. James Webb wrote a letter to his mother in 1845 describing the time he had spent aboard a whaleship. At the Western Islands, he was "glad to get on shore once more," as "the people seemed very kind and tried all they could to entertain us they gave us greate quantenteys of fruit grapes, figs, appels, pairs, peaches, etc." The friendly dispersal of material abundance made a positive impression. Yet the opposite proved true as well. The next stop was "Callio a port in Peru," where Webb spent three days' liberty. Unfortunately, he "did not lik the people as well as I did the Porteguise at the Weston Islands." The disparity hinged on resource availability. At the Azores, people shared with seamen. In Callao, residents helped themselves; they appeared to revel in swindling American travelers. Peru's people had little to offer the men, and the sailors offered up indignation in response.[26]

Yet mariners began to appreciate that as they interacted economically with various societies, the act of trading worked to alter local notions of value. Exchange was a dynamic process that affected all of its participants. As American maritime traffic increased across the nineteenth century, observers fretted that Pacific peoples in particular were becoming too well versed in sharp dealing. One sailor at the Caroline Islands in 1835 complained that natives there had a great talent for "selling to the most satisfactory bidder." They bargained with such avidity "as would put a New York auctioneer to the blush." The seaman expected to bask in the "simplicity" of the Pacific's natives, but instead found a population more reminiscent of urban America's notorious hucksters. Mariners had been prepared by popular culture's rendering of the region to find paradisiacal plenty, but instead they discovered people mostly scraping by. Stephen Rowan, for example, reverted to a domestic racial group to describe business abroad. In Tahiti, he marveled at the commercial acumen of the natives and mourned that "it appears to be characteristic of all Indians as soon as they learn the value of money to become intriguing in all their bargains." A mind to the main chance, he concluded, "prevails very generally among these islands." Simeon Stearns sounded off in similar fashion, fuming in the South Pacific that "I here once and for all remark that an Indian gives away nothing now a days." Another man, again in Tahiti, agreed. "They are no longer pleased with a rattle or tickled with a straw but understand the worthlessness of Toys as well as any down easter in Yankee land." The sailor admitted what others implied: through "their intercourse with us, they lost their former simplicity." Samuel Samuels, at Java, thought "the natives here had been spoiled by the Americans" because they "would no longer exchange their commodities for scrap iron and beads."[27]

Sailors struggled to determine whether or not they would benefit from the onward march of civilization. Many seamen bemoaned the higher costs for goods and savvier swapping on the part of indigenous populations that came with intercultural contact. This is not, of course, to suggest that "static" or "simple" peoples abroad were instantaneously altered by economic forces unleashed on them by sailors. Long-standing exchange networks had united the islands and coastlines of the world before American mariners arrived. But the transformative significance of sustained small-scale maritime contacts is often ignored in histories of parts of the world where missionaries receive the lion's share of scholars' attention. Yet even evangelists criticized loudly the perverse economic influence of seamen. James Watkin, stationed at an outpost on New Zealand's South Island, noted that one "objection to the Missionary is that he will make the natives too knowing, i.e., in matters of trade." But after local residents had engaged in commerce with sailors for decades, Watkin thought "my duty would be to make them less knowing, [for] if they increase their knowledge of this kind this will be a very expensive Mission indeed."[28]

Sailors were the largest population of itinerant peddlers in the world. Discerning observers among them acknowledged that local populations geared at least a portion of their economic existence toward satisfying the demands of that tertiary market. As one diarist noted at Magdalena Bay, Mexico, the "principal wealth" of the inhabitants was the "beef, milk, and cheese . . . collected to be disposed of to the whalers for flour, bread, cloth, &c." Seamen, in other words, sustained frequent, significant economic contact with peoples abroad and were in a position to measure shifts in the nature of that exchange. This did not, however, necessarily guarantee satisfaction. Most mariners seemed to prefer a world described by a whaleman named Frank Cady, where indigenous communities continued to "offer up their all to the white man as an offering to a superior being." Yet the more men traded, the less likely this became. As seafarers and coastal communities exchanged more often and locals began to specialize in swapping with maritime visitors, there was more talk in sailors' letters and journals of their difficulties with navigating the shadow economy. Familiarity did not necessarily breed contempt (though it could), but it did breed complaint about people whose "principal wealth" was increasingly tied to trade with sailors who were necessarily driving harder bargains to remain solvent. Just as much as the sailors who detailed the precise prices cloth commanded in Rio's dolly shops, people overseas knew what they could pull from mariners' pockets and strip from their ships in order to survive. So it was that seafarers abroad often seemed surprised to find only reflections of themselves. Such was Cady's impression of New Zealand, where he described the natives as a "stout robust treacherous voracious gluttinous naked set of wretches." But the most telling observation was his last, for, above all else, he thought Maoris "regular Yankees for trade."[29]

These comments were not complimentary. As sailors bartered in the global undereconomy, the hard bargaining of other peoples around the world became a common source of complaint. This was particularly true during episodes seafarers read as outright theft. Larceny, of course, was already a contested term among the working poor of transatlantic capitalist societies, who sometimes relied on robbery as a subsistence strategy. Sailors were rarely shy about raiding the cargo holds of their own vessels in order to supplement their meager incomes. But the definition of "thievery" achieved greater complexity abroad. What sailors frequently denounced in some places as theft was likely understood by perpetrators as a legitimate claim on the social obligations of visitors. Nevertheless, that misunderstanding generated hostility. As Secretary of the Navy James Paulding warned the nation's merchant fleet in 1836, the "most common cause of collision with civilized visitors is the offence and punishment of theft." Wanting western goods yet "unacquainted with or possessing but vague ideas of property rights," people of "uncivilized" nations readily resorted to robbery. "Treachery is one of the invariable characteristics of savages and barbarians," he ominously concluded, "and very many of the fatal disasters which have befallen preceding navigators, have arisen from too great a reliance on savage professions of friendship." Aware of the foundational nature of property rights to American notions of propriety, Paulding *encouraged* seafaring men to equate a failure to respect those rights with savagery. A distrust of peoples who were unaccustomed to interchange based on western notions of property rights thus emanated from the office of the chief public officer responsible for the nation's maritime affairs.[30]

The reports of mariners reflected the western, U.S.-based viewpoint the navy secretary exhibited. Thomas Harris claimed that Marquesan islanders "are addicted to pilfering, a crime common to all savage tribes." A chagrined Milo Calkin also noted that multiple Marquesans "succeeded in carrying off several articles which we were never able to regain." Despite sailors' efforts to "conceal everything about the ship," local residents would "steal everything they could get hold of." It might have been that the shoreside community sought something like compensation for a banquet thrown earlier in honor of the ship's company, "the stinking fumes" of which had caused the sailors to beat a hasty retreat. Byron Smith remembered Tahitians as "very thievish"; while aboard, the men were required to "watch them narrowly." William Silver, cruising through the Pacific on a whaling voyage, described several different peoples as "willing to steal anything they can lay their hands on weather they know the use of it or not." George Attwater complained that "when our lads got on shore" at Hawaii, "the natives began to steal there clothes and they thought it best to make there way back on board." Protests to the local authorities and several missionaries accomplished nothing, and when the ship sailed away, the mariner could not but rejoice to be "lieving behind a pack of as big thieves and sassy roagues as ever I fell in with." Attwater and his fellow crew members were not able to walk freely among local residents without literally losing the shirts off their backs, and Attwater's retreat into invective revealed the vulnerability of some American seamen ashore.[31]

U.S. sailors in many parts of the world complained of thievery. One unknown diarist aboard the *Samuel Appleton* at Canton described the deck "crowded with Chinese who come on board to trade," but he was wary, noting that "they are the most expert thieves." Visiting the same port only a few months earlier, another sailor remarked that he was always "glad to get away from the crowd" there, especially "a Chinese crowd half lepers, and the rest thieves." Another sailor described the residents of Singapore as a race of "expert thieves," after noting the ship's steward's loss of several articles. Washington Chase was surprised to find even women capable of pillage. While in Coquimbo, Chile, he spoke to the ship's steward, who related how the captain ordered him to "keep a sharp look-out that the ladies do not make free with the knives and forks, the table and tea-spoons, and in fact any thing that is convenient to be carried away." While the mariner expected to discover the "lower class of citizen . . . given to lay violent hands upon what is not theirs," these were "ladies of high-standing." It astonished him to find an entire "society given to purloining." William Phelps did not rate Sydney any higher, claiming that he "looked upon the people as a set of piratical thieves, with whom it was dangerous to have anything to do." At least that was his impression after wandering a city populated by "loafers in general, not pursuing any particular calling," who waited "for something to turn up which brought game to their nets, and especially on the watch for a ship's crew on liberty." Seamen, their prey, were "taken to a by-place, stripped to their nether garments, and left to get to their ship as best they could." Another sailor thought predatory practices common wherever sailors congregated. Men who went ashore, as a rule, "were generally stripped, not only of their money, but the most of their clothes, and so had to be brought on board most pitiable objects, with some old rags of clothing, black eyes, bloody noses, and cut heads."[32]

Perhaps Phelps misspoke, however, when labeling such men loafers. His remarks shed light on a shadowy subeconomy where entrepreneurs converted the pilfered personal effects of mariners into cash at stalls whose proprietors then resold them. It was not quite right to accuse these individuals of practicing no "profession." Exchange zones became the sources of a good deal of wealth not only for merchants but also for fences who dealt in a specific trade in goods appropriated from the bodies of seamen. Residents of foreign ports, in fact, viewed sailors as ideal targets for plunder precisely because their lack of local knowledge made them vulnerable. Often unable to speak the language and faced with local authorities hostile to "unruly" maritime populations, itinerant Americans suffered countless attempted robberies as an occupational hazard. Observers who saw sailors shedding their clothes for ready money declared it improvident and thoughtless behavior. Seamen no doubt saw it as an insurance policy: if ports crawled with people willing to stupefy the mariner's "every sense with liquor, rob him of his wages, and strip him of his only jacket," then why not sell first for something rather than awake later with nothing? Disgruntled seafarers naturally complained about thievery, but for other peoples around the globe (including in American ports) this iniquity was an industry that fed families. Petty crime presented an opportunistic solution to poverty, particularly during seasonal slack times.[33]

Reports reiterated the regularity of robbery, and those descriptions suggest patterns and stratagems deployed by integrated criminal networks hoping to profit from sailor itinerants. Thomas Bennett, carpenter aboard a

Nantucket whaleship, wrote of Valparaiso's people that "it is unsafe to walk the streets by night, [for] they will take the clothes from one's back if they see an opportunity." Roving gangs hunted down "foreigners assembled at a tavern in the evening, [worked] to excite a quarrel, and [hoped] to shed blood." Thomas Roe, a foremast hand aboard the New London ship *Chelsea*, felt fortunate to escape from Paita, Peru, with his life. While on a stroll to see the sights of the town, he was "seized by four men who took all my money shoes neck hankerchef" and then "threatened to stab me if I made any resistance." A pair of runaways from the ship fared no better, "being robbed of all they had" and then "seized by the spanyards, who claimed a reward of 30 dolls." Twenty-five years later, Robinson Warren did not find things much improved in Peru. "In Callao were gathered perhaps as fine a collection of gallows birds as ever were collected in one spot on earth." It was "a delightful spot," Warren sarcastically declared, where the residents "luxuriated in utter lawlessness [and] indulged in the pleasant little excitements of throat-cutting and robbery." He urged a sailor not to think "of moving around at night without having the handle of his revolver in a position to grasp at a moment's notice." Such episodes occurred with enough regularity to be recounted in the shanties seamen sang to pass time or ensure coordinated labor during tasks that required cooperation. The popular tune "Maggie May," for example, spoke of a sailor ashore in port: "Next morn when I awoke, I found that I was broke / No shoes, nor shirt, nor trousers could I find / When I asked her where they were, she said, 'My dear young sir, / They're down in the Park Lane pawn-shop, Number Nine.'" This and other songs make abundantly clear the systemic nature of such swindling, not to mention the larger undereconomy it perpetuated. In matter-of-fact terms, the eponymous swindler makes clear that this was nothing personal; it was a simple matter of the regular business conducted with local establishments that traded in discards, odds, and ends.[34]

The meaning of what constituted "theft" changed as sailors crossed the cultural divide. Those who targeted seafarers were using their relationships with local pawnshops and dolly shops to ensure their own survival or, perhaps, were simply extracting what they considered a just price for hospitality offered to recent arrivals. Some newspaper accounts seemed to acknowledge the mutable meaning of "larceny." In a story circulated through several New England newspapers, a Nantucket shipmaster wrote home about the "entirely friendly" and "peaceable dispositions" of those who inhabited the "Islands of the Pacific." But "if there is one thing they have a predisposition for more than another, it is to appropriate their neighbor's goods to their own use." The flaw, however, ought to be pardoned, because "they do the thing with such apparent innocence, that one could almost forgive them for taking a marlinspike or hatchet without leave." But where officers might be prepared to forgive and forget, others were not. The grievance of many ordinary men overseas was that few (if any) mechanisms existed to ensure either fair dealing or the return of purloined property. This was particularly irritating for waged workers because the "harmless" theft shipmasters reported on often hit sailors hardest. The ship's stores, harpoons, tools, and other such goods native Pacific islanders or Italian longshoremen stole were likely insured and the costs reimbursable. But when individuals stole clothing or personal effects from seamen, the items were simply gone, taken from poorly paid men with little to spare. In addition, Americans laboring abroad discovered that whatever constabulary and consular forces existed were there largely to protect shipping interests, not personal effects.[35]

Some crews hedged against these losses and misfortunes overseas by pooling their resources; in effect, the men formed what historians of the early republic have referred to in other contexts as "housefuls." These were combinations of individuals—both kin and fictive kin—who associated with and assisted one another in order to mitigate the risks associated with adverse economic climates. When observers romanticized the seaman as someone who would "divide his little stock of worldly goods with some ill-furnished acquaintance" or "give away his last shirt to an utter stranger," they actually documented a more widespread subsistence practice among those clinging to the bottom rungs of the economic ladder. It was sometimes necessary for sailors to craft mutually sustaining relationships with at least some shipmates. Middle-class traveler Charles Nordhoff thought the sailor's "last dollar goes as easy as his first," for custom required him to "treat the crowd" to food and alcohol. "So the money goes," and he who "was a gentleman for a day, is a nigger for the next six months." But seafarers themselves rarely described such behavior as irrational; they saw it as a coping mechanism. The pressure to pool resources could be considerable. William Phelps described how "at a sailor boarding-house" in Sydney, men were expected to "keep up our end of the table in every respect, or appear mean." But it was harder for men of precarious means to forgive thievish antics, no matter how innocent the perpetrator's intentions. As a result, one often finds sailors using much harsher language to describe foreign peoples and places than merchants or traders, who were generally more secure in their persons and property. Wealthier observers wagged their fingers over the seeming obstinacy of seafarers' efforts to protect their miniscule property

or their proclivity for engaging in roguish schemes and swindles, but behind such scolding was a certain ignorance about how the underground
economy functioned.[36]

Instead of ruminating about the systemic interdependency of mercantile macroeconomies and "degenerate" shadow economies, well-heeled
observers instead either fixated on the supposedly quaint and quirkily
anti-capitalistic behavior of sailors or warned about how what they called
petty crimes jeopardized larger commercial connections. Wealthy traveler
J. Ross Browne recounted an episode in Madagascar in which the crew
of a whaleship refused to compensate Malagasy vendors, instead forcibly
ejecting them from the ship. As the foremast hands explained to him, this
"was a mode of cheating the natives as common in practice as in theory,"
so common that it became an expression often used in maritime journals,
"paying with the fore-top sail," which meant hoisting anchor and fleeing
one's financial obligations. Charles Erskine, another mariner, recounted that
he and his shipmates intentionally ran up debts with Chinese creditors,
knowing full well that they would never be paid once their ship left port.
Thus, the "bills were squared by the foretop sails, as Jack before the mast has
it." But the habitual and widespread nature of such trickery worried conscientious whalemen. "Such examples will invariably be followed" by native
peoples themselves, Browne lamented, "for where the vices of civilized life
are sown, there they will grow."[37]

One naval officer clearly felt that this prediction had been realized
throughout the Pacific, given the "rascally practices of American whalemen" who touched at places such as Tahiti. There, islanders were "not
disposed to accommodate merchant ships with refreshments owing in a
great measure to" repeated robberies. "I regret to know," he sighed, "that
American whalers are the most common perpetrators of these unhuman
customs." Another observer, this time in Japan, also spoke in a saddened
tone of ordinary sailors at Hakodate "going up and down the streets to
take whatever they came across" and then "march down to the boats with
[their] booty." When local merchants responded by shutting down all trade,
the American lamented that such stealing "tended to create an increased
distrust of us." The events that led to that reluctance to exchange on the
part of swindled natives besmirched the nation's reputation. In addition,
such behavior threatened the viability of a commercial sector that was dependent on the goodwill of peoples overseas for the repair and resupply
of its ships. As the nineteenth century progressed, both sailors and consuls
moving through the world reported escalations in violence between the

maritime community and local populations. Many of these incidents were tied to local residents' increasing savvy about trade, and ships operating with thin profit margins that resorted to unfair practices in response. U.S. naval forces, for instance, assaulted the Fijian island of Waya Levu in 1858 after the murder of two American sailors, Louis Bauer and Henry Homer. This retaliation, however, originated in a dispute between local residents and the two men over a single bottle of coconut oil that had been swapped in small trade.[38]

Newspapers reported on these trends as worthy of documentation and comment. Much like officers and consuls, media outlets scolded sailors as swindlers whose shenanigans imperiled more consequential revenue streams. One 1855 account submitted to the Honolulu *Friend*, for example, discussed barter between American whalemen and the natives of an island east of Fiji. The islanders might have been "the most hideous looking wretches I ever beheld," began the correspondent, but that did not excuse the schemes of the schooner's crew to cheat them. By the end of the vessel's stay, a massive outlay of yams, hogs, and hens had been brought aboard for little in return, leaving this eyewitness to scold that if the men "ever had any conscience, it had little to do in trade with the natives of Horne Island." The *Worcester Gazette* seemed no less troubled by reports from several sailors that attested to similar stunts at Easter Island. "After receiving the various fruits which the natives were able to furnish them with," the ship simply departed, "which was likely to be attended with serious consequences to the next visitors." And, sure enough, the next visitors reported being "attacked with showers of stones from slings . . . with such violence as to nearly kill the Captain." In 1846, the *New-York Observer* detailed the bloody fate of eleven sailors aboard the ship *Sisters* under the headline "Massacres of Seamen in the South Seas." In what was labeled "a disputed barter transaction," the men were killed after a Fijian chief objected to having been whipped with a rope's end. Sensationalistic stories about the Pacific consisting of gruesome violence and, naturally, cannibalism—on this day "four were cooked and eaten"—had long sold papers and perpetuated stereotypes.[39]

Yet these accounts ignored many others that examined the conduct of tertiary economic traffic for clues about how more consequential contacts could be sustained. There were lessons to be learned in the parlors, drawing rooms, and offices where these newspapers piled up, namely, that untrustworthy and undisciplined men sent to trade would not succeed. Seamen served as connective links between the republic and the world, but at the same time, they often presented the possibility of rupture. The *Observer* spelled this out when it claimed that American whalemen, "white deserters on the island," had "urged the natives to these cruelties." Another article entitled "Honesty is the Best Policy" sought to substantiate that maxim's truth for "those from civilized lands who go among savages for the purposes of barter and trade." The reporter's "intercourse among the inhabitants of Micronesia" brought to his attention repeated "instances of well attested fraud and meanness, which if brought before a jury of twelve honest men, would send the perpetrators to State prison." Singling out one such moment, when a man paid for provisions with shredded rope meant to mimic plugs of tobacco, the author launched into a tirade meant to illustrate the broader significance of microeconomic matters. "Think of the enmity that one such act would excite and keep alive among those savages! . . . No wonder their policy has been one of blood and murder towards to white man." And, he continued, "we might multiply examples, almost without end, of the base tricks and little meannesses, dishonest bargains and dishonorable dealings" carried out by the maritime community.[40]

More forthright observers, however, recognized that dishonesty was not a trait monopolized by a particular race, nation, or occupational cohort. Rather, the economic world seamen inherited and inhabited by the middle of the nineteenth century required all parties to approach transactions with an appropriate degree of skepticism. Each group, accordingly, acted with common sense by engaging in trade with a mind to his own advantage. What some sanctimoniously scolded as "dishonesty" was from another point of view simply the reality of what it meant to "scrape by." Merchant Joseph Osborn, for example, complained that the "capers" of sailors often sabotaged his bêche-de-mer business, but the Fijians they traded with were no better. "These savages perfectly understand the art of flattery," he explained, and "with the aid of this they coax many a green horn out of a present and then laugh in secret at his generosity." Seamen did rob Pacific peoples, but they also reported scams where Hawaiians, Maoris, and others would sell half-finished mats rolled up to look complete or hand over woven hats, only to have a confederate steal them back so they could be sold to someone on the next vessel. Angered mariners often called them "the Jews of the South Seas" or complained that they drove "as short a bargain as any Jew of Jerusalem."[41]

Frederick Benton Williams thought the Chinese in Shanghai a hard-bargaining people, "expert thieves," even, "for without coming near you apparently, they will get almost everything you have." Yet, he continued, this was no different from how sailors treated host populations: "Not that

Jack Tar is any too honest in dealing with them either." Williams told of a Chinese vendor aboard his ship who came to sell the men a few bolts of silk. Several of the prospective buyers chose instead to steal some of his wares, and when the "enraged Chinaman chased down his goods," the mariners simply pulled their knives in order to make "such physical arguments [as] sailors frequently use." Pouring salt on the wound, "poor John Chinaman, robbed, insulted, abused, licked, he returned to the main hatch only to find that his other goods had entirely disappeared." Sailors went into the world understanding—or at least learning to accept—that exchange resembled something like a war of all against all. This was a lesson they had learned both in America's rougher waterfront realms of making do and from employers who were willing to swindle their waterborne employees if possible. One could cheat or be cheated, many concluded. Williams admitted as much in claiming that both sailors and their contacts abroad stole when either, in his words, "think it safe to do so." Or, as another man expressed it while trading overseas, "two Cheats is an even Bargain." The expression, this observer noted, was something "the Vulgar say," and was the sailor's "only method to keep pace with [the] faithless villons" they transacted with. Such was the cynical variety of relativism that came to dictate small-scale exchange relations between mariners and peoples overseas by the 1850s. Though maritime observers often refused to see such similarities, the comparably strained circumstances of seamen and the individuals they traded among meant the two populations had more in common than initially met the eye. Yet that strange likeness increasingly became a source of conflict exactly because the makeshift coping strategies each deployed often placed them at odds with one another.[42]

That characterization of the global shadow economy as one defined by poor people on all sides of the color line struggling to survive—stealing, swindling, seeking small advantage—contrasts markedly with the travel narratives of merchants and officers. Only on rare occasions, after all, could seamen speak confidently of their own economic security, of advantages assured and the attendant commercial supremacy of Americans. In the hardscrabble existence of working men overseas, complaints of disadvantage, of having been taken in by the superior acumen of others, abounded. Maritime empire's scions, however, struck a different tone. Their language promised the inevitable supremacy of U.S. mercantile ventures. Yankee acquisitiveness, they saw, could swiftly conquer "indolent" individuals abroad who did not have a suitably commercial spirit. The prophets of profit rarely bothered to consider how life looked different from the bottom rung of the economic ladder. The best that many mariners ever had to say about a place was a report that men had not been robbed and fruit was cheap enough to be purchased. Those bleaker descriptions must be set beside cheery predictions of American financial prowess if we are to appreciate how seemingly separate worlds and vocabularies were actually intertwined.

George Train, an entrepreneur abroad in the 1850s, helps evoke how the merchant class seized on the language of the gospel of commerce to explain Americans to themselves. In a series of letters home from Melbourne that were printed in the *Boston Post*, Train rhapsodized about America's economically creative character. "We must introduce a sprinkling of Yankeeism here and teach the residents the meaning of dispatch!," began one missive. Peoples along the Pacific Rim lacked "the spirit that was the secret of our prosperity." Growth in the United States became the standard by which other places could be assessed: "Look at Lawrence, and Chicago, and Cincinnati, and San Francisco! Babes in the wood in the morning, but full grown men at night!" A later letter revealed an undiminished confidence in the extraordinary capacities of American endeavor. "Go where you will in the world, you can but note some indication of the energy of our people," he rejoiced. "Hang a coffee bag in that place noted for the warmth of its temperature and the morals of its inhabitants, and a Yankee will be sure to find it." It was the scale of American ambition that most impressed him. Although the U.S. mercantile community often entered markets long controlled by the representatives of other nations, "the American defies competition and laughs sneeringly at impossibilities." This being the case, it was not uncommon in ports around the world "to hear the movers of some undertaking that has been dragging its slow carcase along, remark: 'If you want to have [it] finished, you must let the Americans take hold of it.'" It all went to show, Train concluded, "that the Americans are not asleep."[43]

This was all promotional language that brought to a global context the sort of enthusiastic boosterism typically associated with the internal economic transformation attending "revolutions" in marketplaces, transportation, and communication in the nineteenth-century United States. Compare his confident pronouncements with something more ordinary such as the events related by one journal keeper aboard the ship *Concordia*, which was carrying coffee from East Africa. While the merchant master was getting rich, the bartering of the ship's sailors in the shadow economy was filled with regular shortfalls, shortcomings, and quarrels, all recorded with strange exactitude by a common ship's hand. At Mozambique, for example, local vendors came aboard to sell "potatoes and onions honey peanuts etc.," but the mariners "did not make much of trade as they were pretty sharp." Other locations proved equally frustrating. It was rare to find poor sailors who thought the world needed the sort of instruction in better bartering—that "sprinkling of Yankeeism"—that Train prescribed. In the destitute coastal districts where seafarers did business, apparently, there was already plenty of "go-ahead" spirit on display as men and women struggling to scrape by drew mariners into their own commercial schemes. Being driven hard by African marketers, all that those aboard the *Concordia* could do was condemn their counterparts as an "ugly set of men" and a "dirty filthy race." But in denouncing the hard bargaining of others, sailors implicitly deplored their own poverty.[44]

Elite members of the maritime community, meanwhile, seized upon ideas about the era of market revolution. This was not idle commentary. Colonial fantasies underpinned the repeated invocation of a specifically American antidote to underdevelopment abroad. When wealthy traveler Dan Smith stepped off his Newburyport brig in Talcahuano, Chile, around 1850 and remarked that "everything bears the mark of indolence to us Yankees, [and] in our hands the country would be fruitful," he made claims that had imperial overtones. Passengers aboard ships habitually had letters home printed in newspapers to spread speculative fever. In 1847 for example, the Salem *Register* circulated one such missive that described the Juan Fernandez Islands as a place marked by "squalid and detestable idleness" that "in the hands of skillful industry would be a very paradise." Joseph Clark, trading at Mexican-controlled California, spoke in similarly prophetic terms. He concluded on his 1842 voyage that "Yankee enterprise and the spirit and principles of the pilgrims might make this the garden of America," if only the natives were not "too indolent to cultivate the soil." Likewise, Thomas Sherman wrote in Brazil that "Rio Jainerio is not a verey pleasant place" for "the people are Ignorant and Supersticious and in Everey sens of the word a Hundrid year Behind the times of our New England." Naval officer Frederick Schley sardonically stated of Santiago, Chile, that "they are only two or three centuries behind the U.S. in every thing!" To be "behind the times" was to invite American intercession, as Mexico had learned and as Japan would soon after. This was, in the words of cultural theorists, "negative notation," emphasizing all that a particular land did *not* contain, compared to the productive capacities of civilization. The authors quoted above and many others emphasized the potential for improvement that various locales exhibited and the ability of American entrepreneurs to make those possibilities realities. In the climate in which each wrote, the United States became more and more involved in hemispheric and global politics via filibuster movements, diplomatic overtures, naval interventions, and legislative fiats.[45]

But although American merchants claimed to be "taming the savage and making safe the highway of commerce through the world," all this talk of peaceable trade, of civilization advancing at the behest of business interests, could not withstand much scrutiny. The critics of the gospel of commerce reminded readers that "peaceful" exchange often meant bloodshed. Herman Melville, a skeptic of all talk about the inherent benevolence of American economic ambition, explained that "we whites have a sad reputation among many of the Polynesians. They esteem us, with some exceptions, the most barbarous, treacherous, irreligious, and devilish creatures on earth." The sarcastic edge of a rhetorical question pinpointed the source of native disgust: "It may be a mere prejudice of these unlettered savages, for have not our traders always treated them with brotherly affection?" It was difficult to answer in the affirmative when one considered the repeated instances of ships involved in the "indiscriminate massacre upon some poor little village on the seaside—splattering the torn bamboo huts with the blood and brains of women and children, defenseless and innocent." This evocative imagery corresponded with the celebrated author's well-documented opposition to the republic's expansionist ethos, but it also tapped into similar rhetorical strands that decried the abuse of Indians, Mexicans, and others who had been steamrolled by the national juggernaut on North America's western edges.[46]

Melville saw the platitudes of the commercial class as doubly blind, for they also excused or overlooked the abuse and exploitation of seafaring laborers. His novels—from *Billy Budd* to *Moby Dick*—rarely failed to position ordinary sailors as the victims of an elite and grasping class of authority figures. *Redburn* remains most emphatic about that point. In it, the author noticed that sailors "are the true importers and exporters of spices and silks; of fruits and wines and marbles." Were they to disappear, "almost everything would stop here on earth." But even as mariners made money for others, the world's respectable people dismissively deemed them "the refuse and off-scourings of the earth." Perceptive seamen also saw the linkages between the difficult work of being poor and the fantastic wealth amassed by shipping firms. Alonzo Sampson expressed it best in describing sailors' employers as "leeches" who locked laboring men into exploitative relations of debt dependency. "The quicker a sailor spends his hard earnings," after

all, "the sooner he will be ready to ship again, and the more abject his poverty, the better terms for themselves they can get out of him." This was the
prevailing power dynamic between what Sampson called "the ruling class"
and those who scraped by. The functioning of one economy required the
destitution of another. Maritime empire's masters asked their workers to
sacrifice so that they might gain.[47]

Captains, consuls, and shippers (and men were sometimes all three at
once; the line between public service and personal gain disappeared easily
on America's saltwater frontier) complained about sailors stealing and being
stolen from and criticized more generally the disorderly market behavior
among port city underclasses. As one author disapprovingly summarized
what he called "the usual history" of mariners' lives ashore: "They go; fall
into all manner of dissipation; get drunk; are plundered; sell some of their
clothes for more drink; quarrel with the soldiers; come back with blackened
eyes; cut all kinds of antics; become rude and noisy; are thrown into the brig;
and then go about their work." Seafarers were considered backward because
they did not adhere to the accumulative ethic thought to be winning the
world for American businessmen. They rid themselves of shoes, clothes, and
personal possessions and snatched ship's goods to make ends meet; their survival abroad depended on divestment rather than investment. All that beg-
ging, borrowing, and stealing was an annoyance at best, and when it went
wrong, it had the potential to scuttle larger economic connections. But the
witnesses who bemoaned petty thievery in Atlantic and Pacific entrepôts
failed to see people filching from one another largely because they were too
poor to do much else. Observers refused to connect small squabbles over
"trash" and "trinkets" in seaside bazaars with the steady accumulation of
capital in the hands of people who "mattered." A judge advocate could with
a straight face condemn seafarers who swiped shawls worth a few rupees as
men who dishonored their nation and drew "discredit on the ship and service among strangers," even while merchants and warships collaborated to
obliterate entire villages for some act of commercial noncompliance. Such
was the hypocrisy Melville and other critics denounced.[48]

But the naysayers of maritime empire seem to have been outvoted, in
both the court of public opinion and the halls of the national legislature.
In 1846, an obscure, one-term Illinois congressman named Abraham Lincoln stood before the House and declared that his state, and America more
generally, should not rest until "she had the market of the world." When
he spoke and others seconded, they no doubt referred to the more "consequential" dealing of mercantile firms. Broad intersectional support grew

for bills intended to promote the propagation of American trade overseas. Yet the small-scale exchange sailors struck up did as much to familiarize the "market of the world" with the nation's name and products as anything Lincoln conjured. The mariner's world market did not consist of flour barrels, cotton bales, tobacco hogsheads or other U.S. exports, though. Rather, it was an undereconomy that dealt in embezzled rum, old clothing, rusted tools, and rotting fruit. And yet the nation's sailors, the overlooked engines of international exchange in nineteenth-century America, helped pave the way for the more systematic commercial penetration of later periods. The limited economic engagements of the maritime community underwrote much larger policy questions. They linked the nation to the world.[49]

But an American merchant marine that squeezed sailors, forcing them to scrape by both at home and abroad, was an unstable foundation on which to construct maritime empire. Work that was not well paid, that repeatedly shoved seamen into precarious and compromising financial situations, would not be tolerated forever. Sailor Horace Palmer, for example, quit the ocean in 1879 when he realized that after two years of hard labor, he could "expect almost if not quite nothing at the end of the voyage." Ship owners and mercantile brokers were "not the chaps that do the work, break their legs, starve by inches and lose their lives," and yet, he grumbled, they managed to "see that Jack is shorn of all the miserable pennies he earns and pocket all gains." And when in 1848 whaleman James Webb complained to his mother that "I made nothing by the voyage—the owners claimed all when we got home—and I thought I would go to sea no more," he encapsulated the grievances of a much larger class of waterborne workers. Lofty speeches proposing that the United States capture the "market of the world" did little to line the purses of those who risked more and made less as the nineteenth century progressed. Prognostications of prosperity failed to describe the makeshift markets that clothed, fed, and housed more and more of the world's population as it integrated into commercial spheres dominated by moneyed men from Western Europe and the United States. By the 1870s, white American mariners had by and large climbed down from the rigging for good, hoping to try their luck elsewhere. In their stead appeared tourists, men and women who had won out in the Gilded Age's disparate distribution of wealth and who traveled abroad not to make ends meet but to demonstrate that they had already succeeded in doing so.[50]

Epilogue

Out of the Sailor's Den, into the Tourist Trap

In his boyhood, as we have seen, Mark Twain witnessed the height of American maritime expansion. He wrote of national nautical daring and the spectacular achievements of the United States Exploring Expedition as "in everybody's mouths." Its commander, Charles Wilkes, seemed "a marvel" to him and his fellow Missourians, "for he had gone wandering about the globe in his ships and had looked with his own eyes upon its furthest corners." What Twain called the world's "dreamlands"—those "names and places which existed rather as shadows and rumors than as realities"—had been made tangible by sailors and seafaring. The nation's maritime community allowed citizens in what was then one of the young republic's remotest regions an opportunity to feel their connection to the planet and its peoples. The famed writer could not help but ecstatically expound on the magnitude of that event: "How wonderful the glory!"[1]

Writing in 1906, however, Twain acknowledged new realities. Places shrouded in "fogs and mysteries" that had been known to men and women in the United States largely through marine enterprise were by then mundane. The great humorist now proved almost dismissive of America's aquatic feats, for, as he so flippantly phrased it, "everybody visits those places now, in outings and summer excursions, and no fame is to be gotten out of it."

These ruminations capture in succinct terms a major shift in the nation's primary presence throughout the world. During the antebellum era, seafarers had been the largest contingent of Americans abroad. At the peak of maritime empire, over 90 percent of the country's foreign trade was carried in its own vessels, and those ships had been staffed by a sizeable contingent of U.S. citizens.[2]

But in large part as a consequence of the Civil War—during which American merchants filed foreign registries in an attempt to avoid Confederate raiders—far fewer national ships and sailors found themselves abroad at the turn of the new century. International trade provided a larger and larger proportion of the republic's GDP, and yet by 1900 less than 10 percent of those cargoes were carried by American ships. Seamen sought work in shoreside trades or disappeared inland. The nation's maritime "world" was now far less world-oriented. It consisted almost entirely of an internal network of rivers, lakes, and coastlines that Americans exploited to trade with one another in record volume. And in the moment Twain mused, it was Gilded Age sightseers, not seafarers, who were spreading over the face of the earth. These were men and women using the wealth sailors had previously helped to generate to fund their overseas jaunts. As the U.S. deepwater maritime industry began its slow decline across the second half of the nineteenth century, merchants funneled diminishing returns into domestic industries whose profits underwrote a postbellum boom in the business of American tourism. Seafarers, it would seem, had been working toward their own replacement as the country's chief representatives abroad. "Once our emblem floated from the mastheads of vessels seen in every sea, bay, and harbor," one typical obituary for maritime empire read, "and now what are we?" The United States might have become a continental hegemon, but its sails no longer whitened every sea.[3]

The disappearance of American oceanic shipping, however, is more than the economic story most historians tell. It also has social and political dimensions, as well as broader implications for the history of U.S. foreign relations. One major shift, for example, was the change in who went to sea aboard ships flying the stars and stripes. Beginning in the 1830s, and accelerating across the 1850s and 1860s, foreign-born seamen (largely from Scandinavia, northern Europe, and the Pacific) comprised pluralities and then majorities on ships leaving the United States. The navy felt the effects of this phenomenon first, then whaling and the merchant marine. By the early twentieth century, seamen's labor activist Andrew Furuseth could complain, as did many nativists, that maritime labor was entirely "the domain . . . of the sewage of the Caucasian race and of such of the races of

OUR MERCHANT MARINE, THE RIP VAN WINKLE OF THE SEA.

Figure 11. "Our Merchant Marine, the Rip Van Winkle of the Seas." As this 1911 political cartoon observes, a nation that once boasted that its sails whitened every sea was facing new realities. Canvas and flags in tatters, a dormant American merchant marine slept while its ships rotted in port. Such iconography proved a significant contrast to earlier prognostications of U.S. maritime manifest destiny. "Our Merchant Marine, the Rip Van Winkle of the Seas," *Puck*, Nov. 15, 1911, courtesy of the Library of Congress, Prints and Photographs Collection, AP101. P7 1911 (Case X) [P&P].

Asia as felt that their condition could be improved by becoming seamen." Democratic congressman John Edward Raker echoed those observations in 1914, noting that "our own countrymen began quitting the sea fifty years ago," adding that the "white man" had been replaced by "men from India, China, and the Malay Islands." Indeed, exactly fifty years before Raker spoke, the U.S. consul at Tumbes, Peru, had written home to recommend the closure of his office, given the "small number of *American* seamen" who appeared abroad. Even those "few Americans who ship in such vessels at the commencement of the voyage will not be found in them at the end of one or two years," he stated. For "one reason or another," white citizens "deserted, [and] their places [were] filled by Portuguese subjects from the Western Islands, 'Canackers' from the Sandwich and South Sea Islands, and natives of Chili and other South American States."[4]

But while the consul (and others) may have been confused about why, exactly, white American working men were disappearing from the world's shores, many sailors were quite articulate when explaining their abandonment of the ocean. What they noticed, collectively, might be thought of as the closure of America's deep-water frontier, which happened decades before the 1893 moment when Frederick Jackson Turner famously eulogized the passing of its western counterpart. There were many reasons why American citizens chose to leave the ocean. For one, it was simply too hard to scrape by overseas. Shrinking avenues for advancement afloat and emerging opportunities in industry ashore combined to make waterborne labor less attractive to the nation's sons. Because of thinning profit margins in the highly competitive carrying trade, shipowners sought to cut costs wherever possible, and labor usually bore the brunt of those initiatives. Real wages for maritime workers began to crater. Men who had worked aboard ships as only one phase of their lives were being replaced by a "deep-sea proletariat," a permanent underclass of laborers recruited from foreign ports, paid poorly, and used ever more harshly.[5]

A secondary issue, yet one that was connected to the issue of foreign displacement, was the question of race, which also played an important role in discouraging native-born white American men from pursuing employment at sea. Nonwhite peoples, one seafaring narrative fretted, when placed "in positions of authority over men of Anglo-Saxon origin, are apt to treat their subordinates with great cruelty." Another mariner reported that "the practice of promoting foreigners" left "American seamen . . . disgusted with the service, by being compelled to submit to [their] authority." Remarks about the wider world—aboard ships and in countries overseas— as a dangerous space of nonwhite empowerment increased among white sailors. Men commanded by racial subordinates afloat commented on the exoticism, even danger, of such a reversal of the American order overseas. "We want no masters, and least of all no Negro masters," went the popular Democratic chant decrying black suffrage movements in the United States. Although "Negro masters" were held at bay domestically, they made themselves known abroad. This provoked many white working men along the maritime frontier. They wrote in jaded terms of black, Kanaka, or Asian authority overseas. The country's canvas had once been a claim to ownership of the world's oceans; now, these individuals suggested, white sails connoted a kind of exile from all that was authentically American.[6]

Recall sailor William Stetson, who raged that some American men (unequivocally tagged as "white") preferred to abandon ships rather than serve alongside the "barbarian cannibals" and "niggers" captains had hired overseas. Horace Palmer, right before deserting his whaling vessel in the 1870s, complained that while "common sense" on land suggested that "a white man is just a shade in advance of a nigger," a different logic governed life on American ships, where "it is strange to find an officer ... who does not think a nigger a little bit above any other class of being." One captain simply reminded his men that "You've got a driver over you!" and he was it. "Yes, a *slave-driver, a nigger-driver*," and he only wanted to know which of the crew "will tell me he isn't a nigger slave." The "blackness" of conditions under sail, in other words, proved a powerful inducement to make one's living as a free laborer ashore. The republic's mariners began to vanish from the wider world, choosing instead to work in factories. It is ironic that the globetrotting now a symbol of privilege was largely the province of poorer laborers in the early decades of the republic.[7]

But those workshops and mills looked more attractive for a reason. Seafaring was thought to be the destiny of a "black" or "degraded" and altogether "different" caste of men exactly because it looked retrograde in the burgeoning industrial-capitalist order coming to dominate Atlantic seaport cities. Men who labored on ships were subject to what was considered an unusual degree of regulation by public authorities. Sailors were still harshly disciplined in their floating workplaces by masters given broad legal authority to maintain order and compel obedience. Mariners looked like something of a breed apart in this new economic system's growing army of workers: they were not "free laborers" who hired their manpower out to employers. Although a factory worker might, at least in theory, walk away from his job whenever he pleased, a seafarer could be legally ordered to continue serving. Deserting a textile mill was not a crime; deserting a ship, on the other hand, was considered an offense, and the seaman who did so could be arrested, jailed, and forced back on board. This made mariners seem like something closer to slaves or indentured servants. In the late 1860s, seaman Roland Gould explained the increasingly anomalous position of seafaring communities in the liberalizing order of the Atlantic basin by asking his readers an easily answerable question: "What American would ever be content to rivet the chains of slavery upon himself?" The coercive and largely patriarchal command structure of shipboard society were now things to be avoided; Gould's query implied as much. That disciplinary regime marked sailors as odd in a world coming to consensus about the importance of internalized self-discipline—instead of legal and physical coercion—in labor relations. American men thus deserted the maritime trades in droves. Gilded Age autobiographies dissuaded their readers from pursuing a life afloat. With the rise of steam power and telegraphy, "the romance of the sea departed." There are now, Samuel Samuels sighed in

1887, "no new lands to discover." He sounded like many others when he wrote that "I would not commit my memoirs to paper if I felt that they would in the slightest tend to induce a boy to become a sailor." Most of the republic's citizens heeded such warnings.[8]

The United States, in other words, did not "become" international near the end of the nineteenth century. Its first era of internationalism was by then crumbling. But if, as Twain shrewdly noted at the turn of the twentieth century, "summer travels" regularly took Americans to places that had previously been visited only by sailors, then the tenor of the nation's foreign relations must surely have changed as well. To be a "tourist" in a place is in many ways an entirely different proposition than laboring overseas. "Tourism" implies its own way of engaging with the peoples and environments of the world. Perhaps no individual better illustrates that transition than one of the maritime world's most famous dilettantes, Richard Henry Dana Jr. In the winter of 1836, Dana rounded Cape Horn and began his stay along the coast of what was then Mexican-controlled California. "Stay," however, is precisely the parlance of leisure travel that did not apply to the time Dana spent abroad. His life afloat was laborious, and the acclaimed *Two Years before the Mast*, an ethnographic narrative Dana produced, is nothing if not an effort to describe how relentless toil shaped the journeys of working men from the United States. Such was, Dana thought, "the true light in which a sailor's life is to be viewed: plain, matter-of-fact drudgery and hardship." The "typical" antebellum American overseas, implied the author, approached the wider world with a sweated brow.[9]

But Dana's writing career did not end with the publication of *Two Years*. Although they never achieved the notoriety of the original work, his subsequent productions still allowed readers to travel alongside the adventurer *To Cuba and Back* and on *A Voyage Around the World*. In those instances Dana was a passenger and did not labor. Both are testaments to the new touristic sensibilities more and more Americans would adopt as the nineteenth century progressed. Neither, however, quite captures how *different* life abroad looked when one approached it as a traveler in the way his short piece entitled "Twenty-Four Years Later" does. In it, the now-successful Harvard-educated lawyer returns to California in 1859 and reflects on the changes that had taken place in the intervening decades.[10]

The essay is largely a paean to progress. On his first voyage, Dana rarely spent a dry night in the cramped confines of the rickety brig *Pilgrim*. Now he approached San Francisco as a passenger aboard the steamship *Golden Gate*, "brilliant with its lighted saloons and staterooms." The city astounded him. A man who had decried Spanish slothfulness thirty years earlier, exclaiming that "in the hands of an enterprising people, what a country this might be!," stood in awe before urban sprawl he called "one of the capitals of the American Republic, and the sole emporium of a new world, the awakened Pacific." What was once "a vast solitude" now blazed with "bodies of dazzling light." The spectacle reduced Dana to a state of dissociative disbelief. "When I saw all these things"—the lighthouses and fortresses, the towers and steeples—"and reflected on what I once was and saw here, and what now surrounded me, I could scarcely keep my hold on reality at all, or the genuineness of anything, and seemed to myself like one who had moved in 'worlds not realized.'"[11]

American nationhood had brought to California so much of the modernity Dana felt was lacking during his first voyage there. Yet the way he *could* engage with the environment changed alongside the circumstances under which the former mariner traveled. As a foremast hand, Dana found himself confined to the decrepit groggeries of San Diego and dilapidated hide houses of San Pedro. He returned, however, as a gentleman, a paying customer, and a minor celebrity, for "almost every American in California had read my book." Now he spoke of mingling in respectable society, of social calls and parlor visits, of decorous and sumptuous meals. In 1836, Dana had slept atop piles of cowhide beside mission Indians and three Hawaiian boatmen hired as short-term laborers. Twenty years later, he perused "the latest New York papers" while "comfortably abed in a commodious room in the Oriental Hotel." Upon returning, Dana never lingered on the waterfront. Rather, this traveler, like most, quickly left the dockside haunts frequented by sailors—what became San Francisco's infamous "Barbary Coast" red-light district—in favor of the city's "better" parts.[12]

But this was not the Oriental Hotel in Nagasaki that played host to brutal brawling between American whalemen and British sailors, and therein lay the crux of the nation's shifting engagement with the wider world. As tourists and travelers replaced young seafaring men as the nation's primary presence abroad, modes of encounter altered to accommodate the different styles in which each community moved. Luxurious lodgings and policed resorts arose to replace waterfront taverns and bawdy brothels as the places one would most likely find an American overseas. Citizens of the republic abroad would now become known for their prosperity and pretensions to refinement. Such men and women were parvenus, perhaps, but they were a far cry from the rabble-rousing roustabouts whom nineteenth-century consuls complained of as "giving our people a bad name in all the stopping places of the world." This was a major shift in the class composition of the nation's presence overseas and, at some level, in the conduct of its foreign relations. Elites came to replace working people, in larger and larger numbers, as the nation's principal representatives abroad.[13]

And so as Americans disappeared from the globe's tumultuous quays and coasts, they began to reappear in very different areas of cities and towns, places that were attractive to the tourist's eye. Previously, indigenous inhabitants of the world had encountered Americans as gangs of itinerant men who were impoverished, sexually aggressive, and often disposed to violence. These mariners interacted with men and women overseas of very similar circumstance as their own, people who were in many ways dependent on those swarms of young men (among other floating populations) for their livelihoods. By the fin de siècle, most Americans were not paid to enter into the wider world but in fact paid others for the privilege of doing so. A more confident breed of American Anglo-Saxonism followed in the footsteps of these later generations. Unburdened by the "slavish" degradation that so troubled the sailors who had previously traveled around the world, the new travelers preached with more and more certitude the greatness of white men and women in the United States. Later voyagers did not have to suffer the embarrassment of lower-class Americans who jeopardized their country's pretensions to global prestige; they did not need to shake their heads as native peoples fled before marauding sailors, "seeming to believe," as one naval officer worried, "that Americans were a brutal set of savages delighting in rapine, bloodshed, and plunder." As the class composition of Americans overseas became less differentiated, that community became more unified in its attempts to project the nation as a "respectable" place of prosperous persons. Indeed, in the later nineteenth century one rarely finds letters of complaint such as that filed in 1855 by a wealthy American traveler in Canton, who protested that the rowdiness of his maritime countrymen—their tendency to "do great mischief," to "insult and assault" passersby—represented "a great annoyance to respectable people." As "upright" citizens became the larger component of U.S. nationals overseas, debate over what was appropriate behavior in a foreign country congealed into consensus about bourgeois correctness. Americans abroad might be boors, but they were less and less "savage."[14]

The populations later travelers encountered overseas were more often higher-status individuals or laborers who were paid to remain servile for the sake of tourist dollars. Sailors overseas were characterized by the close *proximity* of their relationships with local peoples. Whether out of choice or necessity, seafarers bargained with, had sex with, and fought with the groups they encountered. That proximity strained many of those relationships and created innumerable headaches for consular authorities assigned to oversee the interests of American sailors. Travelers of the later period rarely saw the same types of people sailors had seen. Their approach to voyaging emphasized the cultivation of *distance*. They wandered through what can be thought of as "Baedeker World," a place of structure, order, and routine built by the tourist guidebooks of Karl Baedeker, Thomas Cook, and others. These publications promised to eliminate the "messiness" that had characterized life abroad for poor mariners; indeed, most of them explicitly warned tourists about the need to avoid the districts where American sailors had congregated while roaming the globe. This new ethic of travel was in no way immersive; instead it called for observation from afar. Money and prestige sheltered tourists from the need for close contact with others, while the habit of traveling with husbands, wives, and children limited sexual dalliance. Indeed, it is hugely significant that women were increasingly a part of the American experience abroad. Women brought new sensibilities to overseas travel. For example the brawls that many seamen appeared to leap into with alacrity shocked women who abhorred interpersonal violence. Missionaries, after all, particularly female missionaries, devoted their lives abroad to cultivating what has been called a "gospel of gentility." American observers arriving after their country's sailors had, by and large, cleared out, judged the wider world on very different terms. And, just as likely, other peoples came to different conclusions about Americans based on the increasing prevalence of tourists.[15]

Most people today who interact with Americans overseas know them as businesspeople, as tourists with a camera slung over their shoulders, or as employees of a non-governmental organization. But earlier, hundreds of thousands of American men poured out across the globe in the course of their labor. Only with disingenuousness could later chroniclers maintain the fiction that sailors were a "breed apart," somehow detached from shoreside community and deserving of separate scholarly inquiry. Frank Bullen remarked in 1900 that "the sailor lives in a little world of his own . . . the majority of his days he lives in utmost ignorance of what is going on in the world, and is like the inhabitants of some undiscovered country." By the close of the nineteenth century, sailors were seen as an exotic and disconnected community, but mariners began the era in ways that challenged Bullen's assessment. Not the world unto themselves many thought, sailors were in fact one of the country's principal connective links *to* the wider world, its arteries, one might say. Yet given how much the young republic had depended on the circulatory function of its ships and sailors, it is astonishing to see how quickly their contributions could be forgotten.[16]

After the 1870s, when deep-water oceanic exploits became less and less a part of the nation's lived experience, those writing the history of earlier eras became inattentive to the central role nautical issues had played. As American craft disappeared from Atlantic waterfronts and were replaced by foreign registries and stranger seamen, ships and sailors were gradually excised from the master narrative of the period. In a country that was fond of winners and addicted to triumphal self-imagining, maritime history represented a tale of failure. Even the most committed oracles of the republic's maritime manifest destiny were silenced. Their hush, in turn, reverberated across the pages of history. The country's seaports became mere transit points that directed traffic, by road and rail, into the interior. The United States reconstituted itself as a naval power, content to police international sea lanes populated by ships and sailors from far-off places. Those foreign-registered vessels, flying flags of convenience, enabled the United States to import more and more of the world's commodities and manufactures. But that veritable "consumers' imperium" no longer depended on the labor of American deep-water seamen or national merchant craft.[17]

When Americans did recall the time when the world's oceans were whitened by their sails, it was through the rose-colored glasses of romanticism. In a post–Civil War nation of rapid industrialization, wind power was the quaint and cheery remnant of "pre-modernity." This brand of reminiscing meant that what little maritime remembrance remained in the United States was long on nostalgia and short on substance. The twentieth century's "second discovery of the sea" involved only a growing appreciation for the recreational potential ocean travel presented. More and more leisure travelers made the shore a weekend destination. It was a space for relaxation, for contemplation before the sublime, away from the din of rapidly growing cities. The "sea voyage," no longer an occupation, became instead a metaphor for emerging understandings of economic risk in capitalism's financial sector, or, alternatively, an allegory about one's personal journey through life. Individuals adhered to Henry Thoreau's notion that we "explore the private sea, the Atlantic and Pacific Ocean of one's own being" even as fewer of his countrymen were actually employed atop those bodies of water.[18]

Hubert Howe Bancroft, author of a widely read imperial manifesto entitled *The New Pacific*, divulged the depths of American amnesia about maritime life by 1900. His promotional prose encouraged citizens to appreciate the "windfall" of so many "superb islands and archipelagos," the spoils of war with Spain, "dropping into the lap of the United States all at one time." Echoing Frederick Jackson Turner's contemporaneous conclusion, Bancroft noticed that "we have no longer a virgin continent to develop." And so, because "pioneer work in the United States is done, *now* we must take a plunge into the sea." The *suddenness* of the country's entrance into the international arena amazed him. "Almost since yesterday," he marveled, "from the modest attitude of quiet industry the United States assumes the position of a world power." Thus, in 1898, "the old America"—that is, the continentally contained nation—"passes away; behold a new America appears, and her face is toward the Pacific."[19]

Inattentive to a previous century of global maritime activity, Bancroft found that only when armed with the excuse of overseas empire could Americans accept aquatic ambitions. His model of linear progress across the continent followed by an abrupt leap into the wider world became the template of countless national histories of the long nineteenth century. And as Bancroft made clear, the "new" American overseas empire, even as it constructed colonies, would also be a project dedicated to the erasure of prior American global engagement. In an effort to remedy (and forget) what to high-status persons had been the national embarrassment of a nineteenth-century maritime empire characterized by whoring, theft, and often brutal violence, Americans abroad were now to be dominated by populations dedicated to "uplift." Missionaries, educators, and businessmen labored to undo damage done by the "peculiar class" of men known as mariners, who were actuated, in the words of one U.S. consul, by little other than unchecked "bravado" and who frequently jeopardized "the honor of the flag." Thus, the work of American empire post-1870 would be one of creative destruction in multiple senses: the imposition of United States commercial, political, and military agendas on indigenous populations but also the dismantling of the supposedly discreditable legacy sailors had left as the nation's global intermediaries.[20]

Recapturing the oceanic dimension of nineteenth-century U.S. history reveals the several points of engagement and entanglement between the nation and the world. Far too often, race and nation are treated as somehow fundamentally connected to territorial expansion in the fledgling republic. Detaching those variables from landward movement creates a narrative of far greater complexity and contingency. Ideas about the fitness of American whiteness and nationhood may have—with some exception—proven powerful enough to motivate the subjugation of vast territorial space. But those same concepts did not succeed at sea. American men, in growing numbers, fled an industry that betrayed the promises of *herrenvolk* democracy. Labor afloat and time abroad, which subjected white sailors to harsh punishment at sea and discipline ashore at the hands of "racial inferiors," could not sustain the linkages between lighter skin color and positive self-image that was gathering strength at home in the United States.[21]

A calculus among white American mariners increasingly determined that no matter how onerous one's working life might be ashore, it could not match the degradation a citizen suffered in attempting to toil overseas. Histories that acknowledge the rhetoric of Anglo-Saxonism that propelled people across the North American continent might benefit from the history of marine commerce as an institution that was largely unsupportive of such fantasy; no arena better reveals the tenuousness of racial categories or the bankruptcy of American sloganeering about liberty in the white man's republic. Land and water by the 1840s and 1850s, in fact, attained an inverse relationship. Anglo-American "successes" in the continental context engendered a buoyant confidence in the inherent supremacy and deserved privileges of white citizenry. But as men afloat found that life abroad did not support those values, they chose to remain ashore and further propelled the pressure to expand territorially. Indeed, Bancroft himself noted that the War of 1898 "more clearly than before . . . made manifest the destiny of the Anglo-Saxon race to rise preeminent among peoples."[22]

What white sailor, meanwhile, could pretend to that preeminence? An American maritime enterprise that would not support such lofty rhetoric appeared destined to fail in its efforts to attract anything other than foreign or nonwhite laborers. "White" men at sea were almost exclusively overseers by the end of the nineteenth century, and it became their task to organize and control the diversity beneath them. As one observer noted, ship owners now purposefully hired a "medley of foreigners" rather than white American men exactly because this "made for the safety of the officers." "Brutality," after all, was "much less likely to be resented successfully" when "there could be no banding together for a common purpose of revenge." Sailor Nathaniel Morgan made the casual observation that shipmasters recruited (and beat with impunity) Pacific islanders because they were "ignorant of the language and laws of the Country" and would have "no redress." Of course, it did not hurt that, in the words of another mariner, foreign-born crews "are cheap to feed" and "paid much less than white sailors." The increasingly scientific practice of worksite race management—designed specifically to perpetuate inequalities, divide workers, and prevent the laboring class' collaborative countermeasures—was pioneered not only in factories ashore but also in vessels afloat.[23]

Reconnecting ship to shore, then, simultaneously reveals the transportability and instability of nineteenth-century racial categories. Sailors initially expected to benefit from the white supremacy undergirding manifest destiny. But when conditions at sea caused the country's largest contingent abroad to feel insecure about their own identities as full-fledged white American men, disorder and disaffection were the results. After U.S. nationals abroad attained a more homogenous middle- to upper-class character at the end of the nineteenth century, though, those individuals could more genuinely promote and project a territorial empire overseas predicated on an ideology of race- and status-based supremacy. American maritime empire, however, had sowed the seeds of its own demise by tapping into the era's transatlantic currents of racism and nationalism. The industry was unable to support the claims of its most impassioned advocates. American sails may have "whitened every sea," but the corrosive quality of saltwater left too many men afloat feeling somehow less than white and not quite American. Most historians of the United States write of the destructive effect wrought by burgeoning patriotism and race science, both on the continent and overseas. The maritime world, however, tells a story of the conditions under which that same Anglo-Saxon ebullience and spread-eagle jingoism withered. Curious, then, that Bancroft thought "now," at the turn of the twentieth century, was the time to "take a plunge into the sea." In large numbers, white American working men had already leapt in and found the water little to their liking.

Notes

The following abbreviations are used in the notes:

ISM	Independence Seaport Museum, Philadelphia, Pa.
LOC	Library of Congress Manuscript Collection, Washington, D.C.
MM	Mariners' Museum, Newport News, Va.
MMHS	Marblehead Museum and Historical Society, Marblehead, Mass.
MSM	Mystic Seaport Museum, Mystic, Conn.
NARA I	National Archives and Records Administration, Washington, D.C.
NARA II	National Archives and Records Administration, College Park, Md.
NBFPL	New Bedford Free Public Library, New Bedford, Mass.
NBWM	New Bedford Whaling Museum, New Bedford, Mass.
NHC	Naval Historical Center, Washington, D.C.
NYHS	New-York Historical Society, Rare Book and Manuscript Library, New York, N.Y.
NYPL	New York Public Library, Manuscripts and Archives Division, New York, N.Y.
PEM	Peabody Essex Museum, Phillips Library, Salem, Mass.
PPL	Providence Public Library, Providence, R.I.

Introduction

1. Alexis de Tocqueville, *Democracy in America*, trans. Henry Reeve (New York: D. Appleton, 1904), 2:475; *Southern Literary Messenger* quoted in Reginald Horsman, *Race and Manifest Destiny: The Origins of American Racial Anglo-Saxonism* (Cambridge, Mass.: Harvard University Press, 1981), 290; "The Commercial Age," *De Bow's Review* 7, no. 3 (1849): 236. Maritime boosterism is discussed more broadly in John H. Schroeder, *Shaping a Maritime Empire: The Commercial and Diplomatic Role of the American Navy, 1829–1861* (Westport, Conn: Greenwood Press, 1985), 5–7; and Thomas Hietala, *Manifest Design: Anxious Aggrandizement in Late Jacksonian America* (Ithaca, N.Y.: Cornell University Press, 1985), esp. chapter 3.

2. Cong. Globe, 29th Cong., 1st Sess., Feb. 1846, 8; Cong. Globe, 29th Cong., 1st Sess., Jan. 1846, 293; Cong. Globe, 24th Cong., 1st Sess., Apr. 1836, 261; Cong. Globe, 24th Cong., 1st Sess., May 1836, 338–340. On the last point see Cong. Globe, 29th Cong., 1st Sess., Feb. 1846: "The commerce of the country is no sectional or partial interest." Note that T. L. Hames, from the landlocked state of Indiana, nevertheless was only one among many politicians from non-maritime districts to perceive a vested interest in sail and sailors. Celebrations of the American seaman and U.S. maritime domination appear again in Cong. Globe, 24th Cong., 1st Sess., May 1836, 540–541; Cong. Globe, 30th Cong., 1st Sess., Dec. 1847, 6; and Cong. Globe, 30th Cong., 2nd Sess., Feb. 1849, 133; Cong. Globe, 24th Cong., 1st Sess., May 1836, 338–340: seamen as "our valuable and adventurous citizens."

3. Herman Melville, *Moby Dick, or, The White Whale* (Boston: C. H. Simonds, 1925), 64; *New Bedford Mercury*, Jan. 30, 1829; Cong. Globe, 33rd Cong., 1st Sess., Appendix, Mar. 1854. On the ocean as both a forgotten field of inquiry and a powerful corrective to that amnesia, see John R. Gillis, *The Human Shore: Seacoasts in History* (Chicago: University of Chicago Press, 2013). On territorial expansion, see Mark Rifkin, *Manifesting America: The Imperial Construction of U.S. National Space* (New York: Oxford University Press, 2009); Patrick Griffin, *American Leviathan: Empire, Nation, and the Revolutionary Frontier* (New York: Hill and Wang, 2007); Richard Kluger, *Seizing Destiny: How America Grew from Sea to Shining Sea* (New York: Knopf, 2007); Adam Rothman, *Slave Country: American Expansion and the Origins of the Deep South* (Cambridge, Mass.: Harvard University Press, 2005). Although sailors are the focal point of this study, the celebration of American achievements in shipbuilding and nautical technology demand recognition as an important part of the maritime nationalism that suffused the antebellum United States. See John Curtis Perry, *Facing West: Americans and the Opening of the Pacific* (Westport, Conn.: Praeger Press, 1994), 66–70.

4. "Territorializing vision" appears in Gillis, *Human Shore*, esp. 121–127; "terraqueous" appears on 99. See also Kären Wigen, "Introduction," in *Seascapes: Maritime Histories, Littoral Cultures, and Transoceanic Exchanges*, ed. Jerry Bentley, Renate Bridenthal, and Kären Wigen (Honolulu: University of Hawaii Press, 2007), 1–2. "Continental presumptions" in James D. Drake, *Nation's Nature: How Continental Presumptions Gave Rise to the United States of America* (Charlottesville: University of Virginia Press, 2011). Need for "globalized" antebellum American history in Rosemarie Zagarri, "The Significance of the 'Global Turn' for the Early American Republic: Globalization in the Age of Nation Building," *Journal of the Early Republic* 31 (Spring 2011): 1–37. For a redefinition of "maritime," see Daniel Vickers, *Young Men and the Sea: Yankee Seafarers in the Age of Sail* (New Haven, Conn.: Yale University Press, 2005), 1–6.

5. Cong. Globe, 27th Cong., 2nd Sess., Appendix, 750–751; Cong. Globe, 27th Cong., 2nd Sess., May 1842, 513; congressman quoted in Horsman, *Race and Manifest Destiny*, 289; Cong. Globe, 35th Cong., 1st Sess., June 1858, Appendix, 512–513; Allan B. Cole, ed., *Yankee*

Surveyors in the Shogun's Seas: Records of the United States Surveying Expedition to the North Pacific Ocean, 1853–1856 (Princeton, N.J.: Princeton University Press, 1946), 24; William Dane Phelps, *Fore and Aft; or, Leaves from the Life of an Old Sailor* (Boston: Nichols and Hall, 1871), 259–260; Timothy Dwight, *America* (1790), in *Early American Writing*, ed. Giles Gunn (New York: Penguin Books, 1994), 557; Edward T. Perkins, *Na Motu: or, Reef-Rovings in the South Seas* (New York: Pudney and Russell, 1854), 456. See also *The Sun* (New York), July 24, 1846 ("The riches of the most unlimited market in the world would be thrown open to our enterprise, and . . . our commerce would increase till every ocean billow between us and the China seas would twinkle with our sail."); and *Baltimore American*, quoted in *Picayune* (New Orleans), July 2, 1846 ("The commerce of the world is to be ours, and both oceans are to be subject to us."). Maritime empire also discussed in Norman Graebner, *Empire on the Pacific: A Study in American Continental Expansion* (New York: Ronald Press, 1955).

    6. Oratory in Winthrop L. Marvin, *The American Merchant Marine, Its History and Romance from 1620–1902* (New York: Charles Scribner's Sons, 1916), 37, 262; *Annals of the Congress of the United States*, 12th Cong., 1st Sess. (Washington, D.C.: Gales and Seaton, 1853), 599–602. "Ultimate empire of the ocean" in Anders Stephanson, *Manifest Destiny: American Expansion and the Empire of Right* (New York: Hill and Wang, 1995), 61. On the connection between oceanic and territorial empire, see David C. Hendrickson, *Union, Nation, or Empire: The American Debate over International Relations, 1789–1941* (Lawrence, Kans.: University Press of Kansas, 2009), 285–289; and Schroeder, *Shaping a Maritime Empire*, 62–66. On broader Atlantic discourse of maritime empire, see Anthony Pagden, *Peoples and Empires: A Short History of European Migration, Exploration, and Conquest from Greece to the Present* (New York: Modern Library, 2001), 81–98. Some historians have acknowledged the importance of maritime commerce in early U.S. global engagement; see Ian Tyrrell, *Transnational Nation: United States History in Global Perspective Since 1789* (New York: Palgrave Macmillan, 2007), 4–5, and William Earl Weeks, *The New Cambridge History of American Foreign Relations: Dimensions of Early American Empire, 1754–1865* (Cambridge: Cambridge University Press, 2013), 130–149. Caroline Frank, *Objectifying China, Imagining America: Chinese Commodities in Early America* (Chicago: University of Chicago Press, 2011), 4–5, reminds us that prior to independence, colonial North America had long accessed "a vast extragovernmental, transoceanic circulation of ideas and commodities in which Americans actively participated."

    7. Cong. Globe, 27th Cong., 2nd Sess., Appendix, 750–751. On the sea as frontier, see Gillis, *Human Shore*, 68–98.

    8. This narrowing of nineteenth-century U.S. history to focus solely on continental expansion has been called the "hourglass" formulation. See Carl J. Guarneri, "Internationalizing the United States Survey Course: American History for a Global Age," *History Teacher* 36, no. 1 (2002): 41–42. See also Eric Foner, "American Freedom in a Global Age," *American Historical Review* 106, no. 1 (2001): 1–16; Akira Iriye, "The Internationalization of History," *American Historical Review* 94, no. 1 (1989): 1–10; David Thelen, "Of Audiences, Borderlands, and Comparisons: Toward the Internationalization of American History," *Journal of American History* 79, no. 2 (1992): 432–462. Much of the scholarship is encapsulated in Thomas Bender, *The La Pietra Report: The NYU-OAH Project on Internationalizing the Study of American History* (Bloomington: Indiana University Press, 2000).

    9. For example, see Robert Rydell, *All the World's a Fair: Visions of Empire at American International Expositions, 1876–1916* (Chicago: University of Chicago Press, 1987); Shelley Streeby, *American Sensations: Class, Empire, and the Production of Popular Culture* (Berkeley: University of California Press, 2002); or Kristin Hoganson's discussion of the "fictive travel movement" in *Consumers' Imperium: The Global Production of American Domesticity, 1865–1920*

(Chapel Hill: University of North Carolina Press, 2007), 153–208. On going beyond the study of formal state-to-state relations, see Akira Iriye, "Internationalizing International History," in *Rethinking American History in a Global Age*, ed. Thomas Bender (Los Angeles: University of California Press, 2002), 47–62.

10. *New-Bedford Daily Mercury*, Jan. 5, 1841, 2; Herman Melville, *Redburn* (New York: Harper, 1863), 178. Among a more recent and growing body of books emphasizing America's early international presence are Robert May, *Manifest Destiny's Underworld: Filibustering in Antebellum America* (Chapel Hill: University of North Carolina Press, 2002); Aims McGuinness, *Path of Empire: Panama and the California Gold Rush* (Ithaca, N.Y.: Cornell University Press, 2008); Ian Tyrrell, *Reforming the World: The Creation of America's Moral Empire* (Princeton, N.J.: Princeton University Press, 2010); Gerald Horne, *The Deepest South: The United States, Brazil, and the African Slave Trade* (New York: New York University Press, 2007); Akira Iriye, *Global Community: The Role of International Organizations in the Making of the Contemporary World* (Berkeley: University of California Press, 2002), esp. 1–8. See also "Diplomatic History Today: A Roundtable," *Journal of American History* 95, no. 4 (2009): 1053–1091. Literary scholars in particular have proven key players in examining working peoples' engagement with transnational themes. See Streeby, *American Sensations*; or Gretchen Murphy, *Hemispheric Imaginings: The Monroe Doctrine and Narratives of U.S. Empire* (Durham, N.C.: Duke University Press, 2005).

11. Studies that confine America's "global turn" to the end of the nineteenth century include Frank Ninkovich, *Global Dawn: The Cultural Foundation of American Internationalism, 1865–1890* (Cambridge, Mass.: Harvard University Press, 2009); Walter LaFeber, *The New Empire: An Interpretation of American Expansion, 1860–1898* (Ithaca, N.Y.: Cornell University Press, 1968); Tyrrell, *Reforming the World*; and Matthew Frye Jacobson, *Barbarian Virtues: The United States Encounters Foreign Peoples at Home and Abroad, 1876–1917* (New York: Hill and Wang, 2000). On global commodity flows and domestic consumption in the United States, see Mona Domosh, *American Commodities in an Age of Empire* (New York: Routledge, 2006); Steven C. Topik and Allen Wells, "Commodity Chains in a Global Economy," in *A World Connecting: 1870–1945*, ed. Emily S. Rosenberg (Cambridge, Mass.: Belknap Press of Harvard University, 2012), 593–812; and Sven Beckert, "Emancipation and Empire: Reconstructing the Worldwide Web of Cotton Production in the Age of the American Civil War," *American Historical Review* 109, no. 5 (2004): 1405–1438. On immigration as foreign relations, see Donna Gabaccia, *Foreign Relations: American Immigration in Global Perspective* (Princeton, N.J.: Princeton University Press, 2012).

12. In this narrative arc, there are echoes of the early modern effort to destroy the pirates' nests that threatened the profitability of mercantile firms. See Robert C. Ritchie, *Captain Kidd and the War against the Pirates* (Cambridge, Mass.: Harvard University Press, 1989); and Marcus Rediker, *Villains of All Nations: Atlantic Pirates in the Golden Age* (Boston: Beacon Press, 2005).

13. Winthrop Marvin, *The American Merchant Marine* (New York: Scribners, 1900), 76. "Sensory agents of empire" in Andrew Rotter, "Empires of the Senses: How Seeing, Hearing, Smelling, Tasting, and Touching Shaped Imperial Encounters" *Diplomatic History* 35, no. 1 (2011): 3–19.

14. Estimates of the seafaring population's size in Paul Gilje, *Liberty on the Waterfront: American Maritime Culture in the Age of Revolution* (Philadelphia: University of Pennsylvania Press, 2004), 24–25. Daniel Vickers reminds us that "most sailors spent most of their lives ashore," meaning that "we hang more on the socializing power of the ship . . . than it can possibly bear"; see *The Autobiography of Ashley Bowen* (Ontario, Canada: Broadview Press, 2006), 28–29. On those same points, see also Vickers, *Young Men and Sea: Yankee Seafarers in the Age of Sail* (New Haven,

Conn.: Yale University Press, 2005). On the disconnect between maritime history and broader fields of inquiry, see Daniel Vickers, "Beyond Jack Tar," *William and Mary Quarterly* 50, no. 2 (1993): 418–424; and Matthew Raffety, "Recent Currents in Nineteenth-Century American Maritime History," *History Compass* 6, no. 2 (2008): 607–626, esp. 609.

15. *Benton v. Whitney* (1841), *Federal Cases*, 30 vols. (Rochester, N.Y.: West Publishing, n.d.) 3:258; Vickers, *Young Men and the Sea*, contains the most thorough effort to debunk "sailor exceptionalism," as does Isaac Land, "The Many-Tongued Hydra: Sea Talk, Maritime Culture, and Atlantic Identities, 1700–1850," *Journal of American and Comparative Cultures* 25, nos. 3–4 (2002): 412–415. See also Greg Dening, *Mr. Bligh's Bad Language: Passion, Power, and Theatre on the Bounty* (Cambridge: Cambridge University Press, 1992). Dening argues that "Jolly Jack Tar" was simply an invention: "The more the country became dependent on the exploitation of seamen's brilliant skills, the more sure it became that seamen were 'children'—improvident, intemperate, profligate" (56).

16. Rosemary Ommer and Gerald Panting, eds., *Working Men Who Got Wet: Proceedings of the Fourth Conference of the Atlanta Canada Shipping Project, July 24–July 26, 1980* (St. John's: Maritime History Group, Memorial University of Newfoundland, 1980). For sailor bodies as national symbol, see Simon Newman, "Reading the Bodies of Early American Seafarers," *William and Mary Quarterly* 55, no. 1 (1998): 59–82. See also Newman, *Embodied History: The Lives of the Poor in Early Philadelphia* (Philadelphia: University of Pennsylvania Press, 2003), 104–124; and Myra C. Glenn, "Forging Manhood and Nationhood Together: American Sailors' Accounts of Their Exploits, Sufferings, and Resistance in the Antebellum United States," *American Nineteenth Century History* 8, no. 1 (2007): 27–49.

17. Boyenton quoted in Margaret Creighton, *Dogwatch and Liberty Days: Seafaring Life in the Nineteenth Century* (Worcester, Mass.: Mercantile Press, 1982), 1–2, which further argues for the significance of white American seamen within a diverse industry. On Benson, see Michael Sokolow, *Charles Benson: Mariner of Color in the Age of Sail* (Amherst, Mass.: University of Massachusetts Press, 2003), quoted on 1 and 62. No single study seems able to estimate what percentage of the maritime trades was populated by native-born white Americans. Richard Henry Dana Jr. thought that "more than three fourths of the seamen in our merchant vessels are foreigners"; see *Two Years before the Mast* (New York: Signet Classic, 2000, orig. pub. 1840), 381. But it is important to remember that his estimate (and those of others) were employed to justify the use of flogging aboard merchant ships to discipline "foreign" (read: unfeeling) bodies who could not otherwise be controlled. Vickers, *Young Men and the Sea*, 178n17 cites William McNally's estimate that "not one-third" of seamen were native born. The numbers fluctuated between industries, whaling being, for example, more diverse than the merchant marine. Cabotage laws passed by Congress in 1817 mandated that two-thirds of the crew of any ship registered in the United States were to be citizens, though captains and shipping agents often forged these lists. Jean Heffer notes that while not all sailors aboard U.S. ships were American, "U.S. nationals made up the majority"; see Jean Heffer, *The United States and the Pacific: History of a Frontier*, trans. W. Donald Wilson (Notre Dame, Ind.: University of Notre Dame Press, 2002), 61. Jennifer Schell argues that "the dominant, conglomerate identity [aboard ships] was primarily a white one, and all of the other races, nationalities, and ethnicities working aboard ship were somehow subordinated, managed, and regulated such that their foreign racial and ethnic characteristics simply reinforced white self-understandings"; "'Us Lone Wand'ring Whaling-Men': Cross-Cutting Fantasies of Work and Nation in Eighteenth- and Nineteenth-Century American Whaling Narratives" (PhD diss., University of Pittsburgh, 2006), 18–19. See also Creighton, *Rites and Passages*, 8–15, for crew composition and the viability of concentrating on the diaries of white, literate seamen in an otherwise diverse industry.

18. Gilje, *Liberty of the Waterfront*, xii, provides some precedent for thinking of the maritime community as a coherent whole. On the circulation of revolutionary ideology through black maritime networks, see David S. Cecelski, *The Waterman's Song: Slavery and Freedom in Maritime North Carolina* (Chapel Hill: University of North Carolina Press, 2001); Paul Gilroy, *The Black Atlantic: Modernity and Double Consciousness* (Cambridge, Mass.: Harvard University Press, 1993); Julius Scott, "Afro-American Sailors and the International Communication Network," in *Jack Tar in History: Essays in the History of Maritime Life and Labour*, ed. Colin Howell and Richard Twomey (Fredericton, New Brunswick: Acadiensis Press, 1991), 37–52. On the racial landscape aboard ships at sea, see W. Jeffrey Bolster, *Black Jacks: African-American Seamen in the Age of Sail* (Cambridge, Mass.: Harvard University Press, 1997); David Chappell, *Double Ghosts: Oceanian Voyagers on Euroamerican Ships* (Armonk, N.Y.: M.E. Sharpe, 1997); Briton Cooper Busch, *Whaling Will Never Do for Me: The American Whaleman in the Nineteenth Century* (Lexington: University Press of Kentucky, 1994); David Kazanjian, *The Colonizing Trick: National Culture and Imperial Citizenship in Early America* (Minneapolis: University of Minnesota Press, 2003); Peter Linebaugh and Marcus Rediker, *The Many-Headed Hydra: Sailors, Slaves, Commoners, and the Hidden History of the Revolutionary Atlantic* (Boston: Beacon Press, 2001); Emma Christopher, *Slave Ship Sailors and Their Captive Cargoes, 1730–1807* (Cambridge: Cambridge University Press, 2006); Michael J. Bennett, *Union Jacks: Yankee Sailors in the Civil War* (Chapel Hill: University of North Carolina Press, 2004); Jennifer Schell, *"A Bold and Hardy Race of Men": The Lives and Literature of American Whalemen* (Boston: University of Massachusetts Press, 2013), 169–198; Nancy Shoemaker, "Mr. Tashtego: Native American Whalemen in Antebellum New England," *Journal of the Early Republic* 33, no. 1 (2013): 109–132.

19. On "sea as heterotopia," see Philip E. Steinberg, *The Social Construction of the Ocean* (Cambridge: Cambridge University Press, 2001). As a space of cross-racial, class-based collaboration, see Linebaugh and Rediker, *The Many-Headed Hydra*; and Marcus Rediker, *Between the Devil and the Deep Blue Sea: Merchant Seamen, Pirates, and the Anglo-American Maritime World, 1700–1750* (Cambridge: Cambridge University Press, 1987). These claims have, in turn, inspired a lively debate and substantial qualification. See Eric W. Sager, *Seafaring Labour: The Merchant Marine of Atlantic Canada, 1820–1914* (Kingston, Ontario: McGill University Press, 1989); Vickers, *Young Men and the Sea*; Isaac Land, *War, Nationalism, and the British Sailor* (New York: Palgrave, 2009); Gilje, *Liberty on the Waterfront*; Leon Fink, *Sweatshops at Sea: Merchant Seamen in the World's First Globalized Industry* (Chapel Hill: University of North Carolina Press, 2011); and Matthew Taylor Raffety, *The Republic Afloat: Law, Honor, and Citizenship in Maritime America* (Chicago: University of Chicago Press, 2013). For mutually influential categories of race and masculinity, see Dana Nelson, *National Manhood: Capitalist Citizenship and the Imagined Fraternity of White Men* (Durham, N.C.: Duke University Press, 1998).

20. Coastal or internal versus international shipping quoted in Alex Roland, W. Jeffrey Bolster, and Alexander Keyssar, *The Way of the Ship: America's Maritime History Reenvisioned, 1600–2000* (Hoboken, N.J.: John Wiley & Sons, 2008), 1–2, 110, and passim. "Alongshore peoples" in Gillis, *The Human Shore*, 68, 86–87. Other studies emphasize the primacy of fisheries, coastal transport, and internal waterways, including Bolster, *The Mortal Sea: Fishing the Atlantic in the Age of Sail* (Cambridge, Mass.: Belknap Press of Harvard University, 2012); Christopher P. Magra, *The Fisherman's Cause: Atlantic Commerce and the Maritime Dimensions of the American Revolution* (Cambridge: Cambridge University Press, 2009); David S. Cecelski, *The Waterman's Song: Slavery and Freedom in Maritime North Carolina* (Chapel Hill: University of North Carolina Press, 2001); and Thomas C. Buchanan, *Black Life on the Mississippi: Slaves, Free Blacks, and the Western Steamboat World* (Chapel Hill: University of North Carolina Press, 2004).

21. Melville, *Redburn*, 179.

Chapter 1

1. Mark Twain, *Autobiography*, 2 vols. (New York: Kessinger, 2003), 2:120–121; Paul Lyons, *American Pacificism: Oceania in the U.S. Imagination* (New York: Routledge, 2006), 29n7. See also John R. Eperjesi, *The Imperialist Imaginary: Visions of Asia and the Pacific in American Culture* (Hanover, N.H.: Dartmouth Press, 2005), 26–34.

2. On shift in maritime labor from a norm to a distinct occupation, see Daniel Vickers, *Young Men and the Sea: Yankee Seafarers in the Age of Sail* (New Haven, Conn.: Yale University Press, 2005). For the popularity of seafaring narratives, see Myra C. Glenn, *Jack Tar's Story: The Autobiographies and Memoirs of Sailors in Antebellum America* (Cambridge: Cambridge University Press, 2010).

3. On the growth in the market for nineteenth-century sea voyage narratives, see Jennifer Schell, *"A Bold and Hardy Race of Men": The Lives and Literature of American Whalemen* (Boston: University of Massachusetts Press, 2013); Hester Blum, *The View from the Masthead: Maritime Imagination and Antebellum American Sea Narratives* (Chapel Hill: University of North Carolina Press, 2008); Haskell Springer, ed., *America and the Sea: A Literary History* (Athens: University of Georgia Press, 1995); and Thomas Philbrick, *James Fenimore Cooper and the Development of American Sea Fiction* (Cambridge, Mass.: Harvard University Press, 1961). The perils and profits of using sailor narratives are discussed in Myra C. Glenn, "Forging Manhood and Nationhood Together: American Sailors' Accounts of their Exploits, Sufferings, and Resistance in the Antebellum United States," *American Nineteenth Century History* 8, no. 1 (2007), esp. 28–31; and Blum, *The View from the Masthead*, 2–11 and 20–29. The "representativeness" of literate and reflective individuals is also discussed in Joyce Appleby, *Inheriting the Revolution: The First Generation of Americans* (Cambridge, Mass.: Harvard University Press, 2000); and Ann Fabian, *The Unvarnished Truth: Personal Narratives in Nineteenth-Century America* (Berkeley: University of California Press, 2000). Sailor literacy has been estimated to lie somewhere between 75 and 90 percent for the period discussed. See Blum, *View from the Masthead*, 5.

4. Charles Erskine, *Twenty Years before the Mast* (Philadelphia: George W. Jacobs, 1896), vii; Ralph Waldo Emerson, "American Civilization," *The Atlantic* (Apr. 1862): 502–503. See Kristen Hoganson, *Consumers' Imperium: The Global Production of American Domesticity, 1865–1920* (Chapel Hill: University of North Carolina Press, 2007), 8–12. On the many forms and functions of maritime literature, see Paul Gilje, *Liberty on the Waterfront: American Maritime Culture in the Age of Revolution* (Philadelphia: University of Pennsylvania Press, 2004), 228–258. For the shift from memoirs to travelogues, see Vickers, *Young Men and the Sea*, 188–189.

5. Literary scholars in particular have proven key players in examining working peoples' engagement with transnational themes. See Shelley Streeby, *American Sensations: Class, Empire, and the Production of Popular Culture* (Berkeley: University of California Press, 2002); or Gretchen Murphy, *Hemispheric Imaginings: The Monroe Doctrine and Narratives of U.S. Empire* (Durham, N.C.: Duke University Press, 2005).

6. *Hudson River Chronicle*, July 17, 1838; "Who Remembers the Sailor?," editorial, *Sailor's Magazine and Naval Journal* 10, no. 3 (Nov. 1837): 75–76. See also *New-Bedford Mercury*, Dec. 21, 1838; or *Berkshire County Whig*, Dec. 23, 1841.

7. George Little, *Life on the Ocean, or, Twenty Years at Sea, Being the Personal Adventures of the Author* (Boston: Waite and Peirce, 1846), 369–370 and 379; Jeremiah N. Reynolds, *Voyage of the United States Frigate* Potomac (New York: Harper and Brothers, 1835), preface and 106–109.

8. Little, *Life on the Ocean*, 369–370; "Address of the Workingmen's Party of Charlestown, Massachusetts to Their Brethren throughout the Commonwealth and the Union," *Boston*

Quarterly Review 4 (Jan. 1841): 119–123. On producerist rhetoric and maritime labor, see Schell, "*A Bold and Hardy Race of Men*," 16–41.

9. Kariann Yokota, *Unbecoming British: How Revolutionary America became a Postcolonial Nation* (New York: Oxford University Press, 2011), 115–152, editorial quoted on 119. Sailors, war, and patriotic discourse are covered in Gilje, *Liberty on the Waterfront*, 130–162; and Gilje, *Free Trade and Sailors' Rights in the War of 1812* (Cambridge: Cambridge University Press, 2013). Isaac Land notes that in "songs, petitions, and autobiographies, sailors identified themselves with the cause of imperial expansion and cast themselves as defenders of white honor on a dangerous frontier"; see "'Sinful Propensities': Piracy, Sodomy, and Empire in the Rhetoric of Naval Reform, 1770–1870," in *Discipline and the Other Body: Correction, Corporeality, and Colonialism*, ed. Stephen Pierce and Anupama Rao (Durham, N.C.: Duke University Press, 2006), 92–93.

10. "Communications and Selections," *Sailor's Magazine and Naval Journal* 5, no. 1 (1832): 1–2; "Anniversaries and Reports of Seamen's Friends Societies," New Bedford Port Society quoted in ibid., 15; "Extract of the Report of the Ladies' Bethel Association," *Sailor's Magazine and Naval Journal* 9, no. 3 (1836): 3–4; "Report from the Navy Department," in *Register of Debates in Congress*, 18th Cong., 2nd Sess., Jan. 1, 1825, 56.

11. On postrevolutionary calls for the "common man's voice" in print, see Joyce Appleby, *Inheriting the Revolution: The First Generation of Americans* (Cambridge, Mass.: Belknap Press, 2000); and Gilje, *Liberty on the Waterfront*, 234. On the antebellum explosion in U.S. print culture, see Michael Denning, *Mechanic Accents: Dime Novels and Working-Class Culture in America* (London: Verso, 1987) and Michael Warner, *Letters of the Republic: Publication and the Public Sphere in Eighteenth-Century America* (Cambridge, Mass: Harvard University Press, 1990). The dissemination of "sketches of the foreign" in a later period is covered in Matthew Frye Jacobson, *Barbarian Virtues: The United States Encounters Foreign Peoples at Home and Abroad, 1876–1917* (New York: Hill and Wang, 2000), 105–138.

12. Herman Melville, *Moby Dick, or, The White Whale* (Boston: C. H. Simonds, 1925), 106.

13. Ibid., 108; J. Ross Browne, *Etchings of a Whaling Cruise* (New York: Harper and Brothers, 1846), iv; Winthrop L. Marvin, *The American Merchant Marine, Its History and Romance from 1620–1902* (New York: Charles Scribner's Sons, 1916), 200; William Dane Phelps, *Fore and Aft; or, Leaves from the Life of an Old Sailor* (Boston: Nichols and Hall, 1871), 175–176; "A Sermon Written for the Sailor's Magazine," *Sailor's Magazine and Naval Journal* 9, no. 11 (1837): 329–333. On the relationship between maritime intelligence, science, and commerce, see William Goetzmann, *New Lands, New Men: America and the Second Great Age of Discovery* (New York: Penguin, 1987), 233–234.

14. John Peck, *Maritime Fiction: Sailors and the Sea in British and American Novels, 1719–1917* (New York: Palgrave, 2001); Blum, *View from the Masthead*; Schell, *"A Bold and Hardy Race of Men."*

15. Walter Teller, ed., *Five Sea Captains: Their Own Accounts of Voyages under Sail* (New York: Atheneum, 1960), 226; "Conversion of Seamen," *Sailors' Magazine and Naval Journal* 10 (Feb. 1838): 15.

16. Henry Wise, *Los Gringos: Or, An Inside View of Mexico and California, with Wanderings in Peru, Chili, and Polynesia* (London: George Bentley, 1849), 29; A Roving Printer, *Life and Adventures in the South Pacific* (New York: Harper and Brothers, 1861), 88; George Little, *Life on the Ocean*, 68. Seafaring recreation is further described in Marcus Rediker, *Between the Devil and the Deep Blue Sea: Merchant Seamen, Pirates, and the Anglo-American Maritime World, 1700–1750* (London: Cambridge University Press, 1989), 153–204.

17. Little, *Life on the Ocean*, 128, 137–138; Erskine, *Twenty Years before the Mast*, 39; entries dated Nov. 19, 1858, and May 10, 1859, journal of William Abbe, kept aboard ship *Atkins*

Adams, ODHS Log #485, NBWM. See also Margaret Creighton, "Fraternity in the American Forecastle, 1830–1870," *New England Quarterly* 63, no. 4 (1990): 531–557.

18. William B. Whitecar, *Four Years Aboard the Whaleship, Embracing Cruises in the Pacific, Atlantic, Indian, and Antarctic in the Years 1855, 56, 57, 58, 59* (Philadelphia: J. B. Lippincott, 1860), 27–28; R. B. Forbes, *An Appeal to Merchants and Ship Owners on the Subject of Seamen* (Boston: Sleeper & Rogers, 1854), 6; "A Foretopman" [Henry Mercier], *Life in a Man-of-War or, Scenes in "Old Ironsides"* (Philadelphia: Lydia R. Bailey, 1841), 105–106. See also Blum, *View from the Masthead*, 19–45.

19. *The Life Boat* (Apr. 1860): 253 and quoted in Blum, *View from the Masthead*, 9–10; Nathaniel Ames, *A Mariner's Sketches* (Providence, R.I.: Cory, Marshall, and Hammond, 1830), 241–242. "Narragansett Library Book List" quoted in Blum, *View from the Masthead*, 33–34; Charles Samuel Stewart, *A Visit to the South Seas in the United States Ship Vincennes, during the Years 1829–1830* (New York: John P. Haven, 1833), 25–26. For the literacy rates of sailors, see Blum, *View from the Masthead*, 5; Rediker, *Between the Devil and the Deep Blue Sea*, 158; and Harry Skallerup, *Books Afloat and Ashore: A History of Books, Libraries, and Reading among Seamen during the Age of Sail* (Hamden, Conn.: Archon, 1974), 22–23. By way of comparison, white "common laborers" during the antebellum era are estimated to have had a literacy rate of around 50 to 60 percent, while the (largely free and northern) black literacy rate is estimated at 20 percent. See Lee Soltow and Edward Stevens, *The Rise of Literacy and the Common School in the United States: A Socioeconomic Analysis to 1870* (Chicago: University of Chicago Press, 1981), 50–54; U.S. Dept. of Commerce, Bureau of the Census, *Historical Statistics of the United States, Colonial Times to 1970* (Washington, D.C.: Bureau of the Census, 1975); and Denning, *Mechanic Accents*, 30–31.

20. Dana, *Two Years before the Mast*, 265. On Dana and the use of seafaring narratives by territorial expansionists, see Robert F. Lucid, "*Two Years before the Mast* as Propaganda," *American Quarterly* 12, no. 3 (1960): 392–403; Ronald Takaki, *Iron Cages: Race and Culture in 19th-Century America* (New York: Alfred Knopf, 1979), 156–157; and Amy Greenberg, *Manifest Manhood and the Antebellum American Empire* (Cambridge: Cambridge University Press, 2005), 81. Some of these ideas about the early flow of information are discussed in Tom Standage, *The Victorian Internet: The Remarkable Story of the Telegraph and the Nineteenth-Century's On-Line Pioneers* (New York: Walker & Co., 1998).

21. Alonzo D. Sampson, *Three Times around the World* (Buffalo: Express Printing, 1867), 1; Frederic Stanhope Hill, *Twenty Years at Sea or Leaves from My Old Log-Books* (Boston: Houghton, Mifflin, and Co., 1893), 6–7; John Sherburne Sleeper, *Jack in the Forecastle; or, Incidents in the Early Life of Hawser Martingale* (New York: Worthington, 1886), 9–10.

22. Richard A. Schwarzlose, "Harbor News Association: The Formal Origin of the AP," *Journalism and Mass Communication Quarterly* 45, no. 2 (1968): 253–260.

23. *Boston Courier*, Oct. 2, 1828. For the relationship between dissemination of information and citizenship, see Warner, *Letters of the Republic*; Richard R. John, *Spreading the News: The American Postal System from Franklin to Morse* (Cambridge, Mass.: Harvard University Press, 1995); and Menahem Blondheim, *News over the Wires: The Telegraph and the Flow of Public Information in America, 1844–1897* (Cambridge, Mass: Harvard University Press, 1994).

24. *New-Bedford Daily Gazette*, republished in *New York Star*, Nov. 26, 1835; *New-Bedford Daily Mercury*, Jan. 5, 1841; *New-Bedford Mercury*, Jan. 30, 1829.

25. Original story appears in the *Boston Mercantile Evening Journal*, May 15, 1835. Subsequently reprinted in the *Boston Courier*, May 16, 1835; *Nantucket Inquirer* and *Boston Daily Columbian Centinel*, May 18, 1835; and *Salem Landmark*, May 20, 1835.

26. *Columbian Centinel*, Aug. 9, 1800; the story also appeared in the *Federal Gazette* and the *Daily Baltimore Advertiser*, Aug. 7, 1800; *Nantucket Enquirer*, Mar. 3, 1832; *Lynn Record*, Sept. 24, 1834, and for reprints, see *Salem Observer*, Sept. 27, 1834, and *Salem Mercury*, Sept. 24, 1834; *Salem Mercury*, Apr. 27, 1836; *Essex North Register*, Apr. 29, 1836.

27. *Salem Mercury*, Apr. 27, 1836; *Essex North Register*, Apr. 29, 1836; *Boston Daily Journal*, Aug. 8, 1865.

28. *Nantucket Enquirer*, Mar. 28, 1825. Reprinted in *The Repertory*, Apr. 1, 1825; *New-Bedford Weekly Mercury*, Apr. 1, 1825; *Essex Register*, Apr. 4, 1825; *New England Gazette*, Apr. 5, 1825; and *New England Palladium and Commercial Advertiser*, Apr. 1, 1825.

29. *Boston Daily Advertiser*, May 14, 1836; *Salem Gazette*, June 10, 1870. On letters and the circulation of news, see Eve Tavor Bannet, *Empire of Letters: Letter Manuals and Transatlantic Correspondence, 1688–1820* (Cambridge: Cambridge University Press, 2005); and Konstantin Dierks, *In My Power: Letter Writing and Communications in Early America* (Philadelphia: University of Pennsylvania Press, 2009).

30. *Salem Gazette*, June 2, 1835; *Boston Evening Mercantile Journal*, June 9, 1835; and *Boston Daily Advertiser*, June 15, 1835.

31. On Barbary captivity, see Robert J. Allison, *The Crescent Obscured: The United States and the Muslim World, 1776–1815* (New York: Oxford University Press, 1995). On the United States Exploring Expedition, see Barry Alan Joyce, *The Shaping of American Ethnography: The Wilkes Exploring Expedition, 1838–1842* (Lincoln: University of Nebraska Press, 2001).

32. John Jewitt, *A Narrative of the Adventures and Sufferings of John R. Jewitt* (Middletown, Conn.: Seth Richards, 1815). The associated play and circumstances surrounding its production are discussed in Douglas S. Harvey, *The Theatre of Empire: Frontier Performances in America, 1750–1860* (London: Pickering and Chatto, 2010), 128–132. On nautical plays of Dibdin, see Isaac Land, *War Nationalism, and the British Sailor* (New York: Palgrave Macmillan, 2009), 89–98. On poetry, drama, "sailor captive" plays, and the portrayal of the wider world, see Blum, *View from the Masthead*, 8–9 and 46–70.

33. *Lynn Record*, May 5, 1836; *Providence Patriot*, Apr. 17, 1819; "Last of Vendovi!," *New York Herald*, June 12, 1842; "Important News from the Exploring Expedition," *Weekly Herald*, June 18, 1842. The ordeal of Veidovi is discussed in Ann Fabian, *The Skull Collectors: Race, Science, and America's Unburied Dead* (Chicago: University of Chicago Press, 2010), 121–161.

34. See Paul M. Angle, ed., *Created Equal: The Complete Lincoln-Douglas Debates of 1858* (Chicago: University of Chicago Press, 1958), 22–23, 64, and 156.

35. Bayard Taylor, *A Visit to China, India, and Japan* (London: James Blackwood, 1859), 237–238.

36. Entry dated July 4, 1870, journal of Susan McKenzie, kept aboard ship *Hercules*, MSS 56, Box 46, Series M, Subseries 4, NBWM; entries dated Mar. 8, 1857, and Sept. 26, 1856, journal of Robert Weir, kept aboard *Clara Bell*, Log 164, MSM; Hill, *Twenty Years at Sea*, 119; Thomas Dudley to sister, letter dated Mar. 8, 1856, Thomas C. Dudley Papers, William L. Clements Library, University of Michigan, Ann Arbor, Mich. For sailors' souvenirs as objects of domestic display, see Caroline Frank, *Objectifying China, Imagining America: Chinese Commodities in Early America* (Chicago: University of Chicago Press, 2011).

37. Charles Wilkes, *Narrative of the United States Exploring Expedition during the Years 1838–1842*, 5 vols. (New York: G. P. Putnam, 1856), 2:399–400; entries dated Dec. 23–24, 1866, and Jan. 11, 1867, journal of Charles Judd, kept aboard U.S.S. *Ossipee*, NHC; entry dated Sept. 29, 1853, journal of William B. Allen, kept aboard ship *Vandalia*, MMC-1798, LOC.

38. Ernest Dodge, *Islands and Empires: Western Impact on the Pacific and East Asia* (Minneapolis: University of Minnesota Press, 1976), 77–79. On forgeries, see Alfred Hunter, *An Popular*

Catalogue of the Extraordinary Curiosities in the National Institute (Washington, D.C.: Alfred Hunter, 1855), 49.

39. "A Day in Old Salem," newspaper clipping, Peabody Academy of Science scrapbook, 1875–1879, PEM; entries dated July 27 and Dec. 1, 1854, diary of Edward McCauley, NYHS. See Anya Zilberstein, "Objects of Distant Exchange: The Northwest Coast, Early America, and the Global Imagination," *William and Mary Quarterly* 64, no. 3 (2007): 591–620; and Daniel Finamore, "Displaying the Sea and Defining America: Early Exhibitions at the Salem East India Marine Society," *Journal of Maritime Research* 4 (May 2002): 1–12. Fabian notes that sailors and whalemen "sometimes peddled [exotic objects] to curious collectors"; see *Skull Collectors*, 129. Isaac Land notes the importance of sailor guides in early British museums in *War, Nationalism, and the British Sailor* (New York: Palgrave Macmillan, 2009), 143–152.

40. William Goddard to Joseph Lindsey, letter dated Oct. 7, 1835, Box 6, Folder 8, Joseph Lindsey Collection, MMHS; Edward Shippen, *Thirty Years at Sea: The Story of a Sailor's Life* (Philadelphia: J. B. Lippincott, 1879), 79–80; entry dated Aug., 1842, journal of John Martin, kept aboard ship *Lucy Ann*, KWM Log 434, NBWM; William Dane Phelps, *Fore and Aft; or, Leaves from the Life of an Old Sailor* (Boston: Nichols and Hall, 1871), 117–118. For sailors gathering and transporting specimens, see Christopher Parsons, "Ecosystems under Sail: Specimen Transport in the Eighteenth-Century French and British Atlantics," *Early American Studies* 10, no. 3 (2012): 503–529. On skull collecting and early race science, see Fabian, *Skull Collectors*; and Robert E. Bieder, *Science Encounters the Indian, 1820–1880: The Early Years of American Ethnology* (Norman: University of Oklahoma Press, 1986). On skull collecting and empire more broadly, see Ricardo Roque, *Headhunting and Colonialism: Anthropology and the Circulation of Human Skulls in the Portuguese Empire, 1870–1930* (New York: Palgrave Macmillan, 2010).

41. William Stanton, *The Leopard's Spots: Scientific Attitudes toward Race in America, 1815–1859* (Chicago: University of Chicago Press, 1960), 10. See also Charlotte Porter, *The Eagle's Nest: Natural History and American Ideas, 1812–1849* (Tuscaloosa: University of Alabama Press, 1986); and Joyce, *The Shaping of American Ethnography*, 8–9. William Goetzmann, *New Lands, New Men: America and the Second Great Age of Discovery* (New York: Viking, 1986), 234–236, delimits the centrality of maritime accounts to the accretion of anthropological information and race science. It was also argued that racial diversity within the United States itself made Americans innately inclined toward ethnography: "Nowhere else can we find brought in so close proximity, the representatives of races and families of men, of origins and physical and mental constitutions so diverse. Within the boundaries of our own country, three at least of the five grand divisions into which the human family is usually grouped, are fully represented"; E. G. S., "American Ethnology," *American Whig Review* 9 (Apr. 1849): 385–386. The most comprehensive study of public intellectuals and the spread of scientific racism in the early republic remains Bruce Dain, *A Hideous Monster of the Mind: American Race Theory in the Early Republic* (Cambridge, Mass.: Harvard University Press, 2002), yet even he confines the debate over race largely to the condition of enslaved peoples. On the Indian angle, see Nancy Shoemaker, *A Strange Likeness: Becoming Red and White in Eighteenth-Century North America* (New York: Oxford University Press, 2004). Other overviews of scientific racism in early America include David Roediger, *How Race Survived U.S. History* (New York: Verso, 2008); Reginald Horsman, *Race and Manifest Destiny: Origins of American Racial Anglo-Saxonism* (Cambridge, Mass.: Harvard University Press, 1981), esp. 43–61; and George M. Frederickson, *The Black Image in the White Mind: The Debate on Afro-American Character and Destiny, 1817–1914* (New York: Harper & Row, 1971), esp. 76–82.

42. Journal of N. Byron Smith entitled "History of a Three Years' Whaling Voyage," 28–29, 129, microfilm 16, 747–1P, LOC.

43. Charles Lane to cousin, undated letter (ca. 1855), Box 43, Series L, Subseries 1, MSS 56, Correspondence of Charles Lane, NBWM; entry dated Aug. 5, 1847, journal of Horace Putnam, kept aboard ship *Cherokee*, PEM; Albert Freeman to Charles Cullis, Sept. 2, 1855, Letters of Albert Freeman, Box 1, Folder 3, Collection 118, MSM.

44. "The extinction of the red race upon this continent may be said to be almost consummated; and China, which by a sort of instinct, excluded the whites for thousands of years, is now open to a similar influence, and a crisis is reached in the history of the dark species of man"; "Natural History of Man," *United States Magazine and Democratic Review* 26 (Apr. 1850): 345. See also undated entry (ca. Aug. 1842), journal of John Martin, KWM 434, NBWM; entry dated Feb. 13, 1854, journal of Edward McCauley, NYHS; and Moon-Ho Jung, *Coolies and Cane: Race, Labor, and Sugar in the Age of Emancipation* (Baltimore, Md.: Johns Hopkins University Press, 2006). Other examples of sailors and race science include Francis Allyn Olmsted, *Incidents of a Whaling Voyage* (New York: D. Appleton and Co., 1841), 213; L. Vernon Briggs, *Around Cape Horn to Honolulu on the Bark* Amy Turner (Boston: Charles E. Lauriat, 1926), 134–135; Robert Coffin, *The Last of the "Logan": The True Adventures of Robert Coffin, Mariner, in the Years 1854 to 1859 Wherein Are Set Forth His Pursuit of the Whale, His Shipwreck on Rapid Reef, His Life among the Cannibals of Fiji, and His Search for Gold in Australia, as Told by Himself* (1859; repr., Ithaca, N.Y.: Cornell University Press, 1941), 140; William Williams, "The Voyage of the *Florence*," in *One Whaling Family*, ed. Harold Williams (Boston: Houghton Mifflin, 1964), 289; and William Reynolds, *The Private Journal of William Reynolds, 1838–1842* (New York: Penguin Books, 2004), 145.

45. Josiah C. Nott and George R. Gliddon, *Types of Mankind: Or, Ethnological Researches Based upon the Ancient Monuments, Paintings, Sculptures, and Crania of Races, and upon Their Natural, Geographical, Philological and Biblical History* (Philadelphia: Lippincott and Grambo, 1854). Nott to James H. Hammond and Ephraim Squier on pseudoscience as a justification for slavery is quoted in William Sumner Jenkins, *Pro-Slavery Thought in the Old South* (Chapel Hill: University of North Carolina Press, 1935), 257, 259–260.

46. On maritime conduits of resistance, abolitionism, and black radicalism, see W. Jeffrey Bolster, *Black Jacks: African-American Seamen in the Age of Sail* (Cambridge, Mass.: Harvard University Press, 1997); David S. Cecelski, *The Waterman's Song: Slavery and Freedom in Maritime North Carolina* (Chapel Hill: University of North Carolina Press, 2001); Peter Linebaugh and Marcus Rediker, *The Many-Headed Hydra: Sailors, Slaves, Commoners and the Hidden History of the Revolutionary Atlantic* (Boston: Beacon Press, 2000); and Paul Gilroy, *The Black Atlantic: Modernity and Double Consciousness* (Cambridge, Mass.: Harvard, 1993).

47. Hester Blum reports that sailors' reading materials included an array of magazines and newspapers that elaborated upon race science. See *The View from the Masthead*, 2–11, 20–29. Examples include "Is Man One or Many?," *Putnam's Monthly* 4 (July 1854): 1–14; and "The Negro," *DeBow's Review* 3 (May 1847), 419–422. For sailors who had any schooling to speak of, geography textbooks were a source for racial classification overseas, as noted in Anne Baker, *Heartless Immensity: Literature, Culture, and Geography in Antebellum America* (Ann Arbor: University of Michigan Press, 2006), 130–131. The phrase "habitable globe" appears in Cong. Globe, 27th Cong., 2nd Sess., Appendix, 750–751.

Chapter 2

1. Log of bark *Lagoda*, 1868–1873, ODHS Log #494, NBWM; entry dated Feb. 5, 1857, log of bark *Alto*, KWM 14, NBWM; entries dated Nov. 20 and Dec. 2, 1847, journal of

Frederick Schley, kept aboard ship *Cumberland*, NHC; entry dated Nov. 21, 1858, journal of William Abbe, kept aboard ship *Atkins Adams*, ODHS Log #485, NBWM; entry dated July 28, 1840, journal of Simeon A. Stearns, kept aboard ship *Vincennes*, NYPL; entry dated Oct. 23, 1848, journal of William Henry Weaver, NYHS.

2. Journal of Charles Mervine, reprinted in Charles K. Mervine and Kent Packard, eds., "Jottings by the Way: A Sailor's Log, 1862–1864," *Pennsylvania Magazine of History and Biography* 71, no. 3 (1947): 249; Eric Lott, *Love and Theft: Blackface Minstrelsy and the American Working Class* (New York: Oxford University Press, 1993), 31.

3. "Communications and Selections: The Shipmaster," *Sailor's Magazine and Naval Journal* 8, no. 1 (1835): 9.

4. "Tarantula" quoted in Lott, *Love and Theft*, 3. The life of T. D. Rice is described in Alexander Saxton, "Blackface Minstrelsy and Jacksonian Ideology," *American Quarterly* 27, no 1 (1975): 3–28.

5. Robert C. Toll, *Blacking Up: The Minstrel Show in Nineteenth-Century America* (New York: Oxford University Press, 1974); Lott, *Love and Theft*; Walter T. Lhamon, *Raising Cain: Blackface Performance from Jim Crow to Hip Hop* (Cambridge, Mass.: Harvard University Press, 1998); Alexander Saxton, *The Rise and Fall of the White Republic: Class Politics and Mass Culture in Nineteenth Century America* (New York: Verso, 1990), 165–181; Robert W. Rydell and Rob Kroes, *Buffalo Bill in Bologna: The Americanization of the World, 1869–1922* (Chicago: University of Chicago Press, 2005), 17, 35. It should be noted that several of these scholars describe how minstrelsy became a platform for the ideology of Manifest Destiny and continental expansionism, most notably through Stephen Foster's famed riff "Oh! Susanna," which reached peak popularity during the conquest of Mexico and the subsequent California gold rush. See esp. Saxton, *Rise and Fall of the White Republic*, 172–173. Here I am less focused on the paradigm of territorial expansion; I am attempting to pinpoint the global ramification of the minstrel show.

6. On the popularity of song and dance in maritime culture, see Walter Colton, *Ship and Shore* (New York: Leavitt, Lord, and Co., 1835), 152–154. Michael Bennett discusses minstrel performances onboard naval vessels during the Civil War in *Union Jacks: Yankee Sailors in the Civil War* (Chapel Hill: University of North Carolina Press, 2004), 175–177.

7. Kenneth E. Shewmaker, "Forging the 'Great Chain': Daniel Webster and the Origins of American Foreign Policy toward East Asia and the Pacific, 1841–1852," *Proceedings of the American Philosophical Society* 129, no. 3 (1985): 225–259. On cultural diplomacy and the Perry Expedition, including some discussion of the minstrel show, see Jeffrey A. Keith, "Civilization, Race, and the Japan Expedition's Cultural Diplomacy, 1853–1854," *Diplomatic History* 35, no. 2 (2011): 179–202. Eric Lott also discusses international minstrelsy in "White Like Me: Racial Cross-Dressing and the Construction of American Whiteness," in *Cultures of United States Imperialism*, ed. Amy Kaplan and Donald E. Pease (Durham, N.C.: Duke University Press, 1993), 474–497.

8. Michael Adas, *Dominance by Design: Technological Imperatives and America's Civilizing Mission* (Cambridge, Mass.: Harvard University Press, 2006), esp. 5–6, 12; Peter Booth Wiley, *Yankees in the Land of the Gods: Commodore Perry and the Opening of Japan* (New York: Viking Press, 1990).

9. Wilhelm Heine, *With Perry to Japan: A Memoir* (Honolulu: University of Hawaii Press, 1990), 169; S. Wells Williams, *A Journal of the Perry Expedition to Japan* (Wilmington, Del.: Scholarly Resources, 1973), 150; entry dated Mar. 28, 1854, journal of John Glendy Sproston, kept aboard ship *Macedonian*, MMC-0113N, LOC.

10. Roger Pineau, ed., *The Personal Journal of Commodore Matthew C. Perry* (Washington, D.C.: Smithsonian Institution Press, 1968), 188–189; Francis L. Hawks, *Narrative of the Expedition of an American Squadron to the China Seas and Japan* (Washington, D.C.: AOP Nicholson, 1856), 376, 70. Additional description of the performance is found in entry for Mar. 27, 1854, journal

of Edward Yorke McCauley, NYHS. The "negro concert" is further described in Samuel Eliot Morison, *"Old Bruin": Commodore Matthew C. Perry, 1794–1858* (Boston: Little, Brown, 1967), esp. 348–353; Victor Fell Yellin, "Mrs. Belmont, Matthew Perry, and the 'Japanese Minstrels,'" *American Music* 14, no. 3 (1996): 257–275; Steven Lubar, "In the Footsteps of Perry: The Smithsonian Goes to Japan," *The Public Historian* 17, no. 3 (1995): 54–57; and (most thoroughly) in Gretchen Murphy, *Hemispheric Imaginings: The Monroe Doctrine and Narratives of U.S. Empire* (Durham, N.C.: Duke University Press, 2005), 62–96. The structure of the show itself reveals a shift that took place in minstrelsy from its 1830s inception into the 1850s. Minstrelsy was originally a four-man instrumental operation, but the newer forms had performers arranged in a line where "customary position corresponded roughly to class identification." The end men, who played tambourine and bones, were lower class: by costume and vernacular "the plantation nigger." The middleman, or interlocutor, served as a bogus mouthpiece for high culture. See Saxton, *Rise and Fall of the White Republic*, 170.

11. George Henry Preble, *The Opening of Japan: A Diary of Discovery in the Far East, 1853–1856*, ed. Boleslaw Szczesniak (Norman: University of Oklahoma Press, 1962), 152–153; and Yellin, "'Japanese Minstrels,'" 265–256. On Japanese attitudes toward blackness, see Sherick A. Hughes, "The Convenient Scapegoating of Blacks in Postwar Japan: Shaping the Black Experience Abroad," *Journal of Black Studies* 33, no. 3 (2003): 335–340, quote at 338; J. G. Russell, "The Black Other in Contemporary Japanese Mass Culture," in *Contemporary Japan and Popular Culture*, ed. J. W. Treat (Honolulu: University of Hawaii Press, 1996), 16–40, esp. 20; and Masao Miyoshi, *As We Saw Them: The First Japanese Embassy to the United States* (New York: Kondansha International, 1994), 58–67. On the "theatricality" of imperial encounter, see, for example, Greg Dening, "The Theatricality of Observing and Being Observed: Eighteenth-Century Europe 'Discovers' the ? Century 'Pacific,'" in *Implicit Understandings: Observing, Reporting, and Reflecting on the Encounters between Europeans and Other Peoples in the Early Modern Era*, ed. Stuart B. Schwartz (New York: Cambridge, 1994), 451–483, esp. 455.

12. Hawks, *Narrative of the Expedition of an American Squadron*, 470, 376; Ronald P. Toby, "The 'Indianness' of Iberia and Changing Japanese Iconographies of Other," in *Implicit Understandings: Observing, Reporting, and Reflecting on the Encounters between Europeans and Other Peoples in the Early Modern Era*, ed. Stuart B. Schwartz (New York: Cambridge, 1994), 349. David Roediger argues that sharing humor over blackface minstrelsy became a means to "mutual understanding" in the American working class. It might also be argued that blackface could function overseas to relieve tensions between encountered peoples. See David R. Roediger, *The Wages of Whiteness: Race and the Making of the American Working Class*, revised ed. (New York: Verso, 2007), 115–116, 127.

13. Journal entry dated Dec. 1853; Thomas Dudley to sister dated Nov. 28, 1854; Thomas Dudley to sister dated Dec. 9, 1854; Thomas Dudley to sister dated Dec. 20, 1853, Thomas C. Dudley Papers, William L. Clements Library, University of Michigan, Ann Arbor. For minstrelsy as reform, see Benjamin Reiss, *Theaters of Madness: Insane Asylums and Nineteenth-Century American Culture* (Chicago: University of Chicago Press, 2008), 51–77.

14. J. Willett Spalding, *Japan and around the World* (New York: Redfield, 1855), 220, 80; Sarah Keyes, "'Like a Roaring Lion': The Overland Trail as Sonic Conquest," *Journal of American History* 96 (June 2009): 19–43.

15. Horatio Bridge, *Journal of an African Cruiser by an Officer of the U.S. Navy* (Aberdeen: George Clark and Son, 1848), 20–21; Douglass, *The North Star*, Oct. 27, 1848, quoted in Lott, *Love and Theft*, 15.

16. Undated entry (ca. 1858), journal of Albert Peck, kept aboard ship *Covington*, Paul C. Nicholson Whaling Collection, microfilm reel 17, vol. 187, PPL. Master Juba, or William Henry Lane, was a black performer who toured with a white-owned minstrel company in the 1840s. Charles Dickens graphically described him in his *American Notes*, and his notoriously frantic dance steps received numerous rave reviews. His name became synonymous with African American, or "Juba" dance in the nineteenth century. See Dickens, *American Notes* (Greenwich, Conn.: Fawcett, 1961), chapter 6; and Lott, *Love and Theft*, 113–116.

17. Horatio Bridge, *Journal of an African Cruiser by an Officer of the U.S. Navy* (Aberdeen: George Clark and Son, 1848), 10–11. Minstrel show titles drawn solely from Bennett, *Union Jacks*, 175–177; entry dated Nov. 2, 1864, journal of Charles K. Mervine, Historical Society of Pennsylvania; journal entry dated Mar. 29, 1853, Journal of Thomas Dudley in Thomas C. Dudley Papers, William L. Clements Library, University of Michigan; Henry Wise, *Los Gringos* (New York: Baker and Scribner, 1849), 25.

18. Nathaniel Philbrick, *Sea of Glory: America's Voyage of Discovery, the U.S. Exploring Expedition, 1838–1842* (New York: Penguin, 2004).

19. Charles Erskine, *Twenty Years before the Mast* (Boston: Morning Star Press, 1890), 160–161; Charles Wilkes, *Narrative of the U.S. Exploring Expedition*, 5 vols. (Philadelphia: Lea and Blanchard, 1845), 2:55, 3:130.

20. Wilkes, *Narrative of the U.S. Exploring Expedition*, 2:55, 3:130. On the United States Exploring Expedition and minstrel music, see William Reynolds, *The Private Journal of William Reynolds: U.S. Exploring Expedition, 1838–1842*, ed. Nathaniel and Thomas Philbrick (New York: Penguin, 2005), 147–148. For whites' confused racial classification of Fijians, see Paul Lyons, *American Pacificism: Oceania and the U.S. Imagination* (New York: Routledge, 2006), 74–75; and Barry Alan Joyce, *The Shaping of American Ethnography: The Wilkes Exploring Expedition, 1838–1842* (Lincoln: University of Nebraska Press, 2001), esp. 60–61, 98–100, and 118–121. Some at home in the United States confused blackface minstrels with actual African Americans, and later advertisements took care to show performers both in and out of costume; see Lott, *Love and Theft*, 19–20.

21. Account of the status of black mariners in Fiji contained in "Narrative of John Jackson," in John Elphinstone Erskine, *Journal of a Cruise among the Islands of the Western Pacific* (London: John Murray, 1853), 465–466. Discussions of the question of minstrelsy and audience reception in Dale Cockrell, *Demons of Disorder: Early Blackface Minstrels and Their World* (Cambridge: Cambridge University Press, 1997), 161–162, and William J. Mahar, *Behind the Burnt Cork Mask: Early Blackface Minstrelsy and Antebellum American Popular Culture* (Urbana, Ill.: University of Illinois Press, 1998).

22. Erskine, *Twenty Years before the Mast*, 158–160.

23. Ibid., 47, 136–137.

24. A Roving Printer, *Life and Adventures in the South Pacific* (New York: Harper and Brothers, 1861), 150–2; George Colvocoresses, *Four Years in a Government Exploring Expedition* (1852; repr., Bedford, Mass.: Applewood Books, n.d.), 79; Charles Rockwell, *Sketches of Foreign Travel and Life at Sea*, 2 vols. (Boston: Tappan and Dennet, 1842), 2:260.

25. Charles Rockwell, *Sketches of Foreign Travel and Life at Sea*, 2 vols. (Boston: Tappan and Dennet, 1842), 2:260.

26. Entry dated Jan. 25, 1850, journal of Nathaniel Morgan, kept aboard ship *Hannibal*, Log 862, MSM; entry dated Sept. 20, 1855, journal of William Stetson, kept aboard ship *Arab*, ODHS Log #0507, NBWM.

27. Rockwell, *Sketches of Foreign Travel and Life at Sea*, 2:260; deposition of William Green at the trial of Abraham Lyell, Feb. 21, 1857, RG 125, Records of the Office of the Judge Advocate General (Navy), Records of the General Courts Martial and Courts of Inquiry of the Navy Department, 1799–1867, M273, reel 85, vol. 76, NARA I. See also trial of Lewis Rogers, June 6, 1857, RG 125, Records of the Office of the Judge Advocate General (Navy), Records of the General Courts Martial and Courts of Inquiry of the Navy Department, 1799–1867, M273, reel 87, vol. 78, NARA I.

28. Narrative found in *Boston Daily Advertiser*, Aug. 22, 1840.

29. Erskine, *Journal of a Cruise among the Islands of the Western Pacific*, 351–352.

30. Edward Wakefield, *Adventure in New Zealand from 1839–1844* (London: Whitcombe and Tombs, 1908), 24; James Goodenough, *Journal of Commodore Goodenough* (London: Henry S. King, 1876), 298; Lhamon, *Raising Cain*, 3, 63, and, 186–187. Lhamon believes that minstrelsy, far from a display of bigotry, in fact gestured toward interracial solidarity until it was co-opted by elites and driven toward more divisive ends. These claims are highly controversial, as suggested in Saidiya V. Hartman, *Scenes of Subjection: Terror, Slavery, and Self-Making in Nineteenth-Century America* (New York: Oxford University Press, 1997). Hartman rejects scholarship treating minstrelsy as a subversive expression of cross-racial class solidarity. Language and communication across the Pacific is discussed in Nicholas Thomas, *Islanders: The Pacific in the Age of Empire* (New Haven, Conn.: Yale University Press, 2010), 230–240. For "contact zones," see Mary Louise Pratt, "Arts of the Contact Zone," *Profession* (1991): 33–40.

31. Richard Henry Dana Jr., *Two Years before the Mast* (New York: Harper and Brothers, 1868), 171–172; Richard A. Cruise, *Journal of a Ten Months' Residence in New Zealand* (London: Longman, 1823), 31, 214.

32. A discussion of Pacific peoples' resistance tactics appears in David Chappell, *Double Ghosts: Oceanian Voyagers on Euroamerican Ships* (Armonk, N.Y.: M. E. Sharpe, 1997). On active responses to European arrival, see Thomas, *Islanders*.

33. Bayard Taylor, *A Visit to China, India, and Japan* (London: James Blackwood, 1859), 79–80.

34. Colvocoresses, *Four Years in a Government Exploring Expedition*, 77; John Lloyd Stephens, *Incidents of Travel in Yucatan*, 2 vols. (London: John Murray, 1843), 1:30. See Ryan Dunch, "Beyond Cultural Imperialism: Cultural Theory, Christian Missions, and Global Modernity," *History and Theory* 41, no. 3 (2002): 301–325; and Mary Louise Pratt, *Imperial Eyes: Travel Writing and Transculturation* (New York: Routledge, 2007).

35. "Narrative of John Jackson," 468–469. On the theatre of Pacific intercultural encounters, see Vanessa Smith, *Literary Culture and the Pacific: Nineteenth-Century Textual Encounters* (New York: Cambridge University Press, 1998). On "oppositional representation" or "autoethnography," see Pratt, "Arts of the Contact Zone," esp. 35.

36. "Frank T. Bullen Revives Memories of an Old Whaling Town," newspaper clipping located in journal kept aboard ship *South Boston*, 1851–1853, ODHS Log #761, NBWM.

37. Edwin P. Christy, *Christy's Plantation Melodies No. 4* (Philadelphia: Fisher, 1854), quoted in Alexander Saxton, "Blackface Minstrelsy and Jacksonian Ideology," *American Quarterly* 27, no. 1 (1975): 1. Shifts in minstrelsy are covered in LeRoy Ashby, *With Amusement for All: A History of American Popular Culture since 1830* (Lexington: University of Kentucky Press, 2006), 12–22.

38. On the larger matrix of Pacific cultural interchange, see Matt Matsuda, *Pacific Worlds: A History of Seas, Peoples, and Cultures* (New York: Cambridge University Press, 2012). Caribbean (and especially Cuban) blackface performance is discussed in Jill Lane, *Blackface Cuba, 1840–1895* (Philadelphia: University of Pennsylvania Press, 2005).

39. *Kunchi* is described in Matsuda, *Pacific Worlds*, 88–89.

40. Joseph G. Clark, *Lights and Shadows of Sailor Life, as Exemplified in Fifteen Years' Experience* (Boston: Benjamin B. Mussey & Co., 1848), 124, 138, 166. On *nanban* drag shows, see Toby, "The 'Indianness' of Iberia and Changing Japanese Iconographies of Other," 323–351.

41. The translated playbill is quoted in Heine, *With Perry to Japan*, 155 and described in Keith, "Civilization, Race, and the Japan Expedition's Cultural Diplomacy," 197–199. Justin Martin to brother, Nov. 29, 1844, Letters of Justin Martin, MSM. For men complaining of the "bondage" of nautical life, see deposition of Orville Matthews at the trial of Michael Welch, July 6, 1858, RG 125, Records of the Office of the Judge Advocate General (Navy), M273, reel 88, vol. 79, NARA I; deposition of Lewis Hoffman in the trial of Francis Wray, Dec. 23, 1858, RG 125, Records of the Office of the Judge Advocate General (Navy), M273, reel 91, vol. 72, NARA I.

42. Deposition of Martin Byrne at the trial of William Good, Mar. 4, 1857, RG 125, Records of the Office of the Judge Advocate General (Navy), M273, reel 85, vol. 86, NARA I; Spalding, *Japan and around the World*, 202–203; Hawks, *Narrative of the Expedition*, 470. For theatre and power, see Peter P. Reed, *Rogue Performances: Staging the Underclasses in Early American Theatre Culture* (New York: Palgrave Macmillan, 2009), 4.

43. Mark Twain, *The Autobiography of Mark Twain* (New York: Harper, 1961), 66. The Jack Tar stereotype is discussed in Jesse Lemisch, "Jack Tar in the Streets: Merchant Seamen in the Politics of Revolutionary America," *William and Mary Quarterly* 25, no. 3 (1968): 371–407; and Matthew Raffety, *The Republic Afloat: Law, Honor, and Citizenship in Maritime America* (Chicago: University of Chicago Press, 2013), 96–100. Isaac Land describes the costumed, stage-like performances of sailors ashore in *War, Nationalism, and the British Sailor* (New York: Palgrave-Macmillan, 2009), 39–45. See also Isaac Land, "Customs of the Sea: Flogging, Empire, and the 'True British Seaman,' 1770–1870," *Interventions* 3, no. 2 (2001): 169–185, esp. 174: "the caricatured image of 'Jack Tar' closely paralleled the myth of Sambo."

44. The *Examiner* is quoted in Alex Roland, W. Jeffrey Bolster, and Alexander Keyssar, *The Way of the Ship: America's Maritime History Reenvisioned, 1600–2000* (Hoboken, N.J.: Wiley and Sons, 2008), 238. Paternalistic courts and legislation are described in Leon Fink, *Sweatshops at Sea: Merchant Seamen in the World's First Globalized Industry from 1812 to the Present* (Chapel Hill: University of North Carolina Press, 2011), 61–62.

45. Bayard Taylor, *Eldorado, or, Adventures in the Path of Empire* (New York: Knopf, 1949), 206; J. K. Kennard, "Who Are Our National Poets?" *Knickerbocker* 26 no. 4 (1845): 331–341. See also Murphy, *Hemispheric Imaginings*, 79–81.

46. Eric Lott, "'The Seeming Counterfeit': Racial Politics and Early Blackface Minstrelsy," *American Quarterly* 43, no. 2 (1991): 226; *New York Herald*, Aug. 27, 1837, quoted in Cockrell, *Demons of Disorder*, 65–66 and *Boston Post*, July 26, 1838. On minstrelsy and empire, see Douglas Harvey, *The Theatre of Empire: Frontier Performances in America, 1750–1860* (London: Pickering and Chatto, 2010).

47. Lott, "'The Seeming Counterfeit,'" 226; Carl H. Nightingale, *Segregation: A Global History of Divided Cities* (Chicago: University of Chicago Press, 2013). Blackbirding and the Pacific trade in illicit labor are described in Gerald Horne, *The White Pacific: U.S. Imperialism and Black Slavery in the South Seas after the Civil War* (Honolulu: University of Hawaii Press, 2007); and Thomas, *Islanders*, 237–239. Mutual misunderstanding and middle grounds are described in Richard White, "Creative Misunderstandings and New Understandings," *William and Mary Quarterly* 63, no. 1 (2006): 9–14.

48. Global segregationist initiatives are described in Charles A. Price, *The Great White Walls Are Built: Restrictive Immigration in North America and Australasia, 1836–1888* (Canberra: Australia

National University Press, 1974); and Nightingale, *Segregation*, esp. 135–154. Quotes about the KKK and the blackbird trade appear in Horne, *White Pacific*, 4–5, 41.

49. Philbrick and Philbrick, *The Private Journal of William Reynolds*, 104; Anne Hoffman Cleaver and E. Jeffrey Stann, eds., *Voyage to the Southern Ocean: The Letters of Lieutenant William Reynolds from the U.S. Exploring Expedition, 1838–1842* (Annapolis: Naval Institute Press, 1988), 162.

50. Antarctic minstrels are described in Mike Pearson, "'No Joke in Petticoats': British Polar Expeditions and Their Theatrical Presentations," *The Drama Review* 48, no. 1 (2004): 44–59.

51. For traveling minstrel shows, see Ian Tyrrell, *Transnational Nation: United States History in Global Perspective since 1789* (New York: Palgrave Macmillan, 2007), 111.

Chapter 3

1. Poem in journal kept aboard ship *South Boston*, 1851–1853, ODHS Log #761, NBWM. For a similar example, see William Cullen Bryant's poem "Catterskill Falls," in Richard Henry Stoddard and Harry C. Edwards, eds., *The Complete Poems of William Cullen Bryant* (New York: D. Appleton, 1874), 169–172. Myra C. Glenn notes the pioneer analogy in "Forging Manhood and Nationhood Together: American Sailors' Accounts of their Exploits, Sufferings, and Resistance in the Antebellum United States," *American Nineteenth-Century History* 8, no. 1 (2007): 30. Thomas Philbrick uses Cooper's fiction to propose intertwined oceanic and continental frontiers in *James Fenimore Cooper and the Development of American Sea Fiction* (Cambridge, Mass: Harvard University Press, 1961), vii–xi and 260–266. On the similar theme of a comparison of whalers and backwoods hunters, see Jennifer Schell, *"A Bold and Hardy Race of Men": The Lives and Literature of American Whalemen* (Boston: University of Massachusetts Press, 2013), 199–208.

2. Daniel Vickers, *Young Men and the Sea: Yankee Seafarers in the Age of Sail* (New Haven, Conn: Yale University Press, 2005), 4–5. Works focused on continental expansion in the United States as the site of cultural encounter include Adam Rothman, *Slave Country: American Expansion and the Origins of the Deep South* (Cambridge, Mass.: Harvard University Press, 2005); Patrick Griffin, *American Leviathan: Empire, Nation, and the Revolutionary Frontier* (New York: Hill and Wang, 2007); Peter J. Kastor, *The Nation's Crucible: The Louisiana Purchase and the Creation of America* (New Haven, Conn.: Yale University Press, 2004); and Stephen Aron, *How the West Was Lost: The Transformation of Kentucky from Daniel Boone to Henry Clay* (Baltimore, Md.: Johns Hopkins University Press, 1996). The interplay between working-class culture, expansion, and the flash press is discussed in Shelley Streeby, *American Sensations: Class, Empire, and the Production of Popular Culture* (Berkeley: University of California Press, 2002).

3. The Nantucket whale fishery provides an important counterexample to the more general underrepresentation of Native Americans in the working experience of the nation's seamen. From the colonial period through the early nineteenth century, Nantucket's indigenous population served aboard whaleships and alongside the island's white and predominantly Quaker men, often entangled in usurious relations of debt dependency; see Daniel Vickers, "The First Whalemen of Nantucket," *William and Mary Quarterly* 40, no. 4 (1983): 560–583. Indians who served before the mast did so with excellent reputations, as noted in an early nineteenth-century court case where the judge remarked that a ship's "crew composed of Nantucket Indians [was] known to be among the best seamen in our service"; quoted in Gaddis Smith, "Black Seamen and the Federal Courts, 1789–1860," in *Ships, Seafaring and Society*, ed. Timothy J. Runyan (Detroit, Mich.: Wayne State University Press, 1987), 326. See also Briton Cooper Busch, *"Whaling Will Never Do for Me": The American Whaleman in the Nineteenth Century* (Lexington:

University Press of Kentucky, 1994), 32–50; and David A. Chappell, "Ahab's Boat: Non-European Seamen in Western Ships of Exploration and Commerce," in *Sea Changes: Historicizing the Ocean*, ed. Bernhard Klein and Gesa Mackenthun (New York: Routledge, 2004), 75–89.

4. Karen Kupperman describes the application of extant tropes to Indian bodies in *Indians and English: Facing Off in Early America* (Ithaca, N.Y.: Cornell University Press, 2000). Daniel Richter describes ideological constructions of the Indian that enabled people to rely "less on what they had actually seen than on what they thought they knew" in "'Believing That Many of the Red People Suffer Much for the Want of Food': Hunting, Agriculture, and a Quaker Construction of Indianness in the Early Republic," in *Race and the Early Republic: Racial Consciousness and Nation-Building in the Early Republic*, ed. Michael A. Morrison and James Brewer Stewart (New York: Rowman and Littlefield Publishers, 2002), 28.

5. Thomas Bender, "Historians, the Nation, and the Plenitude of Narratives," in *Rethinking American History in a Global Age*, ed. Thomas Bender (Los Angeles: University of California Press, 2002), 6. See also Bender, *A Nation among Nations: America's Place in World History* (New York: Hill and Wang, 2006); and Ian Tyrrell, *Transnational Nation: United States History in Global Perspective since 1789* (New York: Palgrave Macmillan, 2007).

6. Maritime approaches to world history include Rainer F. Buschman, "Oceans of World History: Delineating Aquacentric Notions of the Global Past," *History Compass* 2, no. 1 (2004): 1–10; and the forum "Oceans of History," *American Historical Review* 111, no. 3 (2006): 717–780. Other works that discuss ideas about Indians in the white mind include Robert F. Berkhofer, *The White Man's Indian: Images of the American Indian from Columbus to the Present* (New York: Knopf, 1978); Elise Marienstras, "The Common Man's Indian: The Image of the Indian as a Promoter of National Identity in the Early National Era," in *Native Americans and the Early Republic*, ed. Frederick E. Hoxie, Ronald Hoffman, and Peter J. Albert (Charlottesville, Va.: University Press of Virginia, 1999): 261–296. On the more global application of Jacksonian ideology, see Thomas Hietala, *Manifest Design: Anxious Aggrandizement in Late Jacksonian America* (Ithaca, N.Y.: Cornell University Press, 1985), esp. chapter 3; John H. Schroeder, *Shaping a Maritime Empire: The Commercial and Diplomatic Role of the American Navy, 1829–1861* (Westport, Conn.: Greenwood Press, 1985), esp. chapter 5; John M. Belohlavek, *"Let the Eagle Soar!": The Foreign Policy of Andrew Jackson* (Lincoln: University of Nebraska Press, 1985); and Reginald Horsman, *Race and Manifest Destiny: The Origins of American Racial Anglo-Saxonism* (Cambridge, Mass.: Harvard University Press, 1981).

7. Walker quoted in Hietala, *Manifest Design*, 91–92, my emphasis; Cong. Globe, 31st Cong., 2nd Sess., Mar. 1851, 757–758, referring to a need for the protection of "our ocean frontier"; *Cincinnati Daily Enquirer*, Nov. 26, 1853. Stephen A. Douglas made similar arguments about maritime expansionism: "The great point at issue, the great struggle is for our maritime ascendancy on all these waters"; Cong. Globe, 29th Congress, 1st Session, Jan. 1846, 259. Other examples of maritime "frontier" boosterism include *San Francisco Herald*, Oct. 27, 1851; "California—Its Position and Prospects," *Democratic Review* 24 (May 1849): esp. 426–427; *Honolulu Polynesian*, Nov. 22, 1851. Daniel Vickers also describes the expansive, oceanic notions of the "frontier" of early Americans; see *Young Men and the Sea*, 249. William E. Weeks briefly urges scholars to consider the "whaling frontier" as a zone of intercultural contact between Americans and foreign peoples in "American Expansion, 1815–1860," in *A Companion to American Foreign Relations*, ed. Robert Schulzinger (Oxford: Blackwell Publishing, 2003), 72–73. The global applicability of Turnerian paradigms is discussed in Dan Jones, "Significance of the Frontier in World History," *History Compass* 1, no. 1 (2003): 1–3. The most recent effort to confine "Indian country" solely to the continent is William Unrau, *The Rise and Fall of Indian Country, 1825–1855* (Lawrence: University Press of Kansas, 2007). Thomas Hietala

hints at the enlarged dimensions of expansionism in arguing that American "concerns were commercial as well as territorial; their ambitions global, not just continental or hemispheric"; see "'This Splendid Juggernaut': Westward a Nation and Its People" in *Manifest Destiny and Empire: American Antebellum Expansionism*, ed. Robert W. Johanssen, Samuel Walter Haynes, and Christopher Morris (College Station: Texas A&M University Press, 1997), 51. In *The Fatal Environment: The Myth of the Frontier in the Age of Industrialization, 1800–1890* (New York: Atheneum, 1985) and *Gunfighter Nation: The Myth of the Frontier in Twentieth-Century America* (New York: Atheneum, 1992), Richard Slotkin provides evidence of the continued dependence on frontier rhetoric in the United States. On the Pacific frontier, see Arrell Morgan Gibson, *Yankees in Paradise: The Pacific Basin Frontier* (Albuquerque: University of New Mexico Press, 1987); Jean Heffer, *The United States and the Pacific: The History of a Frontier*, trans. Donald W. Wilson (Notre Dame: University of Notre Dame Press, 2002), esp. chapter 4; Amy Greenberg, *Manifest Manhood and the Antebellum American Empire* (Cambridge: Cambridge University Press, 2005), 231–268; and David Chappell, *Double Ghosts: Oceanian Voyagers on Euroamerican Ships* (Armonk, N.Y.: M. E. Sharpe, 1997), esp. 4–10.

8. Josiah Quincy, ed., *The Journals of Samuel Shaw* (Boston: William Crosby and H. P. Nichols, 1847), 151.

9. Charles Lane, Guam, to his cousin, 1855–1856, aboard bark *Henry Taber*, MSS 56, Box 43, Series L, Subseries 1, NBWM; entry dated Jan. 7, 1802, journal of William Haswell, kept aboard ship *Lydia*, PEM; A Roving Printer, *Life and Adventures in the South Pacific* (New York: Harper and Brothers, 1861), 98.

10. Undated entry, journal of William Alfred Allen, kept aboard ship *Samuel Robertson* Oct. 1841–Jan. 1846, ODHS Log #1040, NBWM. On the relationship between race and Native Americans, see John Wood Sweet, *Bodies Politic: Negotiating Race in the American North, 1730–1830* (Baltimore, Md.: Johns Hopkins University Press, 2003); or Nancy Shoemaker, *A Strange Likeness: Becoming Red and White in Eighteenth-Century North America* (New York: Oxford University Press, 2004).

11. Undated entry, 1851, journal of Horace B. Putnam, kept aboard the brig *Cherokee*, PEM; entry dated May 6, 1824, journal of David S. Edwards, NYPL; John M. Bullard, ed., *Captain Edmund Gardner, His Journal* (Milford, N.H.: The Cabinet Press, 1958), 7. For similar comparisons, see journal of N. Byron Smith, kept aboard ship *Nile*, 92–93, 95, Microfilm 16, 747–1P, LOC.

12. Kevin S. Reilly, ed., *The Journal of George Attwater* (New Haven, Conn.: New Haven Colonial Historical Society, 2002), 191–194.

13. Entry dated May 19, 1834, diary of Joseph Osborn, aboard ship *Emerald*, PEM; entry dated Dec. 26, 1851, journal kept aboard ship *Fortune*, Log F745/1850L, Paul C. Nicholson Whaling Collection, PPL; entry dated Nov. 29, 1849, journal of William Wilson, kept aboard ship *Cavalier*, Log 18, MSM. John Blatchford located "Female Indians" in Malaysia in *Narrative of the Life and Captivity of John Blatchford . . . a Prisoner of War in the Late American Revolution* (New London, Conn.: T. Green, 1788), 17. On gendered representations of native peoples, see Kathleen Brown, *Good Wives, Nasty Wenches, and Anxious Patriarchs: Gender, Race, and Power in Colonial Virginia* (Chapel Hill: University of North Carolina, 1996), esp. chapter 2; and David D. Smits, "The Squaw Drudge: A Prime Index of Savagism," *Ethnohistory* 29, no. 4 (1982): 281–306.

14. Ussama Makdisi notes that American missionaries abroad often used Indian tropes to legitimate their spiritual labor overseas as akin to initial Puritan forays into the wilderness. See *Artillery of Heaven: American Missionaries and the Failed Conversion of the Middle East* (Ithaca, N.Y.: Cornell University Press, 2008), esp. 4–5, 10–11, 88–89. The public nature of "private" journals

and correspondence in the maritime world is discussed in Margaret Creighton, "American Mariners and the Rites of Manhood," in *Jack Tar in History: Essays in the History of Maritime Life and Labour*, ed. Colin Howell and Richard Twomey (Fredericton, N.B.: Acadiensis Press, 1991), 147; and Hester Blum, *The View from the Mast-Head: Maritime Imagination and Antebellum American Sea Narratives* (Chapel Hill: University of North Carolina Press, 2008), 20–23. Richard Henry Dana noted that while at sea sailors frequently exchanged books, diaries, and letters with shipmates and with sailors aboard other ships they chanced to meet at sea. See Richard Henry Dana Jr., *Two Years before the Mast and Other Voyages* (New York: Library of America, 2005), 202. The editors of Jeremiah Reynolds's sea letters note their much wider circulation; see Anne Hoffman Cleaver and E. Jeffrey Stann, eds., *Voyage to the Southern Ocean: The Letters of Lieutenant William Reynolds from the U.S. Exploring Expedition, 1838–1842* (Annapolis: Naval Institute Press, 1988), ix. On the prevalence of the "Indian metric," see Philip J. Deloria, *Indians in Unexpected Places* (Lawrence: University Press of Kansas, 2004).

15. J. Ross Browne, *Etchings of a Whaling Cruise*, ed. John Seelye (1846; repr., Cambridge, Mass.: Belknap Press of Harvard University, 1968), 333–337.

16. Robert Coffin, *The Last of the "Logan": The True Adventures of Robert Coffin, Mariner, in the Years 1854 to 1859 Wherein Are Set Forth His Pursuit of the Whale, His Shipwreck on Rapid Reef, His Life among the Cannibals of Fiji, and His Search for Gold in Australia, as Told by Himself* (1859; repr., Ithaca, N.Y.: Cornell University Press, 1941), 39; entry dated Sept. 25, 1839, diary of Ezra Green, MM.

17. William B. Whitecar, *Four Years Aboard the Whaleship: Embracing Cruises in the Pacific, Atlantic, Indian, and Antarctic Oceans, in the Years 1855, 56, 57, 58, 59* (Philadelphia: J. B. Lippincott & Co., 1860), 84–85; entry dated Aug. 24, 1839, journal of Simeon Stearns, kept aboard ship *Vincennes*, NYPL. William Herndon also described a lethargic existence as "the Indian fashion" while anchored at Laguna, Mexico, in entry dated Mar. 4, 1848, journal of William Herndon, NYHS. Mary Louise Pratt notes that travelers often rendered foreign landscapes in ways that comported more closely with the home culture; see *Imperial Eyes: Travel Writing and Transculturation* (New York: Oxford, 1992), 204.

18. Undated entry (ca. 1839–1840), journal of Simeon A. Stearns; Joseph G. Clark, *Lights and Shadows of Sailor Life, as Exemplified in Fifteen Years' Experience* (Boston: Benjamin B. Mussey & Co., 1848), 213; entry dated July 12, 1840, journal of William Clark, kept aboard ship *Relief*, PEM. Barry Alan Joyce provides an important account of how the United States Exploring Expedition's ethnologists depended on "Indian" comparisons to classify the various peoples they encountered in *The Shaping of American Ethnography: The Wilkes Exploring Expedition, 1838–1842* (Lincoln, Neb: University of Nebraska Press, 2001), esp. 1–3, 127–128.

19. Nathaniel Philbrick and Thomas Philbrick, eds., *The Private Journal of William Reynolds: United States Exploring Expedition, 1838–1842* (New York: Penguin Books, 2004), 193–202, 241; Cleaver and Stann, *Voyage to the Southern Ocean*, 162; Charles Erskine, *Twenty Years before the Mast: With the More Thrilling Scenes and Incidents While Circumnavigating the Globe* (Philadelphia: George W. Jacobs & Co., 1896), 267. Reynolds, who uses the term "Natives" in this particular passage, used phrases such as "savage," "native," and "Indian" interchangeably in his lengthy diary and his voluminous correspondence. Other seafarers did the same, suggesting a rough contextual likeness among terms meant to designate both a lack of societal sophistication and the absence of any clear nationality among the observed. It was not rare at the time for Americans more broadly to suggest an equivalency among those several terms. Reynolds refers to Pacific Islanders alternately as "Natives" and "Indians" in ibid. 162, 185, 186. William Alfred Allen wrote of his whaleship being "surrounded by half naked indians" in Tahiti and later described "walking among the huts of the kannakas or indians till I was heartily tired"; entries dated Oct. 15 and 17,

1842, journal of William Alfred Allen. Jackson's message to Congress is in James D. Richardson, *A Compilation of the Messages and Papers of Presidents* (Washington, D.C.: Bureau of National Literature and Art, 1908), 3:519–522.

20. Undated entry (ca. 1840), journal of Simeon A. Stearns. On extirpative violence as a tactic used against Indians, see Patrick M. Malone, *A Skulking Way of War: Technology and Tactics among the New England Indians* (Baltimore, Md.: Johns Hopkins University Press, 1993); Jill Lepore, *The Name of War: King Philip's War and the Origins of American Identity* (New York: Knopf, 1998); and John Grenier, *The First Way of War: American War Making on the Frontier, 1607–1814* (New York: Cambridge University Press, 2005). British travelers were often more dependent on the trope of "blackness" to describe aboriginal cultures in Australia, New Zealand, and Oceania, though Captain Cook, for example, also used comparisons to Indians during his circumnavigation. But, Paul Lyons adds, "while Oceanians were often referred to as Indians, [this was] a fact that resonates differently in U.S. contexts than in [Cook's] own." See Lyons, *American Pacificism: Oceania in the U.S. Imagination* (New York: Routledge, 2006), 30. On expansion and "blackness" in Australia and New Zealand, see Inga Clendinnen, *Dancing with Strangers: Europeans and Australians at First Contact* (Cambridge: Cambridge University Press, 2005); Alistair Paterson, *The Lost Legions: Culture Contact in Colonial Australia* (Lanham, Md.: Alta Mira Press, 2008); and Allaine Cerwonka, *Native to the Nation: Disciplining Landscapes and Bodies in Australia* (Minneapolis: University of Minnesota Press, 2004). Vanessa Smith notes that French mariners in the Pacific referred to peoples as Indians but suggests that classical allusions were more common; see "Costume Changes: Passing at Sea and on the Beach," in *Sea Changes: Historicizing the Ocean*, ed. Bernhard Klein and Gesa Mackenthun (New York: Routledge, 2004), 37–51.

21. Arguments about racial tolerance and the maritime world appear in Peter Linebaugh and Marcus Rediker, *The Many-Headed Hydra: The Hidden History of the Revolutionary Atlantic* (Boston: Beacon Press, 2000); and James Farr, "A Slow Boat to Nowhere: The Multi-Racial Crews of the American Whaling Industry," *Journal of Negro History* 68, no. 2 (1983): 159–170.

22. Entry dated Sept. 20, 1855, journal of William Stetson, kept aboard ship *Arab*, ODHS Log #0507, NBWM; entry dated July 24, 1844, journal of William Alfred Allen.

23. See Glenn, "Forging Manhood and Nationhood Together," 38–42; Isaac Land, "The Many-Tongued Hydra: Sea Talk, Maritime Culture, and Atlantic Identities, 1700–1850," *Journal of American and Comparative Cultures* 25, nos. 3–4 (2002): 415; and Isaac Land, "Customs of the Sea: Flogging, Empire, and the 'True British Seaman,' 1770–1870," *Interventions* 3, no. 2 (2001): 169–185. Nathaniel Ames urged the expurgation of Portuguese, Cubans, and other such "detestable material" from the navy for the affront to national and racial decency they presented in *Nautical Reminiscences* (Providence: William Marshall, 1832), 36–38, quoted in Land, "Many-Tongued Hydra," 416. See also Clark, *Lights and Shadows of Sailor Life*, 319–320, for complaints about "foreigners" in the American navy.

24. Elihu Wright to his brother Samuel Wright, letter dated May 23, 1824, Letters of Elihu Wright, MSM. Efforts such as those of Wright and his shipmates to segregate their workplace became more common as the nineteenth century progressed. The infamous whaleship *Essex*, for example, was racially segregated on the insistence of white crew members. See Nathaniel Philbrick, *In the Heart of the Sea: The Tragedy of the Whaleship* Essex (New York: Viking, 2000), 34–35. When Frank Bullen stepped aboard a New Bedford whaleship ca. 1850, he "saw at once that black men and white had separated themselves, the blacks taking the port side and the whites the starboard"; Bullen, *The Cruise of the Cachalot: Round the World after Sperm Whales* (London: Smith, Elder & Co., 1898), 4. Michael J. Jarvis also describes shipboard segregation in "The Material Culture of Ships in the Age of Sail," in *Pirates, Jack Tar, and Memory: New Directions*

in American Maritime History, ed. Paul A. Gilje and William Pencak (Mystic, Conn.: Mystic Seaport, 2007), 61–63.

25. Roger Pineau, ed., *The Personal Journal of Commodore Matthew C. Perry* (Washington, D.C.: Smithsonian Institution Press, 1968), 24. Nancy Shoemaker presents compelling evidence about the regular appearance of Native American seamen in New England vessels; see "Mr. Tashtego: Native American Whalemen in Antebellum New England," *Journal of the Early Republic* 33, no. 1 (2013): 109–132.

26. Amasa Delano, "Narrative of Voyages and Travels in the Northern and Southern Hemispheres" in *Five Sea Captains: Their Own Accounts of Voyages under Sail*, ed. Walter Teller (New York: Atheneum Publishers, 1960), 51–52. On discourses of sympathy regarding Indians, see Laura Stevens, *The Poor Indians: British Missionaries, Native Americans, and Colonial Sensibility* (Philadelphia: University of Pennsylvania Press, 2004); and Renato Rosaldo, *Culture and Truth: The Remaking of Social Analysis* (Boston: Beacon Press, 1989), 68–87.

27. Dana, *Two Years before the Mast*, 234–235.

28. Ibid., 234. See also Rosaldo, *Culture and Truth*, 68–70; Greenberg, *Manifest Manhood*, 250–251. At several points in the narrative, it should be noted, Dana came into conflict with his shipmates over his privileged status. The ship's African American cook, for example, was outraged when Dana mocked his superstitions: "'You think, 'cause you been to college, you know better than anybody'"; Dana, *Two Years before the Mast*, 39.

29. William Meacham Murrell, *Cruise of the Frigate* Columbia *around the World* (Boston: Benjamin B. Mussey, 1840), 177.

30. Manhood and masculinity were obviously in flux during the period considered. As Greenberg notes, class was not necessarily the determining force in the types of manhood a person adhered to, but it was a significant factor. She discusses intersections between class and constructions of manhood in Greenberg, *Manifest Manhood*, 8–17; see also Bruce Dorsey, *Reforming Men and Women: Gender in the Antebellum City* (Ithaca, N.Y.: Cornell University Press, 2002); E. Anthony Rotundo, *American Manhood: Transformations in Masculinity from the Revolution to the Modern Era* (New York: Basic Books, 1993); and Gail Bederman, *Manliness and Civilization: A Cultural History of Gender and Race in the United States, 1880–1917* (Chicago: University of Chicago Press, 1995), 17–18.

31. Francis Allyn Olmsted, *Incidents of a Whaling Voyage to Which Are Added Observations on the Scenery, Manners and Customs, and Missionary Stations of the Sandwich and Society Islands* (New York: D. Appleton and Co., 1841), 127; George Little, *Life on the Ocean* (Boston: Waite and Pierce, 1846), 378–379. For sailor bodies as symbol, see Simon Newman, "Reading the Bodies of Early American Seafarers," *William and Mary Quarterly* 55, no. 1 (1998): 59–82; Simon P. Newman, *Embodied History: The Lives of the Poor in Early Philadelphia* (Philadelphia: University of Pennsylvania Press, 2003), 104–124; and Glenn, "Forging Manhood and Nationhood Together," 38–42.

32. G. R. Thompson, ed., *Edgar Allan Poe: Essays and Reviews* (New York: Library of America, 1984), 1231; Herman Melville, *Moby Dick, or, The White Whale* (Boston: C. H. Simonds, 1925), 104–108.

33. "Frank T. Bullen Revives Memories of an Old Whaling Town," newspaper clipping found in journal kept aboard ship *South Boston*, 1851–1853, ODHS Log #761, NBWM; Winthrop Martin in the *American Merchant Marine*, quoted in J. Wade Caruthers, *American Pacific Ocean Trade* (New York: Exposition Press, 1973), 83; William Dane Phelps, *Fore and Aft; or, Leaves from the Life of an Old Sailor* (Boston: Nichols and Hall, 1871), 106; Irving quoted in Schell, "*Bold and Hardy Race of Men*," 205; George F. Ruxton, *Adventures in Mexico and the Rocky Mountains* (London: John Murray, 1861), 242; *Berkshire County Whig*, Dec. 23, 1841. "Metaphorical

interchange" is described in Schell, "*A Bold and Hardy Race of Men*," 199–208. See also Haskell Springer, *America and the Sea: A Literary History* (Athens: University of Georgia Press, 1995), Introduction. Philbrick discussed interchange between oceanic and terrestrial frontiers in *James Fenimore Cooper and the Development of American Sea Fiction*, vii–xi and 260–266. See also Paul David Nelson, "James Fenimore Cooper's Maritime Nationalism, 1820–1850," *Journal of Military Affairs* 41, no. 3 (1977): 129–132; and Paul Gilje, *Liberty on the Waterfront: American Maritime Culture in the Age of Revolution* (Philadelphia: University of Pennsylvania Press, 2004), 229–249. The popularity of Buntline and Cooper among seafarers is discussed in Blum, *View from the Masthead*, 9–10 and 20–23.

34. Undated entry (ca. Apr. 1787), diary kept by John Hayes aboard the *Asia*, Barry-Hayes Papers, reel 1, ISM. For Indian military strength through the period of the early republic, see Richard White, *The Middle Ground: Indians, Empires, and Republics in the Great Lakes Region, 1650–1815* (New York: Cambridge University Press, 1991); and Gregory Dowd, *A Spirited Resistance: The North American Indian Struggle for Unity, 1745–1815* (Baltimore, Md.: Johns Hopkins University Press, 1993).

35. Olmsted, *Incidents of a Whaling Voyage*, 263; entry dated July 10, 1852 journal of William H. Myers, kept aboard ship *Alpha*, ODHS Log #1054, NBWM. Brian Dippie argues that lamentations over the "vanishing American" were so widespread as to create a "national habit of thought"; Dippie, *The Vanishing American: White Attitudes and U.S. Indian Policy* (Middletown, Conn.: Wesleyan University Press, 1982), 15. On the changing depictions of Indians in popular culture, see Roy Harvey Pearce, *The Savages of America: A Study of the Indian and the Idea of Civilization* (Baltimore, Md.: Johns Hopkins University Press, 1965); Berkhofer, *The White Man's Indian*; Alan Trachtenberg, *Shades of Hiawatha: Staging Indians, Making Americans, 1880–1930* (New York: Hill and Wang, 2004); Shari Huhndorf, *Going Native: Indians in the American Cultural Imagination* (Ithaca, N.Y.: Cornell University Press, 2001); Susan Schekel, *The Insistence of the Indian: Race and Nationalism in Nineteenth-Century American Culture* (Princeton, N.J.: Princeton University Press, 1998); and Marienstras, "The Common Man's Indian," 250–263.

36. Cleaver and Stann, *Voyage to the Southern Ocean*, 12; Erskine, *Twenty Years before the Mast*, 70. On whites wearing Indian costumes and role-playing as Indians, see Philip J. Deloria, *Playing Indian* (New Haven, Conn.: Yale University Press, 1998), chapter 2; Trachtenberg, *Shades of Hiawatha*; Susan Schekel, *Insistence of the Indian*, esp. chapter 3. "Red-face" performance is described in Roediger, *Wages of Whiteness*, 104–105.

37. *Young America on the Pacific*, quoted in Lorraine McConaghy, *Warship under Sail: The U.S.S. Decatur in the Pacific West* (Seattle: Univ. of Washington Press, 2009), 15; undated entry (ca. 1840), journal of Simeon A. Stearns, NYPL. See also Richter, *Facing East*, 189–236; and White, *The Middle Ground*. For imperial continuities across the nineteenth-century United States, see Greenberg, *Manifest Manhood*; and Amy Kaplan, *The Anarchy of Empire in the Making of U.S. Culture* (Cambridge, Mass.: Harvard University Press, 2002). Kaplan rightly prefers to see an "expansionist continuum" across the nineteenth and twentieth centuries in "'Left Alone with America': The Absence of Empire in the Study of American Culture," in *Cultures of United States Imperialism*, ed. Amy Kaplan and Donald E. Pease (Durham, N.C.: Duke University Press, 1993), 17. See Rod Edmond, *Representing the South Pacific: Colonial Discourse from Cook to Gauguin* (New York: Cambridge University Press, 1997) for a discussion of "inevitable racial destruction" and commercial expansion in the Pacific. On the last point, see Bender, *Nation among Nations*, 213–214: "The U.S. was thus reenacting abroad the policies at the heart of its westward expansion."

38. Undated entry (ca. Aug., 1840 and Dec. 10, 1840), journal of William Clark.

39. "Anti-Indian sublime" appears in Silver, *Our Savage Neighbors*, xvii–xx. "Vengeance" as a legal instrument in Jason Opal, "General Jackson's Passports: Natural Rights and Sovereign

Citizens in the Political Thought of Andrew Jackson, 1780s-1820s," *Studies in American Political Development* 27 (Oct. 2013), 1–17. The move from Jeffersonian assimilation to Jacksonian aggression is described in Daniel Richter, *Facing East from Indian Country: A Native History of Early America* (Cambridge, Mass.: Harvard University Press, 2001), 226–236. Militant sailor nationalism and maritime expansion is referred to in the Democratic periodical *The Man*, Apr. 10, 1834 and the *New-York Commercial Advertiser*, Apr. 8, 1834, in an article that coincided with a mayoral election Democrats hoped to curry seafarers' favor in. For shifting emphases in the popular press, see Streeby, *American Sensations*, esp. 91: popular literature in the 1840s and 1850s glorified expansion and "worked to popularize an ideology of imperial U.S. American manhood." On sailors and Democratic politics, see Gilje, *Liberty on the Waterfront*, 242–258.

40. Entry for Oct. 1853, 143, journal of N. Byron Smith; undated entry (ca. Aug. 1848), journals of Midshipman Henry Wise, vol. 7, kept aboard USS *Independence*, RG 45, Records of the Naval Records Collection of the Office of Naval Records and Library, E608 (60), NARA I; Edward T. Perkins, *Na Motu: or, Reef-Rovings in the South Seas* (New York: Pudney and Russell, 1854), iv–v; entry dated Jan. 25, 1847, journal of Elias Trotter, kept aboard ship *Illinois*, ODHS Log #1005, NBWM.

41. A.W. Ely, "The Islands of the Pacific," *De Bow's Review* 18 (Feb. 1855): 213; *Daily Alta California* (San Francisco), Apr. 22, 1851, quoted in Greenberg, *Manifest Manhood*, 241; Seward quoted in Anders Stephanson, *Manifest Destiny: American Expansion and the Empire of Right* (New York: Hill and Wang, 1995), 61. The continental context is discussed in Laura E. Gómez, *Manifest Destinies: The Making of the Mexican American Race* (New York: NYU Press, 2007). Goetzmann notes of the mid-nineteenth century, "For Americans, an era of global Manifest Destiny had begun"; *New Lands, New Men*, 266. Manifest Destiny as applied to the Pacific basin generally and Hawaii specifically is discussed in Greenberg, *Manifest Manhood*, 239–254.

42. William Dane Phelps, *Fore and Aft; or, Leaves from the Life of an Old Sailor* (Boston: Nichols and Hall, 1871), 242, 259–260. Richard Henry Dana Jr.'s *Two Years before the Mast* was another maritime memoir geared toward extending America's continental reach.

43. On the imagining of Indian Territory, see James P. Ronda, "'We Have a Country': Race, Geography, and the Invention of Indian Territory," in *Race and the Early Republic: Racial Consciousness and Nation-Building in the Early Republic*, ed. Michael A. Morrison and James Brewer Stewart (New York: Rowman and Littlefield, 2002), 159–172.

44. Marcus Rediker, *Between the Devil and the Deep Blue Sea: Merchant Seamen, Pirates, and the Anglo-American Maritime World, 1700–1750* (Cambridge: Cambridge University Press, 1987), 154–204. Jesse Lemisch discusses the popular presentation of Jack Tar in "Jack Tar in the Streets: Merchant Seamen in the Politics of Revolutionary America," *William and Mary Quarterly* 25, no. 3 (1968): 372–377. Historians have started to reassess citizenship afloat and the connections between seafarers and the nation. Some of the best work is Isaac Land, *War, Nationalism, and the British Sailor, 1750–1850* (New York: Palgrave Macmillan, 2009), 1–11; Paul Gilje, *Liberty on the Waterfront: American Maritime Culture in the Age of Revolution* (Philadelphia: University of Pennsylvania Press, 2004), 163–178; Raffety, "Recent Currents in Nineteenth-Century American Maritime History," 607–626; and Raffety, *The Republic Afloat: Law, Honor, and Citizenship in Maritime America* (Chicago: University of Chicago Press, 2013); Sarah Purcell sees sailors' narratives as overwhelmingly concerned with asserting both American national identity and the idea of mariners as viable citizens in "John Blatchford's New America: Sailors, Print Culture, and Post-Colonial American Identity," in *Pirates, Jack Tar, and Memory: New Directions in American Maritime History*, ed. Paul Gilje and William Pencak (Mystic, Conn.: Mystic Seaport, 2007), 73–93. For access to narratives of imperial grandeur among marginal people, see Linda Colley, "Britishness and Otherness: An Argument," *Journal of British Studies* 31, no. 4

(1992): 309–329; and Colley, *Britons: Forging the Nation, 1707–1837* (New Haven, Conn.: Yale University Press, 1992). On the British context, see Isaac Land, "'Sinful Propensities': Piracy, Sodomy, and Empire in the Rhetoric of Naval Reform, 1770–1870," in *Discipline and the Other Body: Correction, Corporeality, and Colonialism*, ed. Stephen Pierce and Anupama Rao (Durham, N.C.: Duke University Press, 2006), 92–93. Land similarly notes that in "songs, petitions, and autobiographies, sailors identified themselves with the cause of imperial expansion and cast themselves as defenders of white honor on a dangerous frontier." On "Indian hating" and national citizenship, see Richard Slotkin, *Regeneration through Violence: The Mythology of the American Frontier* (Middletown, Conn.: Wesleyan University Press, 1973); Richard Drinnon, *Facing West: The Metaphysics of Indian-Hating and Empire Building* (Minneapolis: University of Minnesota Press, 1980); Silver, *Our Savage Neighbors*, chapter 9.

45. Alfred Thayer Mahan, *The Problem of Asia and Its Effect Upon International Policies* (Boston: Little and Brown, 1900), 15, 98; and Alfred Thayer Mahan, *Interest of America in Sea Power: Present and Future* (Boston: Little and Brown, 1897), 165–167. For the "Indian past," see Ronald Takaki, *Iron Cages: Race and Culture in 19th-Century America*, rev. ed. (New York: Oxford University Press, 2000), 269. An earlier equation of Native American and Chinese extinction appears in "Natural History of Man," *Democratic Review* 26 (Apr. 1850), 345: "The extinction of the red race on this continent [is] almost consummated . . . and China is now open to a similar influence."

46. Paul Kramer, *Blood of Government: Race, Empire, the U.S., and the Philippines* (Chapel Hill: University of North Carolina Press, 2006); W. L. Williams, "United States Indian Policy and the Debate over Philippine Annexation: Implications for the Origins of American Imperialism," *Journal of American History* 66, no. 4 (1980): 810–831. On the continuity of the "Indian" and "frontier" analogies for the Pacific into the twentieth century, see Lyons, *American Pacificism*, 31: "[It] is reflected in poet Charles Olson's insistence that Oceania is 'part of our geography, another West, prefigured in the plains.'"

47. Samuel Kamakau, *Ruling Chiefs of Hawai'i*, trans. M. K. Pukui (Honolulu: Kamehameha Schools Press, 1992), iv, quoted in Lyons, *American Pacificism*, 30; Lili'uokalani, *Hawaii's Story by Hawaii's Queen* (Rutland, Vt.: Charles E. Tuttle, 1980), 369; petition quoted in Stuart Banner, *Possessing the Pacific: Land, Settlers, and Indigenous People from Australia to Alaska* (Cambridge, Mass.: Harvard University Press, 2005), 141. On Pacific-wide solidarities and the resistance to imperial imperatives, see Chappell, *Double Ghosts*; Thomas, *Islanders*; and Banner, *Possessing the Pacific*, 260–286.

48. For waterfront reform, see Gilje, *Liberty on the Waterfront*, 195–227.

Chapter 4

1. Entry dated Nov. 10, 1852, journal of S. B. Morgan, kept aboard ship *South Boston*, ODHS Log #761, NBWM; journal of N. Byron Smith entitled "History of a Three Years' Whaling Voyage," 116, Microfilm 16, 747–1P, LOC. See also Alonzo D. Sampson, *Three Times around the World: Life and Adventures of Alonzo Sampson* (New York: Express Print, 1867), 54–59; William C. Parke, *Personal Reminiscences of William Cooper Parke, Marshal of the Hawaiian Islands* (Cambridge, Mass.: Harvard University Press, 1891), 35–45; and Thomas Thrum, "When Sailors Ruled the Town," in *All About Hawaii* (n.p., 1920), 62–68. The Honolulu riot of 1852 is discussed more broadly in Briton Cooper Busch, *"Whaling Will Never Do for Me": The American Whaleman in the Nineteenth Century* (Lexington : University Press of Kentucky, 1994), 177–193; and Stan Hugill, *Sailortown* (New York: Dutton, 1967), 271–277.

2. Parke, *Personal Reminiscences*, 35–45, quote at 42.

3. Ibid., 44. See also William Alexander, *A Brief History of the Hawaiian People* (New York: American Book Co., 1891), 274. On the Hawaiian filibusters, see Robert E. May, "Manifest Destiny's Filibusters," in *Manifest Destiny and Empire: American Antebellum Expansionism*, ed. Sam W. Haynes and Christopher Morris (College Station: Texas A&M University Press, 1997), 146–148; and Amy Greenberg, *Manifest Manhood and the Antebellum American Empire* (New York: Cambridge University Press, 2005), 232–243. For militias and the overthrow of the Hawaiian government, see Noenoe K. Silva, *Aloha Betrayed: Native Hawaiian Resistance to American Colonialism* (Durham, N.C.: Duke University Press, 2004); and Eric T. L. Love, *Race over Empire: Racism and U.S. Imperialism, 1865–1900* (Chapel Hill, N.C.: University of North Carolina Press, 2004), 115–158. For Hawaiian relations with Japan, see Matt Matsuda, *Pacific Worlds: A History of Seas, Peoples, and Cultures* (New York: Cambridge University Press, 2012), 241–243.

4. *Publications of the Historical Commission of the Territory of Hawaii*, 4 vols. (Honolulu, 1927), 1:21; Ralph Kuykendall, *The Hawaiian Kingdom*, 3 vols. (Honolulu: University Press of Hawaii, 1938–1967), 1:311. For the "Great Mahele," see Matsuda, *Pacific Worlds*, 241–243.

5. "History of a Three Years' Whaling Voyage," 116. On sailors' rights and the law, see Matthew Raffety, *The Republic Afloat: Law, Honor, and Citizenship in Maritime America* (Chicago: University of Chicago Press, 2013).

6. For example, see Robert Rydell, *All the World's a Fair: Visions of Empire at American International Expositions, 1876–1916* (Chicago: University of Chicago Press, 1987); Shelley Streeby, *American Sensations: Class, Empire, and the Production of Popular Culture* (Berkeley: University of California Press, 2002); and Kristin Hoganson's discussion of the "fictive travel movement" in *Consumers' Imperium: The Global Production of American Domesticity, 1865–1920* (Chapel Hill: University of North Carolina Press, 2007), 153–208. Studies that persistently confine America's "global turn" to the end of the nineteenth century include Frank Ninkovich, *Global Dawn: The Cultural Foundation of American Internationalism, 1865–1890* (Cambridge, Mass.: Harvard University Press, 2009); and Ian Tyrrell, *Reforming the World: The Creation of America's Moral Empire* (Princeton, N.J.: Princeton University Press, 2010).

7. Greenberg, *Manifest Manhood*, esp. 5–17. For a discussion of "low-level" violence between isthmian travelers and Central American peoples, see *Manifest Manhood*, 104–106; Lorien Foote, *The Gentlemen and the Roughs: Manhood, Honor, and Violence in the Union Army* (New York: New York University Press, 2010); and Richard Stott, *Jolly Fellows: Male Milieus in Nineteenth-Century America* (Baltimore, Md.: Johns Hopkins University Press, 2009).

8. Edward T. Perkins, *Na Motu: or, Reef-Rovings in the South Seas* (New York: Pudney and Russell, 1854), 454. For interpersonal violence in the West, see Stott, *Jolly Fellows*, esp. 187–188, 197. For working-class violence and sport culture, see Elliott J. Gorn, "'Good-Bye Boys, I Die a True American': Homicide, Nativism, and Working-Class Culture in Antebellum New York City," *Journal of American History* 74, no. 2 (1987): 388–410; Michael Kaplan, "New York City Tavern Violence and the Creation of Working-Class Male Identity," *Journal of the Early Republic* 15, no. 4 (1995): 591–617; Timothy Gilfoyle, *City of Eros: New York City, Prostitution, and the Commercialization of Sex, 1790–1920* (New York: Norton, 1992), 92–117; and Amy Greenberg, "Fights/Fires: Violent Firemen in the Nineteenth-Century American City," in *Men and Violence: Gender, Honor, and Rituals in Modern Europe and America*, ed. Pieter Spierenburg (Columbus: Ohio State University Press, 1998), 159–189.

9. Entries dated Feb. 11, Feb. 18, and Feb. 25, 1854, journal of William Stetson, kept aboard ship *Arab*, ODHS Log #0507, NBWM. See also Elliott J. Gorn, *The Manly Art: Bare Knuckle Fighting in America* (Ithaca, N.Y.: Cornell University Press, 1986); and Gorn, "Gouge and Bite, Pull Hair and Scratch: The Social Significance of Fighting in the Southern Backcountry," *American Historical Review* 90, no. 1 (1985): 18–43. On performative nationalism, see David

Waldstreicher, *In the Midst of Perpetual Fetes: The Making of American Nationalism, 1776–1820* (Chapel Hill: University of North Carolina Press, 1997); and Simon Newman, *Parades and Politics of the Street: Festive Culture in the Early American Republic* (Philadelphia: University of Pennsylvania Press, 1997).

10. Depositions of George Ormsworth, Ormand Vigno, John Dunn, James Neary, and Thomas Case in *U.S. v. Thomas Case*, RG 84, Records of the Foreign Service Posts of the Department of State, Misc. Consular Court Records, 1859–1869, Nagasaki, Japan, vol. 14, NARA II; depositions of Michael Broderick, Hugh Pritchard, David Anderson, William Caw, John Palmer, and Samuel Luckwell in *U.S. v. Michael Broderick*, RG 84, Records of the Foreign Service Posts of the Department of State, Misc. Consular Court Records, 1859–1869, vol. 14, NARA II; deposition of Robert Lewis at the trial of John Taylor, USS *Powhatan*, May 5, 1858, RG 125, Records of the Office of the Judge Advocate General (Navy), M273, reel 88, vol. 79, NARA I.

11. "The Anglo-Saxon Race," *American Whig Review* 7 (Jan. 1848): 29. The Heenan-Sayers fight is described in Stott, *Jolly Fellows*, 109–112.

12. Alonzo D. Sampson, *Three Times around the World* (Buffalo, N.Y.: Express Printing, 1867), 39, 104–105.

13. Entry dated July 12, 1853, journal of William B. Allen, kept aboard the *Vandalia*, MMC-1798, LOC; Richard Walsh to sister, Aug. 19, 1850, Walsh Family Papers, vol. 2, ISM; William Whitecar, *Four Years Aboard the Whaleship* (Philadelphia: J. B. Lippincott & Co., 1860), 81, 109; Albert L. Freeman to Charles Cullis, Sept. 2, 1855, Letters of Albert L. Freeman, Collection 118, Box 1, MSM.

14. Boleslaw Szczesniak, ed., *The Opening of Japan: A Diary of Discovery in the Far East, 1853–1856* (Norman, Okla.: University of Oklahoma Press, 1962), 129.

15. Thomas Dudley to his sister, May 26, June 12, and June 16, 1852, Thomas C. Dudley Papers, William L. Clements Library, University of Michigan, Ann Arbor. On race and nationalism, see Bruce Dain, *A Hideous Monster of the Mind: American Race Theory in the Early Republic* (Cambridge, Mass.: Harvard University Press, 2002); Ronald Takaki, *Iron Cages: Race and Culture in 19th-Century America* (New York: Oxford University Press, 2000); David R. Roediger, *The Wages of Whiteness: Race and the Making of the American Working Class*, revised ed. (New York: Verso, 2007); and Alexander Saxton, *Rise and Fall of the White Republic: Class Politics and Mass Culture in Nineteenth Century America* (New York: Verso, 1990). These ideas owe something to Matthew Frye Jacobson, who argues that in the context of extracontinental empire, "suspect whites" suddenly became "legitimate whites" when compared to the "barbarian" peoples they encountered; see *Whiteness of a Different Color: European Immigrants and the Alchemy of Race* (Cambridge, Mass.: Harvard University Press, 1998).

16. Entry dated Sept. 23, 1845, journal of Elias Trotter, kept aboard ship *Illinois*, ODHS log #1005, NBWM. On these points, see Isaac Land, "The Many-Tongued Hydra: Sea Talk, Maritime Culture, and Atlantic Identities, 1700–1850," *Journal of American and Comparative Cultures* 25, nos. 3–4 (2002), 415; and Busch, "Whaling Will Never Do for Me," 32–58. David Kazanjian discusses how "racial codification and exploitation began to spill into the [sea]" in the nineteenth century in *The Colonizing Trick: National Culture and Imperial Citizenship in Early America* (Minneapolis: University of Minnesota Press, 2003), 38.

17. Depositions of D. L. Moore, J. W. Davis, C. A. Tanner, and James Cavanagh in *U.S. v. William Baird*, Nov. 26, 1859, RG 84, Records of the Foreign Service Posts of the Department of State, Misc. Consular Court Records, 1859–1869, Nagasaki, Japan, vol. 14, NARA II; Depositions of William Simmons and Peter B. Hawkins in *U.S. v. Peter B. Hawkins*, Jan. 3, 1861, RG 84, Records of the Foreign Service Posts of the Department of State, Misc. Consular

Court Records, 1859–1869, Nagasaki, Japan, vol. 14, NARA II; Sampson, *Three Times around the World*, 46; trial of Thomas Murray, USS *Decatur*, Dec. 21, 1858, RG 125, Records of the Office of the Judge Advocate General (Navy), M273, reel 91, vol. 82, NARA I; David Hottman to U.S. Consul William Lilley, June 19, 1856, RG 84, Records of the Foreign Service Posts of the Department of State, Misc. Consular Court Records, 1859–1869, Misc. Letters Received, Pernambuco, Brazil, vol. 053, NARA II; Depositions of mate, second mate, and steward aboard brig *Fairy*, June 19, 1856, RG 84, Records of the Foreign Service Posts of the Department of State, Misc. Consular Court Records, 1859–1869, Pernambuco, Brazil, vol. 053, NARA II.

18. William Merrill to John Forsyth, Letter dated July 29, 1835, Consular Dispatches from U.S. Consul at Santiago, Cape Verde Islands, microcopy 434, reel 2, NBFPL; Sampson, *Three Times around the World*, 155–157; *U.S. v. John McKenna*, RG 84, Records of the Foreign Service Posts of the Department of State, Criminal Court Case Files, C31-C60, Shanghai, China, NARA II.

19. Depositions of John Jalls and George Howard in the trials of James Collins and Edwin Haley, Dec. 9, 1856–May 28, 1857, USS *Massachusetts*, RG 125, Records of the Office of the Judge Advocate General (Navy), M273, reel 85, vol. 76, NARA I.

20. *Nixon v. Dyer*, 1842, and *Robeson vs. Gray*, 1842, Records of the U.S. District Court for the Eastern District of Pennsylvania, Box 27, National Archives, Mid-Atlantic Division–Philadelphia; entry dated Jan. 6, 1843, journal of Silas Fitch, Log 142, MSM; "Virginia" mentioned in Thomas Dudley to sister, letter dated June 12, 1852, Thomas C. Dudley Papers, William L. Clements Library, University of Michigan, Ann Arbor; *Robinson v. Taylor*, 1841, Records of the U.S. District Court, Eastern District of Pennsylvania, Admiralty Case Files, Box 27, National Archives, Mid-Atlantic Division–Philadelphia; J. Ross Browne, *Etchings of a Whaling Cruise* (1846; repr., Cambridge, Mass.: Harvard University Press, 1968), 107–108.

21. Entry for Mar. 19, 1850, journal of Frederick Schley, kept aboard USS *Cumberland*, NHC; entries dated Apr. 6 and Apr. 11, 1854, journal kept aboard ship *Eureka*, PEM; Washington Chase, *A Voyage from the United States to South America, Performed During the Years 1821–1823* (Newburyport: Herald Press, 1823), 29–31.

22. Trial of Richard Kelly, Michael Garman, and James Quinn, Mar. 3, 1857, USS *St. Mary's*, RG 125, Records of the Office of the Judge Advocate General (Navy), M273, reel 85, vol. 76, NARA I; Cokananto to John B. Williams, Jan. 26, 1848, RG 59, Department of State Records, Despatches from U.S. Consuls in the Bay of Islands and Auckland, New Zealand, Microfilm T49, reel 2, NARA II; Correspondence of Samuel Blackler, MSS 56, Box 9, Series B, Subseries 22, NBWM.

23. Village of Kim Ting to U.S. Consul, Nov. 14, 1843, and U.S. Consul to village of Kim Ting, Nov. 19, 1843, RG 59, Department of State Records, Consular Despatches, Canton, China, M101, reel 3, NARA II.

24. *U.S. v. John McKenna*.

25. Ibid.

26. Though not specifically maritime in nature, recent work on the contemporaneous "Watermelon Riot," including the memory of that incident and its subsequent impact on relations between the United States and Central America, supports such conclusions. See Aims McGuinness, *Path of Empire: Panama and the California Gold Rush* (Ithaca, N.Y.: Cornell University Press, 2008), 123–151.

27. Elisha E. Rice to State Department, June 30, 1858, RG 59, Department of State Records, Consular Despatches, Hakodate, Japan, M452, reel 1, NARA II. Emphasis in original.

28. Undated entry (ca. 1858), journal of Albert Peck, Paul C. Nicholson Whaling Collection, reel 17, vol. 187, PPL.

29. Samuel Blackler to Queen, Aug. 25 and Sept. 7, 1840, RG 84, Records of the Foreign Service Posts of the Department of State, Misc. Letters Sent, Tahiti, Society Islands, vol. 027, NARA II; report of Edward Cunningham, U.S. vice-consul at Shanghai, July 23, 1853, in *Executive Documents of the U.S. House*, 33rd Cong., 1st Sess., vol. 16, Doc. 123, 230.

30. William Merrill to John Forsyth, Letter dated July 29, 1835, Consular Despatches from U.S. Consul at Santiago, Cape Verde Islands, Microcopy T434, reel 2, NBFPL; entry dated Aug. 16, 1828, journal of Stephen C. Rowan, 0536D NHF-25, LOC; Francis Ripley to wife, June 25, 1849, Correspondence of Francis Ripley, NYHS.

31. John B. Williams to State Department, July 6, 1844, RG 59, Department of State Records, Despatches from U.S. Consuls in the Bay of Islands and Auckland, New Zealand, Microfilm T49, reel 1, NARA II; U.S. Commercial Agent at Feejee to Secretary of State James Buchanan, Mar. 6, 1848, RG 59, Department of State Records, Despatches from U.S. Consuls in the Bay of Islands and Auckland, New Zealand, Microfilm T49, reel 2, NARA II; O. H. Perry to Peter Parker, July 14, 1856, RG 84, Records of the Foreign Service Posts of the Department of State, Canton, China, Misc. and Official Letters, vol. 120A, NARA II; Assistant Secretary of State to U.S. Consul Thomas Miller, n.d., RG 84, Records of the Foreign Service Posts of the Department of State, Communications from Dept. of State and Treasury Dept., Hilo, Hawaii, Box 1, NARA II.

32. "From the Chinese Repository: Seamen in the Port of Canton," *Sailors' Magazine and Naval Journal* 7, no. 74 (1834): 37–39; Nicholas Trist, *The Condition of American Seamen in the Port of Havana* (Washington, D.C.: n.p., 1839), 23–24; Charles Samuel Stewart, *A Visit to the South Seas in the United States Ship Vincennes, During the Years 1829–1830*, Vol. 1 (New York: John P. Haven, 1833), 269–270.

33. *North American Daily Advertiser*, Apr. 14, 1843; *Boston Daily Atlas*, Aug. 28, 1843; *Daily Evening Traveller* (Boston), Aug. 30, 1856, 2; *Friend* (Honolulu), Sept. 2, 1861, emphasis in original. See also *Pittsfield Sun*, Aug. 31, 1843; *Salem Gazette*, Feb. 10, 1801; *New-Bedford Daily Mercury*, Sept. 1, 1856, 2; *Friend* (Honolulu), Feb. 1, 1855.

34. John Warren, "An Oration Delivered July 4, 1783," quoted in Dane A. Morrison, "American Expatriates in Canton: National Identity and the Maritime Experience Abroad, 1784–1850," in *Perspectives on Race, Ethnicity, and Power in Maritime America*, ed. G. S. Gordinier (Mystic, Conn.: Mystic Seaport Museum, 2005), 2–25; Dean quoted in Reginald Horsman, *Race and Manifest Destiny: The Origins of American Racial Anglo-Saxonism* (Cambridge, Mass.: Harvard University Press, 1981), 289–303; Cong. Globe, 32nd Cong., 1st Sess., April 22, 1852, 1166; John Elphinstone Erskine, *Journal of a Cruise among the Islands of the Western Pacific* (London: John Murray, 1853), 308–309.

35. The "Gospel of Commerce" is discussed in John Schroeder, *Shaping a Maritime Empire: The Commercial and Diplomatic Role of the American Navy, 1829–1861* (Westport, Conn.: Greenwood Press, 1985), 8–9 and 79–93. "Trade as peace" is described in Paul Gilje, *Free Trade and Sailors' Rights in the War of 1812* (New York: Cambridge University Press, 2013); and Anthony Pagden, *Peoples and Empires* (New York: Modern Library, 2001), 86–87. On the links between commerce and the spread of "civilization," see Jeffrey A. Keith, "Civilization, Race, and the Japan Expedition's Cultural Diplomacy, 1853–1854," *Diplomatic History* 35, no. 2 (2011): 179–202. On the supposed contrast between the American and European empires, see Paul Kramer, "Empires, Exceptions, and Anglo-Saxons: Race and Rule between the British and United States Empires, 1880–1910," *Journal of American History* 88, no. 4 (2002): 1315–1353; and Mona Domosh, *American Commodities in an Age of Empire* (New York: Routledge, 2006), 2–3.

36. *Berkshire County Whig*, Dec. 23, 1841; missionary quoted in Busch, "*Whaling Will Never Do for Me*," 120.

37. The best treatment of waterfront reform movements appears in Paul Gilje, *Liberty on the Waterfront: American Maritime Culture in the Age of Revolution* (Philadelphia: University of Pennsylvania Press, 2004), 195–227. The more general spirit of reform is covered in Bruce Dorsey, *Reforming Men and Women: Gender in the Antebellum City* (Ithaca, N.Y.: Cornell University Press, 2002). Valerie Burton argues that reformers propagated the stereotype of the rowdy sailor as a foil to the sort of workers—soberly inclined, fastidious—they hoped to raise in Britain and the United States; see "'Whoring, Drinking Sailors': Reflections on Masculinity from the Labour History of Nineteenth-Century British Shipping," in *Working Out Gender: Perspectives from Labour History*, ed. Margaret Walsh (London: Ashgate, 1999), 84–101. Stereotypes about sailors, then, tell us next to nothing about maritime lives but rather speak to the imperatives of capitalist development ashore.

38. Samuel Shaw to merchants of Canton, Letter dated May 11, 1795, RG 59, Department of State Records, Consular Despatches from Canton, China, M101, reel 1, NARA II; *Sailor's Magazine and Naval Journal* 5, no. 1 (1832): 1–2, 15 (for New Bedford Port Society); "Communications and Selections: The Shipmaster," *Sailor's Magazine and Naval Journal* 8, no. 1 (1835): 9; "When Shall the World Be Converted unto God?," *The Sailor's Magazine and Naval Journal* 7, no. 67 (1834): 204–205; "Who Prays for the Conversion of Seamen?," *Sailor's Magazine and Naval Journal* 7, no. 75 (1834): 67. As Isaac Land argues in *War, Nationalism, and the British Sailor* (New York: Palgrave-Macmillan, 2009), 77: "Jack Tar ruled the waves, but until he could master himself, he would remain a suspect figure." For the broader importance of character to nineteenth-century reformers, see James Salazar, *Bodies of Reform: The Rhetoric of Character in Gilded Age America* (New York: New York University Press, 2010).

39. Orville Dewey, *The Character and Claims of Sea-Faring Men: A Sermon* (New York: C. S. Francis and Co., 1845), 11; *Christian Herald and Sailors Magazine* 10 (July 19, 1823), 153–154.

40. U.S. Commercial Agent James P. Cook to U.S. Consul O. H. Perry, July 14, 1856, RG 59, Department of State Records, Consular Despatches from Canton, China, M101, reel 4, NARA II; George Kimball to Department of State, Oct. 12, 1854, RG 84, Records of the Foreign Service Posts of the Department of State, St. Helena, British Africa, vol. 001, NARA II. For "zones of law," see Eliga H. Gould, "Zones of Law, Zones of Violence: The Legal Geography of the British Atlantic, circa 1772," *William and Mary Quarterly* 60, no. 3 (2003): 471–510. On the work of consuls more generally, see Charles Kennedy, *The American Consul: A History of the United States Consular Service* (New York: Greenwood Press, 1990); and Charles B. Harris, "The United States Consul's Role in Civil Matters Concerning Seamen," *Cumberland Law Review* 6, no. 3 (1976): 559–587.

41. U.S. vice-consul to R. S. Sturges, May 12, 1855, RG 84, Records of the Foreign Service Posts of the Department of State, Misc. Correspondence 1849–1853, Canton, China, vol. 7; entries dated Oct. 26–28, 1848, journal of Henry Wise, kept aboard USS *Independence*, RG 45, Records of the Naval Records Collection of the Office of Naval Records and Library, E608 (60), vol. 7, NARA I.

42. Entry dated May 15, 1827, journals of Thomas Dornin, RG 45, Records of the Naval Records Collection of the Office of Naval Records and Library, M981, reel 1, NARA I. On the maritime frontier and federal power, see Raffety, *Republic Afloat*, 202–207. For consular reform, see Kennedy, *American Consul*, 71–86; for naval expansion (partly connected to advancing southern interests), see Matthew J. Karp, "Slavery and American Sea Power: The Navalist Impulse in the Antebellum South," *Journal of Southern History* 77, no. 2 (2011): 284–324. For sailors as convict laborers, see Hugill, *Sailortown*, 249–251.

43. Undated entry (ca. 1858), journal of Albert Peck; A Roving Printer, *Life and Adventures in the South Pacific* (New York: Harper and Brothers, 1861), 75–76; Ben-Ezra Stiles Ely, *"There*

She Blows": A Narrative of a Whaling Voyage, in the Indian and South Atlantic Oceans (Philadelphia: James K. Simon, 1849), 39–41, 81–82, 85–86; entry dated June 1, 1853, journal of James Bond, kept aboard ship *John A. Parker*, NBFPL.

44. Charles Erskine, *Twenty Years before the Mast* (Philadelphia: George W. Jacobs, 1896), 264–265; letter from whaleship *Florida* to the U.S. consul at Maui, n.d. (ca. 1855), RG 84, Records of the Foreign Service Posts of the Department of State, Honolulu, Hawaii, Box 31, Folder 1, NARA II.

45. Cyrene M. Clarke, *Glances at Life upon the Sea* (Middletown, Conn.: C. H. Pelton, 1854), 74; entry dated Jan. 19, 1852, diary of John Jones, kept aboard *Eliza Adams*, NBWM; entry dated Apr. 21, 1855, journal of William Stetson, NBWM.

46. Deposition of Thomas Smith at the trial of Abraham Lyell, Feb. 21, 1857, RG 125, Records of the Office of the Judge Advocate General (Navy), M273, reel 85, vol. 76, NARA I; trial of John B. Smith, June 6, 1854, RG 125, Records of the Office of the Judge Advocate General (Navy), M273, reel 80, vol. 71, NARA I. For sailor violence ashore, see Eileen Scully, *Bargaining with the State from Afar: American Citizenship in Treaty Port China, 1844–1942* (New York: Columbia University Press, 2001). The efforts of mariners to portray themselves as "protagonists of empire" are described in Isaac Land, "'Sinful Propensities': Piracy, Sodomy, and Empire in the Rhetoric of Naval Reform," in *Discipline and the Other Body: Correction, Corporeality, and Colonialism*, ed. Steven Pierce and Anupama Rao (Durham, N.C.: Duke University Press, 2006), 90–114, esp. 92–93; Sarah Purcell, "John Blatchford's New America: Sailors, Print Culture, and Post-Colonial American Identity" in *Pirates, Jack Tar, and Memory: New Directions in American Maritime History*, ed. Paul Gilje and William Pencak (Mystic, Conn.: Mystic Seaport Museum, 2007), 73–93; and Myra C. Glenn, "Forging Manhood and Nationhood Together: American Sailors' Accounts of Their Exploits, Sufferings, and Resistance in the Antebellum United States," *American Nineteenth Century History* 8, no. 1 (2007): 27–49.

47. Trial of Richard Warren, June 25, 1840, RG 125, Records of the Office of the Judge Advocate General (Navy), M273, reel 36, vol. 34, NARA I; trial of Henry Allen, USS *Plymouth*, May 15, 1848, RG 125, Records of the Office of the Judge Advocate General (Navy), M273, reel 63, vol. 57, NARA I; trial of James Wright, Sept. 22, 1840, RG 125, Records of the Office of the Judge Advocate General (Navy), M273, reel 37, vol. 35, NARA I; trial of Washington Pearsley, RG 125, Records of the Office of the Judge Advocate General (Navy), M273, reel 35, vol. 35, NARA I.

48. J. Grey Jewell, *Among Our Sailors* (New York: Harper, 1874), 14; trial of William Thacker, May 7, 1858, USS *Cumberland*, RG 125, Records of the Office of the Judge Advocate General (Navy), M273, reel 88, vol. 79, NARA I.

49. Quoted in Horsman, *Race and Manifest Destiny*, 290. As Scully notes, in the eyes of imperial adjudicators, unruly "lower-class" whites abroad "lowered the tone" of empire and disrupted attempts to maintain a careful illusion that western power was comprised entirely of affluent and "respectable" persons. In that sense, sailors became the subject of equal, if not greater, disdain among their so-called white brethren who were charged with policing imperial possessions; see *Bargaining with the State from Afar*, 11–12. On tensions in the only nominally unified community of imperialists overseas, see Ann Stoler, "Rethinking Colonial Categories: European Communities and the Boundaries of Rule," *Comparative Studies in Society and History* 13 (Jan. 1989); 134–161; Stoler argues that "colonizers and their communities are frequently treated as diverse but unproblematic [and] unified."

50. James Burley to State Department, Mar. 31, 1852, RG 59, Department of State Records, Despatches from U.S. Consuls in the Bay of Islands and Auckland, New Zealand, Microfilm

T49, reel 2, NARA II; William Miles to State Department, letter dated Nov. 25, 1854, RG 59, Department of State Records, Callao Consular Despatches, M155, reel 1, NARA II; P. W. Snow to Secretary of State John Forsyth, Mar. 11, 1836, RG 59, Department of State Records, Canton Consular Despatches, M101, reel 2, NARA II; U.S. Consul to Secretary of State, Dec. 1, 1851, RG 59, Department of State Records, Shanghai Consular Despatches, M112, reel 1, NARA II. See also U.S. Consul to State Department, July 28, 1852, RG 59, Department of State Records, Hong Kong Consular Despatches, M108, reel 2, NARA II: "On several instances Masters of Merchant vessels have pursued a course which has stirred up a spirit of discontent amongst their crews in order that they might desert, or refuse duty and be discharged for insubordination, and thus forfeit what wages might be due them."

51. Raffety, *Republic Afloat*, 106–107; Samuel Leech, *Thirty Years from Home* (Boston: Tappan and Dennet, 1843), 22; Charles Rockwell, *Sketches of Foreign Travel and Life at Sea*, 2 vols. (Boston: Tappan and Dennet, 1842), 2:398–399, 419; Ely, "*There She Blows*," 85–86. Seth Rockman argues that "common laborers frequently coped with capitalism by directing violence toward fellow workers and through self-destructive behavior"; see *Scraping By: Wage Labor, Slavery, and Survival in Early Baltimore* (Baltimore, Md.: Johns Hopkins University Press, 2009), 9–10. Sailors on slave ships were also notorious for abusing "inferior" races; see Emma Christopher, *Slave Ship Sailors and Their Captive Cargoes, 1730–1807* (Cambridge: Cambridge University Press, 2006).

52. Daniel Wheeler, *Extracts from the Letters and Journal of Daniel Wheeler* (Philadelphia: Joseph Rakestraw, 1840), 118. Shifts in shipping are noted in Daniel Vickers, *Young Men and the Sea: Yankee Seafarers in the Age of Sail* (New Haven, Conn.: Yale University Press), 163–213.

53. Thomas Nickerson, "Desultory Sketches from a Seaman's Log," in *The Loss of the Ship "Essex," Sunk by a Whale: First Person Accounts*, ed. Nathaniel Philbrick and Thomas Philbrick (New York: Penguin Putnam, 2000), 88. See also Nathaniel Philbrick, *In the Heart of the Sea: The Tragedy of the Whaleship* Essex (New York: Viking, 2000), 34–35. Sailor unionization and race are discussed in Leon Fink, *Sweatshops at Sea: Merchant Seamen in the World's First Globalized Industry, from 1812 to the Present* (Chapel Hill: University of North Carolina Press, 2011), esp. 100–110 and 132–134. Examples of successful cross-national and cross-racial cooperation exist, albeit in diminishing numbers as the nineteenth century progressed. See Niklas Frykman "The Mutiny on the Hermione: Warfare, Revolution, and Treason in the Royal Navy," *Journal of Social History* 44, no. 1 (2010): 159–187; and Linebaugh and Rediker, *Many-Headed Hydra*. As David Roediger insists, multiracial job sites rarely produced fellow feeling; instead, they produced "a desire for color bars at work in order to disassociate jobs from black workers." See Roediger, *How Race Survived U.S. History* (London: Verso, 2008), 87.

54. On gendered and racialized violence and the War of 1898, see Kristin Hoganson, *Fighting for American Manhood: How Gender Politics Provoked the Spanish-American and Philippine-American Wars* (New Haven, Conn.: Yale University Press, 1998); and Gail Bederman, *Manliness and Civilization: A Cultural History of Gender and Race in the United States, 1880–1917* (Chicago: University of Chicago Press, 1995).

55. Trial of Charles Currell, Apr. 4, 1857, USS *Wabash*, RG 125, Records of the Office of the Judge Advocate General (Navy), M273, reel 85, NARA I.

56. Theodore Roosevelt, "The Manly Virtues and Practical Politics," *Forum* 17 (July 1894): 555; and Theodore Roosevelt, "The Strenuous Life," speech before the Hamilton Club, Chicago, Apr. 10, 1899, in Theodore Roosevelt, *The Strenuous Life: Essays and Addresses* (New York: The Century Co., 1905), 6; *Reports of the Mosely Education Commission to the United States* (London: Cooperative Printing, 1904), 13. For the "crisis" in Gilded Age manhood, see Matthew Frye Jacobson, *Barbarian Virtues: The United States Encounters Foreign Peoples at Home*

and Abroad, 1876–1917 (New York, 2000), 3–9; and Michael Kimmel, *Manhood in America: A Cultural History*, 3rd ed. (New York: Oxford University Press, 2012), 59–136.

57. Robert W. Kenny, ed., *The New Zealand Journal of John B. Williams of Salem, Massachusetts, 1842–1844* (Salem, Mass.: Peabody Museum of Salem, 1956), 70–71; Tyrrell, *Reforming the World*, passim. See also Scully, *Bargaining with the State from Afar*, 3, where she argues that extraterritorial courts in the later nineteenth century were dedicated to "harness[ing] their citizens abroad in the service of something called 'the national interest.'"

Chapter 5

1. Entries dated Mar. 6 and Mar. 12, 1831, Patrick Barry Hayes journal, Barry-Hayes Papers, Box 6, Folder 7, ISM.

2. Entry dated May 1, 1831, ibid.; copy of letter dated July 10, 1831, ibid.

3. See Charles Batten, *Pleasurable Instruction: Form and Convention in Eighteenth-Century Travel Literature* (Berkeley: University of California Press, 1978).

4. Patrick Barry Hayes to J. S. J. Grogan, July 22, 1831, Barry-Hayes Papers, Box 6, Folder 7, ISM.

5. Patrick Barry Hayes to unnamed friend, Jan. 1832, Barry-Hayes Papers, Box 6, Folder 7, ISM. On depictions of foreign masculinity and "personal annexation," see Amy S. Greenberg, *Manifest Manhood and the Antebellum American Empire* (Cambridge: Cambridge University Press, 2005), 88–134, esp. 88–91; and Shelley Streeby, *American Sensations: Class, Empire, and the Production of Popular Culture* (Berkeley: University of California Press, 2002).

6. Hayes to Grogan, July 22, 1831; Patrick Barry Hayes to Rob Lynch, Dec. 10, 1831, Barry-Hayes Papers, Box 6, Folder 7, ISM.

7. Hayes to Grogan, July 22, 1831; Hayes to Lynch, Dec. 10, 1831. For connections between gender, sexuality, and politics, see Linda Kerber, *Women of the Republic: Intellect and Ideology in Revolutionary America* (Chapel Hill: University of North Carolina Press, 1997); Rosemarie Zagarri, *Revolutionary Backlash: Women and Politics in the Early American Republic* (Philadelphia: University of Pennsylvania Press, 2007), esp. 1–45; Catherine Allgor, *Parlor Politics: In Which the Ladies of Washington Help Build a City and a Government* (Charlottesville: University of Virginia Press, 2000). Inhibitions about interracial sex was common to narratives of western expansion as well, as seen in Arnoldo De León, *They Called Them Greasers: Anglo Attitudes towards Mexicans in Texas, 1821–1900* (Austin: University of Texas Press, 1983). For the trope of the "irresistible American man" abroad, see Greenberg, *Manifest Manhood*, 123–134.

8. Hayes to Grogan, July 22, 1831, emphasis in original.

9. On racial intermixture and the classification problems it created in early America, see Gary Nash, *Red, White, and Black: The Peoples of Early North America* (New York: Prentice-Hall, 1974), chapter 12; and Kirsten Fischer, *Suspect Relations: Sex, Race, and Resistance in Colonial North Carolina* (Ithaca, N.Y.: Cornell University Press, 2002).

10. Hayes to Lynch, Dec. 10, 1831; entry dated Dec. 25, 1834, Patrick Barry Hayes journal, Barry-Hayes Papers, Box 6, Folder 7, ISM.

11. For relations between sailors and women, see Paul Gilje, *Liberty on the Waterfront: American Maritime Culture in the Age of Revolution* (Philadelphia: University of Pennsylvania Press, 2004), 33–65; Margaret Creighton, *Rites and Passages: The Experience of American Whaling, 1830–1870* (Cambridge: Cambridge University Press, 1995), 162–194; Briton Cooper Busch, *"Whaling Will Never Do for Me": The American Whaleman in the Nineteenth Century* (Lexington: University of Kentucky Press, 1994), 135–157; and Margaret Creighton and Lisa Norling, eds., *Iron Men,*

Wooden Women: Gender and Seafaring in the Atlantic World, 1700–1920 (Baltimore, Md.: Johns Hopkins Press, 1996).

12. As Martha Hodes argues, "The history of racial categories is often a history of sexuality as well"; see Martha Hodes, ed., *Sex, Love, Race: Crossing Boundaries in North American History* (New York: New York University Press, 1999), 2. See also Albert L. Hurtado, *Intimate Frontiers: Sex, Gender, and Culture in Old California* (Albuquerque: University of New Mexico Press, 1999); and Gary B. Nash, "The Hidden History of Mestizo America," in Hodes, *Sex, Love, Race*, 10–32. Intimacy and empire is most thoroughly covered in Ann Laura Stoler, ed., *Haunted by Empire: Geographies of Intimacy in North American History* (Durham, N.C.: Duke University Press, 2006), but see also Kathleen Brown's concept of the "gender frontier" in *Good Wives, Nasty Wenches, and Anxious Patriarchs: Gender, Race, and Power in Colonial Virginia* (Chapel Hill, N.C.: University of North Carolina Press, 1996), 42–74; Nayan Shah, *Stranger Intimacy: Contesting Race, Sexuality, and the Law in the North American West* (Berkeley: University of California Press, 2011); and Laura Briggs, *Reproducing Empire: Race, Sex, Science, and U.S. Imperialism in Puerto Rico* (Berkeley: University of California Press, 2002).

13. Justin Martin to brother, letter dated Nov. 29, 1844, VFM 246, MSM. On male encampments and encounters with women, see Sylvia Van Kirk, *Many Tender Ties: Women in Fur Trade Society, 1670–1870* (Norman: University of Oklahoma Press, 1983); Susan Lee Johnson, *Roaring Camp: The Social World of the California Gold Rush* (New York: W. W. Norton, 2000); Shah, *Stranger Intimacy*; and Richard Godbeer, *Sexual Revolution in Early America* (Baltimore, Md.: Johns Hopkins University Press, 2002).

14. Entry dated Apr. 4, 1842, journal of William Alfred Allen, kept aboard ship *Samuel Robertson*, ODHS Log #1040, NBWM.

15. Entry dated Apr. 21, 1862, journal of Charles Follen Blake, kept aboard U.S.S. *Constellation*, 0536D NHF-Alpha, LOC; entry dated Dec. 26, 1842, journal of George Blanchard, kept aboard ship *Pantheon*, quoted in Creighton, *Rites and Passages*, 158.

16. Undated entry (ca. Mar. 1857), journal of Dan Whitfield, kept aboard ship *Doctor Franklin*, ODHS Log #789, NBWM; entry dated May 3, 1850, diary kept aboard *Samuel Appleton*, Log 631, MSM.

17. Entries dated Mar. 1, 3, and 7, 1847, journal of Ezra Goodnough, kept aboard ship *Ann Perry*, PEM. Isaac Land reconsiders the network of economic relationships that mediated relations between men and women in port in "The Humours of Sailortown: Atlantic History Meets Subculture Theory," in *City Limits: Perspectives on the Historical European City*, ed. Glenn Clark, Judith Owens, and Glenn T. Smith (Montreal: McGill-Queen's University Press, 2010), esp. 20–22. Margaret S. Creighton suggests that "for all their rowdiness, the liaisons between sailors and their prostitutes do not seem to have been simply loose associations"; see *Dogwatch and Liberty Days: Seafaring Life in the Nineteenth Century* (Worcester, Mass.: Mercantile Press, 1982), 61–62. For the centrality of women to port cities, see Ellen Hartigan-O'Connor, *The Ties That Buy: Women and Commerce in Revolutionary America* (Philadelphia: University of Pennsylvania Press, 2009).

18. Hoberley quoted in Busch, *"Whaling Will Never Do for Me,"* 145; entry dated Jan. 29–30, 1848, journal kept aboard ship *Ann Alexander*, ODHS Log #394, NBWM. Some of the ease with which men took and then left "wives" abroad may be attributable to what Clare Lyons has shown to be the similarly fluid marital culture along the Philadelphia waterfront; see *Sex among the Rabble: An Intimate History of Gender and Power in the Age of Revolution, Philadelphia, 1730–1830* (Chapel Hill: University of North Carolina Press, 2006), 55–58.

19. Entries dated June 6 and 10, 1847, journal of Ezra Goodnough, kept aboard ship *Ann Perry*, PEM; undated entry (ca. 1860), journal of Robert Strout, vol. 2, Collection 210, MSM;

Joseph G. Clark, *Lights and Shadows of Sailor Life* (Boston: Benjamin B. Mussey, 1848), 260; entry dated Jan. 3, 1857, journal of William Stetson, kept aboard *Arab*, ODHS Log #0507, NBWM.

20. Undated entry (ca. 1858), journal of Albert Peck, Paul C. Nicholson Whaling Collection, reel 17, vol. 187, PPL; Log 18, entry dated Mar. 9, 1850, journal of William Wilson, kept aboard ship *Cavalier*, Log 18, MSM; entry dated Jan. 16, 1842, journal of John Martin, kept aboard the ship *Lucy Ann*, KWM Log 434, NBWM; Benjamin Doane, *Following the Sea* (Halifax: Nimbus, 1987), 152; entries dated Sept. 19 and Nov. 1, 1816, journal kept aboard ship *Zephyr*, Log 839, MSM; entry dated Nov. 9, 1843, journal of William Alfred Allen, kept aboard ship *Samuel Robertson*, ODHS Log #1040, NBWM; entry dated Mar. 13, 1873, journal of Thomas Morrison, kept aboard ship *Avola*, KWM Collection, NBWM. David A. Chappell argues that "regular contact with white seamen enabled Hawaiian women to become such significant providers that local stores did their biggest business when ships were in port . . . though from the beginning, in places such as Tahiti and Pohnpei, many Island women seem to have been under orders from their male kin or chiefs, who appropriated significant portions of their earnings"; "Shipboard Relations between Pacific Island Women and Euroamerican Men, 1767–1887," *Journal of Pacific History* 27, no. 2 (1992): 131–149. See also Caroline Ralston, "Changes in the Lives of Ordinary Women in Early Post-Contact Hawaii," in *Family and Gender in the Pacific: Domestic Contradictions and the Colonial Impact*, ed. Margaret Jolly and Martha Macintyre (Cambridge: Cambridge University Press, 1989), 64: Hawaiian women "threw themselves into the embrace of foreign sailors in what was an enactment of their established cultural practices and beliefs." This soon became an "avenue to foreign goods and thus one of many agents of widespread cultural change." See also David Igler, *The Great Ocean: Pacific Worlds from Captain Cook to the Gold Rush* (New York: Oxford University Press, 2013), 48–63.

21. Foster Rhea Dulles, *Lowered Boats: A Chronicle of American Whaling* (New York: Harcourt Brace, 1933), 63; entry dated Apr. 26, 1847, journal kept aboard ship *Bowditch*, Log B785/1846j, PPL; Capt. David Porter, *Journal of a Cruise Made to the Pacific Ocean in the United States Frigate Essex* (New York: Wiley and Halsted, 1822), 2:59–60.

22. Undated letter (ca. 1856), Correspondence of Charles Lane, MSS 56, Box 43, Series L, Subseries 1, NBWM; George Harrison to father, Jan. 13, 1840, George W. Harrison Papers, LOC; Alfred Doten, *The Journals of Alfred Doten, 1849–1902*, 2 vols., ed. Walter Van Tilburg Clark (Reno: University of Nevada Press, 1973), 40.

23. Entry dated Oct. 4, 1848, journal of William Henry Weaver, NYHS. Exceptionalist mythology is described in Thomas Bender, *A Nation among Nations: America's Place in World History* (New York: Hill and Wang, 2006), 3–14.

24. Entries dated Oct. 1, 1856, and Jan. 3, 1858, journal of Robert Weir, kept aboard *Clara Bell*, Log 164, MSM. See also E. Anthony Rotundo, *American Manhood: Transformations in Masculinity from the Revolution to the Modern Era* (New York: Basic Books, 1993), 124.

25. Entry dated Apr. 15, 1852, journal of John Winslow, kept aboard ship *Wave*, Log W355/1851j, PPL.

26. Entry dated Dec. 25, 1826, journal of Stephen Rowan, kept aboard ship *Vincennes*, Stephen C. Rowan Papers, LOC. For the idea of adjudicating intimacy, see Ann Laura Stoler, *Carnal Knowledge and Imperial Power: Race and the Intimate in Colonial Rule* (Berkeley: University of California Press, 2002); Stoler, *Haunted by Empire*; Anne McClintock, *Imperial Leather: Race, Gender, and Sexuality in the Colonial Contest* (New York: Routledge, 1995); and Shah, *Stranger Intimacy*.

27. See Helen Lefkowitz Horowitz, *Rereading Sex: Battles over Sexual Knowledge and Suppression in Nineteenth-Century America* (New York: Vintage, 2003).

28. Entry dated Mar. 13, 1873, Journal of Thomas Morrison, kept aboard ship *Avola*, KWM Collection, NBWM; entry dated Nov. 15, 1847, journal of George Blanchard, kept aboard ship *Solomon Saltus*, NBWM; entries dated Mar. 8–11, 1839, journal kept aboard the ship *Reaper*, Log 1637, PEM; *Parachute* quoted in Busch, *"Whaling Will Never Do for Me,"* 140.

29. For the riot by sailors from the *Daniel*, see Ernest Dodge, *Islands and Empires: Western Impact on the Pacific and East Asia* (Minneapolis: University of Minnesota Press, 1976), 82. For the riot on the *Dolphin*, see Hiram Bingham, *A Residence of Twenty-One Years in the Sandwich Islands* (Hartford: Hezekiah Huntington, 1849), 243–249.

30. Entry dated Feb. 21, 1861, Journal of Ambrose Bates, kept aboard *Nimrod*, KWM 330, NBWM.

31. Stephen Curtis, *Brief Extracts from the Journal of a Voyage Performed by the Whale Ship Mercury, 1841–1844* (Boston: Samuel Dickinson, 1844), 34; entry dated June 17, 1843, journal of William Allen, kept aboard *Samuel Robertson*, ODHS Log #1040, NBWM; *Doctor Franklin* quoted in Creighton, *Rites and Passages*, 151; Augustus Earle, *A Narrative of a Nine Months' Residence in New Zealand* (London: Longman, 1832), 49–50.

32. Nayan Shah, "Adjudicating Intimacies on U.S. Frontiers," in *Haunted by Empire: Geographies of Intimacy in North American History*, ed. Ann Laura Stoler (Durham, N.C.: Duke University Press, 2006), 116–139; Daniel Wheeler, *Extracts from the Letters and Journal of Daniel Wheeler* (Philadelphia: Joseph Rakestraw, 1840), 65–66; Bingham, *Residence of Twenty-One Years*, 289. For the shift from "permissive" to "regulated" sexuality, see Lyons, *Sex among the Rabble*.

33. Gautham Rao, "Sailors' Health and National Wealth: Marine Hospitals in the Early Republic," *Common-Place* 9, no. 1 (2008); David Igler, "Diseased Goods: Global Exchanges in the Eastern Pacific Basin, 1770–1850," *American Historical Review* 109, no. 3 (2004): 693–719, quote at 704; Philippa Levine, *Prostitution, Race, and Politics: Policing Venereal Disease in the British Empire* (New York: Routledge, 2003).

34. For the Paita and Fayal cases, see Creighton, *Rites and Passages*, 190–191; trial of John Powers, Nov. 9, 1857, RG 125, Records of the Office of the Judge Advocate General (Navy), M273, reel 87, vol. 78, NARA I. The prevalence of homosexual activity aboard ships remains a debated subject. Eric Sager argues that "rarely did the relationship between men become sexual itself"; *Seafaring Labour: The Merchant Marine of Atlantic Canada, 1820–1914* (Montreal: McGill University Press, 1989), 239. B. R. Burg suggests that it was frequent, in *An American Seafarer in the Age of Sail: The Erotic Diaries of Philip C. Van Buskirk, 1851–1870* (New Haven, Conn.: Yale University Press, 1994). For female prostitution as an "antidote" to homosexuality, see Stoler, *Carnal Knowledge and Imperial Power*, 48.

35. John B. Williams to Secretary of State, July, 1848, RG 59, Department of State Records, Despatches from U.S. Consuls, Lauthala, Fiji, Microfilm T25, reel 1, NARA II; John B. Williams to Secretary of State, Oct. 25, 1847, RG 59, Department of State Records, Despatches from U.S. Consuls, Lauthala, Fiji, Microfilm T25, reel 1, NARA II; Ben-Ezra Stiles Ely, *"There She Blows": A Narrative of a Whaling Voyage in the Indian and South Atlantic Oceans* (Philadelphia: James K. Simon, 1849), 98; "Fourth Annual Report," *Sailor's Magazine and Naval Journal* 4, no. 4 (June 1832): 304–306; "Influence of Wicked Sailors in Foreign Lands," *Sailor's Magazine and Naval Journal* 10, no. 8 (1838): 343–346.

36. For sporting culture and brothel riots, see Timothy Gilfoyle, *City of Eros: New York City, Prostitution, and the Commercialization of Sex* (New York: W. W. Norton, 1992), 76–90, Whitman quoted on 101.

37. *U.S. vs. William Sinclair and John Bray*, RG 84, Records of the Foreign Service Posts of the Department of State, Misc. Consular Court Cases, Nagasaki, Japan, Box 02, NARA II;

I. J. Roberts to U.S. Consul, Dec. 29, 1851, RG 84, Records of the Foreign Service Posts of the Department of State, Canton, China, vol. 7, Misc. Correspondence 1849–1853, NARA II.

38. Entry dated Feb. 19, 1850, journal of William Wilson, aboard *Cavalier*, Log 18, MSM; entry dated Feb. 7, 1851, journal of Orson Shattuck, kept aboard ship *Frances*, ODHS Log #994, NBWM; *U.S. vs. A. Pettersson*, RG 84, Records of the Foreign Service Posts of the Department of State, Consular Court Records, Nagasaki, Japan, vol. 14, NARA II; *Japanese Gov't vs. Douglas Frazar*, RG 84, Records of the Foreign Service Posts of the Department of State, Consular Court Records, Nagasaki, Japan, vol. 14, NARA II.

39. Letter No. 35, RG 84, Records of the Foreign Service Posts of the Department of State, Letters Received, Nagasaki, Japan, vol. 15, NARA II; British Consul to I. G. Walsh, June 12, 1860, and Aug. 8, 1861, RG 84, Records of the Foreign Service Posts of the Department of State, Letters Received, Nagasaki, Japan, vol. 15, NARA II; Roger Pineau, ed., *The Personal Journal of Commodore Matthew C. Perry* (Washington, D.C.: Smithsonian Institution Press, 1968), 219. Other examples include J. Ross Browne, *Etchings of a Whaling Cruise*, ed. John Seelye (1846; repr., Cambridge, Mass.: Belknap Press of Harvard University, 1968), 275–276; and entry dated July 26, 1854, Journal of William B. Allen, kept aboard USS *Vandalia*, MMC-1798, LOC. Some of these concerns are covered in Sharon Block, *Rape and Sexual Power in Early America* (Chapel Hill: University of North Carolina Press, 2006). For the treaty, see *Compilation of Treaties in Force* (Washington, D.C.: Government Printing Office, 1899), 373; and sailor's comments undated journal entry, Thomas C. Dudley Papers, William L. Clements Library, University of Michigan, Ann Arbor.

40. Relations between men and women along the American waterfront are discussed in Gilje, *Liberty on the Waterfront*, 33–65.

41. Greenberg, *Manifest Manhood and the Antebellum American Empire*. On the situational nature of manhood in the maritime community, see Ruth Herndon, "The Domestic Cost of Seafaring: Town Leaders and Seamen's Families in Eighteenth Century Rhode Island," in *Iron Men, Wooden Women: Gender and Seafaring in the Atlantic World*, ed. Margaret S. Creighton and Lisa Norling (Baltimore, Md.: Johns Hopkins University Press, 1996), 55–69.

42. Lisa Norling, *Captain Ahab Had a Wife: New England Women and the Whalefishery, 1720–1870* (Chapel Hill: University of North Carolina Press, 2000); Martha Hodes, *The Sea Captain's Wife: A True Story of Love, Race, and War in the Nineteenth Century* (New York: W. W. Norton, 2007), esp. 119–160; Elaine Crane, *Ebb Tide in New England: Women, Seaports, and Social Change* (Boston: Northeastern University Press, 1998), 98–138.

43. Edward T. Perkins, *Na Motu: or, Reef-Rovings in the South Seas* (New York: Pudney and Russell, 1854), 453; Ian Tyrrell, *Woman's World/Woman's Empire: The Woman's Christian Temperance Union in International Perspective, 1880–1930* (Chapel Hill: University of North Carolina Press, 1991), 191–220, quote on 196. See also Daniel T. Rodgers, *Atlantic Crossings: Social Politics in a Progressive Age* (Cambridge, Mass.: Harvard University Press, 1998); Paul A. Kramer, "The Darkness That Enters the Home: The Politics of Prostitution during the Philippine-American War," in *Haunted by Empire: Geographies of Intimacy in North American History*, ed. Ann Laura Stoler (Durham, N.C.: Duke University Press, 2006), 366–404; and Briggs, *Reproducing Empire*, 46–73.

44. Entry dated Sep. 27, 1817, journal of William Rogers, kept aboard ship *Tartar*, PEM; Richard Henry Dana Jr., *Two Years before the Mast* (1840; repr., New York: Library of America, 2000), 232–233.

45. Richard Settle to wife, letter dated Aug. 10, 1877, Papers of Richard Settle, LOC.

46. Richard Swanston to State Department, Apr. 13, 1857, RG 84, Records of the Foreign Service Posts of the Department of State, State Department Despatches, Apia, Samoa, NARA II.

See also Damon Salesa, "Samoa's Half-Castes and Some Frontiers of Comparison," in *Haunted by Empire: Geographies of Intimacy in North American History*, ed. Ann Laura Stoler (Durham, N.C.: Duke University Press, 2006), 71–93, quote at 78.

47. Misc. Consular Court Cases, *Taka vs. G.W. Lake*, RG 84, Records of the Foreign Service Posts of the Department of State, Nagasaki, Japan, Box 02, NARA II.

48. For "sporting culture" and the glorification of bachelorhood, see Gilfoyle, *City of Eros*, 106–116; "codification of female vulnerability" in Lyons, *Sex among the Rabble*, 4–5 and 390–392.

49. Transcript of Edward Upham to Charles Kittredge in Hugh F. Bell, "'I don't think much of a life on the ocean wave': Homeward Bound from China in 1855," in *Ships, Seafaring, and Society: Essays in Maritime History*, ed. Timothy J. Runyan (Detroit: Wayne State University Press, 1987), 145–165.

50. Murphy McGuire quoted in Busch, *"Whaling Will Never Do for Me,"* 141; entry dated Jan. 23, 1842, journal of Solomon Davis, kept aboard brig *Corporal Trim*, PEM; entry dated Feb. 14, 1855, journal kept aboard the U.S.S. *Savannah*, Papers of Robert L. Browning, LOC; entry dated August 1818, journal of Philander Chase, kept aboard *Guerriere*, 15–16, LOC; Thomas Dudley to sister, letter dated Aug. 18, 1853, Papers of Thomas C. Dudley, William L. Clements Library, University of Michigan, Ann Arbor. Rosemarie Zagarri discusses how U.S. observations of "degraded" women in India had a similar effect of silencing discourse on female empowerment; see "The Significance of the 'Global Turn' for the Early American Republic: Globalization in the Age of Nation Building," *Journal of the Early Republic* 31, no. 1 (2011): 1–37, esp. 24.

51. Browne, *Etchings of a Whaling Cruise*, 397–405; Erskine, *Twenty Years before the Mast*, 251–252. It is difficult to escape Paul Gilje's conclusion that "whether she was in an ephemeral or long-term relationship with a sailor, or whether she exploited or was exploited, Jack Tar's liberty exacted a high cost on a woman on the waterfront"; *Liberty on the Waterfront* (Philadelphia: University of Pennsylvania Press, 2004), 35.

52. Browne, *Etchings of a Whaling Cruise*, 404–405.

Chapter 6

1. Walter Brooks to Samson Brooks, Sept. 18, 1850, Business Records Collection MSS 56, Series B, Subseries 36, NBWM.

2. Ibid. Historical accounts of the economic "gullibility" of supposedly uncivilized peoples remain a focus of scholarship about many places, including early North America and the Pacific. See, for example, Daniel K. Richter, *Facing East from Indian Country: A Native History of Early America* (Cambridge, Mass.: Harvard University Press, 2002); or Gananath Obeyesekere, *The Apotheosis of Captain Cook: European Mythmaking in the Pacific* (Princeton, N.J.: Princeton University Press, 1992).

3. Walter F. Brooks to Samson Brooks, undated letter (ca. Mar. 1850), Business Records Collection MSS 56, Series B, Subseries 36, NBWM.

4. Models for navigating the divide between the macroeconomy and the microeconomy in eighteenth- and nineteenth-century American economic development include Daniel Vickers, *Farmers and Fishermen: Two Centuries of Work in Essex County Massachusetts, 1630–1850* (Chapel Hill: University of North Carolina Press, 1994); Jason Opal, *Beyond the Farm: National Ambitions in Rural New England* (Philadelphia: University of Pennsylvania Press, 2008); and Ann Smart Martin, *Buying into the World of Goods: Early Consumers in Backcountry Virginia* (Baltimore, Md.:

Johns Hopkins University Press, 2008). This scholarship, however, retains a decidedly domestic edge, while the study of sailors offers us insight into how goods changed hands along an international front.

5. The commercial empire is discussed in Thomas Bender, *A Nation among Nations: America's Place in World History* (New York: Hill and Wang, 2006), 186–191, 206–219; and John M. Schroeder, *Shaping a Maritime Empire: The Commercial and Diplomatic Role of the American Navy, 1829–1861* (Westport, Conn.: Greenwood Press, 1985), 65–81. Recent examples that limit our historical view of exchange overseas to the machinations of brokerage firms include James R. Fichter, *So Great a Proffit: How the East Indies Trade Transformed American Capitalism* (Cambridge, Mass: Harvard University Press, 2010); Jacques M. Downs, *The Golden Ghetto: The American Commercial Community at Canton and the Shaping of American China Policy, 1784–1844* (Bethlehem, Pa.: Lehigh University Press, 1996); and Kevin C. Murphy, *The American Merchant Experience in Nineteenth Century Japan* (New York: Routledge, 2003). In a similar vein, Jonathan Levy traces the origins of modern conceptions of risk to its maritime roots in *Freaks of Fortune: The Emerging World of Capitalism and Risk in America* (Cambridge, Mass.: Harvard University Press, 2012). Commercial relations in nineteenth-century America are covered most broadly in Schroeder, *Shaping a Maritime Empire*, esp. 3–10; Thomas Hietala, *Manifest Design: Anxious Aggrandizement in Late Jacksonian America* (Ithaca, N.Y.: Cornell University Press, 1985), 55–94; Ian Tyrrell, *Transnational Nation: United States History in Global Perspective since 1789* (New York: Palgrave Macmillan, 2007), 20–38; and Eric Rauchway, *Blessed among Nations: How the World Made America* (New York: Hill and Wang, 2006). Commodity studies include Jennifer L. Anderson, *Mahogany: The Costs of Luxury in Early America* (Cambridge, Mass.: Harvard University Press, 2012); David Hancock, *Oceans of Wine: Madeira and the Emergence of American Trade and Taste* (New Haven, Conn.: Yale University Press, 2009). For a broader history of commodity chains, see Emily S. Rosenberg, ed., *A World Connecting, 1870–1945* (Cambridge, Mass.: Harvard University Press, 2012), esp. 593–812. For intersections between domestic consumption and overseas empire, see Kristin L. Hoganson, *Consumers' Imperium: The Global Production of American Domesticity, 1865–1920* (Chapel Hill: University of North Carolina Press, 2007); and Kristin L. Hoganson, "Buying into Empire: American Consumption at the Turn of the Twentieth Century," in *Colonial Crucible: Empire in the Making of the Modern American State*, ed. Alfred W. McCoy and Francisco A. Scarano (Madison: University of Wisconsin Press, 2009), 248–259.

6. Epeli Hau'ofa, "Our Sea of 'Islands,'" in *We Are the Ocean* (Honolulu: University of Hawaii Press, 2008), 27. Similar conclusions can be drawn about the U.S. West, where American markets became a crucial connective link between ordinary people. See Andrés Reséndez, *Changing National Identities at the Frontier: Texas and New Mexico, 1800–1850* (Cambridge: Cambridge University Press, 2005).

7. Seth Rockman, *Scraping By: Wage Labor, Slavery, and Survival in Early Baltimore* (Baltimore, Md.: Johns Hopkins University Press, 2009); Steven King and Alannah Tomkins, eds., *The Poor in England, 1700–1850: An Economy of Makeshifts* (Manchester: Manchester University Press, 2003). See also conference papers associated with the Library Company of Philadelphia's 2012 exhibition *Capitalism by Gaslight: The Shadow Economies of Nineteenth-Century America*. For port city economies and survival strategies, see Ellen Hartigan-O'Connor, *The Ties That Buy: Women and Commerce in Revolutionary America* (Philadelphia: University of Pennsylvania Press, 2009). For the boisterous lives of sailors in port, what Paul Gilje terms "The Sweets of Liberty," see *Liberty on the Waterfront: American Maritime Culture in the Age of Revolution* (Philadelphia: University of Pennsylvania Press, 2004), 3–32. On the poverty of sailors more generally, see Ira Dye, "Early

American Merchant Seafarers," *Proceedings of the American Philosophical Society* 120, no. 5 (1976): 331–360.

8. On the increasingly "stressed" or "sweated" nature of nineteenth-century American maritime labor, see Busch, "*Whaling Will Never Do for Me*," esp. 1–31; or Alex Roland, W. Jeffrey Bolster, and Alexander Keyssar, *The Way of the Ship: America's Maritime History Reenvisioned, 1600–2000* (Hoboken, N.J.: Wiley and Sons, 2008). On empire as an agent in the dissemination of smuggling and other "suspect" activity, what can be called "rogue colonialism," see Shannon Lee Dawdy, *Building the Devil's Empire: French Colonial New Orleans* (Chicago: University of Chicago Press, 2008), esp. 1–21. The relationship between mainline and "secondary" or "tertiary" markets is discussed in Wendy Woloson, *In Hock: Pawning in America from Independence to the Great Depression* (Chicago: University of Chicago Press, 2009), esp. 3–5 (for sailors particularly see 90–91); Rockman, *Scraping By*, 2–3; and Scott Sandage, *Born Losers: A History of Failure in America* (Cambridge, Mass.: Harvard University Press, 2005), 5–6. In the modern context, see Sudhir Alladi Venkatesh, *Off the Books: The Underground Economy of the Urban Poor* (Cambridge, Mass: Harvard University Press, 2006). Mona Domosh remains attentive to American empire as something "as much about ordinary commercial transactions as it was about political maneuvers or military interventions"; *American Commodities in an Age of Empire* (New York: Routledge, 2006), 5–6.

9. For the economic behavior of sailors on liberty and for sailor's wages, see Gilje, *Liberty on the Waterfront*, 10–12, 18–23; and Margaret Creighton, *Rites and Passages: The Experience of American Whaling, 1830–1870* (New York: Cambridge University Press, 1995), 139–161.

10. Entries dated Feb. 18, 1854, and Dec. 20, 1856, journal of William Stetson, kept aboard ship *Arab*, ODHS Log #0507, NBWM; undated entries (ca. 1842), diary of John Martin, kept aboard ship *Lucy Ann*, NBWM.

11. Alonzo D. Sampson, *Three Times around the World* (Buffalo, N.Y.: Express Printing, 1867), 45, 155. For interconnected exchange systems, especially in the Pacific, see David Igler, *The Great Ocean: Pacific Worlds from Captain Cook to the Gold Rush* (New York: Oxford University Press, 2013).

12. Andrew Brown, *A Sermon on the Dangers of the Seafaring Life* (Boston, 1793), 39. Traditional academic accounts of sailors ashore have long emphasized that the mariner "was essentially a spender" and that he was "definitely not 'price conscious,' and . . . neither knew much nor cared much about such matters as market value, competitive price, or the going rate"; E. P. Hohman, *Seamen Ashore: A Study of the United Seamen's Service and of Merchant Seamen in Port* (New Haven, Conn.: Yale University Press, 1952), 254–255. On the contrast in travel style between rich and poor, see Charles Tyng, *Before the Wind: The Memoir of an American Sea Captain*, ed. Susan Fels (New York: Viking, 1999), 60–64, where elevated social standing extricated Tyng from financial difficulty. For economic interdependence between port brokers and seamen, see Isaac Land, *War, Nationalism, and the British Sailor, 1750–1850* (New York: Palgrave Macmillan, 2009), esp. 29–55. Gilje, *Liberty on the Waterfront*, 16–21, discusses importance of keepers of boardinghouses for sailors.

13. Undated entries (ca. 1842), diary of John Martin, NBWM. For the "carefree," non-acquisitive sailor, see Gilje, *Liberty on the Waterfront*, 11–13.

14. "History of a Three Years' Whaling Voyage" (journal of N. Byron Smith), 6, Manuscript Archive, Microfilm 16, 747–1P, LOC; Alonzo D. Sampson, *Three Times around the World* (Buffalo, N.Y.: Express Printing, 1867), 23–25; entry dated Sept. 10, 1856, journal of William Stetson. Admiralty court case files that shed light on the underground economy of stolen cargo include *Joseph Harborn v. the* Forest *et al.*, RG 21, Records of District Courts of the United States, Admiralty Case Files of the U.S. District Court for the Eastern District of Pennsylvania

1789–1840, reel 14, NARA Philadelphia; folder *Oliver v. Skillington*, RG 21, Records of District Courts of the United States, Admiralty Case Files of the U.S. District Court for the Eastern District of Pennsylvania 1789–1840, Box 30, NARA Philadelphia.

15. Undated entry (ca. 1858), journal of Albert Peck, Paul C. Nicholson Whaling Collection, reel 17, vol. 187, PPL; Sampson, *Three Times around the World*, 23–25. Nineteenth-century novels, plays, and periodicals emphasized the inherently charitable nature and simple-minded generosity of seamen. See Gilje, *Liberty on the Waterfront*, 195–227.

16. Entry dated Apr. 19, 1853, journal of William Speiden, kept aboard ship *Mississippi*, Microfilm 22 423–1P, LOC; entry dated July 20, 1842, journal of William Clark, kept aboard ship *Relief*, PEM.

17. Undated entry (ca. 1835), journal of Robert Browning, kept aboard ship *Vincennes*, 0536D NHF-012, LOC; entry dated May 18, 1851, journal of William H. Myers, kept aboard ship *Alpha*, ODHS Log #1054, NBWM. For rejection of the native mode of exchange, see J. C. Mullett, *A Five Years' Whaling Voyage, 1848–1853* (New York: Fairbanks, Benedict, and Cleveland, 1859), 20. The trading protocol of the Pacific is described in more detail in Marshall Sahlins, *Islands of History* (Chicago: University of Chicago Press, 1985); and Marshall Sahlins, *How Natives Think: About Captain Cook, for Example* (Chicago: University of Chicago Press, 1996).

18. Walter Teller, ed., *Five Sea Captains: Their Own Accounts of Voyages under Sail* (New York: Atheneum Publishers, 1960), 267–268; Edmund Gardner, *Captain Edmund Gardner, His Journal*, ed. John M. Bullard (Milford, N.H.: The Cabinet Press, 1958), 34; entry dated May 17, 1851, journal of William H. Myers; A Roving Printer, *Life and Adventures in the South Pacific* (New York: Harper and Brothers, 1861), 94–95. Indigenous intermediaries are discussed in Mary Malloy, *Souvenirs of the Fur Trade: Northwest Coast Indian Art and Artifacts Collected by American Mariners, 1788–1844* (Cambridge, Mass.: Harvard University Press, 2000), 3–31. For *taio* friendship, see Vanessa Smith, *Intimate Strangers: Friendship, Exchange, and Pacific Encounters* (Cambridge: Cambridge University Press, 2010), 70–71.

19. Undated entry (ca. 1858), journal of Albert Peck; entry dated Feb. 17, 1848, journal of Oren B. Higgins, kept aboard ship *Ann Alexander*, ODHS Log #394, NBWM; entry dated Feb. 19, 1843, journal of John Martin, kept aboard ship *Lucy Ann*, NBWM. For innkeepers and tavern owners as intermediaries, see Dawdy, *Building the Devil's Empire*, 130–135; and Gilje, *Liberty on the Waterfront*, 16–21. The double-edged sword of interlopers is discussed in Greg Dening, *Beach Crossings: Voyaging across Times, Culture, and Self* (Philadelphia: University of Pennsylvania Press, 2004), 269–315. See also David A. Chappell, "Secret Sharers: Indigenous Beachcombers in the Pacific Islands," *Pacific Studies* 17, no. 2 (1994): 1–22.

20. Herman Melville, *Redburn* (New York: Harper, 1863), 176; William Miles to State Department, letter dated Nov. 25, 1854, RG 59, M155, Despatches from U.S. Consuls at Callao, Peru, reel 1, NARA II. Crimping is covered in Leon Fink, *Sweatshops at Sea: Merchant Seamen in the World's First Globalized Industry, from 1812 to the Present* (Chapel Hill: University of North Carolina Press, 2011), 56–57. The vital and various functions of pawnshops in urban economies is discussed in Alannah Tomkins, "Pawnbroking and the Survival Strategies of the Urban Poor in 1770s York," in *The Poor in England, 1700–1850: An Economy of Makeshifts*, ed. Alannah Tomkins and Steven King (Manchester: Manchester University Press, 2003), 166–198; and Woloson, *In Hock.*

21. This particular transit is described over the course of voyage in "History of a Three Years' Whaling Voyage" (journal of N. Byron Smith). The maritime world of goods is covered in James P. Delgado, *Gold Rush Port: The Maritime Archaeology of San Francisco's Waterfront* (Berkeley: University of California Press, 2009). Waterfront pawnshops often contained particularly

"exotic" goods circulated by transient mariners. See Stan Hugill, *Sailortown* (New York: Dutton, 1967), 77–78.

22. Jeremiah Reynolds, *Voyage of the United States Frigate* Potomac (New York: Harper and Brothers, 1835), 253–254, 256; undated entry (ca. 1835), journal of Robert Browning; Frederick Schley to wife, letter dated July 6, 1848, Correspondence of Frederick Schley, NHC; entry dated June 19, 1853, journal of William B. Allen, kept aboard ship *Vandalia*, MMC-1798, LOC; entry dated Feb. 26, 1844, journal of Burr Kellogg, kept aboard ship *Horatio*, LOC; Charles Roberts Anderson, ed., *Journal of a Cruise to the Pacific Ocean in the Frigate* United States (1844; repr., New York: AMS Press, 1966), 49; Captain David Porter, *Journal of a Cruise*, ed. R. D. Madison and Karen Hamon (1815; repr., Annapolis: Naval Institute Press, 1986), 290.

23. Frank Bullen, *The Cruise of the Cachalot: Round the World After Sperm Whales* (London: Smith, Elder & Co., 1898), 162; Nelson Cole Haley, *Whale Hunt: Narrative of a Voyage in the Ship* Charles W. Morgan, *1849–1853* (New York: Ives Washburn Press, 1967), 192.

24. William B. Whitecar, *Four Years aboard the Whaleship: Embracing Cruises in the Pacific, Atlantic, Indian, and Antarctic Oceans, in the Years 1855, 56, 57, 58, 59* (Philadelphia: J. B. Lippincott & Co., 1860), 106–107. See also Nelson Cole Haley, *Whale Hunt: Narrative of a Voyage in the Ship* Charles W. Morgan, *1849–1853* (New York: Ives Washburn Press, 1967), 30–31; and John Nicol, *Life and Adventures, 1776–1801*, ed. Tim Flannery (1821; repr., Melbourne: Text Publishing, 1997), 171–173.

25. J. Ross Browne, *Etchings of a Whaling Cruise* (New York: Harper and Brothers, 1846), 235–236; entries dated Dec. 7 and 8, 1835, journal of A. H. Beckett, kept aboard brig *Gleaner*, PEM; entries dated Apr. 3 and 5, and June 6, 1841, journal kept aboard ship *Neptune*, Log 1841N2 (B12), PEM; undated entry (ca. May 1818), journal kept aboard ship *Tartar*, Log 1841N2 (B12), PEM. On African American marketplaces in the United States, see Robert Olwell, *Masters, Slaves, and Subjects: The Culture of Power in the South Carolina Low Country, 1740–1790* (Ithaca, N.Y.: Cornell University Press, 1998), 141–180. For the frontier context, see Reséndez, *Changing National Identities at the Frontier*.

26. Letter dated Oct. 4, 1845, Correspondence of James Webb, MSS 56, Box 84, Series W, Subseries 6, NBWM; George Little, *Life on the Ocean* (Boston: Waite and Pierce, 1846), 64. See also Prince Samson to Thomas Kempton, Apr. 3, 1805, Correspondence of Prince Samson, MSS 56, Box 70, Series S, Subseries 4, NBWM. Statements that mixed-race South American populations were indolent and unable to put their land to productive use were widespread; see Amy S. Greenberg, *Manifest Manhood and the Antebellum American Empire* (New York: Cambridge University Press, 2005), 96–106.

27. Undated entry (ca. Dec. 1835), journal of Robert Browning; entry dated Aug. 16, 1828, journal of Stephen C. Rowan, kept aboard ship *Vincennes*, 0536D NHF-025, LOC; entry dated Aug. 29, 1839, journal of Simeon Stearns, NYPL; Anderson, *Journal of a Cruise to the Pacific Ocean*, 60; Samuel Samuels, *From the Forecastle to the Cabin* (New York: Harper and Brothers, 1887), 122. See also entry dated Mar. 8, 1846, diary of John Martin.

28. Entries dated June 14, 1840 and Oct. 7, 1840, journal of James Watkin, quoted in Busch, "*Whaling Will Never Do for Me*," 110–111.

29. Entry dated Nov. 27, 1855, journal of William Stetson; undated entry, journal of F. Cady, kept aboard ship *Julian*, NBWM. On native systems of value and the reappropriation of Euro-American trade goods, see Nicholas Thomas, *Entangled Objects: Exchange, Material Culture, and Colonialism in the Pacific* (Cambridge, Mass.: Harvard University Press, 1991), 7–34 and 83–124. An increasing expertise in trade is described in Ernest S. Dodge, *Islands and Empires: Western Impact on the Pacific and East Asia* (Minneapolis: University of Minnesota, 1976), 77–79.

More recent work has suggested how disease vectors traveled along the local trading networks operated in large part by mariners. See, for example, David Igler, "Diseased Goods: Global Exchanges in the Eastern Pacific Basin, 1770–1850," *American Historical Review* 109, no. 3 (2004): 693–719.

30. R. M. Aderman, ed., *The Letters of James Kirke Paulding* (Madison: University of Wisconsin Press, 1962), 225–227. See also Paul Lyons, *American Pacificism: Oceania in the U.S. Imagination* (New York: Routledge, 2006), 60–61.

31. Entry dated July 31, 1826, journal of Thomas Harris, kept aboard *Peacock*, MMC-2373, LOC; entry dated Oct. 29, 1834, journal of Milo Calkin, MMC-1099, LOC; "History of a Three Years' Whaling Voyage" (journal of N Byron Smith), 128; entry dated Sept. 9, 1834, journal of William Silver, kept aboard ship *Bengal*, PEM; Kevin S. Reilly, ed., *The Journal of George Attwater* (New Haven, Conn.: New Haven Colonial Historical Society, 2002), 200. Complaints about thievery were also common among other traveling populations of America; see Greenberg, *Manifest Manhood*, 101–103.

32. Entry dated May 5, 1849, diary kept aboard ship *Samuel Appleton*, MSM; entry dated Jan. 22, 1849, journal of Frederick Schley, kept aboard U.S.S. *Cumberland*, NHC; July 20, 1842, journal of William Clark, kept aboard ship *Relief*, PEM; Washington Chase, *A Voyage from the United States to South America* (Newburyport, Mass.: Herald Press, 1823), 24; William Dane Phelps, *Fore and Aft; or, Leaves from the Life of an Old Sailor* (Boston: Nichols and Hall, 1871), 149–150; Edward Shippen, *Thirty Years at Sea: The Story of a Sailor's Life* (Philadelphia: J. B. Lippincott, 1879), 28.

The supposed thievishness of the Chinese discussed in Lyons, *American Pacificism*, 222–223; and Downs, *The Golden Ghetto*, 222–255. "Criminal" behavior as entrepreneurship is discussed in Heather Shore, "Crime, Criminal Networks, and the Survival Strategies of the Poor in Early Eighteenth-Century London," in *The Poor in England, 1700–1850: An Economy of Makeshifts*, ed. Alannah Tomkins and Steven King (Manchester: Manchester University Press, 2003), 137–165.

33. John Truair, *A Call from the Ocean* (New York: John Gray, 1826), 19. Shore describes theft "as part of the broader makeshift economy of the poor"; "Crime, Criminal Networks," 138.

34. Thomas Bennett, *A Voyage from the United States to South America, Performed during the Years 1821, 1822, and 1823* (Newburyport, Mass.: Herald Press, 1823), 20–21; entry dated Nov. 20, 1831, journal kept aboard the ship *Chelsea*, Log no. 371, MSM; T. Robinson Warren, *Dust and Foam, or Three Oceans and Two Continents* (New York: Scribner, 1859), 361–362. "Maggie May" and similar shanties are discussed in Hugill, *Sailortown*, 76.

35. *Nantucket Enquirer*, Mar. 3, 1832; *New-Bedford Daily Mercury*, Mar. 5, 1832.

36. Charles Nordhoff, *Nine Years a Sailor* (Cincinnati, Ohio: Moore, Wilstach, Keys & Co., 1857), 227; Phelps, *Fore and Aft*, 155. "Housefuls" in Hartigan-O'Connor, *The Ties That Buy*, 14–15.

37. Browne, *Etchings of a Whaling Cruise*, 263; Charles Erskine, *Twenty Years before the Mast* (Philadelphia: George W. Jacobs, 1896), 249. On paying with the fore-top sail, see also Edward Gray to French Commissioner, letter dated Oct. 29, 1850, RG 84, Records of the Foreign Service Posts of the Department of State, Misc. Letters Sent, Tahiti, Society Islands, vol. 27, NARA II.

38. Entry dated Aug. 16, 1828, journal of Stephen C. Rowan; undated entry (ca. 1858), journal of Albert Peck. The Waya Levu incident is discussed in Francis X. Holbrook, "Come, Papillangi, Our Fires Are Lighted," in *America Spreads Her Sails: U.S. Seapower in the 19th Century*, ed. Clayton R. Barrow (Annapolis: Naval Institute Press, 1973), 112–125. On increasing violence, see Dodge, *Islands and Empires*, 156–165.

39. *Friend* (Honolulu), Feb. 1, 1855; *Worcester Gazette*, Jan. 8, 1812; *New-York Observer*, June 20, 1846.

40. *New-York Observer*, June 20, 1846; *Friend* (Honolulu), Sept. 2, 1861. Similar observations occur in John Jewitt, *A Narrative of Adventures and Sufferings of John R. Jewitt* (Middletown, Conn.: Seth Richards, 1815), 114–115.

41. For references to Pacific islander "scams" and "Jews of the South Seas," see David Chappell, *Double Ghosts: Oceanian Voyagers on Euroamerican Ships* (Armonk, N.Y.: M. E. Sharpe, 1997), 10. "Jerusalem" appears in entries dated Aug. 12–29, 1848, journals of Midshipman Henry Wise, vol. 7, RG 45, Records of the Naval Records Collection of the Office of Naval Records and Library, E608 (60), NARA I.

42. Entry undated, journal of Joseph Osborn, kept aboard ship *Emerald*, 248–249, PEM; Frederick Benton Williams, *On Many Seas: The Life and Exploits of a Yankee Sailor* (New York: MacMillan, 1897), 63–64; entry dated Dec. 25, 1789, journal of Benjamin Hodges, kept aboard ship *William and Mary*, PEM.

43. E. Daniel Potts, ed., *The Letters of George Francis Train, 1853–1855* (Melbourne: William Heinemann Ltd., 1970), 24–26 and 92–94.

44. Entries dated June 21–24, 1856, journal kept aboard *Concordia*, Log 502, MSM.

45. Entry dated Mar. 14, 1850, journal of Daniel H. Smith, kept aboard ship *Ark*, MMC-2760, LOC; *Salem Register*, Nov. 29, 1847; Joseph G. Clark, *Lights and Shadows of Sailor Life* (Boston: Benjamin B. Mussey, 1848), 233–234; entry dated Jan. 21, 1850, journal of Thomas Sherman, kept aboard ship *Euphrasia*, PEM; entry dated Jan. 3, 1848, journal of Frederick Schley, kept aboard USS *Cumberland*, NHC. For connections between "indolence" abroad and American imperial aspirations, see Greenberg, *Manifest Manhood*, 74–78 and 88–134. Visions of progress in the nineteenth-century United States are described in Carol Sheriff, *The Artificial River: The Erie Canal and the Paradox of Progress, 1817–1862* (New York: Hill and Wang, 1997), 9–26; Daniel Feller, *The Jacksonian Promise: America, 1815–1840* (Baltimore, Md.: Johns Hopkins University Press, 1995), 14–32; and Gretchen Murphy, *Hemispheric Imaginings: The Monroe Doctrine and Narratives of U.S. Empire* (Durham, N.C.: Duke University Press, 2005), 1–31. Richard Henry Dana's maritime travelogue was also read as inviting expansionism into California; see Robert F. Lucid, "*Two Years before the Mast* as Propaganda," *American Quarterly* 12, no. 3 (1960): 392–403. Negative notation is described in *Exploration and Exchange: A South Seas Anthology, 1680–1900*, ed. Jonathan Lamb, Vanessa Smith, and Nicholas Thomas (Chicago: University of Chicago Press, 2000), 10.

46. Entry dated Jan. 6, 1836, journal of Milo Calkin, MMC-1099, LOC; Melville quoted in the *Baltimore American*, Feb. 8, 1859. Opposition to territorial expansion coalesced around controversial moments in its history, such as during Indian removal and the U.S.-Mexico War. See, for example, Amy Greenberg, *A Wicked War: Polk, Clay, Lincoln, and the 1846 U.S. Invasion of Mexico* (New York: Knopf, 2012), esp. 177–199.

47. Melville, *Redburn*, 178–179; Sampson, *Three Times around the World*, 32. On the last point, see Arthur Dudden, *The American Pacific: From the Old China Trade to the Present* (New York: Oxford University Press, 1992).

48. George Jones, *Sketches of Naval Life* (New Haven, Conn.: Hezekiah Howe, 1829), 76; trial of Richard Kirton aboard USS *John Adams*, Feb. 20, 1839, RG 125, Records of the Office of the Judge Advocate General (Navy), M273, reel 35, vol. 35, NARA I. For divestment as a survival strategy of the working poor, see Woloson, *In Hock*, 115–116. A shift in attitudes toward the urban poor from objects of sympathy to "irresponsible," "shiftless," "idle," and "disorderly" is discussed in Bruce Dorsey, *Reforming Men and Women: Gender in the Antebellum City* (Ithaca, N.Y.: Cornell University Press, 2002), 51–62. Shannon Lee Dawdy argues that seafarers were among the many poor laborers state-driven imperial enterprise depended on: "Rogues and states were bound together in a volatile interdependency"; see *Building the Devil's Empire*, 18–20.

On the interconnected worlds of the working poor and the prosperous few, see Rockman, *Scraping By*, 2–4. Punitive expeditions performed by the U.S. Navy are covered in Clayton R. Barrow, ed., *America Spreads Her Sails: U.S. Seapower in the Nineteenth Century* (Annapolis: Naval Institute Press, 1973).

49. Lincoln quoted in Morton Rothstein, "The American West and Foreign Markets, 1850–1900," in *The Frontier in American Development*, ed. David M. Ellis (Ithaca, N.Y.: Cornell University Press, 1969), 386, 394. See also Bender, *Nation among Nations*, 212–213.

50. Undated entry (ca. 1879), journal of Horace Palmer, ODHS Log #409, NBWM; James Webb to mother, undated letter (ca. 1848), Correspondence of James Webb, MSS 56, Box 84, Series W, Subseries 6, NBWM.

Epilogue

1. Mark Twain, *The Autobiography of Mark Twain*, 2 vols. (New York: Kessinger, 2003), 2:120–121. See also Nathaniel Philbrick, *Sea of Glory: The U.S. Exploring Expedition, 1838–1842* (New York: Viking, 2003).

2. Twain, *Autobiography*, 2:121. For the decline of the "new," see Frank Ninkovich, *Global Dawn: The Cultural Foundation of American Internationalism, 1865–1890* (Cambridge, Mass.: Harvard University Press, 2009), 27–28.

3. Samuel Samuels, *From the Forecastle to the Cabin* (New York: Harper and Brothers, 1887), 307–308. Daniel Vickers captures much of the significance of this economic transformation in *Young Men and the Sea: Yankee Seafarers in the Age of Sail* (New Haven, Conn.: Yale University Press, 2005), 248–252. See also Alex Roland, W. Jeffrey Bolster, and Alexander Keyssar, *The Way of the Ship: America's Maritime History Reenvisioned, 1600–2000* (Hoboken, N.J.: John Wiley and Sons, 2008), esp. 128–129 and 197–210; and Andrew Gibson and Arthur Donovan, *The Abandoned Ocean: A History of United States Maritime Policy* (Columbia: University of South Carolina Press, 2001), 64–101. As Bolster et al. note (p. 147), the decline in deep-water shipping was more than offset by increased internal maritime commerce (rivers, canals, lakes, etc.): "Americans were now trading with the richest market in the world—themselves." Thus, the "declension narrative" of U.S. maritime history is better understood as a transition away from international and toward coastal or internal shipping. The American maritime decline (including the statistics cited above) is also discussed in Leon Fink, *Sweatshops at Sea: Merchant Seamen in the World's First Globalized Industry, from 1812 to the Present* (Chapel Hill: University of North Carolina Press, 2011), 30–35. The touristic turn is described in Christopher Endy, "Travel and World Power: Americans in Europe, 1890–1917," *Diplomatic History* 22, no. 4 (1998): 565–594; and Endy, *Cold War Holidays: American Tourism in France* (Chapel Hill: University of North Carolina Press, 2004).

4. Denison Card to William Seward, Letter dated Oct. 28, 1864, RG 59, Department of State Records, Despatches from U.S. Consuls in Tumbes, Peru, T353, NARA II. Furuseth and Raker are quoted in Fink, *Sweatshops at Sea*, 106–107. See also Henry T. Cheever, *The Whaleman's Adventures in the Southern Ocean, as Gathered by the Rev. H. T. Cheever, on the Homeward Cruise of the* Commodore Preble (London: W. Kent, 1859), 302–303. See also W. Jeffrey Bolster, *Black Jacks: African American Seamen in the Age of Sail* (Cambridge, Mass.: Harvard University Press, 1997), 224: "Although 'statistics' from the era are not verifiable, the overwhelming impression of every observer was that as the century progressed fewer and fewer white Yankees sailed on American ships."

5. For the "proletarianization" of deep-sea labor, see Marcus Rediker, *Between the Devil and the Deep Blue Sea: Merchant Seamen, Pirates, and the Anglo-American Maritime World, 1700–1750* (Cambridge: Cambridge University Press, 1987); Vickers, *Young Men and the Sea*, 248–251; and John R. Gillis, *The Human Shore: Seacoasts in History* (Chicago: University of Chicago Press, 2012), 112–113. Gillis refers to the period 1850–1950 as the "great era of the proletarianized waterfront."

6. Frank T. Bullen, *The Cruise of the Cachalot: Round the World after Sperm Whales* (1898; repr., New Haven, Conn.: Leete's Island Books, 1980), 24; Joseph G. Clark, *Lights and Shadows of Sailor Life* (Boston: Benjamin B. Mussey, 1848), 319–320. Nonwhite authority aboard ships of sail is discussed in Bolster, *Black Jacks*, 158–175; later impediments to black advancement are described on 175–182. Antisuffrage slogans are described in Roediger, *Wages of Whiteness*, 57. On the difficulty of white seamen accepting that challenge to their assumptions about race, see Bullen, *Cruise of the Cachalot*, 4; when Bullen was accosted by the black fourth mate for an insolent reply to his orders, he "hardly liked his patronizing air," but the black man "snapped me up short with 'yes, *sir*, when yew speak to me, yew blank limejuicer. I'se de fourf mate ob dis yar ship, en my name's *Mistah* Jones.'"

7. Entry dated Sept. 20, 1855, journal of William Stetson, kept aboard ship *Arab*, ODHS Log #0507, NBWM; entry dated Mar. 2, 1880, journal of Horace Palmer, ODHS Log #409, NBWM; Richard Henry Dana Jr., *Two Years before the Mast* (Boston: Fields, Osgood, & Co., 1869), 116–117, Dana's emphasis.

8. Vickers, *Young Men and the Sea*, 214–247; Roland Gould, *The Life of Gould, An Ex-Man-of-War's-Man; With Incidents on Sea and Shore, Including a Three-Year's Cruise on the Line of Battle Ship Ohio, on the Mediterranean Station, Under the Veteran Commodore Hall* (Claremont, N.H.: Claremont Manufacturing Company, 1867), 191; Samuel Samuels, *Forecastle to the Cabin* (New York: Harper and Brothers, 1887), 1–2.

9. Richard Henry Dana Jr., *Two Years before the Mast, and Other Voyages* (1840; repr., New York: The Library of America, 2005), 347.

10. Ibid., 365–395.

11. Ibid., 166, 365–367.

12. Ibid., 367, 369. On genteel travelers turning away from waterfronts as "danger zones," see Gillis, *Human Shore*, 112–113.

13. Francis Ripley to wife, June 25, 1849, Correspondence of Francis Ripley, NYHS. Of course, there were singular or exceptional spaces where working people continued to exercise authority over international affairs, the Panama Canal Zone chief among them. See Julie Greene, *The Canal Builders: Making America's Empire at the Panama Canal* (New York: Penguin, 2010).

14. Entry dated Nov. 6, 1853, Journal of William B. Allen, MMC-1798, LOC; U.S. Vice Consul to R. S. Sturges, May 12, 1855, RG 84, Records of the Foreign Service Posts of the Department of State, Consular Posts, Canton, China, Misc. Correspondence 1849–1853, vol. 7, NARA II.

15. On touristic forms of travel, particularly pertaining to Twain's generation, see Jeffrey Alan Melton, *Mark Twain, Travel Books, and Tourism: The Tide of a Great Popular Movement* (Tuscaloosa: University of Alabama Press, 2002); and Eric J. Leed, *The Mind of the Traveler: From Gilgamesh to Global Tourism* (New York: Basic Books, 1991), 285–293. For the "gospel of gentility," see Jane Hunter, *The Gospel of Gentility: American Women Missionaries in Turn of the Century China* (New Haven, Conn.: Yale University Press, 1984). On women, bourgeois belief, and the reshaping of travel, see Amy G. Richter, *Home on the Rails: Women, the Railroad, and the Rise of Public Domesticity* (Chapel Hill: University of North Carolina Press, 2005); for the journeys of women

and "traveling domesticity," see Amy Greenberg, *Manifest Manhood and the Antebellum American Empire* (Cambridge: Cambridge University Press, 2005), 197–230. The terms "Baedeker World" and "Baedeker Land" appear in Thomas Pynchon, *V.* (New York: Perennial, 1963).

16. Frank T. Bullen, *The Men of the Merchant Service* (New York: Stokes, 1900), 251–253.

17. Roland, Bolster, and Keyssar, *The Way of the Ship*, 4–5; Gibson and Donovan, *Abandoned Ocean*; Daniel Vickers, "Beyond Jack Tar," *William and Mary Quarterly* 50, no. 3 (1993): 418–424; Kristen Hoganson, *Consumers' Imperium: The Global Production of American Domesticity, 1865–1920* (Chapel Hill: University of North Carolina Press, 2007).

18. Henry David Thoreau, *Walden* (New York: Thomas Crowell and Company, 1910), 425. For nostalgia for sailors during the industrial age, see Isaac Land, *War, Nationalism, and the British Sailor, 1750–1850* (New York: Palgrave Macmillan, 2009), 131–158. "Second discovery of the sea" appears in Gillis, *Human Shore*, 128–157; and Alain Corbin, *The Lure of the Sea: The Discovery of the Seaside in the Western World, 1750–1840* (Berkeley: University of California Press, 1994). For "voyage" as metaphor for economic risk, see Jonathan Levy, *Freaks of Fortune: The Emerging World of Capitalism and Risk in America* (Cambridge, Mass.: Harvard, 2012).

19. Hubert Howe Bancroft, *The New Pacific*, 3rd ed. (New York: Bancroft Publishers, 1915), 13–14.

20. U.S. Consul George Kimball to Secretary of State William Marcy, Jan. 5, 1857, RG 84, Records of the Foreign Service Posts of the Department of State, St. Helena, British Africa, NARA II. For a critique of linear imperial progress, see Amy Kaplan, *The Anarchy of Empire in the Making of U.S. Culture* (Cambridge, Mass.: Harvard University Press, 2002).

21. See Reginald Horsman, *Race and Manifest Destiny: The Origins of American Racial Anglo-Saxonism* (Cambridge, Mass: Harvard University Press, 1981).

22. Bancroft, *New Pacific*, 15.

23. Frank T. Bullen, *A Whaleman's Wife* (London: Hodder and Stoughton, 1902), 44; entries dated Oct. 20, 1849, and Jan. 29, 1850, journal of Nathaniel Morgan, kept aboard ship *Hannibal*, MSM; Edward Shippen, *Thirty Years at Sea: The Story of a Sailor's Life* (Philadelphia: J.B. Lippincott, 1879), 10. For scientific race management, see David Roediger and Elizabeth D. Esch, *The Production of Difference: Race and the Management of Labor in U.S. History* (New York: Oxford University Press, 2012). Eric Lott, "'The Seeming Counterfeit': Racial Politics and Early Blackface Minstrelsy," *American Quarterly* 43, no. 2 (1991): 226

Index

Please note that page numbers in *italics* refer to figures.